# Catholic Social Thought
# and
# Liberal Institutions

# Catholic Social Thought
## and
# Liberal Institutions

## Freedom with Justice

## Michael Novak

*With a new introduction
and concluding chapter
by the Author*

**Second Edition**

**Transaction Publishers**
New Brunswick (U.S.A.) and Oxford (U.K.)

New material this edition copyright (c) 1989 by Transaction Publishers, New Brunswick, New Jersey 08903
Originally published in 1984 by Harper and Row

Library of Congress Catalog Number: 88-23351
ISBN: 0-88738-763-2
Printed in the United States of America

**Library of Congress Cataloging-in-Publication Data**

Novak, Michael.
   [Freedom with justice]
   Catholic social thought and liberal institutions / Michael Novak: with a new introduction and concluding chapter by the author.
   p. cm.
   Previously published as: Freedom with justice. c1984.
   Bibliography: p.
   Includes index.
   ISBN 0-88738-763-2
   1. Sociology, Christian (Catholic)   2. Sociology, Christian (Catholic)--History of doctrines--19th century.   3. Sociology, Christian (Catholic)--History of doctrines--20th century.
4. Liberalism.  I. Title.
BX1753.N67  1988
261.8--dc19

                                        88-23351
                                             CIP

*For all who love, and wish to advance,*
*Catholic social thought*

# Contents

Part III

ETHOS, VIRTUES, AND INSTITUTIONS:
THE FUTURE DEVELOPMENT OF CATHOLIC SOCIAL
THOUGHT

# Preface to the
# Transaction Edition

The worldwide reception of the hardcover edition of this book gave me much satisfaction. Even some who had found its predecessor[1] strong meat praised this volume, despite disagreement with parts of it. Given the traditional Catholic antipathy toward liberalism, those reviews were heartening. They offer good reason to hope for another look at the liberal classics, old and new, by Catholic scholars.

The fact remains that, for good reasons and bad, Catholics have been taught a certain ambivalence concerning liberal philosophy. On the one hand, they have learned to love such institutions as they have come to share in the United States and a few other places on earth. On the other hand, Vatican documents and many polemical or catechetical writings harshly criticize liberal philosophies, and tend to use the word "liberal" pejoratively. And many aspects of liberal philosophy and practice do deserve criticism.

Oddly, this ambivalence is found both among left-wing and among conservative Catholics. From the left, some form or other of socialist vision is preferred to a liberal vision. In truth, most Catholics who call themselves "socialists" – such as Arthur J. McGovern, and John C. Cort – are plainly *non-Marxist* socialists.[2] They are eager to protect the right to private property, the virtue of enterprise, and the free activities of at least small-scale businesses. Others on the left seem simply anti-capitalist. They cannot bear to call themselves "capitalist," or to admit to being in favor of a capitalist system. They insist upon occupying a position adversarial to the system in which they live. When pressed however, they supply either reformist notions of what needs correction in it or warmly utopian visions of something better, but ill-defined.

On the other flank, among religious conservatives, there are three further types of anti-capitalist thought. First, especially in the literary world, there are many religious minds of a Tory, aristocratic, and agrarian bent who loathe the churning turmoil that capitalism launched into the earlier and tidier order of the pre-capitalist world. For many such, the eighteenth century (or the thirteenth) represents the high point of humanism. G. K. Chesterton, Hilaire Belloc, George Will, the Southern Agrarians, Russell Kirk, and others are in this number.

Other highly orthodox Catholics, especially those of non-English background subliminally think that capitalism is infected with English individualism and spiritual "thinness"; that it is insufficiently spiritual and deep; and that it is vulnerable to shallow materialism and the smugness of a satisfying lunch at an all-male club. Overlooking the tacit presuppositions of an English sense for order, good form, and social sensibility (queueing up respectfully for a bus, for example), they like to speak of "raw self-interest" and "savage liberalism." Their image of the archetypal liberal is Scrooge–or, perhaps, Lord Beaverbrook. They share the visceral antagonism to the word "liberal" expressed often in papal documents. Their feeling about it has an ethnic dimension. They do not like the Protestant temper. They read Max Weber with morose delight; for them, Calvinism is a nasty word.

The third group of conservative anti-capitalists–having been educated by such eminent anti-capitalists as Christopher Dawson, Matthew Arnold, Irving Babbitt, Charles Beard, and Vernon Parrington–have come to despise liberal philosophy both for its aesthetic vulgarity and for, as they see it, its international failings. Although they are by no means socialists, they share many of the socialists' critiques of multinational corporations overseas. They do not like "mass civilization," rock music, jeans, and tee shirts. They would like local aristocracies to be more paternal toward and understanding of the poor, and the poor to act with dignity without aspiring to modern acquisitiveness and ugly tastes. Their "option for the poor" does *not* consist of helping the poor to enter the vulgar middle class.

In brief, my own dream of undergirding the humaneness of liberal institutions with (as I see it) the more adequate Catholic philosophy of the human person, its deep sense of community, and its long-experienced respect for "intermediate associations" or "mediating structures," has been attacked both from the left and from the right. Curiously, the reasonings of the left and of the right are often similar. (Left and right have in common their passionate opposition to liberal institutions.)

Just the same, I have been moved by the essentially positive echo this book has received from both the right and the left. World events are apparently moving rapidly in the direction of liberal institutions, not so much for ideological reasons as because reality is on their side. In order to secure human rights, for example, more and more people are now convinced that liberal institutions are indispensable. Why? Because experience teaches that neither "parchment barriers" nor the good will of individual leaders can be relied upon. Again, in order to achieve real economic progress, even General Secretary Gorbachev and Party Chairman Deng Xiaoping publicly confess that liberal institutions are indispensable: chief among them, the unshackling of private initiative and creativity.

Institutionally, "liberalization" has become the central word of political economy in our time. The hypothesis undergirding liberal institutions is being daily vindicated in experience. The "system of natural liberty" – the set of institutions that most favors the flowering of the innate capacities of the human being – really does work for the common betterment of humankind, if not absolutely, at least in comparison to any known alternative. The liberal hypothesis, the liberal *défi* (as the French say), is experimental: Try it and see.

Its temper is empirical. Its presuppositions reach deep into the workings of human liberty and creativity.

In reading over the notices and reviews of the hardcover edition, however, I have discovered two types of misreadings. Even when some reviewers have grasped the book's main axis, they have not yet thought through its full power. That axis may be stated as follows. There is a difference between liberal philosophies and liberal institutions. Consider an analogy. In the creative arts, there is often a large distance between what an artist has achieved in his work and the interpretation of it given by that artist. One may admire and appropriate for oneself the meaning of a work of art, without accepting (or even knowing) the express interpretation that moved its creator. So also one may cherish liberal institutions, without embracing in all respects the philosophies of the liberal thinkers who first promoted them. Often those institutions have a greater human significance than their first progenitors discerned. Often there was a tacit wisdom in what they did whose full dimensions escaped their attention. The intellectual resources embodied in institutions, their historical fecundity, their unintended consequences, and their capacities for unplanned adaptation exceed the imaginative capacities of a single generation. When some institutions, like some works of art, have a truly universal dimension, they belong to all the generations and to all human beings.

Failing to grasp this, some reviewers have tried to fault me in one of two ways. Professor James Hanink wrote in *The National Catholic Register* that John Stuart Mill was a utilitarian, and surely (he writes with sarcasm) utilitarianism is no philosophy for the Catholic church or anyone else to recommend as a philosophical basis for human rights. Others, such as Peter Steinfels in *The Commonweal* and Joseph Walsh in *The Catholic World*, make the opposite accusation. I do not pay enough attention, they say, to the institutional, even political, struggle that has been necessary to bring about the historical modifications of "liberal capitalism" that they join me in welcoming. Both these types of criticism overlook my main point. The first confirms one side of my thesis: Liberal philosophy *is* often inadequate as a grounding for liberal institutions, particularly as the latter have developed. The second confirms the other side of my thesis: Liberal institutions have grown out of trial and error, out of struggle and conflict, out of the bloody experiences of many generations; but what commends them to our love and admiration is their internal capacity to undergo alteration and reform.

In one sense, then, I am trying to call attention to the way institutions have a life of their own in history, an intelligible life that permits of growth and genuine development from the germ of earlier intuitions. Institutions are full of tacit and not always articulable wisdom, just as works of art are. They bear study. But they do not yield up all their secrets to any one generation or body of thought—not, at least, if they are consonant with the depths of human personality. In all great achievements of the human race, as in human personality, there is an inexhaustibility that rewards fresh philosophical reflection in every generation. Among human works of art, political and social institutions are most noble. This is especially true regarding institutions of liberty.

In another sense, I am trying to provide a set of insights–a theory, an interpretation–that brings to light the inner intelligibility of liberal institutions in a way that has never before been attempted. Any readers moderately attentive to Reinhold Niebuhr's mature writing on the American experience will recognize here his dictum, expressed in *The Irony of American History,* that America's basic institutions contain a deeper, truer wisdom than any of the limited and inadequate theories we have about them.[3] Similarly, Jacques Maritain chided American philosophers, writing that we have never yet articulated an ideology worthy of our institutions.[4] I have always thought that making explicit what is tacit in common experience is a major part of the philosophical vocation.

My interpretation, of course, by no means exhausts the subject. But it is, so far as it goes, a true interpretation, making intelligible in liberal institutions aspects that have not been brought to light before. That at least is its claim.

One aspect of this originality (one only) is that I have taken phrases almost always used pejoratively in Catholic social thought ("liberal," "liberal individualism," "bourgeois individualism," "liberal capitalism") and shown their limitations. In nearly all cases, such locutions in official Catholic social teaching refer to specific philosophical propositions. Those philosophical propositions may well be rejected. But do they adequately describe the tacit wisdom, the inner intelligibility, of liberal institutions? I am certain that they do not.

Is official Catholic social thought opposed to the institutions of religious liberty found in such nations as Switzerland, West Germany, and the United States? To such political democracies as are found in the United States? To such liberal institutions as the separation of powers? To an independent judiciary? To a free press? To labor unions and other free associations independent of state control? To private universities, independent institutes of study and research, philanthropic foundations? Joseph Cardinal Hoeffner, probably the single most respected scholar of Catholic social thought among the bishops of the world, has written quite explicitly: "The proponents of Catholic social doctrine deem the market economy to be the right basic form for the economic system."[5]

Thus, to repeat myself, my distinction between philosophical propositions and living institutions is vital. Catholic socialists today absolutely rely upon it. When Pius XI said that "No one can be at the same time a sincere Catholic and a true socialist,"[6] they say, the Pope was condemning certain propositions of some socialists, but not necessarily the institutional developments sometimes described by that name today. What is good for the goose is good for the gander. If socialists can employ that distinction, so may liberals. Philosophies described as liberal have different histories in Italy, Spain, and Latin America from their histories in France and Germany; and different histories again in the United Kingdom and the United States. I am offering a definition of "liberal" that ties it to specific sets of institutions.

Since this point is so basic to my argument, it should not seem immodest to cite Aaron Wildavsky's grasp of it, when he wrote in the *New York Times*

*Book Review*: "To Michael Novak's great credit, he has placed at the center of his analysis a proper appreciation of the combinations of institutions necessary to approximate the disparate visions of Catholic social thought." This emphasis upon concrete institutions is basic to this book.

Wildavsky, however, makes a further point, on which we are in some disagreement. He seems to embrace the view that "there cannot be one moral rule for the church and another for society." In other words, a person who favors liberal institutions in the worldly society should also favor them in the church. Wildavsky poses an either/or situation: either the church will remain hierarchical, and therefore remain uncomfortable with an egalitarian conception of authority; or it will become egalitarian in its concept of authority and more in tune with the patterns of the liberal society.

From my viewpoint, Wildavsky errs in thinking that both the secular order and the religious order are better served when both have the same conception of authority. To keep alive the vital tension between two different conceptions of authority seems to me much more fitting to human reality. Indeed, the tension between these two different conceptions of authority is uncommonly fruitful for human creativity. I would not *want* a church that operated with the same conception of authority in the domain of faith and morals that the larger secular society employs. There are many areas of life in which truth is not determined by majority rule or individual preference. Scientific truths are not settled that way. Neither are facts. People are entitled to their own opinions. They are not entitled to their own facts.

A democratic, liberal society in particular needs to protect from erosion the fundamental truths by which it lives. For democratic societies (as the framers of the Constitution knew) are not threatened solely by tyrants; they are vulnerable, too, to temporary majorities that would override reason, virtue, and the rights of minorities. The dignity of the human person must be held sacred—not negotiable, not subject to human expedience, not vulnerable either to arrogant majorities or to slipsliding changes in public philosophy. Some truths are well held to be absolute, if democracies are not to be destroyed by their own inner weaknesses. I do not say that Professor Wildavsky needs to share my belief in the necessity of grounding the truths that our framers held to be "self-evident" in an absolute and unshakeable foundation. But he may find it good for democracy that many of us do share such a belief. Many of us do believe that democracy is rooted "in the nature of things"; truly a "system of natural liberty," and rooted in natural law.

At the same time, I am glad that government is forbidden laws about how such truths shall be defined, or by what reasonings they shall be articulated and defended. The state is not equipped, and should not be equipped, to impose truths and values of that sort. Neither may the state forbid minorities, churches, and seekers of truth from articulating, cherishing, and defending such truths, or from protecting their foundation in an authority as awesome and as ultimate as the Author of Life, Creator of the World, and Origin of Truth, of whom the framers of the American experiment did not hesitate to speak openly. In short, the institutions with authority in moral and religious matters need not, and should not, be organized in the same patterns as the civic institutions designed for worldly matters. Civil society should not be organized as the Catholic church is; the Church should not be organized as civil society is. The two different patterns of internal organization can, however, complement one another in ways highly creative for both.

Two or three other matters brought up in the reviews deserve comment. A few reviewers found the treatment of liberation theology in chapter ten too brief. Actually, three long chapters had been devoted to Latin America in *The Spirit of Democratic Capitalism*; when a revision of these chapters appeared as "Why Latin America is Poor" in *The Atlantic Monthly* (March 1982), *The Atlantic* received one of the largest volumes of letters to the editor in its entire history. Meanwhile, I was preparing a full-length treatment of the social reconstruction needed by Latin America if the poor are actually to become more affluent and free, to appear as the third volume of the trilogy, under the title *Will It Liberate? Questions About Liberation Theology*.

Each of these three volumes is intended to stand by itself. But together they offer a full study of new possibilities for Catholic social thought in our generation. Volume one, besides appearing in French, Italian, Korean, and Bengali, has already gone through several printings in Spanish and Portuguese (one translation in Brazil, another in Portugal). A large section of the present volume was translated in Spanish in *Estudios Publicos* (No. 20 [Spring 1985] Santiago, Chile). Volume three will soon be published in Spanish in Mexico.

Further, one reviewer, while agreeing that the treatment of John Stuart Mill in this volume worked quite well, opined that I would have a more difficult time showing the consonance between important themes in Catholic social thought and the thought of John Bright, one of the two most famous of the "Manchester liberals." Actually, I may be the only theologian who owns five volumes of the collected writings of John Bright (and four of Richard Cobden). While I have not had the occasion to complete a study of these volumes, I have already collected many texts from John Bright illustrative of the preeminence he gave Christian and humanistic values over merely economic considerations. For example, he was a resolute foe of those British textile manufacturers who for the sake of cotton sided with the Confederacy in the American Civil War. He argued that questions of religion and morality regarding the dreadful institution of slavery override considerations of profits, supply and demand. His arguments against protectionism and in favor of free international trade were based both upon moral principles of peace and justice and upon the practical superiority of an international as opposed to a nationalist approach to the common good.

Perhaps a long citation from his lecture "On the Distribution of Land," given in Edinburgh on January 26, 1864, will give a flavor of his general philosophy:

> I ask you if I am wrong in saying to the rich and the great, that
> I believe, if they knew their own interests, that it would be

worth their while to try to make this country a more desirable country for the labourer to live in. If they disregard this great question, we, who are of the middle, and not absolutely powerless class, shall have to decide between the claims of territorial magnates and the just rights of millions of our countrymen . . . . It may be so in this country. We build up a system which is injurious to our political freedom, and is destructive of the interests of our producing and working classes. Now, am I the enemy of any class, when I come forward to state facts like these, and to explain principles such as these? . . . I want our country to be populous, to be powerful, and to be happy. But this can only be done–it never has been done in any country–but by just laws justly administered. I plead only for what I believe to be just. I wish to do wrong to no man. For twenty-five years I have stood before audiences–great meetings of my countrymen–pleading only for justice. During that time, as you know, I have endured of abuse. I need not tell you that my clients have not been generally the rich and the great, but rather the poor and the lowly. They cannot give me place and dignities and wealth; but honourable service in their cause yields me that which is of far higher and more lasting value–the consciousness that I have laboured to expound and uphold laws, which, though they were not given amid the thunders of Sinai, are not less the commandments of God, and not less intended to promote and secure the happiness of men.[7]

There are many comparable passages in Richard Cobden. These two actual "Manchester liberals" – as distinct from the German group who took that name – are much closer to Catholic social thought on several cardinal points than has so far been noted by scholars.

Finally, a handful of readers chided me with referring too seldom to biblical texts. They failed to notice, however, that the texts of the Bible have powerful meaning under any and every system of political economy. With the great Jesuit theologian-economist, Heinrich Pesch, I am firmly of the belief that no one can deduce a system of political economy from the texts of the Bible alone.[8] In order to discover a system that actually works, to wit, that actually realizes the vision of humankind revealed in the Bible, a great deal of hard institutional discovery and worldly experimentation is required.

Biblical fundamentalism has often been a mischievous force in the story of actual human liberation, leading to murderously utopian policies, and justifying dreadful abuses of the rights of dissenters. To read the Bible intelligently, in the light of the best available human disciplines, and with a certain humility concerning one's own capacities for interpretation, is to draw upon far more intellectual disciplines than private meditation alone. One needs to add to study of the Bible a profound study of political philosophy, of social institutions, and of economic experiments throughout history. This is especially true regarding practice or, as the Marxists prefer, *praxis*. One of the central motifs of biblical realism is the pervasive sinfulness of human beings. Partly because of sin, and also for other reasons, one must think clearly about what actually does work—in a sinful world—to achieve the liberation of peoples and persons.[9] For institutions often work in counterintuitive ways that are best discerned by trial and error. Such is the irony of history. Biblical simplifiers have often before led their followers into tragedy.

I am grateful to the many reviewers of the hardcover edition, and look forward to dialogue with the readers and reviewers of this new and enlarged paperback edition.

In its hardcover edition, the descriptive subtitle of this book, *Catholic Social Thought and Liberal Institutions,* fell in second place. The publisher of the paperback edition wisely suggested that this part of the title describes the work's essential thesis better than the earlier title, *Freedom with Justice.* In the paperback edition these two titles have accordingly been reversed. It remains true, though, that the original title (now the subtitle) does catch well both the essence of the liberal pledge of "liberty and justice for all" and the inner development of Catholic social thought. For the latter has, in fact, been moving at first slowly but now with accelerating speed from a solitary emphasis upon "social justice" to the more balanced pairing of "freedom with justice." No justice is worthy of the human person that does not respect the seat of human dignity: human freedom. And the American word "freedom" (which presupposes a culture of "ordered liberty") is a more exact word than the simple Latin-root "liberty," whose Continental cultural presuppositions may include either libertarianism or even libertinism—or both.

Further, in preparing this new edition, I have thought it wise to bring it up to date (for reality moves "ever more swiftly," as Pope John Paul II has recently remarked). Thus, I have appended a quite long chapter on Pope John Paul II's new encyclical, *Sollicitudo Rei Socialis,* officially dated December 30, 1987, but actually released late in February 1988. At the risk of repeating myself, I also include an account of Cardinal Ratzinger's two Instructions on Liberation Theology, issued respectively on September 3, 1984, and April 5, 1986. Longer accounts of both are at hand in my *Will it Liberate? Questions about Liberation Theology.*[10]

Although all three drafts of the U.S. Catholic Bishops' Pastoral Letter on the U.S. Economy were issued after the hardcover edition of the present volume went to press, the predictions I made about it at the end of chapter three have held up pretty well, at least as regards the bishops' final (much amended) draft. Those who wish to inspect the long two-year debate culminating in that final version can easily do so. Even while the hardcover edition of the present book was in press, I was invited to take part with other Catholic lay persons in publishing the *Lay Letter on Catholic Social Thought and the U.S. Economy,* which was issued in advance of the bishops' first draft under the title *Toward the Future*. Archbishop Rembert G. Weakland, chairman of the bishops' drafting committee, preferred that we publish our letter before, rather than after, the bishops' first draft appeared. We respected his wishes. (Afterwards, many supporters of the bishops' draft accused us of having launched a "preemptive" strike. We took that description as a compliment. They would not have so described it if we had fallen on our faces.) The bishops' pastoral, the lay letter, and the accompanying literature are easily accessible.[11] There is little need to summarize these matters here, for they fall within the scope of the larger argument mapped out in this volume.

I should probably underline, however, the historic and international significance of these events. Ironically, many on the Catholic left, who usually celebrate lay initiative, were surprisingly unwilling to celebrate *this* exercise of lay initiative. Few even applauded it "in principle." True, it is not usual for lay persons to issue their own "letter" in conjunction with that of their bishops, even concerning matters that do belong "preeminently" to lay persons in the Church. On the whole, however, the U.S. bishops reacted very well to the lay letter and took it in stride. They wrote—and re-wrote—their own three drafts, always taking criticisms from all sides into account. It was a better final product because of their admirable openness.

To summarize, this volume may be read as the second volume of a trilogy: coming after *The Spirit of Democratic Capitalism* and before *Will It Liberate*? It is, further, part of the much larger body of work on basic questions of religion, philosophy, and public policy that it has been my privilege to direct during this past decade at the American Enterprise Institute.[12] But it is intended also to stand on its own, as a one-volume survey of Catholic social thought since 1891, whose fruitful development it is intended to further.

The motto of AEI, "The competition of ideas is essential to a free society," is lived out every day among my many colleagues. Once again, I want to express my gratitude to them for their fellowship, many criticisms and profound suggestions—and especially to the successive presidents of AEI, William J. Baroody, Sr., William J. Baroody, Jr., and Christopher DeMuth, each of whom has exemplified both the liberal spirit and the cherishing of community that liberal institutions take as their ideal.

Michael Novak

## Notes

1.    *The Spirit of Democratic Capitalism* (New York: Simon & Schuster, 1982).

2.  See Arthur F. McGovern, *Marxism: An American Christian Perspective* (Maryknoll, New York: 1980), esp. ch. 9, "Personal Reflections: Marxism, Socialism, and the United States." McGovern criticizes "*concentration* of ownership [original emphasis], not private ownership as such. Some socialists/Marxists seem to argue as if private ownership by its very nature is alienating because it encourages individualism. I do not agree with this. American pride in the self-made person, and reward for personal responsibility, hard work, and initiative, are not misplaced values, nor should they be equated with selfish individualism" (p. 317). John C. Cort has criticized Gustavo Gutierrez for taking socialism in a Marxist direction. See Cort, "Christ and Neighbor," *New Oxford Review*, January-February 1985; and "Reply," *New Oxford Review*, May 1985.

3.  America's "experiences in domestic politics," Niebuhr writes, "represent an ironic form of success. Our success in establishing justice and insuring domestic tranquility has exceeded the characteristic insights of a bourgeois culture." He adds: "The unarticulated wisdom embodied in the actual experience of American life has created forms of justice considerably higher than our more articulate unwisdom suggests." *The Irony of American History* (New York: Charles Scribner's Sons, 1962), pp. 89, 105.

4.  Maritain devoted an entire chapter of his *Reflections on America* (New York: Charles Scribner's Sons, 1958) to "The Need for an Explicit Philosophy": "You are advancing in the night, bearing torches toward which mankind would be glad to turn; but you leave them enveloped in the fog of a merely experiential approach and mere practical conceptualization, with no universal ideas to communicate. For lack of adequate ideology, your lights cannot be seen" (p. 118).

5.  See Joseph Cardinal Hoeffner, "Economic Systems and Economic Ethics," *Crisis*, June 1986, p. 15.

6.  *Quadragesimo Anno*, 120.

7.  James E. Thorold Rogers, ed., *Speeches on Questions of Public Policy by John Bright, M.P.*, 2nd ed., 2 vols. (London: Macmillan; reprint ed., New York: Kraus, 1970), 2:336-7.

8.  See *infra*, ch. 4, "The Architects of Catholic Social Thought," esp. p. 71.

9.  In the first chapter of *Moral Man and Immoral Society* (New York: Charles Scribner's Sons, 1960), Reinhold Niebuhr gives a dozen reasons why a collective's conduct cannot be as moral as a person's. Prudential judgment and the careful study of institutions are crucial.

10.  See Novak, *Will It Liberate? Questions About Liberation Theology* (New York: Paulist Press, 1986), ch. 11, "Epilogue: The Second Vatican Instruction on Liberation."

11.  For the text of the bishops' pastoral letter, see *Origins*, 27 November 1986. For the Lay Commission on Catholic Social Teaching's texts, see *Toward the Future: Catholic Social Thought and the U.S. Economy* (Lanham, Maryland: University Press of America, 1984); Lay Commission, *Liberty and Justice for All* (Notre Dame, Indiana: Brownson Institute, 1986). See also Novak, "Toward Consensus: Revising the Bishops' First Draft," *Catholicism in Crisis*, March 1985; "Blaming America: A Comment on Paragraphs 202-204 of the First Draft," *Catholicism in Crisis*, July 1985; "Economic Rights: The Servile State," *Catholicism in Crisis*, October 1985; "To Promote the General Welfare: Catholic Principles for Welfare Policy," in John W. Houck and Oliver F. Williams, eds., *Catholic Social Teaching and the United States Economy: Working Papers for a Bishops' Pastoral* (Washington, D.C.: University Press of America, 1985); "Where the Second Draft Errs," *America*, 18 January

1986; "Economic Rights," *National Catholic Register*, 16 February 1986; "The Option for the Poor: Clarifications," *Saint Louis University Public Law Review* 5 (1986): 309-328; "The Rights and Wrongs of 'Economic Rights': A Debate Continued," *This World*, Spring 1987. Two panel discussions should also be consulted; see *Catholic Social Teaching and the U.S. Economy: A Conversation with Archbishop Rembert Weakland* (Washington, D.C.: American Enterprise Institute, 1985); and "Catholic Bishops' Pastoral and the American Economy," *This World*, Winter 1985, with contributions by Walter Berns, Michael Novak, John Langan, Brian Benestad, and Donald Warwick.

12. I have edited the following studies at AEI: *Capitalism and Socialism: A Theological Inquiry* (1979); *The Denigration of Capitalism: Six Points of View* (1979); *Democracy and Mediating Structures: A Theological Inquiry* (1981); *Liberation South, Liberation North* (1981); *Latin America: Dependency or Interdependence?* (1985); and *Liberation Theology and the Liberal Society* (1987). See also Bernard Murchland, *Humanism and Capitalism: A Survey of Thought on Morality* (1984); Muhammad Abdul-Rauf, *A Muslim's Reflections on Democratic Capitalism* (1984); Peter L. Berger and Michael Novak, *Speaking to the Third World: Essays on Democracy and Development* (1985); and Michael Novak, *The American Vision: An Essay on the Future of Democratic Capitalism* (1978); and *Toward a Theology of the Corporation* (1981).

# Acknowledgments

This book came into existence through many cooperators; I thank them all.

Terry Hall was my research assistant during the early stages of preparation; after January 1984, Scott Walter filled his place. Both performed heroically, Terry especially on Mill, Scott especially on Pesch and Ketteler. During early 1984, Daryl Borgquist helped a great deal with many details.

During the summer of 1983, as student interns, Warren Meyer and Scott Walter began collecting materials for Part II. Also, interns Dennis David, from the National Journalism Center, and David Seymour lent a hand.

The following persons read sections of earlier drafts of this manuscript and made valuable suggestions: Charles Curran, Gertrude Himmelfarb, James Finn, Robert Spaeth, Edward A. Marciniak, Monsignor John Tracy Ellis, Edward M. Littlejohn, Thomas Langan, Henry Briefs, Jude Dougherty and, above all, Thomas M. Gannon, S.J., who carefully read the whole manuscript and made many good suggestions. I am especially indebted to Franz H. Mueller for many detailed, critical comments; because of him, the book is far better than it would have been, even though not up to his measure.

A friend and editor, Neal Kozodoy, once again lent me his rich skills in reducing the penultimate draft by many pages.

Through all this, Gayle Yiotis typed and re-typed, freely and cheerfully proffering sensible advice.

And Clay Carlson and John Loudon of Harper & Row, as they have so often, midwived these many efforts to publication.

The end, for democracy, is both justice and freedom.
—JACQUES MARITAIN *Man and the State*

... where political regimes do not allow to private individuals the possession also of productive goods, the exercise of human liberty is violated or completely destroyed ... in the right of property, the exercise of liberty finds both a safeguard and a stimulus.... This explains the fact that socio-political groups and associations which endeavor to reconcile *freedom with justice* within society, and which until recently did not uphold the right of private property in productive goods, have now, enlightened by the course of social events, modified their views and are disposed actually to approve this right.
—POPE JOHN XXIII *Mater et Magistra*

We have realized that the modern experiment, originally conceived only as an experiment in freedom, had to become also an experiment in justice. We know that the myopic individualism of modernity led it into other errors, even into a false conception of the problem of the state in terms of the unreal dichotomy, individualism vs. collectivism.
—JOHN COURTNEY MURRAY *We Hold These Truths*

# Introduction

*What does it profit a man if he liberate the whole world, and suffer the loss of his soul?*

—A single word is changed in Matthew 16:26

More and more, the religious leaders of the world are addressing problems of political economy. Their attention is focusing on this world.

How did this shift happen? Which directions should pioneers now explore for the future?

This book answers these two questions by inquiring into Catholic social thought and the institutions of liberalism. Its thesis may be simply stated: Although the Catholic Church during the nineteenth and early twentieth centuries set itself against liberalism *as an ideology*, it has slowly come to support the moral efficacy of liberal *institutions*. Most clearly, it has come to support institutions of human rights. But it has also—more slowly—come to support institutions of democracy and market-oriented economic development.

There is a profound consonance (although not identity) between the Catholic vision of social justice and the liberal institutions which, in this poor and broken world, have better than others allowed the human spirit to flourish. Catholic social thought, learning from experience, will almost certainly continue in this direction.

Although I focus upon the Catholic social tradition, all who are concerned with the moral and religious quality of human systems should find that tradition both instructive in itself and parallel to developments in their own intellectual histories. Before we can establish common ground, each of us needs to delve as deeply as we can into our own intellectual roots. As Paul Tillich once observed, it is in the depths of each religious tradition that we come closer together, in the Source of all our lives, than on the thinner and more conventional surfaces.

My aim in Part I is to proceed from the general to the concrete: First a discussion of religion and economics; then a chapter on realism in both the liberal and the Catholic social traditions; then a chapter on two concrete problems in a contemporary liberal society. The U.S. Catholic bishops will address these two concrete problems, among others, in a pastoral letter on the U.S. economy to be issued in 1985.

In Part II I undertake detailed work on the main texts both of Catholic social thought and of the liberal tradition as represented in John Stuart Mill. In Latin cultures, including the Vatican, *liberalismo* is mainly known through the anti-clerical, often materialistic tradition which goes from Jean-Jacques Rousseau to Marx. Anglo-American liberalism is oddly ignored. Yet the liberal *institutions* which Catholic social thought has come increasingly to appreciate owe much of their development to Anglo-American liberals, of whom Mill is an early prototype.

In Part III I address some of the problems with which Catholic social thought is bound to be wrestling during the rest of this century. These problems are preeminently practical. How does one build institutions that actually protect human rights? Which institutions must be established to protect "the consent of the governed"? Which ethos, which virtues, and which institutions must be prized and nourished in order to ease the sufferings of the poor? We must help the poor. But how?

In such matters, words and theories are not enough. Actual results must be produced, in a sustainable and progressively advancing way. The two ancient enemies of the human race are poverty and tyranny. Both must be vanquished in the harsh arena of reality.

In the pursuit of such goals, both Catholic social thought and liberal institutions are drawn towards a "marriage made in heaven," but far from being realized on earth. It is our vocation, in our generation, to move it toward happy and mutual consummation.

Many call an approach such as mine "neo-conservative." The proper designation for it, I believe, is "neo-liberal" or "realist." I prefer to call the approach, as a whole, "biblical realism." But labels do not finally matter so much as realities. For this reason, I have tried my best to focus debate on institutions rather than on ideology. Of such institutions, the central one is the family—an institution too much taken for granted in liberal thought, but happily foremost in Catholic thought. To focus on institutions rather than on ideology, and on the family rather than the individual or the state, is part of what I mean by realism.

MICHAEL NOVAK

*May, 1984*

# Part I

## CATHOLIC AND LIBERAL

Nor is prudence a knowledge of general principles only: it must take account of particular facts, since it is concerned with action, and action deals with particular things. This is why men who are ignorant of general principles are sometimes more successful in action than others who know them ... [often] men of experience are more successful than theorists.

—ARISTOTLE *Nicomachean Ethics*

All virtue is necessarily prudent.

—ST. THOMAS AQUINAS *On the Virtues in General*

Nothing less than the whole ordered structure of the Occidental Christian view of man rests upon the preeminence of prudence over the other virtues.

—JOSEF PIEPER *Prudence*

# CHAPTER 1

# Theology and Economics: The Next Twenty Years

The practical task of social science is to give prudence access to a more enlightened condition. Thus the progress of social science is well in line with the requirements of prudence, whose duty it is to extend, in the obscurities of contingency, the work of the reason down to immediate contact with the world of action.
—YVES R. SIMON *The Tradition of the Natural Law*

Since Prudence has for its matter, not a thing-to-be-made, an object determined in being, but the pure use that the subject makes of his freedom, it has no certain and determined ways or fixed rules; . . . for applying the universal principles of moral science, precepts and counsels, to the particular action to be produced, there are no ready-made rules; for this action is clothed in a tissue of circumstances which individualize it and make of it each time a truly new case.
—JACQUES MARITAIN *Art and Scholasticism*

In her doctrinal affirmations the Church is confident, even optimistic. . . . On the other hand, the Church is prudent, even cautious, in the area of practice. Her concrete counsels to her children have not the same confidence as her doctrinal statements; they are touched with an accent of warning, even of fear. She boldly urges the truth; she carefully guides action.
—JOHN COURTNEY MURRAY *We Hold These Truths*

During the past four years, a voracious reader would have encountered more articles and books on matters of political economy than at any earlier period in his life—including a mounting number of statements on economics by religious leaders. Whether the subject is tax policy, capital formation, monetarism, unemployment, welfare, infrastructure, "supply side," "industrial policy," or international trade, those not formally trained in economics have rather suddenly had to do considerable homework.

Religious leaders and theologians are awakening to the fact that their accustomed periodicals have ill-prepared them for this hour. Books on church and state, religion and politics, religion and the arts, religion and psychiatry, and religion and sex outnumber books on theology and economics by a very large factor. Moreover, concerning even elementary concepts of economic thought, religious leaders and theologians commonly find themselves without exact and clear definitions. To create a new subdiscipline of theology, "a theology of policital economy," will take a generation of hard work.

## 1. THREE "HABITS OF THE MIND"

Some of this work has already been done, particularly in the Catholic tradition. Since the soon-to-be Bishop von Ketteler of Mainz (1811–1877) first raised the "social question" in his lectures of 1848, a distinguished line of German scholars, several of them Jesuits, has maintained a vital tradition of critical reflection on the interpenetrations of economic and religious realities.[1] Among the most distinguished names of this tradition are Heinrich Pesch, S.J. (1854–1926), Oswald von Nell-Breuning, S.J. (b. 1890), Gustav Gundlach, S.J. (1892–1963), Goetz Briefs (1889–1974), and Franz Mueller (b. 1900).[2] One American scholar, Father John A. Ryan (1869–1945), quite independently of the Europeans, also created a distinguished body of work (including *A Living Wage, Distributive Justice,* and *The Reconstruction of the Social Order*) which had considerable impact upon the administration of Franklin Delano Roosevelt, as is suggested in the title of Ryan's biography, *Right Reverend New Dealer.*[3] Joseph Schumpeter has described the European branch of this tradition in his *History of Economic Analysis.*[4]

Since 1891, moreover, the Roman Catholic popes have discussed the connections between religion and economics in a series of official letters addressed to all Catholics of the world (this is the meaning of the term "encyclical"). Cumulatively, these letters have created a self-conscious tradition of concepts and descriptive analyses, basic principles and prudential judgments, about existing political economies. They form a running commentary on the flow of worldly events during the last one hundred years. Among the basic landmark texts, usually issued on anniversaries of the first, are Leo XIII's *Rerum Novarum* (1891), Pius XI's *Quadragesimo Anno* (1931), John XXIII's *Mater et Magistra* (1961) and *Pacem in Terris* (1963), Paul VI's *Populorum Progressio* (1967) and *Octogesima Adveniens* (1971), and John Paul II's *Laborem Exercens* (1981).[5] The first two of these focus, for the most part, on the political economies of Western Europe. The later ones assume worldwide perspectives. Since over half the world's Catholics now live in so-called Third World nations, the latter emphasis may be expected to continue.

For more than one hundred years, meanwhile, the "social gospel" movement in American Protestantism, like the many movements of Christian socialism in Europe, has also developed basic texts in religion and economics.[6] In successive generations, the writings of Walter Rauschenbusch (1861–1918) and Reinhold Niebuhr (1892–1971) became the focal points of extensive discussion and remarkable activism.[7] The life-work of Walter Muelder (b. 1907) of Boston University, one of the teachers of Martin Luther King, Jr., has also been an important intellectual force.[8] In 1937 the Oxford Conference, a subsequent set of eleven volumes on religion and economics, and many other study projects of the World Council of Churches and the National Council of Churches have created a potent Protestant corpus on this subject.[9] In the period 1960–1980, the preoccupations of Protestant social thought, at least in the United States, turned to other matters, such as race and civil rights, the war in Vietnam, feminism, and the environment. But in recent years there has been a marked return to economic questions, led by adversarial work on the multinationals, dependency theory, the Nestlé boycott, and studies of "corporate responsibility" and "business ethics."

In recent years the Presbyterians, Methodists, and others have maintained high-level study groups on various economic issues. Finally, the evangelical churches, too, are being drawn into fierce public debates that carry them well beyond the traditional individual experience of faith and into activism concerning issues of political economy.[10]

For at least three reasons, moreover, we can expect religious leaders —and lay study groups, universities, and the religious press—to devote yet more attention to religion and economics. First, the continuing struggles of the developing nations will weigh heavily on the consciousness of all. Second, the twenty or so democratic capitalist nations (some would say "mixed economies" or "welfare states") of the world have had unprecedented success in bringing the great bulk of their populations far above the levels of subsistence known in 1891. This sudden rise to affluence has altered the terms of the debate and raised new questions. Third, the "welfare states" themselves seem to have reached the upper limits of the state-guaranteed benefits they can *easily* offer to their citizens. From now on, they may safely be expected to face increasingly difficult choices in which, frequently, one good will have to be traded off for another.

For these and other reasons, political leaders will continue to spend a disproportionate amount of their time facing economic difficulties. Citizens will become engaged in intense public arguments concerning taxes and benefits, ends and means. The churches will become, to some extent, activist pressure groups on various economic issues.

This movement of social forces may, or may not, proceed with intelligence, civility, and practical wisdom. It will surely proceed in many different voices and styles. To help establish a workable framework for discussion, three typical habits of mind will here need to be distinguished, since each bears in a different way upon public policy. Let me call these habits of mind the charismatic, the scientific, and the prudential.

*The charismatic habit.* Often at religious study centers one hears that all should be "converted" to "peace and justice." This habit of mind deserves the name *charismatic* precisely because of its appeal to conversion, as if from outside-in. This approach seems to have arisen in Latin America, in the experience of *conscientization,* in which ordinary people in prayerful reflection on their political-economic circumstances (it is said) burst into a gospel-filled "analysis" of their situation. Whatever its origin, this charismatic habit of mind must be distinguished from the religious habit of mind in general, since obviously most religious persons do not share it and have to be "converted" into it. It must also be distinguished from another sense of "charismatic" becoming common in evangelical and nowadays in Catholic circles, by which is meant an individual "moved by the Holy Spirit" in a sudden rush of deeply felt experience. Typically, the evangelical sense of the charismatic leads to concern with one's own soul in relation to God and one's neighbors. By contrast, the charismatic habit of mind I have been pointing to is aimed at social activism in political and economic matters: "peace and justice."

*The scientific habit.* Among professional economists, the scientific habit will need little exposition. It is the habit of disciplining one's perceptions, procedures, and judgments according to established canons of inquiry, in such a way that one's own activities may be replicated by similarly disciplined others. These canons are often summed up by the word "objectivity." They make possible the confirmation or disconfirmation of theories in accord with rules for presenting evidence.

*The prudential habit.* As all political economists have traditionally observed—witness John Stuart Mill in the preface to his *Principles of Political Economy*[11]—the scientific investigator employs a habit of mind different from that of the statesman or man of affairs who is an activist in the same field. The statesman faces pressures of time, since he must often act (or fail to act) before a scientific account of the circumstances can possibly be executed. Moreover, he must make estimates of how various other free agents may react, if he himself acts thus or so. He must make decisions about human character, current circumstance, and future probabilities, about which science cannot afford him certain judgments in advance. Yet, although the statesman cannot be held to scientific standards, he is not thereby released to standards that take no account of rationality at all. On the contrary, wise decisions are still distinguished from foolish. The standard of rationality applied in such cases has long been called by the classical name of *prudence* (Aristotle's *phronesis*).[12] The prudential habit of mind is the acquired skill of recognizing and doing the right thing at the right time and in the right way, so as to be judged by history as having acted wisely rather than foolishly. Since prudence must cover decisions made in all circumstances, under all contingencies, it is not easy to define its workings through some fixed set of standardized procedures. Its presence or absence is, nonetheless, remarked in every human decision.

There is a reason for keeping these three habits of mind distinct. Some, but not all of those who are most active in bringing religious judgment to bear on economic matters operate from within the charismatic habit of mind. Sometimes, but not always, economists who, as fate would have it, are engaged in argument with them, argue from within the scientific habit of mind. Typically, the issue to be addressed can be wisely approached only within the prudential habit of mind.

Economists need desperately to begin paying attention to claims about economic reality being made among religious leaders and by theologians. For when the churches become gripped by certain ways of thinking and feeling, they do move public opinion; the campaign for the nuclear freeze may serve as an instance. Simply as teachers, economists have a right and a duty to protect the integrity of their field. Moreover, the fate of millions of the poor is involved. Ideologies whose predictable result is economic misery and political tyranny need to be criticized while they are still in infancy, before they assume gigantesque proportions. A thorough review of the economic teachings of the World Council of Churches, the National Council of Churches, and the papacy is very much in order and desperately needed.

On the other hand, too narrow a view of the vocation of the scientist removes the professional economists from this task. An economist may concentrate on his scientific work as a shoemaker sticks to his last. Second, and rather less likely, an economist may imagine that his scientific discipline contains all that needs to be known or recognized in dealing with matters of political economy. Pope John Paul II refers to this narrow perspective as *economism*.[13] This is the vice of making a science into an ideology, a vision of ends, a denial of the legitimacy of other methods of inquiry. In practice, few economists seem vulnerable to this charge; most point out frequently that they canot tell others what they ought to do, but can, through their methods, help to calculate material (and sometimes other) costs and benefits of any such choice. Typically, the economist *qua* economist knows that he is a scientist, not a statesman nor even an investor or a businessman. And he commonly recognizes that when he is acting as either of the latter, he assumes the prudential habit of mind.

In any good argument, it is crucial for all participants to find their way into the same habit of mind, so that the rules of discourse and the canons of evidence are clear and mutually agreeable. In the sorts of arguments religious persons are eager to have with economists, this typically means that the argument is not supposed to be *scientific*. The alternative is *not* that it must then become *charismatic* in the sense described above. The proper alternative is that it should become *prudential*. In that case the economist will not be expected to argue merely as a scientist (although he will be expected not to forget his science), but, rather, as a statesman or person of affairs: as a prudent person facing concrete cases and the contingent circumstances of decisions about future policies. This seems fair enough. On the other side, the religious leader or theologian must be subject to exactly the same expectations.

No doubt each party to the debate will go often to his own strength, the religious leader to religious principles or ideals about the future, the economist to economic principles and his own ideals about the future.

## 2. DEFINING THE TERMS

The problem is that here, too, there is considerable slippage. On occasion, the same words are used with different meanings rooted in quite diverse intellectual traditions. Four examples of such systematic verbal miscommunication are "self-interest," "acquisitiveness," "profits," and "markets."

### 1. SELF-INTEREST

When an economist uses this term, he means autonomous choice. He says nothing at all about the moral content of the choice; in the eyes of the economist, that frame is deliberately kept empty. Self-interest means *whatever* a person has chosen, whether it is sanctity or truth, pleasure or material benefit. The concept is as general and empty as possible, in order to be universalizable.

The very same word, however, has quite different meanings in theology. In Islamic and Jewish traditions, for example, "self-interest" does not typically have negative connotations. It is understood as an elemental commonsense duty to oneself, quite reasonable and basic. In this context, the commandment "Love thy neighbor as thyself" has a sound basis. A fundamental and proper love of self (including love for one's family and community, one's duties, and one's vocation) is no cause for moral uneasiness.

In the Christian tradition, however, "self-interest" has acquired a pejorative connotation. There are two reasons why this is so. First, Christianity strives to go "beyond the law." Under this impulse, which is not necessarily orthodox, Christians often feel obliged to reject (or to disguise) self-interest as imperfect, flawed, self-enclosed. Secondly, the Christian understanding of love, especially as *agape* (self-sacrificial love), seems to some Christians to be *opposed* to self-interest. A Christian should be like Christ, who was "a man for others." An appeal to self-interest seems, in this symbolic network, directly contrary to the Christian appeal to the denial of self-interest in order to love God and neighbor.

Adam Smith was a professor of moral philosophy who praised sympathy and fellow feeling as the highest human qualities, while observing how, in practice, "self-interest" may serve the common good. When Smith speaks of the "self-interest" of the butcher and the baker, however, this "self-interest" is seldom individualistic merely. The butcher tolerates the blood and the baker bears the heat, not for themselves alone but for their families and their dependents. They sacrifice their own present for a future which only their children may enjoy.

Thus care must be taken in discussions of religion and economics to unpack the misleadingly simple concept of self-interest, so as to specify its exact moral meaning in each and every context. Without such care, conflicting meanings may frustrate understanding. Theologians will naturally question whether businessmen work for altruism, as George Gilder says, or for personal advantage. Erik Erickson has developed the concept of "basic trust" (which he does not scruple to relate to biblical love) to mean a psychological attitude toward reality which permits the self to reach out, to act, to take risks, to create new events—as opposed to psychological withdrawal, mistrust, inability to affirm, and self-enclosure.[14] "Basic trust," Erickson believes, is the root impulse of creativity, love, faith, and affirmation. This, I think, is what Gilder is getting at. The opposite to the person of basic trust is the miser, the hoarder, the Scrooge. The Belgian sociologist of economics Leo Moulin[15] holds that one reason why Judaism and Christianity were indispensable conditions for the discovery of capitalism is that they taught human beings that creation is good, that God is good, that humans are made in the image of the Creator—and, therefore, that they should be bold, free, inventive, exploratory, and creative. When Dante wrote of "the love that moves the sun and all the stars," he similarly used "love" in this general meaning of affirmation, movement, act.

Thus theologians and economists both would do well to study the depths hidden behind the word "self-interest." It is a word of many meanings and profound associations. Unexamined, it causes unnecessary mischief.

## 2. ACQUISITIVENESS

R. H. Tawney, the socialist historian, was the decisive force in selecting acquisitiveness as the fundamental motive of capitalist economic activity; he did not do so for friendly reasons.[16] This word confuses two quite different motivations. Truly, the miser is acquisitive; he hoards, holds, wants to possess. The miser's behavior is quite different from that of the investor, the entrepreneur, and the inventor. Two key words in a capitalist civilization are "new" and "improved." Business reaches out to create new things and often fails. Technological invention in one place also means obsolescence in another. It is not *having* and *grasping* that characterize the capitalist spirit, but *letting go* and *venturing, creating* and *rendering obsolete*. Max Weber was far more penetrating than Tawney:

The impulse to acquisition, pursuit of gain, of money, of the greatest possible amount of money, has in itself nothing to do with capitalism. This impulse exists and has existed among waiters, physicians, coachmen, artists, prostitutes, dishonest officials, soldiers, nobles, crusaders, gamblers, and beggars. One may say that it has been common to all sorts and conditions of men at all times and in all countries of the earth, wherever the objective possibility of it is or has been given. It should be taught in the kindergarten of cultural history that this naïve idea of capitalism must be given up once and for all. Unlimited greed for gain is not in the least identical with capitalism and is still less its spirit.[17]

What does define a capitalist order is, rather, the habit of abstaining from consumption and from miserly hoarding, in order to invest in creative ventures. The aim is to produce new wealth in a sustained way—which new wealth is then again similarly invested. Why should one do this? Individuals each have their own purposes; but clearly the economic development of the planet demands it, so long as poverty abides. Individuals drink different draughts of this restless creativity, this capitalist spirit, whose aim is not to live sumptuously or even comfortably, as was the spirit of pre-capitalist persons of wealth, but to create ever new wealth in a sustained and systematic way.[18] "Acquisitiveness" and "possessiveness" name this spirit badly.

### 3. PROFIT

The semantic confusion is just as great with "profit." Most persons confuse profit with mark-up. They further intuitively confuse profit with cash taken out of the business by owners or managers. They think that the capitalist spirit is "Buy cheap, sell dear," and that profits "go into the pocket" of those who make them.

Religious leaders need to understand the ways in which profit is another word for development. Not to earn profit is to be economically stagnant or going backwards. In our day, perhaps as many as half of all Americans whose family income is more than $30,000 a year are engaged in activities of government, teaching, research, and other activities that earn no profit. No wonder many have an inadequate conception of profit; they have no experience in earning it in a sustained, creative, venturesome way. If they did, they would see that most profit is a cost of doing productive work. Some of it goes to retire the loans used to start up a business. Some of it is invested in improving the product or in finding new markets for it. By far, the largest proportion of profit is reinvested. Typically, only a small proportion of it is used in paying dividends to the original investors (to whom the business is in debt) and in raising salaries. One may say that dividends and salaries go "into someone's pockets," but often enough that money, too, is reinvested.

Religious leaders may retort that this is how "the rich get richer." Yet, as John Stuart Mill pointed out in *The Principles of Political Economy*, there is a keen difference between wealth and capital.[19] Wealth merely hoarded or used for consumption is unproductive. Capital is that portion of wealth which is reinvested in productive activities. Wealth may or may not be socially useful. But capital provides many social benefits in the form of new employment, goods, services, invention, and new wealth. It provides the funds which are paid both into nonprofit activities and into taxes. Profit is also the source of funds for the research and development on which future prosperity depends.

Those who are in favor of doing away with profits are necessarily in favor of halting the production of new wealth (that is, development). If they retort that their wish is rather to "socialize" profit, by yielding all profit to the state, they subordinate the economic system to the political system. Does such subordination serve the common good? Such experiments have been widely tried. Empirical surveys are in order. Is not profit, in any case, best understood as the margin of new wealth created by the prudent investment of old?

## 4. THE MARKET

In theological circles, the word "market" has been surrounded by many symbolic overtones. It is treated as a question of faith or ideology; whether to *trust* "the magic of the marketplace" or not. In addition, some seem to harbor fears about the market; if it is left free and untrammeled, things will spin out of control, no one will be in charge, irrationality and abuse will spread, anarchy will ensue, the strong will take advantage of the weak.

Of course, there is no one "market." There are only many particular markets. A market for home computers is an aggregation of those who want to purchase home computers now and those who manufacture and distribute them for sale. A short while ago, no such market existed. Markets come and disappear (although antiquarians sometimes keep markets going long after fashion passes by). Some are large, especially those designed for potentially every family and person, and some are small, especially those for very expensive or highly specialized goods or services. Some markets are easy to find or to establish, some quite difficult. Some goods and services are not marketed. Air, though an indispensable good, did not have a market in John Stuart Mill's time, although he foresaw its potential marketability in places where air was absent. Sometimes the word "market" is used metaphorically, as in "the free market of ideas" or even "the market for religious belonging in a pluralist society." In such cases, one does not mean literally that persons actually "purchase" religious belonging. Yet even commitments of the spirit must be "exchanged" from person to person and are subject to autonomous choice; hence, the metaphor.

In summary, economists need to know that words they use as familiar coin may strike the ears of religious leaders with echoes economists do not intend. The translation of meaning from one intellectual tradition to another is no easy task.

## 3. THE ANTI-LIBERAL TRADITION IN THE CHURCHES

During the nineteenth century religious leaders and theologians often defended the *ancien régime* and traditional values, being rather skeptical about political democracy and cultural pluralism. But their hesitations with respect to politics and culture were as nothing compared to their virtually unanimous disapprobation of capitalist economics. Max Weber argued in *The Protestant Ethic and the Spirit of Capitalism* that certain Protestant conceptions and habits were indispensable to the emergence of the new capitalist ethos. This is quite different from suggesting that Protestant (or any other religious) leaders actively promoted the new capitalist ethos in speech and book. In fact, few did; and Weber could cite very few. Typically, even those "Catholic liberals" of France who, like Lamennais, were in favor of political democracy, were quite opposed to "individualism" in the economic and cultural spheres. Such religious "liberals" may not have joined the Christian socialists. But most were, in varying degrees, anti-capitalist. In England, the motto of the Christian socialists was: "Christianity is the religion of which socialism is the practice." Paul Tillich said that socialism "is the only possible economic system from the Christian point of view."[20]

This tendency in religious thought, it is worth noting, is sometimes more exactly described as "anti-capitalist" than as "pro-socialist." Thus, for example, the influential British writers Hilaire Belloc *(The Servile State)* and G. K. Chesterton *(The Outline of Sanity)* opposed both socialism and capitalism, in the name of what they called Distributism.[21] Furthermore, many religious writers employed a *pre*-capitalist point of view. While they favored traditional institutions such as private property and free markets, they did not like certain features of the capitalist *spirit,* its ethos, its liberal "philosophy." This is true of Chesterton and Belloc, of many non-Marxist Christian socialists, clearly so of Popes Leo XIII and Pius XI, and probably, as well, if one takes their work as a whole, of such American critics of capitalism, sometimes more or less loosely calling themselves socialists, as Walter Rauschenbusch and Reinhold Niebuhr.[22]

If we date the beginnings of the democratic capitalist era from Adam Smith's *Inquiry into the Nature and Causes of The Wealth of Nations,* in 1776, it becomes evident that two streams which are analytically quite separate were often in reality intermixed. In front of one's face was the complex reality of the newly emerging social system of political economy. (By parity of designation, this new system is fairly called "democratic" in its political part and "capitalist" in economy.) Flowing through one's head was the body of theory—the vibrant ideology, usually called "liberalism"—advanced by those who promoted this system. Quite often, the ideology did not match the reality. Yet, for those immersed in the movements of that time, the carriers of the ideology were simultaneously the chief activists shaping the new realities. Pity their opponents, of the right or of the left. It was not so easy to attack what one disagreed with in the ideology, while defending what one agreed with in the new realities. It was easier to attack "Capitalism" and "bourgeois liberalism" *en bloc* than to make nice distinctions.

Today, our situation is rather different. We can more calmly assess the real achievements of the liberal era—of the capitalist economy and the democratic polity—while sharply distancing ourselves from this or that bit of analysis, theory, and philosophy, set forth by way of bringing them into existence. We may take issue, for example, with the extreme individualism of Bentham, with the abstractness of Ricardo, with the sentimentality in parts of John Stuart Mill, and also with particular portions of their economic analysis. In this sense, one can imagine the articulation of a theory of democratic capitalism different from theirs and more closely tied to what actually happened. As artists are often not the best interpreters of their own creations, so activists are not always the best expositors of the realities they helped to bring into being. We can distinguish, that is to say, between the realities of democratic capitalism in the nineteenth century and the theories put forward in its promotion.

The anti-capitalist tradition has typically attacked both the reality and the ideology, although not always distinguishing between the two. For example, "possessive individualism" is attacked, often through an analysis of the writings of Bentham or others. But care is not taken to see whether, in fact, persons in democratic capitalist societies *are* actually "possessive" or "individualistic," by comparison with persons in other cultures. The two phenomena are quite distinct. Bentham may have been wrong in his theories. His theories, further, may have been out of tune with the realities of democratic capitalist cultural developments. Again, when Popes Leo XIII and Pius XI attack certain principles of liberal societies, it does not follow either that specific writers actually held the principles ascribed to them or that those principles accurately described the real nature of events. The principles attacked may, indeed, be false. Whether any author actually held them, or whether they were in fact operative in historical events, must be shown, not merely asserted. In a word, debates in these matters are sometimes about theories and sometimes about facts. The two sorts of debate must be carefully distinguished.

The roots of the anti-capitalist tendency in religious thought are many. Just as nineteenth-century liberals perceived religious leaders to be conservative, so many religious leaders denied that liberalism—whether in theory or in social reality—represented true human progress. From the beginning, questions were raised about the break-down of community, excessive individualism and "alienation," the proletarianization of the largely rural peasant populations of Europe as they flocked to industrial sites, the breakdown of the family, child labor, the loss of rural independence before the onrush of wage-dependency, and the growth of urban slums. The evil results that capitalism brought in its train were denounced; the good it did or might yet do was dis-counted.

Perhaps most profoundly of all, the rise of commerce and industry precipitated great changes in the moral-cultural order: in morals, in ways of thought, in aesthetics, and in ordinary behavior. Traditional authorities—whether of the landed aristocracy or of the church, both in public and in domestic life—lost ground. Whereas the traditional ethic counseled sufficiency, the new ethos urged each to try to "better his condition." Whereas the older ethos pictured the desire for wealth as the root of all evils, the new ethos taught that the production of wealth is a noble task, a moral obligation.

A capitalist economy brings with it—has as its precondition—a new morality. A capitalist economy is not merely a functional relation to production. It has its own spirit and social logic, conveys new ideals, offers a new set of commandments and prohibitions. These impera-tives, far from being identical to classical wisdom, whether of stoic hu-manism or of Jewish-Christian provenance, seem to run counter to known and familiar traditional moralities. Some thought of the new morality as liberation; others found it an abomination.

There is another point. Many of the central propositions of the new political economy of democratic capitalism not only run counter to re-ceived wisdom; they seem wrong on their face. From classical times, the main treatises concerning justice dealt almost exclusively with "distribu-tive justice." In a world which had not yet inquired into the cause of wealth, there was no question of "productive justice." The notion that, given the suffering inherent in almost universal poverty, economic de-velopment is a moral obligation could not arise. The feeling that an economy is a zero-sum game, in which the wealth of some is a cause of the poverty of others, seemed intuitively sound. The notion that a free, untrammeled market must necessarily end in anarchy, abuse, and dog-eat-dog acquisitiveness seemed intuitively as plain as a steeple in the sky. The opposite and truer notion, that persons seeking to benefit from a free market would be constrained to adapt themselves to the desires and actions of others, and thus learn cooperative habits, had to be arrived at counterintuitively, by watching how markets actually worked.

Again, it seems intuitively obvious that the best way for a small nation to avoid waste, concentrate its efforts, and produce efficient results is to allow a group of the most intelligent planners in its midst to set priorities, lay down guidelines, and command multifarious activities. It seems intuitively obvious that a planned socialist economy must be, at the very least, "less wasteful" than a free market economy. (This was, at the turn of the century, one of the socialist arguments most telling even to those who were not socialists.[23]) The lesson that what is intuitively obvious works less well than the counterintuitive principle—that free markets exert their own cooperative disciplines—must be acquired through experience.

Today, the many experiments in political economy now being conducted by the 160 nations of the world render moot the ideological arguments of past generations. John Stuart Mill, for example, *suspected* that socialist designs would not work out exactly as socialists hoped, while his wife, Harriet Taylor Mill, was full of enthusiasm for socialism.[24] Poor Mill had to make decisions concerning experiments that had not yet taken place. Many such experiments have passed before our eyes.

Nonetheless, religious thinkers, in the main, have not assessed economic history. In few seminaries are courses in economics mandatory, although courses in politics, sociology, and psychology increasingly are. Theologians, therefore, face two challenges simultaneously. First, they need to acquire some of the basic concepts and methods of economic analysis, and to see through some of the conventional, intuitively acquired notions that do not withstand analysis.[25] Second, they must master factual materials concerning domestic and international economic activities, about which they are concerned to render judgment.

To meet this need, I hope that a significant number of economists will turn their attention to the economic questions being raised by official and unofficial church bodies. As religious leaders make more and more pronouncements about economic matters, they must receive prompt and effective feedback. Otherwise, unchallenged assertions will begin to acquire the weight of conventional wisdom and official tradition. If mistakes are being made, they need to be corrected before they solidify. For the churches represent not only a legitimate but also a significant institutional force within democratic capitalist societies. The elites of economics and of religion have weighty responsibilities each toward the other.

# CHAPTER 2

# Perfect Enemy of Good:
# Against Utopianism

... The temptation becomes stronger to risk being swept away toward
types of messianism which give promises but create illusions. The result-
ing dangers are patent: violent popular reactions, agitation towards in-
surrection, and a drifting towards totalitarian ideologies.
—PAUL VI *Populorum Progressio*, 11

A real evil should not be fought against at the cost of greater misery.
—PAUL VI *Populorum Progressio*, 31

Nor should [good men], under pretext of seeking what is best, meanwhile fail to do what they can do.   —JOHN XXIII *Mater et Magistra*, 238

It must be borne in mind that to proceed gradually is the law of life in
all its expressions. Therefore, in human institutions, too, it is not possible to renovate for the better except by working within them gradually.
—JOHN XXIII *Pacem in Terris*, 162

In "Why I am Not a Conservative," the justly famous Postscript to *The
Constitution of Liberty*, Friedrich Hayek remarks that it is impossible for a
person such as himself, committed to a liberal political economy, to call
himself a "conservative." Liberal institutions, political and economic,
are designed to be dynamic and continuously to change history. Yet
Hayek cannot call himself a "progressive," either, since this term is
nowadays a euphemism for socialism. Much the same is true of "liberalism"; in the United States today, the word suggests reliance upon "big
government." Hayek does note, however, that his intellectual lineage
includes St. Thomas Aquinas, Burke, Macaulay, Tocqueville, Glad-
stone, and Lord Acton. His is a tradition committed to progress, realism, a higher law, and close reflection upon actual experience.[1]

Thus Hayek's Postscript affords a clue to the central point of contact
between Catholic social thought and liberal institutions; three of the
thinkers (Aquinas, Tocqueville, Acton) with whom he associates his
thought are self-consciously Catholic. *Both traditions are centrally commit-*

ted to the virtue of practical wisdom. Both hold that the perfect is the enemy of the good. Both are anti-utopian. Both recognize the frailties and weaknesses of human beings and the unpredictability of history. These shared characteristics are especially marked in the Anglo-American tradition of liberalism.[2]

It was on the Continent, though, that Catholic social thought learned from bitter experience to think ill of liberalism.[3] Because of such experience, liberalism even in Britain seemed to the Vatican to be identified with doctrines of human perfectibility, with "the survival of the fittest," and with a version of laissez-faire that meant no moral constraint upon individual self-interest. For such reasons—and because liberalism of this sort leads by a direct path to socialism[4]—Hayek, too, wished not to be called a liberal. Were such assertions true, neither would I. Such assertions violate a Catholic sense of realism, learned through a long social history.

## 1. BENEDICTINES AND FAMILIES

In the lush, green rolling countryside of southwestern Germany, hidden in a remote village, there stands the magnificent Benedictine church and monastery of Ottobeuren, the first Benedictine establishment on German soil, dating from A.D. 764. A visitor to Ottobeuren for the "Catholic Day" celebrated during the summer of 1983 would have sought shelter from the unseasonably cold June air in the smoky neighborhood taverns or brightly lit and crowded hotel dining rooms. Images of rural plenitude, stolid simplicity, and green countryside would remain in his memory. The next morning, entering for the first time the rich pink rococo interior of the huge basilica, which dominates the village, the visitor would be stunned by its grandeur and riotous brilliance. How did such a sensibility, so much white and pink and gold, spring from the neighboring farms and plain stucco houses? The kaisers of the region, imitating Bourbon France, had much to do with it. But there are other contrasts, too. Beneath the cheery cherubs which adorn the swirling altars of the transepts, protected by glass, lie the ghastly skeletons of saints and martyrs, their skulls smiling grotesquely under the weight of bejeweled velvet robes and honorific crowns of gold. Death conquering riches, holiness death, in disturbing metaphors of the vanity of this world.

Many scholars believe that such Benedictine monasteries are the cradle of Western civilization—of its libraries, sciences, arts, agriculture, democratic self-governance, and multinational commerce. St. Benedict himself (c.480–c.542) is regarded by the Catholic church as the patron saint of European civilization, together with St. Cyril (c.825–869) and St. Methodius (c.825–885), the founders of Christian civilization in the Eastern half of Europe. If Christianity is to be regarded as yeast in dough, quietly inspiring every aspect of culture, these monasteries are the institutions which gave that yeast its thrust and its staying power in region after region of the world.

Such monasteries lived on profits. They proved that by hard and prayerful labor *(laborare est orare)* Europeans could live beyond subsistence and earn the leisure which is the basis of culture: the leisure to pray, to study, to teach the arts of civilization, and to nourish the human spirit in song and stone and manuscript. The monasteries, too, taught Christian living. In their surrounding lands they taught families their dignity, their obligations, and the secrets of fruitful agriculture and early industrial craftsmanship.

Like the monasteries, the Catholic church has been interested not only in the souls of humans, but in the shape of their civilization: in their family life, above all, but also in their economic welfare and political advancement. On the one hand, this has sometimes laid the Catholic church open to charges of worldliness. On the other hand, since the monasteries have been a chief institutional means of expressing Catholic concern for the world, critics such as Max Weber have also accused the Catholic church, by comparison with the Protestant churches, of otherworldliness. What cannot be denied is the church's perennial involvement in the sciences and the arts, in economics and politics, in orphanages and other charitable institutions, in questions of peace and war, and in general in all questions affecting the dignity and the welfare of human beings. The maxim guiding the church is, while not being *of* the world, certainly to be engaged in its every struggle.

The phrases I would prefer for the Catholic ideal of life in this world are "biblical realism" (the phrase of the American Protestant theologian Reinhold Niebuhr) and "integral humanism" (the phrase of the French Catholic philosopher Jacques Maritain). In the former, one captures the irony, the tragedy, the sinfulness of human life, as we have been taught through the biblical tradition to expect to encounter it. In the latter, one captures the instinct of natural law and the (flawed) impulse to human progress and development, as we have been taught in the tradition of St. Augustine and St. Thomas Aquinas to expect to encounter it. When he regards the immense human tragedies of Western history, the sins, the errors, a Catholic cannot help feeling, along with pride in heroic virtues and achievements of beauty, a sense of humility and contrition. The long journey of the Catholic church through time has included sin and virtue, corruption and a striving for holiness, tragedy and glory. Extremes of darkness and of light are mixed with long stretches of mediocrity: it is an immensely human story, marked everywhere by the grace and the forgiveness of God.

A visit to Ottobeuren—like similar visits to Strasbourg and Trier, other centers of very early Catholicism in central Europe—reminds one that there have been tragedies in every century; that blood has been shed in every century; that great currents gather force, sweeping all before them, sowing destruction and division, while giving birth to renewed life. One cannot meditate during a Catholic liturgy in Central Europe, reliving the bloody death and the resurrection of Jesus Christ, and rise from such worship a utopian. The imperfect, the broken, are perduring realities of life. The impulse to banish them in the name of a premature utopia, even a religious utopia, has so often been murderous.

The Catholic church survives by humble charity. Wind and waves have too often broken over her; only humble charity stands firm. One sees in Central Europe why the key metaphor for the church is rock. One sees why the basilicas and churches are appropriately fashioned of great stones. They must endure vicissitudes, marching armies, and virulent plagues of the body and the spirit.

Humble charity is also the key phrase for the most basic institution in which the Catholic faith has its roots, even more so than in the monasteries: the Christian family. The strength of the church lies in its families. Its concern for families is the main justification for the concern of the church in every other social institution. In the beginning, such families gathered around the monasteries for instruction.

## 2. THE CATHOLIC CRITIQUE OF LIBERALISM

A sophisticated European could have been forgiven in the year 1800 for believing that Catholicism belonged to the past and lay dying a lingering death. Thomas Jefferson believed it one of the corruptions of the human race. In Europe, Napoleon's troops seized churches and monasteries, seminaries and convents, and used their living quarters for rowdy barracks, their naves for stables. In Britain, Catholics were relatively few and still disdained. In Northern Europe, the cultivated were learning to despise religion, Catholicism most of all, and the secular and laical spirit rode high. Southern Europe seemed backward and still asleep, Catholicism held to be its retarding weight. "Progress" seemed to be an anti-Catholic word, just as the Catholic "Dark Ages" were held to be yielding to modern "Enlightenment." Catholic intellect and Catholic intellectual circles seemed at a low ebb. One can cite major Catholic intellects, artists, and thriving intellectual institutions, but it can scarcely be denied that during the hundred years from 1750 to 1850, Catholicism was in retreat. In the middle of that period, as the nineteenth century began, the pope himself was in demeaning captivity under Napoleon. The thousand years since the coronation of Charlemagne in A.D. 800 had ended in searing humiliation.

In 1864, in his famous "Syllabus of Errors," Pope Pius IX seemed to some to be sounding the death-knell of Catholicism. He hurled anathemas at every thesis of European liberalism. He seemed to condemn democracy, free speech, the free press, and virtually every other principle of the liberal order. He seemed to point the Catholic church in a direction utterly reactionary.

And yet the unexpected happened. As Josef Schumpeter points out in his *History of Economic Analysis,* a renewal of faith and intellect began among the younger Catholics of Europe. In 1848, a young priest who had attracted public esteem for a funeral oration in Frankfurt, Wilhelm von Ketteler (1811–1877), was invited to preach six key sermons on "The Social Question" in the Cathedral of Mainz. From Germany, a new era of "social Catholicism" took birth. Concern for the family was to be its hallmark.

By 1891 one of the greatest popes of all time, Leo XIII, calling Ketteler his "great predecessor," committed the Catholic church (in Pius XI's phrase) to the "reconstruction of the social order" in an encyclical which opened a new age in Catholic thought. Its roots, of course, were ancient. The same Leo XIII committed the Catholic church officially, for the first time in its history, to the great teacher St. Thomas Aquinas (1225–1274), whose books had been publicly burned after his death by order of the bishop of Paris. This choice was immensely significant. For Aquinas was, par excellence, a theologian of this world, an "integral humanist," a "biblical realist." He taught the church to take seriously every question of this world—from war and peace to international law, from natural science to logic and natural-law ethics. No theologian before or since has thought so systematically and so synthetically about every question of thisworldly experience and Catholic faith. He denied neither one. He affirmed both.

One may assert that the choice of a thirteenth-century thinker for guidance in nineteenth-century problems was a backward step. In reality, it was not. For the great temptation for Christians in every age is to deny one half or the other of the true Christian tradition. In every age, some wish to attend wholly to the biblical message, to questions which are specifically Christian because evangelical. In every age, some wish to concentrate their attention upon the secular city, upon questions relevant to the most inquiring of the nonbelievers of the age. These twin instincts may be labeled the "fundamentalist" and the "progressive," respectively. In the mid-1960s, for example, we saw these two tendencies in their starkness at the time of the "death of God" controversy; some Christians turned sharply away from philosophy to the study of the Scriptures, and others broadmindedly sought to interpret faith in God in terms consistent with contemporary agnosticism. In the 1980s, this choice is again dividing modern Catholics. Some ground themselves almost solely in Scripture; others argue the case of reason, natural law, and prudence.

The genius of Thomas Aquinas was to refuse this choice. Instead, he tried to show that Catholic faith emanates from the same Creator who made the world and who, as Providence, is Lord of history; and that the Christian life includes within itself, while not being wholly captured by, every moral and truthful achievement of human beings. He did not identify, so to speak, Christ and Aristotle. But he did hold that Catholic faith heals, builds upon, and includes within itself every truth and every moral achievement which the Creator implanted in his creation, reached by no matter whom.

This is a bold systematic claim. It afforded Leo XIII a way of thinking accessible to all persons of good will, even while setting his thoughts in the specific context of Catholic faith. In the world of 1891, it was no longer possible to assume that a pope's words would go only to Catholics. On the contrary, not only were Protestants dominant in many nations of Europe, but in every nation many who were not Christians at all, but of other religions and of no religion, played decisive roles. Nonetheless, all without exception are bound by certain truths of human nature and historical experience. These are basic norms of social justice for which sound arguments can be made in terms that do not require their hearers to accept biblical wisdom as normative. For it is one of the advantages of natural law theory, as articulated by Thomas Aquinas, that it proceeds by way of the lessons of human experience and by way of reasoned argument. One does not have to accept all of it, or agree with every argument made by others, to be caught up in a mutual pursuit of sound reasoning.

Thus Leo XIII set forth arguments against those forms of socialism which deny the right to private property. In terms of human experience, he argued that the practice of social ownership leads typically to certain abuses,[5] whereas the practice of private property leads typically to certain advantages shared by the community as a whole.[6] In other words, the common good is better served by the practice of private property. To this, Leo XIII added other traditional arguments.[7]

Above all, Leo XIII argued, private property is important to the family. It affords each family an inheritance to pass along to its children. It affords protection against the state. It nurtures important Christian virtues.

For it is a most sacred law of nature that a father must provide food and all necessaries for those whom he has begotten; and similarly, nature dictates that a man's children, who carry on, as it were, and continue his own personality, should be provided by him with all that is needful to enable them honorably to keep themselves from want and misery in the uncertainties of this mortal life. Now, in no other way can a father effect this except by the ownership of profitable property, which he can transmit to his children by inheritance.[8]

The family—nearly all Leo XIII's arguments come down to this. In 1891 there was no "socialist bloc," only a tide of socialist ideas and parties, some Marxist, some not. On the one hand, Leo XIII saw that even as an idea socialism threatens to aggrandize the state exorbitantly at the expense of the family. On the other hand, he watched unchecked liberalism and industrialization run roughshod over families, cruelly uprooting them and placing them in situations of extreme uncertainty, and forcing upon them a moral corruption more visible in urban than in earlier rural settings. The social order Leo XIII saw unfolding in Europe in 1891 was causing misery for families. It was not consistent either with the full Christian vision of a just society or with basic claims of natural justice.

Condemning socialism outright, Leo XIII also severely criticized the dominant liberal capitalism of Northwestern Europe. Following Thomas Aquinas, he tried to affirm whatever was good and sound in modern life, while raising his voice to inspire a redirection of the social order yet to be accomplished. He challenged leaders and peoples to bring the modern order into conformity with basic principles of natural justice and, rather more than that, with higher Christian ideals. Not wishing to place the Catholic church in the camp of any ideological body—neither Marxist nor socialist, neither liberal nor reactionary—he launched the ideal of what came to be called "the Catholic middle way."

## 3. THE FAILURES OF LIBERALISM

It is, nonetheless, an odd experience for an American brought up to admire liberal institutions and liberal values to learn of the bitter struggle waged by the papacy against liberalism in the nineteenth century. The term "liberal" is consistently used in the literature of the papacy, even today, as a pejorative. The Spaniard Sarda y Salvani encapsulated this tradition succinctly: *Liberalismo es pecado.*[9] On the European continent, the term was associated with particular conflicts, political currents, personalities, and doctrines of such varied and complex types that sorting them out would require a very long history. Moreover, when a European reads the works of British and American liberalism, the very words tend to be understood through lenses colored by continental experience; misinterpretations are multiple.

It is important, even so, to distinguish between the word *liberal* as designating an attitude or spirit, of which almost everybody speaks well, and as denoting a specific set of principles: political, economic, and moral. A person of liberal spirit is open, generous of mind, genial in argument, inquisitive, experimental in temper. The Second Vatican Council was praised, for example, for being "liberal," "opening the church," and "bringing it up to date" through new questioning and experiment. As every virtue has its characteristic vices, so the vices into which the liberal spirit regularly falls have long since been classically identified: from permissiveness arising from flabbiness of judgment, on the one hand, to decadence of will, as when a person becomes so "open" that decisive action of any sort causes alarm. The classic Vatican term for the latter is "indifferentism"; the colloquial description of the former is "wishy-washy."

There is a further point here. The root meaning of "liberal" is "liberated from," and so there inheres in the liberal attitude a complex relation to authority. The liberal tradition, for example, has a certain authority of its own, together with a pantheon of great liberators; so one cannot say that liberals lack all respect for authority, status, and prestige. To be liberal, however, generally implies that one questions authority, values dissent, appreciates early what seems at first to be heresy, moves rather more quickly to favor what is new, and enjoys challenging regnant standards.

Yet it is not in its attitudinal component that liberalism attracted the animosity of the Catholic church in the nineteenth century. After all, many churchmen have been known to be latitudinarian; the critical complaint of the Protestant Reformers against Catholic churchmen had been excessive laxity, not excessive fidelity. The Protestant revolt against authority in the name of individual conscience was not, in essence, an offspring of a liberal so much as of a more tightly observant spirit: ruled by the self rather than by the pope but not, to be sure, for the sake of worldly laxity. In the Catholic mind, "liberal" often became confused with "Protestant" and even with "Puritan," not because of some tendency toward moral laxity, but because of its stress upon subjectivism and individualism. From the Catholic point of view, if each man is to be his own pope, what is to protect the true faith from mere personal opinion? What Protestant and liberal have in common is radical individualism.

The Catholic tradition held that liberalism as a *moral* doctrine too lightly valued authority and tradition in religion, and yielded too much to individual conscience, which after all is prey to whim, the spirit of the age, and unreliable contrariety. Furthermore, excessive individualism destroys the family, as "looking out for number one" destroys the national community. The distorting tendency of radical individualism is narcissism, which diminishes the moral stature of every person who yields to it.

As a *political* doctrine, liberalism is a preference for republican institutions, for bills of rights, for democracy, for universal suffrage. The nineteenth-century popes—Pius IX, in particular—had some ugly experiences with liberal activists (he had to flee the Vatican for his life), and they were skeptical of liberal claims to moral superiority. Pius IX condemned the proposition that "the Roman pontiff can and ought to reconcile himself to and compromise with progress, with Liberalism, and with modern civilization."[10] Under him and succeeding popes (until Vatican Council II), the papacy explicitly resisted the American form of separation of church and state, as well as American conceptions of religious liberty. The popes leaned to the proposition that unchecked liberty does sometimes harm public morals, and that states ought sometimes to restrict liberties accordingly.

As an *economic* doctrine, finally, liberalism has caused Catholic social teaching very grave difficulties and continues to do so.[11] It is not that the Catholic church has been tempted to socialism. If anything, its more serious temptation has been a kind of nostalgia for a simpler, more agrarian world of the traditional type, the type found often enough in Catholic regions from Ireland and Belgium to Bavaria, from Italy to the Philippines, from Portugal to Brazil, from Spain to Central and South America. The fondest memories of the Catholic church seem to reside in the humble charity of rural village life, recalling the days when even major cities were small in scale, and run by guilds. Still today such images haunt the Catholic social imagination. Words like "organic community" occur frequently in Catholic prose. The "Distributism" made famous by G. K. Chesterton, Hilaire Belloc, and Eric Gill is but one example of a larger genre.[12] Rural cooperatives, credit unions, and corporativist experiments of many sorts continue to express around the world an almost distinctively Catholic inclination. The ambiance is typically agrarian. Although, as Josef Pieper shows, the Catholic imagination runs toward the *civitas* or small city rather than toward the isolation of agricultural life, and although Catholicism has been historically a religion strongest in cities (the word "pagan" long meant country folk), the modern city, like the modern economy, seems still to offend the Catholic imagination.[13] The works of two Catholic historians, Carlton Hayes[14] and Newman C. Eberhardt[15] afford many examples of this tendency.

It has seemed wrong to Catholic social thought to judge human life by economic criteria alone, and to leave individual human beings to the mercy solely of economic laws. Indeed, Pope John Paul II has encapsulated such vices in the succinct name "economism,"[16] as if in conscious parallel to the distortion of science called "scientism." As a science, economics has much to contribute to human understanding and to a fuller human life. But an economic system is not, and cannot become, the whole of life. Typically, Catholic social thought sees a large role to be played by moral and cultural institutions, guiding and directing economic practices. It also sees a role for political systems—for the state—in protecting the weak and the dependent.

Yet, liberals today also accept these principles. It is not illiberal to have compassion for the poor and the needy, or to favor the formation of labor unions, or to assign important roles in the economy to the state. Quite the contrary. Like socialism, liberalism too is an intellectual movement always in evolution, benefiting both by self-criticism and by trial and error. One must distinguish between liberalism as a set of doctrines at a given date and their intellectual evolution over time.

One must also distinguish between liberalism as a set of doctrines and liberalism as a set of institutions. It is not always the case that philosophical theories keep up with, or accurately describe, the institutions they are intended to explain. This is especially not the case in cultures committed to pragmatic adjustment rather than to theory and ideology. Again, theories intended as partial and abstract are bound to diverge from the full context of concrete life. It must be understood that academic specialization typically leads economists to dwell on the economic system, political scientists to dwell on the political system, and humanists to dwell on literature and manners. In concrete life, however, these matters come together. The dearth of philosophical and theological thinking about actual, concrete experience within liberal societies leaves such societies intellectually inarticulate.

The Catholic tradition of social thought has not itself attempted to elaborate a theology of the liberal society: that is, of a society pluralistic in its moral and cultural institutions; democratic in its political institutions; and capitalist in its economic institutions. (Certain important pieces of this work have been done, in the United States especially, by John A. Ryan, John Courtney Murray, and Jacques Maritain.[17]) This is an odd gap in Catholic social thought. For no other set of social institutions owes as much to fundamental Jewish and Christian insights about the nature and destiny of human societies, and none shows as much promise for the full flowering of Jewish and Christian ideals. Liberal societies are, as it were, the children of such ideals. Some theologians, alas, would abandon them as orphans.

## 4. SOCIAL JUSTICE

Once it becomes clear, as it has, that human beings have the capacity to choose and to shape the social order under which they will agree to live, Catholic social teaching must necessarily set forth an *ideal* of social justice in keeping with the Jewish and Christian vision of the human vocation and with the natural law embodied in history by the Creator. The term "social justice" has here three purposes. First, it calls attention to the fact that the practice of justice in private and personal life does not entirely acquit the responsibilities of Christian or Jew. If humans can shape the social order, they bear further moral responsibilities in so doing. "Thy will be done on earth as it is in heaven." Jews and Christians bear religious responsibilities for the sort of "kingdom" they struggle to build on earth. Their vocation is terrestrial and this-worldly, as well as transcendent and focused upon the salvation of their immortal souls.

Second, the term "social justice" suggests that the entire social order is subject to a vision shared by Jews and Christians of the sort of order worthy of the Creator, to whose co-creation they are called. This "new creation" will not ever be realized within history; so long as history lasts, human beings will only be striving towards it. Its vision of justice and of love, of liberty and of truth, of universal community and of peace, beckons to them as an "impossible possibility," a vision that can always be approximated but never fully reached.

In large measure, this inadequacy is due to the limitations of human intellect. To an even greater degree, it is due to our sinfulness. We do not always act at our highest possible levels. Sometimes we betray our highest ideals. Often we depart from the ways of grace and of reason. Moreover, misusing human liberty, some persons positively choose the ways of selfishness and evil. The power of evil in this world is more terrifying than we like to imagine.

Third, the term "social justice" means that in the face of injustice, passivity is not enough; the excuse that "everyone else" is implicated affords no excuse. Encountering something unjust in the social order, just persons must *organize* themselves socially to begin to set it right.[18] Where a lonely individual may not prevail, over time and with patience associations organized to achieve reform may eventually give birth to more just social practices. In any case, every step in this direction expresses social justice in action. It is not required that such acts succeed; but they must be set in motion. One must sometimes be content with small beginnings.

It is in this context that Jewish and Christian wisdom has always seen that the perfect is the enemy of the good. Maintaining the highest possible human vision is always in order, but patience in trying to realize it is inevitably necessary. This is because, in our haste, even our ideals are often ill-chosen or badly designed. Were we to realize them, the result would sometimes be tragic beyond imagining. It is also because, even when they are well-designed and well-chosen, human weakness and human malice often sabotage them. Anyone who has tried to build a utopian community learns such lessons. Indeed, everyone who has tried to create an ideal family life learns hard lessons of daily realism.

This is yet another reason why biblical realism so cherishes family life: It is the school of humble charity. Husband and wife discover in each other faults and quirks beyond numbering. The love of friend for friend, until death doth them part, is not given but hard-earned. Their children teach them further lessons in realism. Their relatives supply vivid models both of human heroism and of human frailty. Misunderstandings, pettiness, rivalry, conflict, emotional turmoil, illness, and personal disasters of every sort are part of the normal pattern of family existence. Each person has a personal cross to bear, and each is in many ways a cross to others. Much mutual charity, humility, and forgiveness are demanded of each.

If all this is true in the family, it is even more true in society at large. Much is made these days, not only on the left of the political spectrum, of the "sinful structures" in society at large, "structures of domination" and "structures of oppression." Libertarians, holding that that government is best which governs least, share with many on the contemporary left a chaste sense of the sinfulness of institutions. Often such terms are used in innocence, as if after some "liberation" there would be no more such "sinful structures." This is an error. Many on the left maintain a stubborn vagueness about the institutions that will follow upon "liberation." Usually, they draw heavy drafts upon the account of socialist ideology, imagining a social order which has nowhere yet been put into existence. They imagine a society in which "cooperation" will replace "competition," and "participation" will replace "authority," and "equality" will replace "inequality." It is only when you ask them to describe the *institutions* through which they intend to realize such dreams that they take refuge in "we don't know yet," "things will have to evolve," "we must work toward it."[19] These are the utopian revolutionaries. They know the ideals they seek better than they know their own society. They know better the institutions they hate than the institutions they would wish to conserve.

Catholic social thought is more modest. As the Church itself is never perfect in its ministers and people, so it realizes that no social order in history will represent the full kingdom of God. Therefore, it devotes much of its energy to preventing the worst. It seeks checks and balances. It fears the pretenses and illusions even of self-proclaimed prophets, since there are always many more false prophets than true. Visionaries abound. Demagogues abound. In politics, Aristotle writes, we must be satisfied with a tincture of virtue; we must expect in each kind of reality only the sort of perfection it can bear.[20] Practical wisdom is the heroic (and rare) virtue of realizing the maximum good achievable at any one moment, no more, no less.

The perfect is the enemy of the good. We have learned in our time, Albert Camus writes in *The Rebel*, that abstractions are murderous, and that virtue lies in the imperfect best.[21] This is, in any case, the overwhelming testimony of the Jewish and the Christian faiths.

From two quarters, this testimony is likely to be denied today. The Marxists, first, have murderous use to make of the illusion of "the paradise of the proletariat," after the end of "class struggle," after "the withering away" of the state. The Marxists *intend* the perfect to be the enemy of the good. So do many contemporary Christians who are in politics best described not as Marxists, but, to use Eric Voegelin's word, as gnostics.[22]

It is altogether orthodox to discern and then to denounce the sinfulness of this world and its institutions. But to suggest that some new worldly structures will be sinless goes beyond Jewish and Christian belief. Gnostics do not describe the imperfect, sinful institutions *they* will create. Were they to address proximate questions, with practicality and realism, they would have to argue in terms of mere comparatives, thereby surrendering their absolute claims to moral righteousness. Gnostics often say that theirs is a "prophetic" voice. They speak of politics as though its mode of consciousness were that of religious "conversion" and they typically invoke the charismatic habit of mind, rather than the prudential.

For the most part, the modern papacy has been spared this temptation. Developing through the need to administer the papal states amid wars, terrors, invasions, and conspiracies of many sorts, the popes learned more than most religious leaders the lessons of statecraft. Furthermore, the Catholic church is itself a community of sinners, no sect of purely spiritual striving, a quite visible, quite human, quite bureaucratic, and quite worldly-wise institution. It is incarnate in political reality. Weighted down with flesh and human experience as it is, it cannot credibly be tempted to gnosticism.

Just as God did not make the world perfect, but shot through with contingency, failure, error, evil, and malice, so the Catholic church has seen God's governance as Providence, that is to say, Prudence. "Nature succeeds only for the most part," Aristotle observed. The Creator, making the world, saw that it was good, not perfect.

Human beings cannot foresee the undesirable consequences of their own actions. Thus even well-intended acts often have consequences that are evil, while, through no merit of their own, similar acts by other individuals or nations may be favored by history. Moreover, at the moment of making decisions, human beings of noble character, or nations acting on the whole justly, bring themselves to ruin through flawed decisions of their own making. Anyone who acts in history does well to do so in humility, awaiting the mercy of God, since all human acts are tinged with irony and tragedy.

Acting well is no easy task for human beings, not in our personal lives and certainly not in politics. Indeed, when the actions of entire groups are included within the scope of human decisionmaking (as is always the case in political action), potential sources of irony and tragedy are multiplied. Political actions typically inspire counteractions by other groups and other leaders. Problems of accurate communication (and tactical wisdom all up and down the ranks) *within* groups and *between* groups often give large-scale political actions the character more of darkness than of light. "Ignorant armies," in the justly famous line of Matthew Arnold, "clash by night."

In *Moral Man and Immoral Society* (1932), Reinhold Niebuhr lists nearly a dozen reasons why the actions of groups are more complex and less morally lightsome than actions by individuals.[23] His point is not that there is one morality for individuals, another morality for groups. It is, rather, that there are so many more ways in which the political actions of groups may go awry that one must be conscious of their immensely more problematic moral character. For good leaders with the highest moral intentions may, through oversimplification (or, on the other hand, through excessive complexification), set in motion actions whose moral outcomes they themselves may come to abhor. Indeed, the extreme difficulty of successful moral action by political groups often induces in leaders a sort of paralysis, as when every proposed action seems to entail so many foreseeable evil consequences worse than the present that simple inaction seems to them preferable. Such difficulties, of course, do not provide a moral excuse. Inaction, too, has moral consequences. Wisdom in political leaders—wisdom married to courage—is, therefore, a virtue most highly prized in all societies, in part because it is so rare. It is akin, in fact, to genius.

As in all things human, however, we must each do the best we can with what we have. Our liberty obliges us to live without excuses, accepting responsibility for our reversals as well as for our successes and for our omissions as well as for our acts. As mercy is the attribute in which God's divinity is most manifest, so do human agents most often have recourse to God in his mercy. For such reasons, the Catholic church most carefully bids us to pray often for our leaders, both in the Church and in the world, because their needs are endless, and for ourselves.

In this context, the concept "social justice" receives its just complexity. If justice is so difficult in personal life, how can we expect to find it in an entire society? How will the laws eliminate the sinfulness in the hearts of humans? How will institutions, staffed by fallible human beings, be always just? How should institutions be designed, so as to minimize expectable and recurring injustices and so as to elicit from human beings the maximal virtue and creativity of which they are capable?

The modern Catholic tradition of social justice began in Leo XIII as a *cri de coeur,* protesting against the massive suffering of families. This cry from the heart rested, to be sure, on ancient and proven traditions, particularly upon the thought of St. Thomas Aquinas. This tradition has not been static. It has been developing, decade by decade. Yet anyone can see in it, while recognizing its power and its beauty, certain profound gaps.

Its main deficiency is that it is not yet, at this point, very positive. It is clearer in what it condemns than in what it commends. It is most deficient in its vision of *institutions.* This is a great failing in a theory of social justice, for social justice must mean institution-building if it is to do more than commend a set of private virtues.

More clearly in the 1980s than in the 1890s, Catholic social thought now recognizes two overarching ideals, in the pursuit of which institutions need everywhere to be built. These are the ideals of "development" and "human rights" (the "dignity" of the "human person" and of "human associations"). Are there, or are there not, institutions most likely to serve these ends?

Institutions cannot be built in a cultural vacuum. They depend for their appropriate functioning, first, upon the *ethos* within which the persons who staff them live (the culture) and, second, upon their ordinary practice of the relevant *virtues*. Courts in which the judges are ordinarily corrupt can scarcely be considered institutions of justice. An ethos within which family ties overrule standards of equality before the law is bound to produce institutions flawed by favoritism, nepotism, and respect, not for rules of equality, but for rules of family belonging. One cannot argue in favor of institutions in abstraction from questions of cultural ethos and habitual virtues.

It is plain that peoples differ not only in the institutions they maintain, but also in their ethos and in their favored range of virtues. Each culture may have moral qualities lacking in others. It does not follow, however, that each reflects equally the Catholic vision, or that each is to be judged morally adequate just because it is what it is. On the contrary, it is normal to expect that each falls short of the full Catholic vision, although each may fall short in a different way. Furthermore, it is normal to expect that some come closer than others to realizing the full Catholic vision, however imperfectly.

Very few nations today are "confessional" states, in which the Catholic religion is the official religion of the state. But we may say that some two score nations are "Catholic nations" in terms of the religious affiliation of a majority of their citizens. This is true of most of the nations of South and Central America, of Ireland and Spain, Portugal and Italy, the Philippines, Poland, France perhaps (described today as "mission territory," since so many are only nominally Catholic), and at the very least large portions of Germany, Austria, Belgium, the Netherlands, Luxembourg, Hungary, Lithuania, and other states. Leaving aside those under the militant anti-religious control of the Soviet Union, and apart from those in Western Europe, it can hardly be said that most of these Catholic nations have yet lived up to the full Catholic vision of development and respect for human rights.

In fact, a majority of the remaining Catholic nations, those in South America and Central America and the Philippines, are today involved in bitter political struggles in the light of these two ideals. Why should this be so?

By and large, Catholic cultures have not been leaders in discovering and designing the institutions of democracy or the protection of human rights, but have come rather late to these traditions. Further, Catholic cultures seem on the whole rather more vulnerable to the traditional style of single-person leadership, as in the monarchies of old and in the dictatorships of today. Again, Catholic cultures—and not solely Latin ones—seem especially vulnerable to extremist and terrorist forms of political romanticism, neither much admiring pragmatism nor much committed to the arts of compromise and the habits of a loyal opposition.[24] It has been noted even in Europe, for example, that Catholic youths made up a disproportionate share of the various terrorist groups operating in many nations of Europe during the period 1960–1980.[25] Aristocratic cultures are more mercurial, passionate, and romantic than bourgeois liberal cultures. The moral advances Montesquieu[26] foresaw once the culture of commerce and industry would take hold in Europe— advances in moderation, in tolerance, in respect for order and law, in prudent habits, in a close watch over small losses and small gains, in peaceable ways—come slower in aristocratic/peasant cultures. Catholic cultures, finally, tend rather markedly toward broad swings between populism, on the one hand, and the charismatic rule of the strong man, on the other.

Thus, although Catholic social thought is *intellectually* committed to the prudence, rationality, and realism of St. Thomas Aquinas, nonetheless, in the concrete, Catholic cultures—again, not solely the Latin ones —seem to maintain a very strong romantic streak in their political traditions. They are, perhaps, closer to the medieval traditions of chivalry, heroism, and derring-do, even (perhaps especially) in lost causes. This is not without its own beauty. The most Catholic of the peoples of Eastern Europe, the Poles, are known as the most romantic of the Slav nations. What is historically most striking about Solidarity, in fact, is its triumph over the politics of gesture, its hardheaded and bloodless restraint, its sustained and measured realism.

In these days, poignantly aware of its minority status among world religions (Catholics number a little less than 800 million among the world's population of 4.6 billion), the Catholic church is in no position to impose its own social teaching on the world. It cannot claim that most persons in the world share fundamental Catholic beliefs or expectations. On the whole, the record of Catholic nations, while not the worst in the world, is not one which inspires emulation. Everyone may concede that Catholic social thought makes some excellent points. But one is bound also to note that many of these points are derivative from other traditions. For example, not only were the rights of religious liberty, the rights of the free press, and other similar rights not pioneered by papal thought; their establishment was at times and under peculiar circumstances explicitly opposed by papal thought. On many such matters Catholic social thought has experienced a great reversal in recent decades.

For these are, in the end, questions of practical wisdom. It is not enough to voice beautiful ideals, calling them "progressive" and "liberal"; one must look to how they are institutionalized and to the long-term effects of their institutionalization. Some ideals, which at first one opposes on philosophical grounds, turn out, in institutional practice, to have effects quite different from those one feared. Further, practical institutions sometimes turn out to have philosophical justifications quite different from those in whose spirit they were first advanced. In politics, the human race learns better by experience than by ideology. It is, therefore, no disgrace to resist an ideology in the beginning, while later changing one's mind about the practical institutions in whose origins that ideology was prominent.

In this sense, too, the perfect is the enemy of the good. This world, as it is, is never perfect; but, as the Creator himself judged, it is good. To imitate God, it is necessary to resist the perfectionist impulse, and to learn to discern the good in humble things that others reject and despise. That is, ironically, the way God is perfect. So when we are told, "Be ye perfect, as God is perfect," we must imitate God. The Lord God could have created a perfect world, but did not; He allowed for the disobedience of Adam and Eve and all the rest of us. It is our vocation to bring the good things of creation, which are never perfect, to fruition. To do so with practical wisdom is the highest attainable human perfection.

## 5. POLITICAL ECONOMY

There is good news, then, about Catholic social thought, and bad. The good news is that Catholic social thought calls us to a sustained vocation in politics and in economics. It is not enough to accept history; we must be active in changing it. The bad news is that Catholic social thought, at this point in history, has established only vague outlines of the institutions which best realize its ideals in practice. In particular, it has not resolved its own uncertainties about political economy.

The very phrase "political economy" is relatively new. Although its first use seems to have occurred in the seventeenth century,[27], it did not represent a proper field of study until the end of the eighteenth, achieving its classic shape a half-century later with the publication in 1848 of John Stuart Mill's first edition (of seven) of *The Principles of Political Economy*. This early classic statement has been subjected to many criticisms and modifications. Moreover, its two components, political science and economics, for many years have gone their separate ways as two different disciplines and professions.

Political economy was, at first, a "liberal" conception. It focused on the newly perceived possibility of development—that is, of producing new wealth in a sustained and systematic way. It was preoccupied with defeating two ancient enemies of the human race, poverty and tyranny.[28] From these, it sought liberation for all peoples everywhere and drew thence the name "liberalism."

Liberalism's fundamental move was to diagnose the extent to which the state was the source both of tyranny and of persistent poverty. Liberalism was not anarchic and did not seek the elimination of the state. It was realistic and recognized substantial roles for the state, even while seeking to limit the state more narrowly than had ever been achieved before. It established the tradition of individual rights, structures of due process, and the principle of constitutional government dependent on the consent of the governed.

The philosophers who championed the new ideals of "liberalism" and "progress" were in some cases anti-religious and, in many more cases, anti-clerical; in particular, most (although not all) were anti-Catholic. For most, Catholicism represented not only a perverse union of church and state, but also a legitimation of the virtually omnipotent state of the *ancien régime*. They thought of it as a contributor both to tyranny and to traditional poverty (that is, economic stagnation).

Although there were some liberal Catholics, liberalism (especially in Italy) included many who were ferociously anti-Catholic, both in their opposition to the papal states and in their rejection of Catholic moral teaching. Thus, although the pontificate of Pope Piux IX (1846–1878) seemed at first auspicious for a reconciliation between Catholicism and liberalism, the uncontrolled violence of the liberal assault upon the temporal power of the popes and upon Catholic doctrine drove Pio Ñono bitterly to reject liberalism.[29] That poisonous experience has continued to be reflected in papal teaching. Virtually every use of the world "liberal" in papal documents is pejorative. The opinion that liberal writers like Adam Smith, Thomas Jefferson, James Madison, and others in France and Germany entertained about Catholicism came, alas, to be reciprocated.

This was a tragedy both for Catholicism and for liberalism. Liberalism needed the Catholic sense of community, of transcendence, of realism, of irony, of tragedy, of evil. And Catholicism needed the institutions of liberalism for the incarnation in society of its own vision of the dignity of the human person, of the indispensable role of free associations, and of the limited state respectful of the rights of conscience.

Hardly a generation after the founding of liberalism as the classic approach to political economy, a countertrend began among the printers and publicists of France; by 1832, it was being called "socialism."[30] In the beginning it appealed to the inherited and primeval sense of community; almost as early, it began to attack property as theft. (Again, the basic idea was communal, in this case with respect to ownership.) On the face of it, socialism was much more consistent with the old order than liberalism was. Yet it was, at least in France and Germany, even more radically anti-religious and anti-clerical than liberalism. On the surface one would think that the Catholic sense of "organic" community had more in common with socialism than with liberalism. Nonetheless, even though socialism remained until 1917 an ideal existing chiefly in books and manifestoes, rather than a realized social system, Catholic social thought vigorously resisted it. Leo XIII could not have been more clear in 1891:

To remedy these evils the *Socialists*, working on the poor man's envy of the rich, endeavor to destroy private property, and maintain that individual possessions should become the common property of all, to be administered by the State or by municipal bodies. . . . But their proposals are so clearly futile for all practical purposes, that if they were carried out the working man himself would be among the first to suffer. Moreover, they are emphatically unjust, because they would rob the lawful possessor, bring the State into a sphere that is not its own, and cause complete confusion in the community.[31]

Fourteen years after the founding of the Soviet Union, before the purges and the enforced famine in Ukraine which killed some 7 million (mostly Catholic) Ukrainians, Pius XI was even clearer:

If socialism, like all errors, contains some truth (which, moreover, the Supreme Pontiffs have never denied), it is based nevertheless on a theory of human society peculiar to itself and irreconcilable with true Christianity. Religous socialism, Christian socialism, are contradictory terms; no one can be at the same time a good Catholic and a true Socialist.[32]

The popes resisted four features of socialism in particular. First, they feared the sustained and systematic atheism of most of its proponents, socialist as well as communist.[33] Second, they rejected its mischievously false illusion of equality.[34] Third, they saw that its concept of the state was unlimited and exceedingly dangerous.[35] Fourth, they held that its rejection of private property infringed upon a basic human right and was doomed to result in much suffering for the poor; it ran contrary to the common good.[36]

In its clearsighted rejection of socialism (and especially of Marxism), Catholic social thought was also eager to establish its distance from liberalism. It was for many decades after Piux IX and Leo XIII suspicious of, and at times directly hostile to, democracy (notably so in Italy). Its treatment of capitalism was not symmetrical to its outright condemnation of socialism. After all, the popes were defenders of at least a limited concept of private property. Still, Catholic social thinkers strongly opposed some main "tenets" (as they called them) of liberal thought: individualism, laissez-faire, the universal moral supremacy of market considerations. They also criticized some practical concomitants of industrialization: reflexive opposition to labor unions, the neglect of the poor and the unemployed, hard labor for women and children, and the like.

But if Catholic social thought condemns both socialism and capitalism, even if not symmetrically, what vision of political economy does it put in their place? Here is where the phrase "social justice" becomes a catch-all. It is true that individual Catholics have social and political obligations, as citizens, in addition to personal, individual ones. The term "social justice" reminds them of these obligations; if they discern abuses, they ought to organize with others to overcome them. It is also true that every social order is subject to moral judgment, in the light of the common good. But without a vision of particular political, economic, and moral-cultural institutions—without a worked-out vision of a functioning political economy—"social justice" remains a vague and partly gnostic phrase, disembodied and merely idealistic. For, in the real world, it is not enough to appeal to the perfect; one must propose a workable alternative.

It is an urgent task for theologians and other social thinkers of the present generation, therefore, to add specificity to the general concept of social justice. This can only be done by working out a Catholic vision of political economy: of those institutions and their appropriate relationship which best realize the Catholic vision of development and human rights.

## 6. FROM SOCIAL JUSTICE TO POLITICAL ECONOMY

Consider Latin America. Much in the future depends upon the directions taken by the peoples of South and Central America. What vision of political economy should the Catholic church of the future hold out to them (and, beyond them, to Asia and to Africa)?

The move from "social justice" to "political economy" is crucial. For the principles of social justice represent a very high degree of abstraction, relevant to all times and places and to every social order. But the principles of political economy move decisively toward concretion. To choose a political economy is to choose a fundamental *ordo* or ordering of basic institutions. And principles of order are decisive. They determine routine recurrences. They supply (or fail to supply) effective checks and balances. They organize human activities creatively or dysfunctionally.

In a sense, the United States was the first new nation of the underdeveloped world beyond Europe. Its founders were the first to grasp the primacy of questions of order. The motto they chose for the seal of the United States—*Novus ordo seclorum* (New order of the ages)—signifies their self-consciousness. Their aim was to defeat tyranny and poverty, to release the creative energies of humans as never before, and to create a new community, a "second Israel," a "city on the hill." The decisive insight of their construction was the separation of systems. They wished to build a polity, a federal governmental system. Separate from it but interdependent with it they wished to build moral and cultural institutions: churches, a free press, universities, and associations committed to the works of the human spirit in the arts, in architecture, and in labor. Separate yet again, but again interdependent, they wished to build relatively free economic institutions of enterprise, of labor, and of capital. Free moral and cultural institutions and free economic institutions would limit, check, and balance the federal government. Such limited government, based on the consent of the governed, would balance, check, limit, and regulate the other two systems.

The two words, political economy, reflected their awareness of the two more easily specified systems, the polity and the economy. Implicit in those two words—explicit in the writings of the political economists of the time—are the ethos and the virtues (or "moral sentiments") required of any people that would hope to live free, committed to liberty and justice for all. To specify the exact nature of this ethos and the range of virtues required to sustain free institutions was difficult for them, since they were determined to allow for religious and spiritual liberty. In a parallel fashion, the Catholic church, since it is a church by intention universal and multicultural, finds it difficult to specify the exact nature of any one political economy which it would champion.

Nonetheless, whoever designates an end must also designate the means. For liberal societies, the last quarter of the twentieth century has imposed the harsh instruction that flabbiness of conscience and decadence of will can be fatal. If moral relativism triumphs, free societies will perish. For liberty itself depends for its fruition upon moral clarity, courage, and restraint. It is not a matter solely of freedom "from"; freedom is itself the fruit of self-discipline, a fully formed character, and communitarian responsibility. Free societies depend upon specific virtues and a specific ethos.

In parallel fashion, the Catholic church, in designating as its social goals the achievement of economic development among the poor of the world and the protection of human rights in all societies, must also designate the institutional means of realizing such goals. To achieve the designated ends, only certain specific forms of political economy can be the means. No one today argues that Soviet-style Marxist societies can protect human rights. It is common today to say that Marxism-Leninism of the Soviet type is a dead faith, a hollow although militarily powerful shell. No one defends, either, a political economy based upon slavery. No one morally approves of apartheid. It is a little less clear that the modern substitute for absolute monarchy—the dictatorships either of the left or of the right—win universal disapproval, since a majority of nations on this planet are still governed by them. But political economies based upon dictatorship have flaws of enormous moral, economic, and political consequence in practice—and few advocates in theory. In short, it is not true that all systems of political economy are morally equal. They are certainly not so in the eyes of the Catholic church.

While it would demand too much to urge the Catholic church to single out one *univocal* form of political economy as a standard for all nations, it seems clear enough today that there is a *middle range* of types of political economy which might serve as the means for realizing a

Catholic vision of social justice. Any political economy, for instance, which may be said to represent the dignity of the human person must, in some effective fashion, rest upon the *consent of the governed*. The word "participatory" may be used in this sense, if one wishes to avoid the ambiguities in the current usage of "democracy," so fraudulently claimed by many dictatorial regimes.

Any commitment, further, to the protection of the human rights of persons, their associations, and their communities must also be a commitment to institutions which actually afford such protections. If one surveys the political economies so far realized in history, the types that produce such successful institutions are very few in number. Of the 160 nations in existence today, a bare thirty or so afford admirable examples of such institutions.

Logically, then, the commitment of Catholic social thought to economic development and to the protection of human rights has already narrowed the gate and made strait the way through which any acceptable political economy must pass. Moreover, in recognition of the frailty of human beings and of the human weaknesses of every institution (well known to the Church itself, in the light of its high calling), the Catholic church in its realism recognizes that *every* political economy will bear the scars of human sinfulness. Therefore, high on its list of criteria for an acceptable political economy must be the capacity of the latter for orderly and peaceful self-reform, for sustained progress in the light of transcendent values, and for institutional checks and balances against all concentrations of power.

In brief, the commitments which the Catholic church has already made to economic development and to the protection of human rights have logically committed her—implicitly rather than explicitly, to be sure—to a conception of political economy at least very like that expressed by the practice of liberal institutions.

For numerous reasons, many theologians, especially in the Protestant world, prefer democratic socialist versions of such a political economy. At least after Stalin, most such thinkers place heaviest emphasis upon the democratic part of their vision. Regarding the socialist part, most seem to reject such classical socialist notions as the state ownership of the means of production, a doctrinal imperative to nationalize industries (they may accept practical reasons in some cases), a complete elimination of private property, the abolition of money as a means of exchange, and the total abolition of markets. In most respects, democratic socialists, at least among theologians, tend also to champion liberal institutions, especially of human and civil rights.

In my own view, such democratic socialists have conceded all the main disputed points of fifty years ago. As a political theory, democratic socialism adds little to liberal democracy. As an economic theory, democratic socialism has little to say that is distinguishable in principle from democratic capitalism; the important economic arguments between them tend to turn on practicalities. As a moral-cultural theory, democratic socialism can no longer pretend to be a secularized version of Christianity or Judaism, for pluralistic religious currents run through it as through democratic capitalism.

In this sense, then, it is true to say with Irving Kristol and other former democratic socialists that the great story of our time is not the crisis of capitalism, but the death of socialism.[37] Nonetheless, as a moral impulse, a specific angle of vision for criticizing liberal institutions, democratic socialism still has strong appeal for intellectuals and, not least, for theologians involved in social ethics.

Even more clearly than democratic socialists, Catholic social thought has slowly but steadily come to embrace the basic institutions of the liberal society, in the economic, the political, and the moral-cultural systems. It is time for that process to become more self-conscious, self-confident, and boldly imaginative. I do not believe that Catholic social thought should serve the liberal society. On the contrary, I hold that the liberal society, among known and workable present and future societies, best serves Catholic social thought: best uplifts the poor, institutionalizes the dignity of the human person, makes possible the growth and manifold activities of human associations of every sort, and conspires to establish a more voluntary and open and communitarian form of life than any society of the past, present, or foreseeable future.

In praising liberal institutions, one must also note their many and persistent failings. Thus the Catholic bishops of the United States decided in 1980 to address a pastoral letter to "Catholic Social Thought and the U.S. Economy." They planned, as of early 1984, to stress four persistent problems: poverty and welfare; employment; international trade; and planning. All four questions are prickly and complex and all four involve trade-offs and partial gains. The bishops have already invited theologians—indeed, all citizens—to give thought to these themes. The fact that the bishops are writing such a letter, the open manner of their doing so, and the sorts of subjects they are tackling illustrate an important feature of liberal societies.

# CHAPTER 3

# An Awareness of Sin:
# The US Catholic Bishops
# and the US Economy

The American as a whole possesses, or has within reach, that minimum of material abundance which is necessary for the practice of virtue. Here is a greatly human goal. The shackles of a secular fear, that has weighed heavily on mankind throughout its history, have been struck off, or loosened, in one vast quarter of the globe ... This raises the question, what is to be the Christian judgment upon that great *res humana*, that sprawling product of human energies, the American economy, which has wrought this human achievement and reached this human goal?

—JOHN COURTNEY MURRAY *We Hold These Truths*

In earlier generations the American Catholic bishops made modest attempts to show that American institutions were compatible with Catholic ideals. The Third Council of Baltimore, for example, said in 1884 that the founders of US institutions "built better than they knew," and pointed out the consonance of basic principles of the Declaration of Independence and the Constitution with the political thought of St. Thomas Aquinas.

Nonetheless, the American bishops have been a little defensive about being Catholic in America, as well as about being American in Rome. The effective intellectual boundaries of official Catholic social thought until about thirty years ago seemed to be limited to the quadrant formed by Rome, Munich, Brussels, and Paris.[1] In recent years, the problems of the developing world (in which most Catholics now live) have loomed larger. The Anglo-American tradition has largely been ignored, except for an occasional pejorative reference.

This is odd. For what Catholic social thought seems now to desire for the Third World is, roughly, what the United States has achieved: institutions of economic development and institutions of human rights. Through the tireless and often lonely work of John Courtney Murray,

S.J., it is true, the Second Vatican Council (1961–1965) approved a statement on religious liberty, endorsing institutions such as those pioneered in the United States.[2] Further, the support given to human rights by recent popes is, implicitly, an endorsement of other human rights institutions pioneered by the United States. Finally, the acceptance by the popes of the idea of economic development is a long step beyond the classical Catholic vision of a society in stasis, patiently accepting whatever Providence grants.

Yet my point is not that Catholic social thought ought to take the United States as an example. On the contrary, Catholic social thought ought to demand still more from the United States, as even the ideals of this nation do, demanding "liberty and justice for all." In history, the agenda of social justice is never closed; there is always more to be accomplished.

Furthermore, it is characteristic of liberal societies that they thrive by self-criticism, by the prod of new dreams, and by public accusation and public ridicule. The theaters in liberal societies are packed with persons applauding burlesques that savage their morals, their manners, and their institutions. Artists often play the role of social critics. Dissident philosophers set their accusations in dramatic form. To see the many faults of liberal societies is not considered disloyalty; on the contrary, critics are often lionized as the true representatives of the tradition. Liberal societies are so open to their critics that some of the latter complain of "repressive tolerance."[3]

Thus, when the Catholic bishops of the United States step forth to criticize the US economy for whatever sins, it is unlikely that they will voice accusations not already voiced by others. In today's world, not least at the United Nations, not only is every fault of the United States given universal airing, but more faults are attributed to the United States than the United States actually has. There is no shortage of criticism of the United States, either in the US media or in the world at large. It would be truly surprising, and truly courageous, if the US bishops were actually to praise the US economy for such things as, with all its faults, it may do well. That would be almost unheard of. A grace note is struck by John Courtney Murray, S.J.:

In sheer point of fact, the Church in America has accepted this thing which is the American economy. Her life, the life of grace, is tied to it in multiple respects. It is, in fact, the thing that has given peculiarity both to certain institutions of the American Catholic Church and to certain forms of Catholic life. The major instance is the whole system of Catholic education, supported by the voluntary contributions of the faithful, who have found in it a means of professing their faith and expressing their spirit of charity and sacrifice. Catholic education in its present many-storied structure would be impossible apart from the American economy, the wealth it has created, and the wide distribution of this wealth that it has operated.[4]

In practice, the four subjects announced by the bishops in 1983—welfare, employment, international trade, and planning—do not lend themselves to simple moralism. In each case the issues are complex. In each, part of the problem is human ignorance, and part is its intrinsic intractability. Even among persons who have the best will in the world to do whatever is necessary to "solve" such problems, there is considerable puzzlement about *what* to do. The bishops are to be commended for selecting such puzzlements. A look at two of these subjects in this chapter—and at a third in Part III—will help to instruct us in what liberal institutions mean in the concrete.

## 1. POVERTY AND WELFARE

The figures on poverty in the United States derived annually by the Census Bureau are based upon a strictly monetary calculation. This calculation presents a problem: many Americans have experienced life in a low-income family without feeling "poor."[5] Again, one way of looking at the Census Bureau reports emphasizes the good already achieved by federal and state programs to assist the poor. Another emphasizes the magnitude of poverty if such assistance is not counted. Thus one method counts all in-kind benefits received by the poor (food stamps, housing assistance, medicaid, etc.), while the other does not.

The monetary definition of poverty for 1982 specified nearly $10,-000 for a non-farm family of four ($9862, to be exact). Any family or person falling below that line counts as poor, whether they have chosen to live at that income or do so involuntarily, and no matter where or in what circumstances they live. Although an annual income of $9862 in a small town in Iowa or Minnesota is quite different from the same income in New York City or downtown Milwaukee, the Census Bureau counts all alike.

Furthermore, if a non-farm family of four earned $9000 in 1982, it would still count as poor, even though it came very close to *not* being so. This point reminds us that most of the poor do earn *some* income. In fact, as a group, the poor earned enough cash to come within $45 billion[6] of lifting the entire group completely out of poverty. This is the so-called "poverty shortfall." In calculating it, in-kind benefits already received are not counted. The political reason for not counting these benefits is to stir the American people to give more benefits to the poor. The political effect of not counting these benefits is to deprive the American people of any satisfaction that poverty programs are working. These political aims are contradictory.

In any case, taking the figures that exaggerate the magnitude of poverty in the United States, the Census Bureau provides the following profile (see Table 1).

These figures illustrate that only 19 million of the 34.4 million poor

## TABLES 1: PROFILE OF THE POOR IN THE UNITED STATES[7]
(1982, numbers in thousands)

| | |
|---|---:|
| Total poverty population | 34,398 |
| White | 23,517 |
| Black | 9,697 |
| Hispanic | 4,301 |
| Children under 15 | 11,587 |
| Young singles (15–24) | 6,606 |
| Other adults (25–64) | 12,454 |
| Person 65 or over | 3,751 |
| Unrelated persons | 6,458 |
| Persons living in families | 27,349 |
| Number of families | 7,512 |
| Single female heads of households | 3,434 |
| Ill or disabled | 2,809 |
| Householders looking for work | 1,327 |
| Located in Northeastern states | 6,364 |
| Located in North Central states | 7,772 |
| Located in Southern states | 13,967 |
| Located in Western states | 6,296 |
| Outside metropolitan areas | 13,152 |
| Inside metropolitan areas | 21,247 |
| In central cities | 12,696 |

are between the ages of 15 and 64. Of these, more than 4.3 million are keeping house. Another 3 million of the poor are ill or disabled. Thus only about 12 million of the poor are potentially able to work. Of these, 9 million worked for pay during at least part of 1982.[8]

The vast majority of the poor are truly dependent. Through no fault of their own, most are not, and cannot be, self-reliant. Other studies show that *individuals* typically move into and out of the poverty ranks with considerable volatility. A study by the University of Michigan showed that only 17 percent of the poor (in the ten years surveyed) had been in poverty for as long as two years running.[9] Poverty for most, the researchers conclude, tends not to be a permanent condition. Individuals in vast numbers fall into it temporarily and rise again. (Many graduate students, numbering 1.6 million nationwide, can testify to that.)[10] This is important in countering the myth of "a permanent underclass."[11] Many of the poor are temporarily down on their luck, and help received can start them on an upward path again.

What we don't learn from these figures is that federal expenditures for the poor have increased by *twenty-one times* the amount spent in 1960 for the poor.[12] This does not count state or private assistance. Federal dollars targeted solely upon the poor exceed the $45 billion "poverty shortfall" by a considerable margin—a factor of nearly 2:1.[13] The American people have been amazingly generous. It is clearly their will that a "safety net" or "floor" be placed under every American citizen. They have, through their representatives, voted more than enough federal funds alone to have achieved this long since.

In short, the "problem" of poverty does not consist of a lack of funding, certainly not as long as poverty is defined solely as a monetary aggregate. The "problem" is not one of money alone. The *design* of social welfare spending for the poor seems to be faulty. More money is being spent than would be necessary to eliminate poverty as a monetary measure simply by giving the money directly to the poor.

Nonetheless, something is missing in the above figures. That "something" is the effect of an intact family. (An intact family is one in which both husband and wife are together; i.e., the natural alternative to the single-parent household.) For it turns out that the maintenance of an intact family is among the surest roads out of poverty. Indeed, social welfare reform in 1962 began on just this premise. President John F. Kennedy launched this reform in his budget message of February 1, 1962, with the words: "It must stress *the integrity and preservation of the family unit.*" He added: "It must contribute to the *attack on dependency,* juvenile delinquency, *family breakdown, illegitimacy,* ill health and disability."[14] The *New York Times* editorialized the next day on the expected result, "the long-term reduction of the need for government help."[15]

These high ideals were not vindicated by the Census Bureau report twenty years later in 1982. Welfare programs whose first criterion in 1962 was to "stress the integrity and preservation of the family unit" seem to be correlated with precisely the reverse results. Devastating results have been experienced in white and hispanic welfare families; even more devastating results have been experienced in black families.

In 1960, before the federal government became involved in the "War on Poverty," white mothers with dependent children constituted 6 percent of all white families with children, while the equivalent figure for black families was 20.7 percent. By 1970, these percentages had grown to 7.8 percent and 30.6 percent, respectively. By 1980, they had leapt again: to 13.4 percent and 46.9 percent.[16] Clearly, each time many of these mothers have another child, the poverty figures will rise. Each poor young girl aged fifteen to nineteen who has a child will also add to the figures. The birth rate among poor teenagers keeps growing.[17]

In 1982, 15 percent of Americans were counted as poor. But if single mothers with dependent children had remained at the same rate as in 1960, the percentage of poor persons would have fallen to 13 percent (from 34.4 million to 29.9 million).[18] This is in part because intact husband-wife families among blacks between the ages of 25–34 have income levels at 89 percent of similar white couples.[19] Of the 9.7 million blacks who are poor, more than half (5.7 million) are in female-headed households. This portion of the poverty population continues to grow at a rapid pace. The following table illustrates the composition of the black poor.[20]

TABLES 2: POVERTY STATUS OF BLACKS IN THE UNITED STATES
(1982)

| *(In Thousands)* | | Below Poverty Level | |
| --- | --- | --- | --- |
| | Total | Number | Percent |
| All blacks | 27,216 | 9,697 | 35.6 |
| Under 18 years | 9,401 | 4,472 | 47.6 |
| 22–64 years | 13,458 | 3,578 | 26.6 |
| 65 years and over | 2,124 | 811 | 38.2 |
| Black families | 6,530 | 2,158 | 33.0 |
| Married couples families | 3,486 | 543 | 15.6 |
| Female householder, no husband present | 2,734 | 1,535 | 56.2 |

These figures show clearly that the presence of both a mother and a father in the home is the most certain road out of poverty. Only 15.6 percent of such black families are poor. On the other hand, 56.2 percent of black female-headed families are poor. Whatever is causing the growth in female-headed households is slowly multiplying the numbers of the black poor: 1.5 million female heads of households and approximately 4 million children, nearly half the black poor, fall in this growing class.[21] This incidence never happened in the past, when blacks were far poorer; it is new. This is a human-made tragedy, caused by neither nature nor nature's God. It should not be beyond the wit of humans to halt what they have set in motion.

It seems worth pausing to mention that a similar deterioration is taking place in white and hispanic welfare families. Of the 5,118,000 white families who are poor, 1,813,000 (35 percent) are headed by a female householder, no husband present.[22] Of the 916,000 Spanish-origin families who are poor, 425,000 (46 percent) are headed by a female householder, no husband present.[23] These numbers, too, keep growing.

Furthermore, it must be added that a growing percentage of single mothers are now abandoned by males even before marriage; a growing percentage of childen every year is being born illegitimate. In 1970 the percentages of illegitimate births were as follows: among whites 5.7 percent; among blacks 37.6 percent. By 1980 these percentages had climbed to 11 percent and 55.2 percent, respectively.[24] Worse still, the *age* of young women giving birth is also declining. Between 1970 and 1980, the proportion of illegitimate births among women aged 15–19 rose from 17 percent to 33 percent among whites and from 63 percent to 85 percent among blacks.[25]

Questions of poverty, therefore, are today inextricable from questions of family life. The so-called "feminization of poverty" is, as the figures show, mostly a problem of abandoned single women, many of whom have never formed families. It is better described as the "masculinization of irresponsibility."

Moreover, this deterioration in the struggle against poverty is growing just as progress is being made in other areas. In 1959 35 percent of the elderly were poor.[26] By 1982 advances in social security (especially in indexing payments to inflation) had lowered this percent to under 15 percent, and non-cash programs like food stamps, housing assistance, and medicare had ameliorated the lot even of these.[27] Similarly, poverty rates for intact husband-wife families had been lowered considerably, although much remains to be done. Finally, the numbers of adult poor persons living alone had been lowered to 6.458 million.[28]

The great disappointment has been with regard to family life. Here welfare programs have seemed to have perverse effects, exactly opposite to those intended. Since so many children are involved, and since a sizeable proportion of their young mothers are not much more than children, the problem is heart-rending and acute.

Catholic social teaching offers no pat remedy for this problem. It does command the Catholic conscience to attend to it. To assert merely that the federal government should distribute more benefits to single mothers with dependent children is not likely to lead to a decrease in the number of single mothers and their dependent children. On the contrary, the number seems to be increasing from decade to decade in correlation with the advent of social welfare programs designed, purportedly, for the opposite effect. Something seems wrong in the design.

The chief reason for Catholic involvement in "the social question" is the one John F. Kennedy gave in 1962: "the integrity and preservation of the family unit." Yet the United States remains the only major industrial nation without a family policy. For two centuries, liberal social thought has tended to focus upon the two new realities of modern life, the emergence of the individual and the emergence of the state. The family has been taken for granted, little studied, little attended to. Yet the family is the fundamental social unit for the inculcation of the virtues necessary to preserve liberal institutions: a sense of civic responsibility; honesty; hard work; and the acquisition of a broad range of social skills, including teamwork, cooperativeness, tolerance, and habits of association and creative initiative. Neglect of the family in social policy has wreaked terrible consequences.

What is to be done? The first step would be to bring the dependency exemption traditionally allowed by the Internal Revenue Service (currently $1000 per dependent) in line with inflation. The $600 allowed in 1948 would have to amount to $5600 per dependent to meet the havoc of inflation. It seems unconscionable that poor persons should pay income taxes, as many of them now do. They should be allowed to keep the money they earn at least until their circumstances improve. A doubling of the dependency exemption would be a beginning, but to reach the historical level set two decades ago, accounting for the intervening inflation, would require approximately a quintupling. Even a doubling would immediately improve the income of millions of poor and near-poor families. Since such families typically save little, this cash flow would go immediately into the active economy, generating at least a small return in new taxes. More important, by this single step a significant proportion of all the families now in poverty would be lifted above the poverty line.

A second step is more controversial. It would be to institutionalize a practice common to most other democratic capitalist societies, a child allowance. Such an allowance could be paid to each family with children. The principle involved is that children are a nation's best single investment in the future.

Not all adults take on the burdens of raising children, but those who do perform an important task for the nation. Families are the best single department of health and human services a society has. When the family works well, the need for state-supplied activities in health and human services is much diminished. When the family functions poorly, the need for state-supplied remedies multiplies rapidly.

Conceivably, child allowances could be taxable, in such fashion that, above a certain income level, less needy families would return a large proportion of the allowance in taxes, while the poor and the near-poor would retain the whole (or virtually the whole) amount. Child allowances might in this way supplant the concept of educational vouchers for each child.

Third, special attention needs to be given to the rapidly growing number of single-parent households. A growing proportion of such households does not result from marital breakup, separation, divorce, or death. The rise in the numbers of children born out-of-wedlock is a dramatic indication of male irresponsibility. Such families do not "break up"; they were never formed in the first place. It is difficult to be certain how to restore incentives, and to eliminate the disincentives that lie behind the growing incidence of such irresponsibility. The situation is neither commanded by nature nor common to ordinary social life. It need not be acceptable to a good society.

On the other hand, it is somewhat easier to imagine programs designed to help the growing number of young women who, while still between the ages of 14 to 19, become heads of single-parent households. Here churches, neighborhood associations, and civic groups might provide local centers, especially in high-welfare urban areas where such households seem to be concentrated. One or two meals a day might be offered at such centers, together with day care for the children and classes for the young parents. Government funds currently aimed at helping *individuals* in such circumstances might be redirected toward establishing such *social learning centers*, which could meet several needs simultaneously: food assistance, day care, instruction and help in parenting, and training for self-sufficiency.

A welfare policy designed to meet the needs of families seems to offer a higher prospect of success than current efforts directed solely to individuals. A family-centered welfare policy would certainly be more in keeping with Catholic social thought, as we shall see in Part II.

Finally, three principles of Catholic social thought might profitably be recalled. First, the basic unit of society is neither the state nor the individual, but the family. Second, according to the principle of subsidiarity, higher levels of social action ought not to be called upon except as a last resort, when the social units closer to the concrete realities cannot meet their own responsibilities. Third, human dignity requires as large as possible a measure of self-reliance, free of dependency. Being poor is no disgrace, but only self-reliance affords the sense of inner pride essential to human dignity.

Two centuries ago, poverty was a virtually universal condition. The very idea that sufficient wealth could be created to make the dream of eliminating poverty plausible was much disputed, even after Adam Smith first articulated it.[29] Today, seeing the incredible vitality of free economies—by which, for example, the United States *doubled* its gross national product in real terms between 1960 and 1983—we see full well that the elimination of grinding poverty is within reach. Indeed, a great deal has been accomplished, despite the vast work yet to be done, at home and abroad.

From these realities, six characteristics of a good society are derivable.

1. The numbers of the poor should decrease generation by generation.
2. The standard of what counts as poverty should rise decade by decade.
3. The free circulation of individuals in both upward and downward mobility should respond in significant measure to individual talent, effort, and opportunity.
4. Each individual over a lifetime should have opportunities to see improvement in his or her condition.
5. A decent floor or safety net should be set under the unlucky, the disabled, and the needy.
6. Invention, creativity, and personal liberty should flourish; talent should be sought and nourished among persons born poor.

Most Catholic immigrants arrived in the United States desperately poor. They have reason to see how a well-designed political economy can and does meet these six conditions. They also have reason to meet the failures of the system, as manifested in the 1980s, by a social creativity worthy of their forebears.

## 2. THE CREATION OF EMPLOYMENT

Given today's tremendous population growth, agriculture alone can no longer employ all willing workers. That is why images of vast new urban agglomerations color our imagination of Third World cities symbolized by Rio de Janeiro, Lima, and Mexico City. As Peter Berger writes:

It is easy to contrast the turbulence and undeniable misery of these places with the supposed tranquility and relative contentment of the villages from which most of their inhabitants have only just arrived. But there is another side to the picture. The overwhelming majority of the people in these urban agglomerations have come to the cities voluntarily. What is more, they have come knowing full well what to expect: Third World peasants are no less rational than Western intellectuals in making important decisions for themselves and their children, and the networks of clan and caste insure that highly reliable information is fed back to home villages. Why do they keep coming? The answer is very simple: because they have reason to believe that their chances of a better life are greater in the cities than at home.[30]

Analogous pressures caused the immense migrations of peasants from Central Europe during the nineteenth century. Small plots of land cannot sustain large families, especially when their children start families of their own. Millions have no choice except to migrate from the land toward jobs in urban areas. The creation of such jobs is perhaps the greatest of all social tasks for the next fifty years.

Projections for Latin America, for example, are staggering. In 1950 Latin America's labor force (the employed plus those seeking work) was 55 million. By 1975 it had reached 99 million. By 2000, based on the fact of children already born, it will reach 197 million. By 2025, it can be projected to be 300 million.[31] How can all the needed jobs be created in such slowly growing economies?

Compared to the immense problems of Latin America, those of the United States seem petty indeed. Given declining birthrates and a steadily aging population, some demographers have been predicting labor *shortages* in the United States beginning at the end of this decade. Nonetheless, unemployment in the United States during 1981–1983 reached levels frightening to those who remembered the Great Depression, especially those engaged in suddenly vulnerable industries like steel and autos. Before labor shortages set in, during the next five years the United States will have to create another 10 million jobs in order to find work for all those who wish to work. This task requires creativity.

The goal of an economic system is to afford each citizen material wherewithal for the good life. In this sense, as Pope John Paul II (echoing Abraham Lincoln) put it, "labor is prior to capital." Yet there is another sense, an instrumental sense, in which "capital is prior to labor." It is the usual condition of non-farm labor that it requires to be paid even before its products can be completed and sold. In this temporal and instrumental sense, capital expenditures are prior to labor. Prior also are abstention from consumption, savings, inventions, and organizing ideas. These turn wealth into capital, a static economy into a dynamic and productive one. Thus the creation of jobs begins in a spiritual transformation, within which the future is given higher salience than consumption in the present, savings are accumulated and directed toward creative use, and the social cooperation of many persons and associations of a wide range of skills and occupations may be assumed.

Not all cultures have undergone such a transformation of the spirit. Where governments are unstable, where monetary and fiscal policies cannot be relied upon, where habits of social cooperation are not present, where basic rules of honesty and mutual contract are not respected, the building of a creative economy cannot go forward.

In 1970 there were 78.7 million civilians employed in the United States. The labor force was not much larger; only 4.9 million persons who sought work were unemployed. A moderate majority of married women (57 percent) sought no work outside the home. Yet, in that year, two tremendous changes in the US workforce were underway. The unusually large cohort of babies born during the 1950s ("the baby boom") was nearly of age to flood the job market. Nearly 10 million married women in addition to the number already employed began to seek employment. Pessimists predicted that the US economy could grow only by about seven million new jobs if it was lucky, thus falling some 15 million jobs short of demand. They based these projections solely upon the demographics of the baby boom.[32]

The US economy performed better during the period 1970–1984 than anybody expected. It created an unprecedented 24 million jobs, raising the number of employed civilians from 78.7 million to 104.1 million by March, 1984. In short, the number of new civilian jobs grew by 25.4 million, a herculean increase of 32 percent. No other nation came even close to that.

Middle-sized industries of an entrepreneurial nature and small businesses accounted for nearly all these new jobs. The great corporations of the *Fortune* 500 lost three million jobs from 1965 to 1983. Many of the new jobs were in the service sector, and there was a slight decline in the proportion of manufacturing jobs.[33]

By the end of 1983, the number of the employed had climbed decisively above the 100-million mark for the first time in US history (it had touched that number briefly in 1979); and the percentage of employed Americans between the ages of 16 and 65 (almost 60 percent) was at an all-time high. The work ethic is alive and well in America; more adults than ever wish to work.

The magnitude of the "baby boom," however, brought temporary distortions into the profile of income earners. The huge bulge at the younger cohorts, typically at the low end of their lifetime earning capacity, outbalanced the smaller cohorts of older workers at the peak of their earning capacity. As "the pig passes through the python," this bulge will move toward the middle and higher income levels, and within a decade or so will assuredly tilt the national profile of income earners upwards (incidentally raising revenue levels for the government).

Although most of the baby boom generation has already entered the labor market, and although some experts believe that the number of married women entering the labor market may not rise much higher and may slightly decline, a substantial task of job creation still looms ahead during the next ten years.

To see just where these jobs will be needed, it is useful to study the profile of the currently unemployed. As of March 31, 1984, there were 8.772 million persons unemployed. Half had been unemployed 8.3 weeks or less. The average length of unemployment was 19 weeks. One-fifth (20 percent) had been unemployed 27 weeks or more.[34]

What was their reason for unemployment? 53 percent lost their jobs. Almost nine percent had quit their jobs. (This figure shows a measure of confidence). 25 percent were reentering the job market, after an absence. Almost 14 percent were seeking jobs for the first time.[35]

To put these figures in historical perspective, Geoffrey H. Moore of Columbia University has compared joblessness in 1929 and in 1982.[36] In 1929, in the population aged 16 and over, 58 persons out of 100 were employed, two unemployed, and 40 were neither working nor seeking work. In 1982 58 out of 100 were employed, six unemployed, and 36 neither working nor seeking work. The difference between the two years is that in 1929 only one out of 20 persons not working was seeking work, whereas in 1982 about three out of 20 were. Unemployment rose because more people wanted to work. This is especially true, Moore notes, because of the large numbers of women who now seek work.

In 1982 five out of every 10 unemployed women had either left their jobs voluntarily (10 percent), were reentering the job market after an absence (33 percent), or were new entrants (five percent). The frequency with which women leave and reenter the job market inflates the unemployment figures by at least a percentage point. To some extent, a free and mobile job market shows up in the statistics as millions of persons each year quitting and reentering. By contrast, a large majority of unemployed men (78 percent in 1982) did not leave their jobs voluntarily; they lost them. In 1982 those losing their jobs included almost 4 million men and almost 2 million women.

For many families, the loss of employment is devastating. It destroys the financial plans of the family, depletes family savings, threatens mortgages, and forces changes in the educational plans of children. Its psychological costs are especially wounding. No matter how hard the individual has worked, or how much pride he or she has taken in the job, employment is simply taken away. That seems immensely unfair. Since the loss of a job usually derives from large systemic forces—such as international competition—individuals feel particularly helpless. Often, too, the loss is quite sudden. The dread of losing further jobs spreads to associates and others in the family. This sense of unfairness is compounded when others do not seem to share an equivalent fate, and again when no other jobs of comparable reward (if any at all) seem to be available. Personal merit seems to play no role.

Unemployment insurance is intended to cover such emergencies. In the large and well-organized industries, it typically does. Yet it is in precisely such industries that much unemployment would seem now to be permanent. The US auto companies will never again, experts (who are sometimes wrong) predict, go back to their employment levels of a decade ago. Still, only about 40 percent of the unemployed in 1982 actually qualified for unemployment insurance, even though 93 percent of all workers were supposedly covered by it.

A compensating factor is that a majority of the unemployed (58 percent) have a spouse or other family member who is employed. At the end of 1983 there were 61 million families in the United States and 104.4 million jobs. More than 60 percent of husband-wife families had at least two members employed, and more than 70 percent of the entire labor force lived in married-couple families. Thus married men accounted for only 36 percent of the labor force. The vast majority of such husbands were employed; only 6.1 percent were not.[37]

In the early days of Catholic social thought, it was expected that men would be employed outside the home, married women not. The ideal was for each husband to be employed at a "living wage," sufficient to maintain a family in decent circumstances relative to the time. But today's shift to multi-worker households adds a new dimension to labor, and so does the expectation of an income far above the level of subsistence. Education and health care are vastly more demanding upon family budgets than a hundred years ago. Automobiles, television sets, refrigerators, telephones, and other new technologies are, if not quite necessities, nevertheless within the bounds of "a decent living." So also are vacations and other expenditures for recreation. Modern labor is, moreover, considerably lighter than the labor of a century ago. Teenage employment and the employment of women are thus regarded in new ways. Finally, the impulse governing the economic life of families has changed. The drive to "better one's condition" and, in general, to raise "standards of living" from decade to decade is considered both natural and good.

Catholics are not encouraged to be content in poverty; poverty is regarded as an ill to be overcome, and this is now an attainable goal.

Implicit in this new way of thinking is a commitment to social systems sufficiently creative to overcome poverty—and also to afford to all secure and full employment. These are new moral possibilities.

The roots of that portion of unemployment in industrial societies which is "structural," that is, which results from the obsolescence of entire technologies or from failures in international competition, lie in the dynamism of creative societies. The birth of new technologies often spells death for the manufacturers of the old. The competitive gains of dynamic manufacturers and marketers such as the Japanese often spell equivalent losses for industries in other lands. The comparative advantage of lower labor costs in developing countries often implies that goods manufactured there may be produced at similar quality (and by similar machines), but at lower cost. Such economic factors favor the developing nations, which are desperately in need of jobs for their mushrooming populations, but often at the expense of similar industries in the developed nations. These considerations bring us to the threshold of topics of international economics, which will be discussed in chapter twelve.

The problems that result for the U.S. economy in the next few years must, nonetheless, be met. When a large industrial firm closes operations in a city or small community, removing from that community several hundred jobs, the disruption of social life affects virtually every surrounding institution, including schools and churches, other commercial establishments, and the general well-being of the community. What can be done?

Most thinkers will admit that the technologies embodied in any particular firm are bound to grow obsolescent over time. Huge capital expenditures are needed on a recurrent basis to keep firms modernized. Thus industrial facilities cannot be merely taken for granted. It is important for virtually all communities to give much thought and effort to the future of economic development in their localities. Creativity means, in practice, the constant re-creation of the economic base of the community. Cooperative efforts of many sorts are needed, not only from the local media (which have a stake in the continued economic health of the community) and local sources of capital, but from community leaders in every walk of life, including the churches.

Thus the ancient notion of "the common good" seems to have a powerful empirical correlative in the achievement of a sound economy. From this, some infer that the institution through which the common good is best defined and regulated is the state. This seems to be a mistake, best exemplified by the political economies of the Soviet world, which have followed the model of the command economy quite rigorously. From the factors cited above, it is obvious that governments—national, state, and local—do have terribly important roles to play. But theirs are not the only roles.

It is easy enough to call for "national economic plans," or even "international economic planning." Yet the sources of economic dynamism, invention, and progress are typically serendipitous, depending upon the creativity of talented members of a free citizenry. In turn, such persons depend upon a strong supporting social environment, cooperative, open, and encouraging to their efforts. So a sound economy is not chiefly a matter of laissez-faire or "rugged competition." Competition, it is true, is a spur and a discipline. Yet it must also benefit the entire community or else lose its social base.

Much more can be done than has been done in the past to think through the pattern of gains and losses from the necessarily shifting face of economic life, in a rapidly changing, innovative era. When a given firm or industry loses its technological edge, capital can, and for the common benefit should, move elsewhere. But laborers left behind sometimes cannot move. A cycle of good times and hard times is probably implicit in every industry and in every locality, for material things wear out and economic advantages shift rapidly from place to place. Most people are realistic and see sufficient gain in progress not to be nostalgic for days gone by. Still, a good nation must think about those persons who are vulnerable under sudden economic shifts. To require the state to compensate for such shifts would place a dead hand on everything the state touches. To require individual firms or industries to bear the whole load would weaken them in world competition. The key seems to lie in the entire human resources of regional and local communities, committed to maintaining their local economic vitality amid the shifting sands of fortune. In the domain of creativity, there is no substitute for persuasive, farsighted civic leadership engendering civic cooperation for the future.

In this respect, although Catholic social thought is well developed in encouraging political activisim, it needs a vigorous development in encouraging economic activism: savings, productive investments, invention, and enterprise. For these, too, are acts of creation that benefit the common good, particularly in generating employment. There are 15 million corporations and partnerships in the United States, an average of nearly one for every seven employed people. Most are very small, but their vigor affords the real basis and creativity of our economy. Such economic activists need religious encouragement, guidance, and criticism. They further need local leadership and organization. In generating employment locally and in the nation as a whole, their contribution is disproportionately great.

There is one further point about economic development in which Catholic leaders might take the lead. Just as the Homestead Act was designed to prevent the US Middle West from developing in the pattern of Latin America—a few large landed estates, worked by peasants —in favor of a policy promoting as many property owners as possible;

so also the time is now ripe to consider methods for broadening the ownership of industry and commerce. It is both sound American practice and an ideal of Catholic social thought that ownership should be diffused as broadly as possible. To a striking extent, this is already true in the ownership of homes, automobiles, and multiple personal resources. It is not so broadly true in participation in the ownership of industry.

Two experiments come to mind. First, payment for labor might in favorable circumstances take the partial form of participation in stock ownership. Such a device might help to keep wages in line with international competition, while substantial financial benefits still flow to workers. Long-term considerations would be strengthened. Second, corporations of sufficient size might establish credit lines, to be repaid by future contributions made by the corporation in the name of each employee paid out of shared future earnings. On the one hand, these credit lines would establish new sources of internally generated capital. On the other hand, employees would share in the creation of new capital wealth held in their own names. The net worth of employees would grow throughout their employment. Modestly significant annual income from dividends might accrue to them either for reinvestment or for income. Employees, in turn, would own assets against which they might borrow for other needs. To at least a modest extent, they would become owners as well as employees.

The principle is that employees ought to share in capital ownership as well as in wages, and as broadly and substantially as is feasible. Their stake in the financial health of the corporation would thereby be tangible. And a new source of capital investment would become available to the corporation. This principle implies a fresh way of looking at the financing and ownership of corporations. It could be introduced gradually. It is a voluntary principle, and need not be thought of as mandatory universally. There are arguments against it and, as always, practical difficulties. Yet experiments conducted now might reveal great benefits twenty years from now.

## 3. TEMPTATIONS IN THE DESERT

One of the constraints the Catholic bishops will face is a need to seem "progressive," in part for their own most ardent activists, in part for the sake of a favorable press. The conventional wisdom among many intellectuals and publicists virtually requires that the bishops must in part seem to be anti-business; the prophet motive is quite as powerful as the profit motive. The irony is, however, that what passes as "progressive" in much of the press is a quite old pre-capitalist idea: Increase the power of the state. The similarity between socialist and traditionalist societies cannot be too often remarked; both are statist. But are existing socialist or traditional societies just? Do they engender dynamic economies, social mobility, high levels of opportunity, and the diminishment of poverty? The US bishops are not likely to urge the United States to move in the direction of the statist economies of Latin America and Eastern Europe, or even in the direction of Sweden or President Mitterand's France. The US bishops are Americans; they are likely to appreciate the dynamism of a free economy. After four years of intense study, they are likely to extend Catholic teaching on economics to new ground. They are likely to emphasize savings, investment, productivity, invention, and economic dynamism in precedent-making ways.

Of old, even American bishops might have been tempted to stress security rather than creative risk. Even today, the closing of factories in industrial centers with large Catholic populations, such as Youngstown, has had a traumatic effect on many of them. Yet despite the influence of Europe upon Catholic social thought, few American bishops are likely to take a European, rather than an American, approach to job security. In social welfare countries such as West Germany, jobs are protected at high social cost. On the face of it and in the short term, such insistence upon security may seem just. Yet two evil effects follow. First, government intrusion into the economy slowly but inexorably induces economic decline, such as is now widely feared in Europe, and inhibits both new investment and research. Second, employment opportunities decline. Thus, the social welfare economies of Western Europe, excessive in their concern for stability, have *lost* jobs during the period 1970–1984, at a time when the seemingly less "compassionate" but far more dynamic US economy was generating 26 million new jobs. In addition, Western European research, innovation, and entrepreneurship appear rapidly to be losing position to Japan and the United States in the new post-industrial revolution. Catholic habits since medieval times used to prefer the stationary to the dynamic society. The American bishops are likely to show significantly greater philosophical clarity about the importance to the social justice of the dynamics of economic growth.

Second, the Catholic bishops used to be tempted to understate the importance of profits. There is a long Catholic tradition of deriding credit as usury and scorning profit. This tendency has aristocratic and peasant roots, as well as foundations in static, pre-capitalist Catholic societies. Given the American experience, American bishops will scarcely overlook the fact that profits are another name for development. As the pre-capitalist proverb goes, "It is better to play for nothing than to work for nothing." Perhaps it is not so for saints, or even for those less than saints, who receive their share of profits only under nonprofit auspices. But for most persons, incentives are necessary to elicit the herculean efforts and sustained drudgery required to create new wealth, where it did not exist before. Absent profits, nonprofit institutions will be diminished. Worse, new funds for research and development, for the new industries of the future and for dynamic growth, will not be created. As the identification of justice with excessive security unintentionally stultifies the just society, so the identification of justice with disdain for profits assigns itself its own punishment. The main reason that the bishops of the United States are powerful in the world-wide church is that they live in a society which recognizes the creative role of profit, whereas the bishops of Latin America, to choose but one example, do not.

Third, Catholic bishops of old exhibited a traditional discomfort apart from authority, and were at times romantic about the state. In the recent past, some have vaulted from the proposition that there is a *social* need to the proposition that the government has a duty to meet it. The second proposition, however, does not follow from the first. There are other social agencies, besides the state, more effective and less danger-ous. One used to meet often in Catholic theological writings, as well as in the testimony of the bishops before the US Congress, an idealized portrait of government. Recently, however, the bishops have become critical of governmental corruption, inefficiencies, and disincentives as they have been critical of profits and corporations. Is it not more just to be critical of *both*? For example, in discussing factory closings, some bishops are already on record attacking the heedless behavior of some corporations, while also attacking the role of legislation concerning de-preciation, regulation, taxation, and other costs. It is not the case that whatever government does is wise, good, and mothering, whereas what-ever private business corporations do is inherently flawed. How, if so, could one explain the relative backwardness and manifest injustices of state-directed economies, whether of the socialist or of the traditionalist type (as in most Catholic countries)? Succinctly put: *social* does not mean *statist*. At root, Catholic thought favors the limited state.

Finally, American bishops will hardly be triumphalist, as if Catholic social thought possessed a superior record in the actual achievement of social justice in Catholic countries. In fact, Catholic social thought, for all its many achievements, is still incomplete. The record of specifically Catholic countries—as in Latin America—suggests that candid humility is in order. Had the US been a Catholic nation, would its record today be superior to that of Latin America? There are wisdom and grace in the US economic system to be affirmed and before which to be humble, even as one reminds Americans of their own as yet unrealized ideals and their all too frequent betrayals of the best that is in them.

There is some reason to believe that the US bishops will avoid past temptations in 1985. The power of the past will make such avoidance, if it becomes evident, all the more remarkable.

Liberal institutions may seem to some to work as if merely by "mud-dling through," but that description alone does not render them unfit for the muddled processes of social history. On the contrary. The con-sensus arrived at through the complex workings of liberal institutions does not come easily, nor as directly as that of a command society. Such consensus is not, for all that, without its own practical wisdom and human beauty.

Again, liberal societies are not without sin. (Let those without sin cast the first stone.) But this saying points not only to some generic sinfulness shared by all other societies; it points, rather, to sins specific to liberal societies. Socialists are fond of identifying these specific sins as greed, possessive individualism, practical materialism, abuse of physical environment, and alienation. Yet available evidence does not indicate that such sins are specific to liberal societies, or more frequently observed within them than elsewhere. On the contrary, it seems that the specific sin of liberal societies is the sin abundantly manifested in abuses, personal and social, of available liberties. Given magnificent opportunities, so many free persons squander their advantages and live at a much lower level of excellence and virtue than they ought. Superficial, vulgar ideas dominate the airwaves and the press. Many hustlers appeal to what is lowest in humans, not to what is best. The sins inherent in an unprecedented abundance of liberty seem to constitute the specific moral weakness of the liberal society, and are apparent in all spheres of liberty.

The task before us in Part II is to show how a quiet respect for liberal institutions has been slowly developing within the body of Catholic social thought in its most authoritative exponents, the popes. The best way to do that is to begin with an analysis of the work of two of the pioneers whose thinking lies behind the formulations of the popes since Leo XIII, Bishop Wilhelm von Ketteler and Heinrich Pesch, S.J. These two leaders—it is important to note that both were Germans, fighting against a liberalism decisively anti-Catholic, Protestant, and sometimes atheist—were quite clear about what they opposed within liberalism. For this reason, it will be useful to examine how well their own vision meshes with that expressed in the most celebrated liberal text of the nineteenth century, John Stuart Mill's *Principles of Political Economy*. We shall then look at the tradition of papal social thought from Leo XIII to John Paul II. There are many surprises in what follows.

# Part II

# THE DEVELOPMENT OF CATHOLIC SOCIAL THOUGHT (1848–1982)

Some anti-clericals reproach the Church with being on the side of the rich and the powerful and with social stagnation. Some apologists, in an attempt to magnify the Church's work in social progress, insist, on the contrary, on the "revolutionary leaven" which she brings to the world. They describe the Church as having no other end or mission than that of transforming the earthly conditions of peoples' lives and of creating peace, prosperity and happiness in the world. In the opinion of Catholics, both these schools of thought are suffering from illusions. . . .

—JACQUES MARITAIN *Redeeming the Time*

# CHAPTER 4

# The Architects of Catholic Social Thought

Indeed, the early Christians, in preferring the *corona martyrum* to the *corona militum*, preferred to run the risk of an unjust death rather than revolt against the tyrannical power of the persecuting emperors. And yet, again, the ideas and desires which Christian revelation caused to rise up in the soul of man, ceaselessly exert their influence at the very heart of society and transform it gradually. As far as the Church herself is concerned, it is not her task to descend to undertakings directly temporal in the ebb and flow of political activities. Hers is the treasury of energies of another order, more hidden and more powerful. It is justice and love, and Christian revelation, that she must keep alive. Once they have been conveyed into the substance of history, these energies have their own action which unfolds in a measure of duration quite different from the rhythm of time.

—JACQUES MARITAIN *Redeeming the Time*

As the nineteenth century began, Catholic intellectual life, as if beaten down by the French Revolution and its aftermath, was organizationally at a low ebb. By mid-century, however, one could discern in Britain, in France, and in Germany a rebirth of organized Catholic intellectual life and, with returning self-confidence, the beginnings of a new Catholic vision of social justice. To the right and to the left, Catholics opposed liberal individualism and collectivist socialism. They feared the latter because it was militantly atheistic. They feared the former because, as they perceived it, its amorality would lead to socialism.

Two of the early architects of this long renaissance in Catholic social thought deserve special study because of their considerable influence upon future popes, scholars, and practitioners. Both were Germans, from western areas much influenced by the current of new ideas from France. First came the activist priest, later bishop, Wilhelm von Ketteler (1811–1877), whose famous sermons on "the social question" during Advent of 1848 opened the key discussion of the century.[1] The second was the greatest light in the history of Catholic economic thought, Heinrich Pesch (1854–1926), a Jesuit whose monumental five-volume *Lehrbuch der Nationalökonomie* (1905–1926) helps Anglo Saxons to grasp at least part of the distinctive background of the German "social market economy" established by Ludwig Erhard after World War II.[2]

## 1. WILHELM EMMANUEL VON KETTELER (1811–1877)

From 1850 until his death in 1877, Wilhelm von Ketteler was the bishop of Mainz, the recognized spiritual leader of German Catholics, and the founder of the German Bishops' Conference that began at Fulda (1867) and has continued its worldwide influence ever since. Because von Ketteler was so great a model for the thought of Pope Leo XIII, the latter spoke of him to G. Decurtins, a Swiss Catholic sociologist, as "my great predecessor."[3] Before he began his studies for the priesthood at the age of thirty, von Ketteler had taken a law degree and entered government service as a law clerk (1835). He resigned from the government in protest against Prussia's treatment of the Archbishop of Cologne in a celebrated marriage dispute in 1838. He was influenced while studying theology in Munich by the work of the famous predecessors of the modern liberal Catholic revival, Johann Möhler and Ignatius von Dollinger, the great friend and ally of Lord Acton. (Perhaps through such influence, von Ketteler was one of the moderates concerning the declaration of Vatican Council I on papal infallibility.) As a priest, von Ketteler attended the National Assembly in Frankfurt as a representative in 1848; and, as a bishop, he served in the German Reichstag from March to December in 1871.

From the earliest days of his ministry in rural country parishes, von Ketteler committed himself to "the social problem," arguing that the spiritual life of Christians was intimately linked to the material conditions of their social life. Like Karl Marx, who was born not long after him in the city of Trier and who deplored the dissolution of older ties under the solvents of the "cash nexus," von Ketteler deplored the breaking of the "organic" ties of medieval society by the new "atomism" championed by liberalism. He identified liberalism with two chief forces: it stripped human beings down to nothing but individualism; and it supplanted their earlier organic ties with mechanical, rationalistic principles of organization, chiefly the unrestrained free market and unrestrained competition. He became, in this sense, an arch-foe of liberalism. In the Germany of his period, he detested the alliance between liberalism and the Protestant powers of Germany. He opposed the *Kulturkampf* of Bismarck, even within the Reichstag itself.[4]

The year 1848 was decisive for von Kettler, as it was for Marx.[5] That September, at Frankfurt, von Ketteler delivered an ardent appeal for social reform. At the Catholic Congress at Mainz two weeks later, he urged the Church to turn its full energies to the workers' question. Then, during Advent of 1848, he delivered a set of six classic sermons on the position of the Catholic church on the social question.[6] In 1864, by then Bishop of Mainz for fourteen years, he published *The Labor Problem and Christianity*. He was not at that time deeply involved in the writings of Marx, but he had read socialist authors voraciously, especially Ferdinand Lassalle, and countered them with his own study of the social principles of Thomas Aquinas. As for Marx, so for von Ketteler, one of the cardinal ideas was the "organic" nature of human communities—as of the plant world and the animal world—witnessed especially in the full, organic life of the medieval guilds. On these natural, organic connections, von Ketteler judged liberalism to be pouring the destructive solvent of individualism. He feared unfettered immigration and social mobility, the dissolution of the family in easy and casual divorce, and the merciless working of merciless economic laws. Liberalism would inevitably result, he predicted, in the immiseration and starvation of the working class.

Increasingly, von Ketteler also feared the rise of socialism. It would have been easier for him, it appears, if socialism had been inspired by Christian principles. But most socialists, alas, and not only the Marxists, seemed equally as atheistic, anti-Christian, and anti-clerical as did the Continental liberal rationalists. In the straightforward materialism of most socialists, he discerned the same ultimate logic as he perceived in atheistic liberalism. Those who claimed to speak for the working classes, he believed, frequently enough simply wanted to use them for partisan purposes, only to abandon them in their misery.[7]

During von Ketteler's lifetime, liberals in Germany were often explicitly anti-religious, holding that the Enlightenment had rendered religion a residue of the Dark Ages. He conceded that liberals often intended, in the name of "Progress," to make life better for all; but he believed that the principles on which they built were inherently flawed. He conceded that liberals spoke a great deal about "cooperation," but held that this was in flat contradiction to their own principles of atomic individualism. For liberalism to appeal to "cooperation" was, in his eyes, a *non sequitur* forced upon it by the facts of life, not by its own theory.

Liberals, if they wish to be fully consistent, ought to outlaw cooperatives rather than foster them. They stand in open defiance of the purity of modern economics and have a definite, darkly medieval, even ultra-montane flavor; which only proves that nature is more powerful than theoretical nonsense![8]

It is difficult to detect which writers actually represented liberal thought for von Ketteler. He clearly had in mind antagonists within Germany. He seems not to have known Adam Smith's *Theory of the Moral Sentiments* (1769), with its recognition of the fundamental force of fellow-feeling, benevolence, sympathy, and due regard for the viewpoints of objective spectators. Nor did he seem to know of the powerful associative principles active in American life, so tellingly discerned by Alexis de Tocqueville in *Democracy in America* (1835, 1840). It is possible that the German liberals of his era were excessively rigorous in their use of the logic of radical individualism and rationalism, but even this seems not to be the case, since von Ketteler regularly faults them for being in practice untrue to their own principles. He complains of the many organizations, festivals, and self-help associations they sponsor even on the Lord's day, in the name of worker uplift.[9]

There are, perhaps, three major differences between the history of liberalism in Great Britain and in Germany of which scholars must take account. In the first place, Continental liberalism seems to have been systematically anti-religious, in a way in which Anglo-American thought was not. Second, Anglo-American thought, while celebrating individualism, simultaneously took at least tacit account of the moral sentiments of fellow-feeling and respect for the common law. By contrast, German thought has nearly always placed extraordinary weight upon the "organic" connectedness of medieval life, upon the importance of social discipline (which von Ketteler, for example, praised in the Prussian army), and upon the inviolability of home and fatherland.[10] In German thought, British individualism is perceived as unusually abhorrent.

Third, during the lifetime of von Ketteler, the German aristocracy was still in full flower, building huge new palaces to rival that of Versailles, as did Ludwig II of Bavaria. In Germany, revolutions which had occurred over time in Great Britain were telescoped within the same generation. Aristocratic values—in Prussia, military values—flourished even as a new culture of smokestacks and industrial innovations took root. The secular unification of Germany, modernization, and the stirrings of democracy competed against strong attachments to the *ancien régime*. Moreover, religious differences within Germany between Catholics and Protestants were acute, as were those between unbelievers and believers.

To some degree, von Ketteler's critique of German liberalism reminds one of Edmund Burke; he stands clearly among the conservative critics of liberalism. Thus, in appealing to an "organic" sense of German peoplehood, von Ketteler was appealing not only to a still vital ideal, especially in Bavaria, but to a traditional way of life under threat from many diverse sources. Bishop von Ketteler may have been correct in discerning that the spirit of liberalism—the vehicle of scientific and technological progress—was the most powerful of all these threats. In preparing the church for the modern social reconstruction, von Ketteler helped confirm German Catholicism, and later the papacy, in opposition to liberalism. (Even after World War II, the theoreticians behind the "economic miracle" led by Finance Minister, later Chancellor, Ludwig Erhard, were adamant in distinguishing their own conception of the "social market economy" from the "liberal market economy." The

Christian Democrats were not socialists; but they were not liberals, either. The very term was to them disagreeable.[11])

In any case, the model of the medieval guild—in his eyes, an "organic," not "merely mechanical" model of social association—remained a guiding light of von Ketteler's social diagnosis. A long passage goes to the heart of his thought:

The principle of organization which brings people as well as raw materials together into powerful unity is a principle that is operative in the plant and animal world, as well as for man and for the human race, and, for that matter for the entire universe. It originates, of course, in the eternal intelligence and power and love of God, and it shows up on earth in two forms. There is a merely mechanical, external type of organization bringing things together in a superficial, accidental manner; and there is the organic unification which brings things together in a lasting substantial way. The modern cooperative principle would fasten men together in mechanical fashion, whereas God unites men organically as cooperatives formed by men in ages past were united organically.[12]

Bishop von Ketteler gives four examples of the "organically united cooperatives," which, in his eyes, are favored by nature and by God. His thought here is akin to that of the East, of the Slav and the German peoples, so different in tone and image from that of the Anglo-American world.[13] He minimizes individual will and choice, regarding "contract" as morally inferior to primordial bonds of memory and belonging. He cites the family, the ethnic local community, the state, and the medieval guilds as "organically united cooperatives," sharing not only kinship and memory, but also a destiny given rather than chosen. All four, he holds, will be destroyed by secular liberalism.

The family, he asserts, will be destroyed by "the unconditional and unrestricted right to marry and to divorce." The local ethnic community will be destroyed by "the unconditional right to move into and out of an area."[14] The nation will be destroyed by the liberal abolition of all national boundaries, by that kind of liberal and "cosmopolitan world citizenry where every stranger would have as much right in any German community as the native inhabitants."[15]

These objections to liberalism, voiced by a German bishop, have an unsettling quality in the light of later history. Bishop von Ketteler has a very strong view of a superior Germanic purity of morals, which he does not hesitate to set in contrast to the corruptions of the Romans and, by extension, others. His strictures against freedom of movement and cultural pluralism have, indeed, been reversed in twentieth-century Catholic declarations.[16] One cannot condemn von Ketteler, of course, for currents of ideas that flourished after his death. Yet one must note that he always imputed to liberalism an extremist logic, but did not fully grasp the extremes to which his own "organic unities" might be taken.

Moreover, von Ketteler uses the words "spiritual" and "moral" in an unusual way. He seems to mean by them connections of kinship, memory, and tradition which one does not choose, which are inherited by birth. In Anglo-American thought, the sentiments described as "moral" (by Adam Smith, for example, in *A Theory of the Moral Sentiments)* are quite different. Germanic and Slavic thought give far less place to individual choice, idiosyncracy, and the personal pursuit of happiness. Even Max Weber cherished the romantic Eastern sense of belonging and the bold, heroic, brotherly spirit of the Teutonic Knights.[17] Many Easterners abhor as "decadent" the desire of the individual to follow his or her own personal preference. Without some primordial sense of belonging, the center does not hold; life falls apart; mere mechanization takes over. Friedrich Neitzsche tried to articulate the immense difference he felt between the German mind and the English mind.[18] George Santayana, who as a cultivated and cosmopolitan Latin was unusually alert to such profound and inarticulate nuances, also assayed the differences.[19] An Anglo-American reading von Ketteler encounters these on every page. Indeed, the German immigrant Catholics in the United States felt inwardly at war not only with Anglo-American liberalism, but with Anglo-American attitudes and sensibility.[20] Introducing the category of "organic unity," von Ketteler obliges the reader to attend closely to such ethnic histories.

Yet is it especially the contrast between liberal contract theory and the "organic unity" of the medieval guilds that von Ketteler most falls back upon in analyzing the "social question." One of his fundamental images is that of the homogeneous ethnic village; another is that of artisans and craftsmen bound together, not only in the similarities of their work, but also in their religious, spiritual, and cultural lives.

The merchant guilds and craft guilds were organic unities in the best sense of the term. They bound together the common material interests, which the latter day so-called self-help is supposed to foster, with countless moral and spiritual forces into a genuine living organism. These guilds have been all but universally abolished. The obsession of the liberals would seem to be to destroy anything that unites people organically, in living and spiritual and moral and, therefore, truly human fashion. Then these redeemers of the human race would bind men together again by the superficial mechanical structures which they themselves contrive. What they propose would be like reducing by some chemical process all plants and trees and animals—all living organisms found in nature— to atomic particles, and then to put them all together again mechanically. That, in truth, is the kind of experimentation that the liberals would engage in with the human race.[21]

Honesty obliged von Ketteler to qualify his high praise of the ideal of the guilds. "I wish to make it clear," he wrote, "that I do not propose indiscriminately the restrictions imposed by the guilds, especially as these eventually developed in their period of decline. Nor am I opposed to all efforts on behalf of greater freedom in enterprise."[22] He elaborates:

Authority was abused—which is no reason to overthrow authority. Guilds were guilty of not keeping up with changing circumstances, thus they became quite abusive. They all too often came to support inertia and selfish interests. Prices became unconscionably high and quality often suffered so that the consumer's rights were lost sight of. Guilds needed to be updated and reformed. The principle behind guild regulation, however, remained sound, and it should have been preserved.[23]

Guild restrictions, von Ketteler admits, are like regulations concerning free enterprise:

Each is legitimate up to a point, and then each is subject to certain restraints. Guild restrictions became abusive and archaic to the point where they represented mere class egotism; and that is what triggered the cry for free enterprise. Free enterprise served to increase immeasurably the output of goods, to bring down excessive prices, and to improve the quality of goods. Thus it became possible for the poorer classes to enjoy certain goods and services that were formerly beyond their reach. But free enterprise too has its limits, its golden mean; and when these are transgressed, unwholesome consequences result just as they did when guild restrictions became irresponsible.[24]

Thus von Ketteler seems clearly to be seeking a "third way," a golden mean between socialism and liberalism, and between too much regulation and too little. He does not recognize that some liberal thinkers (at least in Great Britain and the distant United States) sought also to check the economic system through political institutions and moral-cultural institutions. In his eyes, liberalism was extremist. Since Ketteler believed strongly in the power of fundamental premises, he proceeded to analyze liberalism *as if it were a set of philosophical doctrines.* He took very little account of the way pragmatic, liberal leaders would adapt these doctrines to fact and circumstance. When they did so, he accused them of *non sequiturs.*

Bishop von Ketteler accepted Ferdinand Lassalle's analysis of "the iron law of wages" (which Marx also accepted). If local labor were required to compete with immigrant labor, and if all human laborers were required to compete against machines, then the law of competition would demand in every case that the cheapest labor would win. Moreover, the cost of labor would be held down to the minimum required to keep a laborer alive. In times of an excessive supply of labor, laborers would mechanically be condemned to starvation. This, von Ketteler thought, is simple logic, the explicit logic of the liberal party. The atomization of human beings "to the status of identical, individual, nuclear particles—an approach that is in perfect harmony with our materialistic outlook—would warrant the winds of chance scattering these particles in haphazard fashion anywhere on earth." He continues:

People are not mere numbers, nor are they all of identical value. . . . absolute social equality is errant nonsense which contradicts nature. The manifold physical and intellectual capacities of men are of infinite variety, and they are immeasurably increased by the different cultural influences which operate in a vast variety of environmental circumstances.[25]

Bishop von Ketteler agreed "that man must support himself inasmuch as he is able, and that God has given him the capacity to accomplish this end." But he denied that each and every individual is actually in a position where he can provide for himself, and that each man is just as capable as every other man to take care of his needs. There are an "immeasurable range of bodily and mental capabilities of different people, as well as differences in their cultural formation, all of which also change with age in the same person." For such reasons, nature and history supply a wide variety of organic structures in which humans find help and protection.

Therefore, even though it may not be done deliberately, it is a crime against humanity to do away with all of these aids and to abandon man in his individual differences and varying external circumstances to some naked, daily competition with the rest of humanity. If the entire human race is to be organized along the lines of such principles of unrestricted free enterprise, unlimited free entry and freedom of movement, as well as complete freedom to form and dissolve the family structure as one wishes, and if this liberal-rationalistic computerized* society is then allowed to run its inevitable course according to ineluctable mathematical laws, the absolutely inevitable outcome would be that each day those digits which do not perform up to a certain uniform level of efficiency would have to be sorted out and eliminated in the general free-for-all competition. Such a first principle of society can scarcely offer a cure for the problems which beset the working class. It will rather aggravate an already intolerable situation by calling into play the cruelest kind of competitive struggle. Without fail, the worker's wage will be driven to the lowest level possible—the level of sheer subsistence; and indeed, even this wage will be paid only to those workers who are at the peak of their physical and mental powers. That would be the mathematical consequence of such a purely mechanical-mathematical process![26]

Honesty obliged von Ketteler to note that some of the promises of a liberal political economy had already come true. The quantity of goods had undeniably increased. The types of goods available to the working class had dramatically improved. Wages had improved. The history of the next hundred years would further demonstrate that his own dire predictions were extreme. Both Wilhelm I and Hitler, the latter returning to primordial ideals of German collective purity, left the German economy in ruins in successive generations. Then, on the ashes of World War II, combining the ideals of social democracy and those of

---

*So the translation aptly, but unhistorically, reads.

the free market in "the social market economy," Germany swiftly became one of the most free and prosperous nations of the world.

Bishop von Ketteler might have taken some pleasure in that mix as an example of the "middle way" he had tried to imagine. So great was the need for labor (in part because of immense losses of life during the war) that Germany for a time needed abundant supplies of foreign labor. Far from the working classes being immiserated, they are today blamed for having become affluent and bourgeois. The immense productivity of the free western part of the nation contrasts vividly with the gray oppression of the eastern part. Great emotional tides of mutual belonging still churn in the German breast, nonetheless; the German story is not complete.

Bishop von Ketteler remains a great figure in Catholic social thought. He saw quickly that Catholic faith is incarnational, and that the care of souls inevitably involves a care for human material needs. He became a chief architect of the later papal assault upon "liberalism," understood as Ketteler understood it. Through him and the legion of Catholic social theorists in Germany, Austria and Switzerland, German Christianity was to have a disproportionate role in the historical evolution of papal social thought. It was to become the model through which political economy was chiefly understood.

## 2. HEINRICH PESCH (1854–1926) AND SOLIDARISM

> Catholicism gives to the world no economic system, it is committed to no definite economic position, is tied to no particular economic system.
> —HEINRICH PESCH[27]

> Still even from the relatively best organization of economic life no paradise can be expected. Considering the weakness of men and the inadequacy of all models, flaws will always arise. The ideal of theory is hardly completely realized, and even the programs of practical economic policy are no magic formulae, even if they move along the proper path. —HEINRICH PESCH[28]

> The economist, like anyone else, must concern himself with the ultimate aims of man. —ALFRED MARSHALL *Principles*

> A person is not likely to be a good economist who is nothing else.
> —JOHN STUART MILL *Auguste Comte's Positivism*

At the peak of his career, Heinrich Pesch was a compelling man with a long gray beard, a taker of snuff despite a poor heart that required vapors at his elbow as he worked, and a man of sparkling warmth and humor. He studied law before entering the Jesuits, and was sent for four years of study in Britain where, observing the distressed lot of the Lancashire workingman, he became, like Marx, deeply involved in "the labor problem." Returning to Germany, not long after von Ketterler's death in 1877, Pesch made economics his life study. He lived in von Ketteler's former home while acting as spiritual director at the seminary in Mainz, and worked for various periods in Luxembourg and Berlin. Honored by many universities, Pesch read and commented at great length on all the great economists of all the schools. Yet he refused to accept any view of economic science that excluded all normative considerations or that claimed to be independent of social philosophic principles. He refused to separate economics as a science from economics as a policy and as an art. He held that values and goals are always implicit in both and should be made explicit in a reasoned and critical fashion.

Young Father Pesch had become, like Bishop von Ketteler and more than most young priests at that time, a student of scholasticism. He wished to write about the human being as a whole, not as economic man. He wished to study economics as part of the whole of human social life. He was quite conscious of the difference that set him apart—a difference that once led to a sharp objection from Max Weber.[29] Pesch stated his position clearly:

Medieval scholasticism, as well as present day moral philosophy and moral theology, deals with the facts of economic life from a moral point of view. That is not the job of the economist. He will not, of course, oppose the demands of ethics, but neither will he lose sight of the fact that economics has become a [relatively] autonomous science, which treats of the economic life of nations from a viewpoint different from that of ethics. The decisive viewpoint of the latter is that of moral goodness, while for economics it is that of national prosperity. The material object may be partially the same for both, but their respective formal object definitely differs and that is why they are to be regarded as independent sciences.[30]

Pesch nonetheless criticized those economists who did not take account of the goals and values necessarily implicit in the achievement of "natural prosperity." His own ambition was to place economic thought within a context larger than that of wealth, productivity, welfare and price alone. He believed that, eventually, all economists would have to face the sorts of questions he was raising, and that they would have to expand and to enlarge some of the basic concepts and methods of economics as they did so. He argued that without honest work, honest dealings, cooperative attitudes, and other virtues among its citizens, no economy could function well. Further, if it did not produce a society esteemed by its members to be roughly moral and just, no economic system could attain its purposes. Every system of economics, he held, rests on a moral-cultural consensus in belief and in action. Economists should openly state those *moral* requirements without which their own systems cannot function. (Contemporary business ethics could learn much from him.) Pesch had great respect for economics as a science, and went to great lengths to avoid confusion between his work in social philosophy and his scientific analysis of economic policy, while insisting on their relation.

By and large, the historians of economic thought ignore Pesch. Yet Schumpeter highly commends Pesch's monumental work in *History of Economic Analysis;* Sombart is a little less kind and a little more brief.[31] Pesch had the classical Thomist ambition to uncover all the assumptions of economic science through a sustained philosophical inquiry. But he respected, too, the autonomous canons of economics. He saw inevitable connections between morality (and religion) and economics, but he kept them distinct:

Religion cannot produce grain; it cannot do away with physical ills. Morally advanced peoples will, no doubt, profit economically from the active, especially the social, virtues of their citizens and will be better prepared to endure physical evil and hard times. But this does not mean that the economist should theologize or moralize in the treatment of his subject matter or, what is worse, try to derive an economic system from Holy Scripture.[32]

Even today, there is philosophy enough in the everyday practice of economists such that not all the differences between disputing economists can be resolved by scientific methods. In the prose of John Kenneth Galbraith, one can take the pulse of a theology quite different from that of Milton Friedman.[33] Most of the time, economists do not argue about these background differences. They try to focus as much attention as possible on those issues that may be resolved by scientific methods. As for the rest, they assign it to "preferences," to be argued about within another frame of reference. But this is exactly the frame of reference that Pesch wanted to make explicit.

In the real world, Pesch believed, in the daily clash of argument and choice of preferences, more is at stake between human beings than scientific method alone can bring to light. Philosophies clash. Theologies jangle one another. These are as real to human beings as material things. In their daily interchanges, human beings are deeply affected by the philosophies of teachers, friends, the climate of the time. Pesch believed that no one can properly understand the daily choices made in family life, in politics, and in economic transactions without grasping the ideas and moral impulses which suffuse them.

According to Richard J. Mulcahy, S.J., Pesch thought of his own work as an evolutionary development within welfare capitalism "in the tradition of Smith, Pigou, and Marshall."[34] Pesch, like Adam Smith,[35] entered economics from moral philosophy. As Smith had first done a study of those settled dispositions which he called "the moral sentiments," linking them to "nature," so Pesch had first steeped himself in the study of the "virtues" (intellectual and moral) and "natural law" in scholasticism. Smith, a Protestant in background, did tend more, but not entirely, to emphasize the individual; Pesch, a Catholic, did tend more, but not entirely, to emphasize the community. Yet one of the aspects of Smith's thought that Pesch especially admired was his emphasis upon the wealth, not of individuals, but of nations. Indeed, the central concept of Pesch, *Nationalökonomie*, the "national economy" figures in the title of his masterwork as an allusion to *The Wealth of Nations*. Just as Smith in his projected but uncompleted trilogy wished first to treat of the moral-cultural system, then of the economic system, and finally of the political system, so Pesch also in his concept of *Nationalökonomie* embraced all three.

The proper formal object of economics, Pesch held, has three parts: (1) the material welfare of a whole people, united both through (2) a political system and through (3) the practice of certain moral and cultural values. While economics as a science doesn't pretend to study everything, it is situated in practice in various nations. The impact of politics and culture on economic activities is felt at every point. Mulcahy summarizes these points succinctly:

Adam Smith's classical title, *An Inquiry into the Nature and Causes of the Wealth of Nations*, epitomizes the general approach of Pesch to the study of economics. His concern is the general welfare rather than private profit. He thus defines economics: "The science of the economic life (the process of providing material goods) of a people, considered as a social unit, bound together by the politico-social community life." Or, with direct application to the modern economy: "The science of the economic life of a politically united community, on the level of a developed exchange economy, in relation to the national material welfare as a goal required by the social purpose of the political society."[36]

Adam Smith's question about "the wealth of the nation" is, for Pesch, the central question. Pesch takes great pains to define even the term "material wealth" in its full human context. He places his own definition in italics:

*To the prosperity of the nation appertains the permanent providing of the material means sufficient, in accord with the requirements of a progressive culture, for the satisfaction of the expanding wants of a nation increasing in population, so that along with a rather larger number of moderately wealthy persons, an extensive and capable middle class will be maintained, a living at least worthy of human dignity and corresponding to the degree of culture attained will be secured for all the members, even the lowest classes, permanent poverty remaining excluded—all of this, at the same time, with the protection of the higher values of the person, the family, the political society.*[37]

Pesch rejects the later, post-Ricardian liberalism which surrenders individuals to naked competition, because he does not believe that every individual has the same talent, character, health, history, or will to make an effort. For the same reason, he is not an egalitarian. As his italicized definition shows, he holds that different social strata, not fixed and permanent, but fluid and open to talent and effort, are appropriate to all free societies. Moreover, he sees that national wealth depends in good measure on the outstanding effort of persons of talent and character. A society that would reduce the effort of everyone to indolence, indifference, or mere narcissism would soon collapse of its own moral mediocrity.[38] Thus even "material wealth" has moral presuppositions.

Further, without the many activities of the political system to stimulate, empower, regulate, and constrain economic activities, Pesch believes, an economy would collapse from civic disorder, bureaucratic corruption, and incompetence. One would soon see the capture of the state by narrow interests indifferent to many of their fellow citizens; and all would suffer from the inadequacy of roads, utilities, sanitation, and other empowerments, which today we call "infrastructure." A healthy economy depends on *polity* as well as on *morality*.

As Pesch, according to Mulcahy, several times makes clear, his main argument is less against the early Smith, whose large social view he finds more congenial (although not quite right philosophically), than against Ricardo, Bentham, and some other individualists who followed later. Pesch strenuously resisted such later liberalism, believing that it had placed the system of private property, free exchange, and relatively free markets—of which he heartily approved—upon a false philosophical basis, with demonstrably evil results for the material welfare of nations.

Pesch believed that the liberals made three great mistakes. First, they focused too much attention on the individual, to the neglect of family, associations, the national sense of peoplehood, and other forms of common social life. Second, they focused too much attention on the more easily quantified material aspects of economic transactions, and too little upon equally important moral motivations and purposes and impulses. Third—and this point is the most subtle and difficult to grasp exactly—Pesch believed that the liberals praised liberty and pluralism so much and trusted so much that individual actions, taken merely in their individuality, would meet in single purpose, that they neglected to identify the common good, or raise the common sights, or give a purpose to national enterprise.[39] Excessive individualism, methodological materialism, and a failure to think about common purposes—these, Pesch thought, would eventually empty liberalism of spiritual power. Encountering such emptiness, many within liberal cultures would be blown by dangerous winds of many sorts, including the most dangerous of all, a passionately uplifting Marxism.

Pesch understood that Marxism, as well as the lesser forms of socialism, were quasi-religious forces, and strong exactly at the places where liberalism was weak. Liberalism ennobled human beings by emphasizing their individual liberty, but it also left them lonely and often empty.[40] Its methodological materialism often heightened the appetite for spiritual challenge, which Marxism, while masquerading as materialism, offered in abundance, through metaphysical belief in an irresistible tide of history. Finally, Marxism linked every remote detail to history's common purpose.

Pesch was a lifelong foe both of liberalism and of socialism. He feared the latter more, and what he most disliked in the former were the weaknesses that made it easy prey to its enemy.[41] To these two philosophies, Pesch proposed one of his own. He called it solidarism. To the Anglo-American ear, this name is not felicitous. But on the continent, "solidarity" has a ring to it as ancient as the villages along the Rhone, the Neckar and the Rhine; it is a term powerful even today in Poland. Pesch understood clearly that Marxism is not a science, but a religion. He judged the weakness in liberalism to lie precisely in its *not* being a religion or a holistic view or an organic vision. He invented solidarism as a better answer to Marxism than liberalism is.

The objections which Pesch launched against both Marxism and socialism are not particularly original, but they have well stood the tests of time. From both, he fears materialism and the destruction of the human soul. He fears state power going to excess. He fears the loss of economic dynamism. He understands quite clearly that socialist conceptions of human motivation are out of keeping with reality and, therefore, doomed to frustration.[42] It is not hard for him to reject socialism. It is far harder to state exactly what he means by solidarism.

This difficulty arises because Pesch wants to argue that solidarism is a "middle way" beyond both liberalism and socialism. But this is not an accurate way of describing what Pesch actually sets forth. His rejection of socialism is virtually total. So far as institutions go, Pesch is almost entirely on the side of liberalism. He is in favor of private property,[43] markets,[44] competition,[45] the limited state,[46] and freedom of association.[47] On all such matters of institutional design, he has some things to say that distinguish his views from those of classical liberals. He begins, after all, from an Aristotelian and Thomistic base, rather than from Smith's concept of tradition and moral sentiment or from Bentham's utilitarianism. Nonetheless, his views do not differ much more from classical liberal views than such views differ from one another. In a sense, Pesch is trying to deepen the liberal view, in order to save it from shipwreck.

In reading today the solidarist alternatives to liberal thought, I find myself of two minds. In some respects, solidarism gives a more accurate, or at least less misleading, account of certain human realities than does classical liberalism. For example, human beings are never really atomic individuals in the way that so much of classical liberalism imagines; and even if they were, for many long years of their lives—in infancy, childhood, and adolescence—they are not. In our formation as moral beings, family may be more important to us than reason itself, having shaped in so many subtle ways the manner in which we imagine, perceive, inquire, and reflect. On many key points, I believe Pesch offers a more satisfying account. But, for the most part, his are friendly amendments, and may be accepted without any damage to liberalism at all; on the contrary, to its fuller health.

On the other hand, there are times when I think that the ambitions of Pesch—and, in a sense, of a certain type of Aristotelianism and Thomism generally—are too grand. Pesch sometimes lacks a certain self-abnegation. At such moments, I believe the classical liberal tradition in its studied modesty may be more correct. For example, feeling the organic vision that once suffused the village life of his ancestors, Pesch wishes to argue that human associations such as labor unions, the professions, and the corporations are not merely assemblages of atomic individuals but, rather, substantive communities in a fuller and more connected sense. About this, Pesch reflects the Continental sense of communal history. He has in mind partly the bond that tied together the members of the medieval guild. They were not simply individuals who happened to join together; in older days, guild members knew one another's families, shared the same faith, and had been part of one another's history for generations.

Almost anyone can sense the difference between these two conceptions, and most of us feel at least some (not too much) nostalgia for the older. Yet, on reflection, the supposed moral superiority of the old-fashioned sort of organic community, compared to the modern sort of pluralistic association, does not entirely hold up. Village communities, guilds, and strong families can be stifling organisms; they are sometimes carriers of xenophobia and intolerance. On the other side, modern pluralistic associations can be suffused with intense charity, friendship, openness, and candor. Not all good is on the one side or the other.

It may be objected, however, that when Pesch speaks of "natural bonds" between persons who happen to work in the same trade or industry, he means nothing so close-knit as family or village life, only the mutual habits and interests of persons similarly occupied. But this would seem to be a very weak bond, indeed, hardly worthy of the title "organic," which he weightily assigns to it. In liberal societies, there may be less community in such occupational ties than in many other voluntary associations. But trade associations, manufacturers' associations, and other occupational groupings are in fact common in liberal societies, without benefit of solidarism.

Solidarism has special meaning for Pesch when it comes to "the people." For many generations now, the Germans have spoken more mystically about the "folk" than most other westerners. For Pesch, "people" is a relatively simple notion, almost identical to "nation." Yet Pesch is thinking neither of race nor of biological homogeneity, but of habits and history and culture. For Pesch, "people" is a natural and intuitive concept, in a way it cannot be for Americans of such diverse stock. One senses today an inwardly burning magnetism between the war-separated East Germany and West Germany, a feeling of things out of joint, wrong, against the very nature of things.

Among the Slavs and among the Germans, there have historically been strong appeals to organic ties, mystical unity, unquenchable solidarity, and deep communion, by comparison with which the Anglo-American instinct for individual breathing space seems thin, alienating, and lonely. In recognizing such feelings as realities, in Germany and the Slav territories, Pesch wishes to channel them into the ways of reason and liberty. But such feelings and such traditions need the liberal critique at least as much as liberalism needs theirs. There is a German mysticism about connectedness which it seems wrong to hold up as an ideal, however deep and primitive its tradition.

If, in conclusion, we were to ask ourselves what institutions dominate the "third way" Pesch has imagined, we find that in virtually every case they are the institutions of the liberal society, transformed by the larger sense of community, spiritual value, and common purpose Pesch wishes to bring to them. Actually, most of the reforms Pesch proposes for liberalism are reforms in its theory about itself and in the criteria by which it guides its conduct. He does not actually offer many practical reforms. On at least one occasion, he said it was a matter of principle with him not to do so. Asked for technical advice by the German Finance Minister, Father Pesch refused to help. He held up his fingers and, smiling, merrily said: "We Jesuits are often accused of meddling in worldly affairs. Well, not so far as to get our fingers burned!"[48] The philosopher's role, he thought, was to set down principles. How best to fulfill them is a matter for persons of practical wisdom acting upon matters of fact. He believed profoundly that principles matter and that ideas have consequences; but the philosopher ought not to pretend to be the man of practical doing.

At the publication of *Rerum Novarum,* Pesch was only thirty-six. Having served as spiritual director in von Ketteler's seminary and lived in von Ketteler's very house, Pesch was warmed by it; it confirmed him in his Thomism and in his philosophical quest for "a middle way." He knew of Leo XIII's praise for von Ketteler. He had no way of knowing that his own work would later be regarded as the bridge between Leo XIII and *Quadragesimo Anno* of Pius XI, which one of his students would help draft. On the whole, his "solidaristic economic system may be conceived as operating in a framework of capitalism as this term is usualy understood in current literature"; so writes Mulcahy in 1952.[49] Pesch delighted in the "variety, freedom, particular aims, autonomy and self-responsibility of private enterprise."[50] He never failed to defend individual rights.

Men have . . . as men in themselves, natural tasks and goals and, consequently, natural rights: the right to exist, the right to work, to acquire property, to activate their personal capabilities, the right to found a family, etc.[51]

And then again:

I have put down free enterprise as the rule, public enterprise as the exception. I have said: Every freedom of economic trade is justified, which is consistent with the goal of the economy, with the material welfare of the people.[52]

Pesch distinguishes three senses of "capitalism," two of which he accepts. He accepts as a technical condition common to every modern progressive economic system (1) the intensive use of means of production financed by large capital expenditures. He accepts (2) private ownership of the means of production, in which production is executed at the risk and under the guidance of the entrepreneur. Pesch always keeps in mind the needs of a large middle class composed of many small entrepreneurs, owners, and artisans; and also the needs of large amounts of capital for heavy industries.[53] He would, however, prefer cooperative ownership and management when feasible.

The third sense of capitalism, which Pesch rejects, is "the embodiment of certain abuses which arose in the historical development of the capitalistic enterprise, specifically in the 'capitalist epoch' but which are not essential to the capitalistic epoch and are not found in every capitalistic enterprise."[54] Using italics, he defines exactly what he rejects:

*An economic system arising from the individualistic freedom of striving for gain, ruled by the principles of exchange and the practices of the liberal economic epoch, serving in the first line not the whole welfare of the people, but the owner of capital and his money interests.*[55]

Pesch holds that the welfare of all must be served. A sound economy can function only in a sound social order, with political unity and stability based upon moral and cultural legitimacy. As he often points out, liberal thinkers did not so much deny these conditions as fail to articulate them. He believed his own work "gives to the Smithian industrial system a *solidaristic* foundation through the social regulation of the economic process."[56]

That regulation occurs both through political institutions and through moral-cultural institutions. Fearing state tyranny, Pesch always favored action through the latter, so far as possible. Pesch wanted to inspire a new *mediating institution* between the individual and the state. He developed the traditional idea of the "vocational group" or the "corporatist group." He believed that every branch of commerce, industry, and the professions shares a common set of interests and a special "spirit." He encouraged everyone involved in one of these vocational groups to form a common association, which would unite persons of all classes: owners, managers, workers, even customers, on local regional, and national levels.

Here Pesch encountered a dilemma, the same one which had wrecked the guilds. These vocational associations were intended to institutionalize a sense for the common good across all social classes. What would prevent them from becoming special interest groups, protecting their own privileges and advantages with respect to other associations?

Pesch was himself an irenic man. He did not like the adversarial principle. He placed enormous weight on a social *Geist* or "spirit"—an attitude, an aspiration, a personal commitment to the common good.[57] Typically, however, such associations became jealous of their own interests. Toward the end of his life, as Mulcahy notes, Pesch felt considerable discouragement concerning this problem.

His idea was picked up, however, by his student, Oswald von Nell-Breuning, S.J., who was called upon to draft *Quadragesimo Anno* for Pius XI. This involved an attempt to replace the adversarial relation between labor and management, shareholders and public, with a cooperative relation. Clearly, the aim of "corporatism," as it was called, like the aim of the competitive principle in Anglo-American thought, was the protection of the common good.

Alas, just at the time Pius XI was speaking of corporatism, both Hitler and Mussolini were boasting of the superiority of "corporatist" fascism to the "decadent individualism" of liberal societies. Pius XI had his own battles with Mussolini, whose state-directed corporatism he explicitly opposed; just before his death he condemned German Nazism.[58] The word "corporatism" fell into disrepute, except in Latin America, where it has had a checkered career.[59]

Two final comments may be in order. If one can accuse the Germans (including Pesch) of too much ignoring the evolution of liberalism in Britain and America, it is also something of a scandal that at least the still relevant portions of Pesch's great work have never been translated into English.

Second, the philosophy of solidarism which he put in place of liberalism has continued to exert powerful influence upon younger Jesuits and other Catholic social thinkers, as is shown in the name chosen for the Polish workers' union under Lech Walesa. "Solidarism" and "solidarity" figure prominently in official Catholic documents and commentaries of the last three decades.

Nonetheless, the metaphor implicit in "solidarism" is troubling to the Anglo-American ear. Evelyn Waugh, the English novelist, once commented after the liturgical reforms of Vatican Council II that if the Germans wished to sing in unison and clap their hands in church, that was all right with him. As for himself, he preferred silence before God, communal solitariness. To English ears, although not to European, solidarity suggests collectivism; it seems not to encourge personal autonomy and dissent. Yet, Anglo-Americans are fond of the *practice* of association, of internalized law, of public respect for others, of "good order." Anglo-Americans cherish a high level of public spiritedness and civic consciousness. Beyond that, "solidarity" sounds a shade excessive.

Thus, too, contemporary Catholic social thought, especially since John XXIII, places compensating emphasis upon the dignity of the individual human person. Some have called this emphasis "personalism." So modified, solidarism seems a little less threatening. No threat to the dignity of the human person, it simply emphasizes the social bonds that knit each person to various mediating communities and to the whole human race.

If this is true, however, it seems plausible that German resistance to liberalism is based upon a parallel misapprehension. Germans do not grasp the social bonds which, for Anglo-Americans, are implicit in the practice of the individual. The distinctive invention of liberal societies is not the individual but the corporation; and, beyond that, a rich multiplication of associations of many varied kinds. The actual texture of life in liberal societies is highly associative and quietly ordered by law and civic consciousness. Perhaps Anglo-Americans take such things so much for granted that they do not feel the need to mention them. Still, the Anglo-American concept of "association" is significantly different from the German concept of "solidarity." The former seeks to highlight the realm of the person, the latter the realm of the common good.

This contrast has some relevance today. At the United Nations, there is much talk about "the rights of peoples." This right is construed as a "collective right," contrasted with "individual rights." Typically, the Soviet bloc and Third World delegations favor the affirmation of "the rights of peoples," while Great Britain, the United States, and other Western nations do not. A clarification might break the impasse. If the "rights of peoples" are construed as rights of *association*, founded in the individual and already more than once affirmed in the Universal Declaration of Human Rights, and if these rights of association may be exercised *against the state*, then the danger of collectivism disappears. An example, which ought to appeal to Pope John Paul II, would be Solidarity in Poland. Solidarity is certainly an association, freely entered into, social in character, that makes justified claims against the Polish state. The "rights of peoples," construed in this way, are clearly liberal; rooted in the rights of individuals, they express both the liberty and the social nature of the human person. They go beyond mere individualism, but are *not* collectivist.

The American philosopher John Dewey has remarked that the personality types nourished in a culture of associations need to be highly tolerant, respectful of others, able to function both in teams and in personal responsibility.[60] Walter Muelder, the American Protestant ethicist, speaks of "communitarian personalism."[61] But most Anglo-American writers, praising the individual, leave such social virtues tacit. By contrast, some Catholic cultures that scorn individualism and praise corporatism seem to nourish personality types that have difficulties with tolerance, compromise, teamwork, and the practice of "loyal opposition." Is it a characteristic of theological discourse that the qualities explicitly stressed in theory are opposite to those most commonly observed in practice? Catholics who are said to stress "works" seem frequently to be less obsessive about strict observance. Protestants who stress "faith alone" give evidence, as Max Weber put it, of an intense commitment to an asceticism of works. Catholic societies which praise solidarity suffer from social division, as for example from fragmented political parties, low tolerance for compromise and dissent, and such political-moral passions as make a "loyal opposition" difficult to maintain. By ironic contrast, American society, said to suffer from rampant individualism, proliferates associative behaviors of many types. In translating the thought of Pesch into Anglo-American realities, it may well be that the *operational* meaning of solidarism is not nearly so foreign to Americans as the images it conjures up. To such considerations we shall return in chapter eleven.

Meanwhile, it seems useful to introduce one of those "liberals" against whom von Ketteler and Pesch were in such visceral reaction. In Catholic social thought, one finds painfully little analysis of concrete, historical "liberal" texts. We should, therefore, ask at least one liberal figure to step forward from the mythology in which "liberal" has been surrounded. Does John Stuart Mill match the profile of the liberal von Ketteler and Pesch warned us against?

# CHAPTER 5

# A Quintessential Liberal: John Stuart Mill

It is indeed true that the actual state of things was not always and everywhere as bad as the liberalistic tenets of the so-called Manchester School
might lead us to conclude.

—PIUS XI (1931)[1]

Pius XI—who had earlier written of "the tottering tenets of liberalism"[2]
—ascribes the following to liberalism:

Capital . . . claimed all the products and profits and left to the laborer the barest
minimum necessary to repair his strength and to ensure the continuation of his
class. For by an inexorable economic law, it was held, all accumulation of riches
must fall to the share of the wealthy, while the workingman must remain per-
petually in indigence or reduced to the minimum needed for existence.[3]

A fair-minded reader might be led to ask: Just who held such a view?
Who belonged to "the so-called Manchester School"?

## 1. THE "MANCHESTER LIBERALS"

In a textbook prepared by a professor at Harvard University in 1884,
in a long sketch of "The History of Political Economy," we find the
following reference to the German scholar, Prince-Smith:

As Cobden had an influence on Bastiat, so both had an influence in Germany
in creating what has been styled by opponents the "Manchester school," led by
Prince-Smith (died 1874). They have worked to secure complete liberty of commerce and industry, and include in their numbers many men of ability and
learning. Yearly congresses have been organized for the purpose of disseminat-
ing liberal ideas, and an excellent review, the "Vierteljahrschrift für Volkswirth-
schaft, Politik, und Kulturgeschichte," has been established. They have devoted
themselves successfully to reforms of labor-laws, interest, workingmen's dwell-
ings, the money system, and banking, and strive for the abolition of protective
duties. Schulze-Delitzsch has acquired a deserved reputation for the creation of
people's banks, and other forms of co-operation. The translator of Mill into
German, Adolph Soetbeer, is the most eminent living authority on the produc-

tion of the precious metals, and a vigorous monometallist. The school is represented in the "Handwörterbuch der Volkswirthschaftslehre" (1865) of Reutzsch. The other writers of this group are Von Böhmert, Faucher, Braun, Wolff, Michaelis, Emminghaus, Wirth, Hertzka, and Von Holtzendorf.[4]

Most Anglo-American readers will not have ranked Richard Cobden among the great liberal political economists. With John Bright, Richard Cobden was active in the repeal of the Corn Laws in Britain.[5] Although a lesser figure, he became, especially in Germany, a symbol of free trade, as opposed to protectionism. Joseph Schumpeter's long *History of Economic Analysis* has several references to this "Manchester School" in Germany. According to Schumpeter's account, it does not seem that this school held the views attributed to it by the pope. Schumpeter distinguished several different kinds of individualism, among them "Political Individualism," by which the Germans meant "simply a laissez-faire attitude in matters of economic policy, the attitude that was dubbed Smithianism or Manchesterism in Germany."[6] Schumpeter observes, however, that many economists who merely *described* the results of the free interplay of self-interests in the behavior of individual households and firms were unfairly "under suspicion of *recommending*" these results, a quite different matter, beyond the scope of their science.[7]

Since Schumpeter is writing a history of economic *analysis*, he has no room for anything but a mention of Cobden and Bright, "the two heroes of the Anti-Corn-Law League," activists rather than theoreticians. But Schumpeter does marvel that in the repeal of the import duties on grains, landholders and farmers led by Cobden and Bright supported a policy *contrary* to their own economic interests. ("Interpret it as you please, but do not forget to ponder this most interesting phenomenon of political sociology."[8]) A free trade policy affects much more than foreign trade; it is linked to "something that is more comprehensive still, namely, a general political and moral attitude or vision."[9] Schumpeter adds:

This attitude, which has come to be called *Manchesterism* by its enemies, was in fact Cobden's and Bright's.... Colonies used to be acquired for the sole purpose of being ruled and exploited in the interest of the mother country and of keeping other nations from doing the same thing. From the Manchester school standpoint there is not even an economic argument in favor of doing this. Still less is there a political one. Colonies exist for themselves just as do any other countries; they should be self-governing; and they should neither accord to, nor be accorded by, the mother country any particular commercial advantages. Nor did all this remain in the realm of either philosophy or agitation. Some practical progress was made toward the goal.[10]

Schumpeter applauds this sort of large international vision, so moral—and practical—in outlook. Schumpeter gives credit to Manchesterism for "its refusal to see English interests in whatever happened anywhere on the globe," and for the adoption of the principle "to side with na-tions, 'struggling to be free.'" Furthermore, he writes, "though the pe-riod witnessed a number of wars, others were prevented by the new attitude.... Most important of all, attempts at sowing the seeds of war by arousing a spirit of either aggression or suspicion, which of course occurred throughout, were also under criticism throughout: as an ex-ample I mention Cobden's highly characteristic struggle for a better understanding of France ..."[11]

Pius XI, of course, was not judging the whole of "Manchesterism," only its alleged doctrine on wages, and he was interested in pointing out doctrinal dangers rather than in a balanced moral assessment. (In a similar spirit, no doubt, liberal writers tended to write quite bitingly about the economic practices and doctrines of the medieval Catholic era, asking what Catholic teaching had ever done to raise up the poor.) Moreover, the most exhaustive commentary on this encylical, *Reorgani-zation of Social Economy,* published by a student of Pesch, the Jesuit Fa-ther Oswald von Nell-Breuning, cites as the main authority for the al-leged doctrines of this "so-called Manchester School" the *socialist* writer, Ferdinand Lassalle, who first described "the Iron Law of wages."[12] Las-salle, he notes, formulated this theory by reliance on David Ricardo's labor theory of value, which "starts from a false assumption, and there-fore, because followed through logically, leads inexorably to false conclu-sions."[13] The views ascribed by Pius XI to the Manchester School, then, are actually those of a socialist, although derived from a Londoner, Ricardo.

This point deserves fuller elaboration. Pope Leo XIII had formulat-ed the heart of capitalist economy in an elegant Latin sentence, *"Nec res sine opera, nec sine re potest opera consistere:* Capital cannot do without labor, nor labor without capital."[14] Holding firm to this balanced view, both Leo XIII and Pius XI wished to reject two extremes: the extreme which held that all profit belongs to capital, and the extreme which held that all profit belongs to labor. Pius XI, as the text cited at the beginning of this chapter shows, understood quite well that in actual practice in capitalist economies, things had never been as bad as the extreme theory held. Still, even in practice, he held, "Capital was long able to appropriate to itself excessive advantages; it claimed all the products and profits."[15] So the abuse, in his eyes, was not only theoretical but practical. Nell-Breuning comments: "We know that the liberalist bourgeoisie first devel-oped a practice and then sanctioned it by the theory of classical economic Liberalism."[16] Here Nell-Breuning does not seem to be correct; in Brit-ain, at least, liberal texts gave rise to new laws, new liberties, and new energizing forces which, both in intention and in practice, much bettered the condition of the poor.

Throughout, however, Pope Pius XI's purpose is plain. Defending the rights both of capital and of labor, he writes: "It is therefore entirely false to ascribe the results of their combined efforts to either party alone and it is flagrantly unjust that either should deny the efficacy of the other and seize all the profits."[17] This is the matter of principle. That principle cannot be said to be anti-capitalist.

Just the same, Pius XI does give pejorative weight to the phrase, "the so-called Manchester School." Father von Nell-Breuning is said to have been the original drafter of *Quadragesimo Anno* or, at the very least, to have been influential in its shaping. His lengthy commentary on this passage does not mention Cobden or Bright, only Ricardo. The phrase "Manchester School" must therefore be intended very loosely. Nell-Breuning is, furthermore, rather more harsh in his commentary than is Pius XI. He attributes these thoughts to Pius XI: "To be just, he wishes to concede that actual practice did not live up to the brutality of the theory. But he considers it necessary to state that it was not a case of practice deviating from theory, but rather an attempt of practice to meet the demands of theory. . . . In an individualistic society capitalistic economy inevitably manifested 'a steady drift' in this direction."[18]

A remark by Schumpeter seems apposite: "Contemporaneous and later critics, German exponents of *Sozialpolitik* in particular, have accused the English 'classic' economists of cold indifference to the fate of labor. The first thing to be said about this is that the indictment reveals a lack of historical sense."[19] Most classic economists supported factory legislation; Cobden came out strongly on behalf of the protection of women and children. J. S. Mill and Alfred Marshall found it not inconsistent to favor certain aspects of socialism. Recalling the unprece- dented successes of the recent adoption of the liberal theory in Britain, moreover, in the early and middle railroad age, Schumpeter recalls how "the removal of the fetters that crowded into business pursuits" had an undeniable "energizing influence." However inadequate, he remarks, the liberal theory was "far from being wholly wrong." And he comments:

But let us remember that much of all that offends us now was in the nature of childhood diseases—some of which were passing even at the time of Marx's glowing indictments—and that the economic promise, which the system of free enterprise held out to *all*, was not an empty one: the standard of living of the masses remained low, but it rose steadily almost all the time; ever-growing num- bers were absorbed at increasing real wages. . . . Also, contemporaneous and later critics, both conservative and socialist, have never adequately realized the extent to which the welfare policies of the next period were rendered possible by the developments of the first three quarters of the nineteenth century and by the policies that fostered them. So far as this goes, there is no reason for discounting either the honesty or the competence of the economists of that time, or for voting them victims of ideological delusion.[20]

These remarks seem more just than those of von Nell-Breuning.

Thus it is an oddity of papal thought that for several generations it took its definition of liberalism from *German* interpreters; that only the

Manchester School, but not the mainstream Londoners and Scots, were considered; and that the claims even of Cobden and Bright were misconstrued. Alarmingly, this historical misunderstanding seems never to have been challenged. Thus, even in his Christmas Message of 1954, Pius XII repeated it:

One hundred years ago, the advocates of systems of free trade expected to harvest admirable results from it. They saw in it an almost magical power. One of the most ardent of them went so far as to compare the power of the principle of free trade in the moral order to that of gravitation in the physical. From free trade he expected unity and peace among men and an end to antagonisms of race, belief and language. History has shown how much of an illusion it was to expect that peace could come from free trade alone.[21]

This text refers to a specific passage in Cobden's *Speeches on Questions of Public Policy*. This passage, available in a collection assembled in 1870, is from an extempore speech Cobden gave in Manchester on January 15, 1846. Pius XII's footnote led me to look up Cobden's concluding paragraph:

But I have been accused of looking too much to material interests. Nevertheless I can say that I have taken as large and great a view of the effects of this mighty principle as ever did any man who dreamt over it in his own study. I believe that the physical gain will be the smallest gain to humanity from the success of this principle. I look farther; I see in the Free-trade principle that which shall act on the moral world as the principle of gravitation in the universe,—drawing men together, thrusting aside the antagonism of race, and creed, and language, and uniting us in the bonds of eternal peace. I have looked even farther. I have speculated, and probably dreamt, in the dim future—ay, a thousand years hence—I have speculated on what the effect of the triumph of this principle may be. I believe that the effect will be to change the face of the world, so as to introduce a system of government entirely distinct from that which now prevails. I believe that the desire and the motive for large and mighty empires; for gigantic armies and great navies—for those materials which are used for the destruction of life and the desolation of the rewards of labour—will die away; I believe that such things will cease to be necessary, or to be used when man becomes one family, and freely exchanges the fruits of his labour with his brother man. I believe that, if we could be allowed to reappear on this sublunary scene, we should see, at a far distant period, the governing system of this world revert to something like the municipal system; and I believe that the speculative philosopher of a thousand years hence will date the greatest revolution that ever happened in the world's history from the triumph of the principle which we have met here to advocate.[22]

Does Pius XII hold that Cobden was too materialistic, or narrowly individualistic? Such a charge will not stand. If he charges that Cobden's vision was a large one, looking ahead a thousand years into the future, and that Cobden hoped too much of a single principle, that of free trade, so much would be true. Cobden's principle does not, however, deserve contempt; surely, his dream of one single human family does not.

Clearly, free trade did not prevent World War I or World War II. Just as clearly, the pattern of protectionism which developed between the wars played no little part in the "new nationalism" to which the Axis powers (including the USSR, until Hitler's betrayal of the Ribbentrop-Molotov Accord) so strongly appealed. No one, not even Cobden and Bright, was so sanguine as to believe that free trade *alone* would bring instant peace and justice. But a policy of free trade, carried out pragmatically and not as an absolute, was regarded by Cobden and Bright as having several moral advantages. It required each state to treat every other as an equal. It required a fundamental openness and mutual cooperation. It was rooted in mutual consent and subject to constant mutual negotiations and adjustments. It is a method of peace, not of war, of voluntary action rather than of imposition or coercion. As a general pragmatic principle, it is consistent with the protection of special industries or special needs, since exceptions based on sound reasons do not overturn the principle.

Because of renewed interest in Marxism among many Catholic social thinkers today, it may be worth dwelling on its root in the labor theory of value. Leo XIII was himself accused of adopting the labor theory of value, unjustly so in the view of Pius XI and Nell-Breuning.[23] The theory derives from David Ricardo, who was on this matter and others the mentor of Karl Marx. It was soon rejected by later liberal economists. In Ricardo's view, value derives from labor, from the physical and nervous effort which humans expend to fashion useable products out of nature. Marx used this analysis to argue that all the fruit of labor belongs to labor; any profit to capital is "stolen" from labor. This was never the meaning of Leo XIII, and Pius XI intended to make the point crystal-clear.

What gave rise to the misunderstanding of *Rerum Novarum,* according to Nell-Breuning, was Leo XIII's sentence: "It is only by the labor of the workingman that states grow rich." The Latin phrase used by Leo XIII was *divitias civitatum,* "the wealth of nations." Nell-Breuning believes it indicates "some sympathy with Adam Smith."[24] He further points out that Pius XI was careful to add to Leo XIII's formulation the importance of the assistance supplied by capital. Speaking of the worker, the pope added the words, "toiling either unaided or with the assistance of tools and machinery which wonderfully intensify his efficiency."[25] Finally, Pius XI was also careful to note that any nation which wants to grow in wealth requires the utmost efforts in *mental* as well as manual labor, on the part of "both employers and employees." Intellectual labor and manual labor are equally labor. The contribution of capital involves creative intelligence, and this in turn is the source of great productivity and much value.

What is odd is that, rhetorically, Pius XI hardly says a good word for liberalism, while nonetheless absorbing into his analysis a great deal that had entered the liberal tradition, both in theory and in practice, by 1931. That year, of course, lay in the trough of the Great Depression. Germany itself was in the last stressful days of the Weimar Republic, having suffered under unbelievable inflation. Mussolini was already on the scene in Italy, building a corporatist state along lines uncomfortably close to the ideas expressed in the last part of Pius XI's encyclical, so close that Pius XI had to distinguish his corporatism explicitly from that of Mussolini.[26] Yet events were to show that corporatism or solidarism, toward which German *Sozialpolitik* led the church in its critique of liberalism, was also in need of critique. Many Catholic thinkers, such as Emmanuel Mounier of *Esprit,* were too easily taken in by the "corporatism" and anti-liberal appeals of the Fascists.[27]

In theory, Catholic social thought is nicely balanced as between the individual and society, avoiding excesses at both extremes and drawing on what is important in both. In practice, Catholic nations seem all the more vulnerable to both political tyranny and economic stagnation as they are insistent on averting their eyes from the crucial importance of liberal institutions.

It may, therefore, be of high interest to look more closely at John Stuart Mill, whose *Principles of Political Economy*[28] was the basic bridge between the first and second halves of the nineteenth century. Published in 1848, the year of Marx's Manifesto and von Ketteler's first Advent sermons on the social question, Mill's book went through six editions by 1866 alone. If Catholic social thought desires a mature and classic liberal text against which to define itself, it could hardly locate a better.

## 2. MILL'S *PRINCIPLES OF POLITICAL ECONOMY*

To move into Mill's *Principles of Political Economy* is to enter a world of spacious intellect, clear writing, and generous temperament. Even in 1848, Mill is clearly attracted to socialist conceptions; and although he voices straightforward doubts about whether they can work in practice, he observes that the issue must be decided by actual experiments. Moreover, Mill writes from the point of view of a man who can remember both worlds, both the pre-capitalist world of large landed estates and agricultural workers, and the budding new world of investment, factory-building, and proletarian labor. With sharp eye, he observes the changes in attitudes and values already chronicled by his father, James Mill. A contemporary of Mill's father, Adam Smith, had published his groundbreaking *Inquiry into the Nature and the Causes of the Wealth of Nations* only in 1776.[29] Many of the policy recommendations Smith had made were novel; Smith thought of himself as, and was perceived to be, calling for a new order. In 1776 factories were few in Britain and the mercantilist philosophy—the traditional statism—dominated thought and practice; Britain was still predominantly rural and aristocratic. A professor of morals, Smith was a humanist, not a materialist, and the same may be said of Mill. Mill had the advantage of systematizing all the arguments on political economy developed between 1776 and 1848, one of the liveliest periods of fresh thought on economic matters and rapid practical transformation the world had ever experienced.

In summarizing Mill's major points (those, at least, that bear comparison with Catholic social teaching), I have used the critical edition of Mill's great work, which traces its many revisions. But I have also consulted an American abridgment of Mill's work, interlaced with commentary on actual American experience at that time, prepared as a textbook for American college students by Professor J. Lawrence Laughlin at Harvard University and published in 1888, not long before Leo XIII's *Rerum Novarum* (1891).[30] The critical edition may be said to represent the fluid state of the art in Anglo-American political economy during the formative period of Catholic social thought. Further, the many charts, graphs, maps, and timely concrete examples added by Laughlin afford a fascinating picture of the America of a century ago. Laughlin's introductory fifty-page "Sketch of the History of Political Economy" is a jewel.

Mill divides his two-volume work (which the Laughlin abridgment compresses into a single volume) into five books. The first, which treats of production, Mill regards as scientific, since the laws that promote or defeat production are closely tied to natural and human limits.

The second book, which treats of distribution, is explicitly less scientific, since patterns of distribution are subject to decisions made by societies through the shape of their customs, traditions, institutions, and changing purposes. (In his *Autobiography,* Mill regards this distinction as the most important contribution of his work.[31])

In Book III Mill devotes more than twenty chapters to conceptual and relational questions of exchange: to value, labor, rent, money, credit, price, supply, international trade, foreign exchange, currency, interest rates, international competition, and the like.

Book IV considers the influence of social progress upon production and distribution. Mill spends many pages on *cooperation,* particularly in his longest chapter on "The Future of the Laboring Class." He includes sections on "Distributive Cooperation," "Productive Cooperation," and "Industrial Partnership."

The fifth book is devoted to government. Among the main topics are taxation, the national debt, and protectionism.

With this outline firmly in mind, Mill opens with some preliminary remarks. Political economy is a large but limited science, which investigates the nature of wealth and the laws of its production and distribution. Its aim is to discover "directly or remotely, the operation of all the causes by which the condition of . . . any society of human beings . . . is made prosperous or the reverse."[32] Its object is the study of economic development.

Political economy offers its results "to the *statesman,* who reaches a conclusion *after* weighing them in connection with *moral* and *political* considerations."[33] Political economy itself "does not *include* ethics, legislation, or the science of government," although these are essential fields in themselves and indispensable to the statesman. Political economy is only part, then, of a larger vision. Moreover, political economy is a *practical* science, and must observe that any economic force, or tendency, is normally acted upon by other influences working at the same time, which may "prevent the expected event from following its cause."[34] This circumstance requires the political economist to bring forward a vast stock of concrete examples, taken from around the world, examples which sometimes illustrate a law and sometimes show how a law is frustrated in the real world. At times, political economy proceeds like a narrative of concrete cases, treated with common sense, illustrating the complexity of abstract laws. In Mill, as in Smith, the British empirical habit and love of the *thisness* of things, classical ever since Duns Scotus, is everywhere evident.

Mill sets himself firmly against the system which had prevailed in Europe prior to about 1780, the mercantile system, which "assumed, either expressly or tacitly, in the whole policy of nations, that wealth consisted solely of money; or of the precious metals."[35] The error lay in zero-sum thinking: "The commerce of the world was looked upon as a struggle among nations, which could draw to itself the largest share of the gold and silver in existence; and in this competition no nation could gain anything, except by making others lose as much."[36] Mill regarded zero-sum thinking as primitive, doomed to fall once "men began, even in an imperfect manner, to explore the foundation of things."[37] "Money, as money, satisfies no want; its worth to any one consists in its being a convenient shape in which to receive his incomings of all sorts," and "the difference between a country with money, and a country altogether without it, would be only one of convenience; a saving of time and trouble."[38]

As an instrument, money may be regarded as wealth, but so is "everything else which serves any human purpose, and which nature does not afford gratuitously." Air, though the most absolute of necessities, is obtained gratuitously and is thus not wealth, but "it is possible to imagine circumstances in which air would be a part of wealth . . . as in divingbells sunk in the sea." Wealth is the subject of political economy. It consists in "all useful and agreeable things except those which can be obtained, in the quantity desired, without labor or sacrifice."[39] From the beginning, the concept of human creation defines the concept of wealth.

Mill opens Book I on production with a discussion of its three requisite parts: labor, appropriate natural objects, and capital. The identification of capital as a cause of production marks the intellectual originality of capitalism, distinguishing it from earlier stages of human understanding. Capital is distinguished from wealth as that part of wealth which is withdrawn from consumption and invested in production.[40] The transition from wealth to capital begins when private consumption is converted to production. Thus abstinence gives rise to capital, as labor is defined by sacrifice. Each has roots in the human spirit.

Labor is either bodily or mental; or, to express the distinction more comprehensively, either muscular or nervous; and it is necessary to include in the idea, not solely the exertion itself, but all feelings of a disagreeable kind, all bodily inconvenience or mental annoyance, connected with the employment of one's thoughts, or muscles, or both, in a particular occupation.[41]

To which Professor Laughlin adds: "The word 'sacrifice' conveys a just idea of what the laborer undergoes, and it corresponds to the abstinence of the capitalist."[42] During earlier centuries, neither roads nor markets being available, the landed aristocracy consumed most of its wealth by maintaining large retinues, entertaining friends, and raising small armies. Meanwhile, many of the lower classes spent a good portion of each year in idleness. Then, slowly, came a transition. The wealthy turned from private consumption to investment in the production of goods and in the employment of the idle. More and more citizens turned from idleness to everyday labor. Thus both the wealthy and the poor sacrificed an easier life for a harder—the "thisworldly asceticism" Max Weber was later to describe—to the benefit of the larger community. Thence arose, beginning about 1780, sustained economic growth in Britain, at a rate of at least 1 percent per year for almost 150 years.[43]

A new decisive factor emerged in economics: *time.* Until a factory is built, its products completed, and their first sales registered, both investors and laborers experience costs, but not income. The investors lose the use of such wealth as they invest. The laborers need food and maintenance, plus an incentive to choose labor. During this period, capital must pay for both factory and wages. Money, therefore, acquires a new relation to time. This is because, once sustained progress is possible, money acquires fecundity. Money becomes creative, at least if the venture is successful; for, the disciplines of the market being met, it creates greater wealth—not only in goods which would otherwise not be produced and in the wages which would not otherwise be paid, but also in the returns gained by efficiency in production. In short, new wealth can be created from existing wealth, provided the latter is saved and invested, not merely wasted. Neither the individuals who participate, nor the nation as a whole, are obliged to remain at an earlier level of wealth; economic development can occur. New wealth is produced. Wealth invested and labor intelligently accomplished are together creative. Nature itself is improved. "Agreeable and useful" goods, which could not be produced apart from such sacrifice, add to personal and to cumulative national wealth.

Mill shows that such wealth is a *social* product, since its production depends not only on the direct labor of inventors, designers, investors, managers, and laborers, but also on the builders of roads, transporters, marketers, suppliers of the necessary materials and machinery and raw materials, organizers of all such elements, government officials, police officers who protect property and life, teachers of the skills and arts and branches of knowledge required for all these manifold activities, and others who contribute, directly or indirectly, to the final product. "All these indirect laborers receive, in the way of remuneration, a fraction, some more, some less (the farther they are removed from the direct process), of the value of the final result."[44]

Nearly all productive labor must be continued for some time before its fruits are obtained. Thus current labor always rests on the capital saved up by earlier labor. At the very least, food and water for today's laborers must have been stocked; so also must the investments in tools and materials, ploughs and seeds.

If a person has a store of food, he has it in his power to consume it himself in idleness, or in feeding others to attend on him, or to fight for him, or to sing or dance for him. If, instead of these things, he gives it to productive laborers to support them during their work, he can, and naturally will, claim a remuneration from the produce. He will not be content with simple repayment; if he receives merely that, he is only in the same situation as at first, and has derived no advantage from delaying to apply his savings to his own benefit or pleasure. He will look for some equivalent for this forbearance: he will expect his advance of food to come back to him with an increase, called, in the language of business, a profit; and the hope of this profit will generally have been a part of the inducement which made him accumulate a stock, by economizing in his own consumption; or, at any rate, which made him forego the application of it, when accumulated, to his personal ease or satisfaction.[45]

"The accumulated stock of the produce of labor is termed Capital."[46] Capital is that portion of wealth which is employed in the production of new wealth.

Care must be taken to distinguish among wealth, capital, and money. Imagine wealth as a large circle. Some part of it is withdrawn from consumption and devoted to fresh production; this (a smaller circle) is capital. Capital is socially useful, essential to production, and creative. But money is only a small part of the capital so invested. In times of depression, for example, a perfectly good factory may stand empty, having no exchange value, and be neither convertible into money nor, at least for the time, countable as wealth.[47]

In Mill's time, many peasants of Europe were only half employed and half fed (Mill, having studied the famine of 1842, mentions the Irish). A hardware manufacturer with a stock only of iron cannot feed laborers on iron. But if he invests moneys earlier spent on new porcelain, jewels, and other ornaments of his household in wages to such laborers, the latter will have money for food. This change in incomes will not automatically make more food available, and shortages may at first keep the laborers on short rations. Yet in the next year the changes in demand will have led to more food being produced, in addition to the procelain, jewels, and ornaments. The hardware manufacturer did not *directly* cause more food to be produced; the change in the commodities produced (i.e., more food) does not constitute capital. The *decision* of an investor to invest in producing more food, however, changes a mere stock of idle wealth into productive capital. Capital springs from a decision of will.[48]

Mill next turns to "Fundamental Propositions regarding Capital": "The first of these propositions is that industry is limited by capital."[49] Capital is an indispensable condition for employing labor. "Every increase of capital gives, or is capable of giving, additional employment of industry; and this without assignable limit."[50] Naturally, much capital is fixed in machinery, buildings, improvements, and the like: but capital available for maintaining labor is indispensable to employment. "If there are human beings capable of work, and food to feed them, they may always be employed in producing something."[51] The common notion of pre-modern societies "that the unproductive expenditure of the rich is necessary to the employment of the poor" is exactly wrong. It is by this *productive* investment that employment is given to the poor.[52]

Common opinion holds that too much production will cause goods to be unsold. Mill holds that when the investing classes "turn their income into capital, they do not thereby annihilate their power of consumption; they do but transfer it to the laborers to whom they give employment."[53] Either the number of employees will increase to spend these funds, or "the laborers become consumers of luxuries . . . the difference being, that the luxuries are shared among the community generally, instead of being confined to a few."[54] "Every addition to capital gives to labor either additional employment or additional remuneration."[55] Professor Laughlin adds:

No one ever knew of a community all of whose wants were satisfied: in fact, civilization is constantly leading us into new fields of enjoyment, and results in a constant differentiation of new desires. To satisfy these wants is the spring to nearly all production and industry. There can, therefore, be no stop to production arising from lack of desire for commodities. "The limit of wealth is never deficiency of consumers," but of productive power.[56]

The source of capital lies in saving. For this, a provident, self-sacrificing ethos is indispensable. Persons who save choose future over present satisfaction, and often enough the satisfaction not of their own wants but of those of later generations. But saving is not the same as hoarding, as capital is not the same as wealth. Hoarding and wealth are self-centered, consumption-oriented. Saving and capital are defined by the investment of wealth in production; they are, and are intended to be, generative of new wealth. This creativity explains how nations recover in a surprisingly short time from devastations of nature or war.[57] It also explains how expenditures on production differ from expenditures on consumption, although in both cases what is expended is gone and the material things in which it is invested (wine, clothes, machines) wear out and are used up. Productive investment not only produces its own replacement, but a certain creative surplus as well. Professor Laughlin appends a note on the situation in Massachusetts, in which the annual average per capita supply of capital in 1880 totaled a little less than $600, whereas the average annual product per capita was about $200; "so that the total capital is the product of only two or three years' labor."[58]

Mill goes on to show how fixed capital, invested in the means of production, can be in conflict with the circulating capital which passes from the capitalist to the laborer and is replenished by sales. Large, sudden infusions of new capital in new technologies can displace workers still caught in suddenly less efficient technologies. Such infusions temporarily drain away the circulating capital, which pays workers, and diminish natural prosperity. Typically, such improvements are introduced gradually and are drawn from annual increases in revenue rather than from circulating capital. Yet every advance in "the state of the arts of production" ultimately makes room for a larger amount of circulating capital and gross produce "than could possibly have existed otherwise." Proof "of the ultimate benefit to laborers of mechanical inventions, even in the existing state of society, will hereafter be seen to be conclusive."[59] Investment in new instruments of production does disturb the settled habits of society, but for the better: a proposition susceptible of proof.

Many causes affect the efficiency of production. Fertility of the soil—affording an abundant food supply—is one. Most of the other causes arise from qualities of the human spirit. The regular and habitual energy of labor, e.g., is the second cause. The skills, knowledge of the arts of life, and the practical good sense of labor is a third. Fourth is the moral quality of laborers, their temperance, steady habits, trustworthiness, and the reliable continuity of their work.[60] Moral qualities are radically important. A fifth important element is "the completeness of the protection which society affords its members."[61] Yet perhaps most important of all is "co-operation, or the combined action of numbers." The needs of humans in modern societies are so many that no one person can alone produce all the goods required to meet his own, and the production of each of them is so interdependent on the production of others that cooperation is the fundamental mode of a modern political economy. Feeding sheep; dressing wool; spinning it into thread; weaving cloth; dyeing cloth; making it a coat; transporting, merchandising, and altering it—all these tasks afford multiple occupations in the making even of a simple garment. A social order in which cooperation has become second nature is indispensable.[62]

It is important, too, that the division of labor affords to persons of different skills, strengths, and inclinations employment suitable to their dispositions. Invention is liable to be stimulated by close attention to one's own specialization. Variety in work is also critical to the release and pleasure of "animal spirits," so that muscles and nerves are replenished by employment first of one sort, then another.[63] Mill stresses the crucial importance to industrial firms of management of above-average intellectual gifts, "persons of a degree of acquirement and cultivated intelligence," who may be attracted to otherwise pedestrian work by larger salaries. Indeed, "it is a common enough practice to connect their pecuniary interest with the interest of the employers, by giving them part of their remuneration in the form of a percentage of the profits."[64] Production on a large scale requires immense degrees of human cooperativeness, intelligent leadership, and a large investment of capital to sustain the enterprise in good times and bad. This, too, is a cooperative effort, best accomplished in practice through joint stock companies, since what is required is typically "an amount of capital beyond the means of the richest individual or private partnership," and government, for reasons "tolerably well known, is generally one of the least eligible of resources when any other is available."[65]

Against Malthus, Mill further observes that as production increases, population grows; but popular advances in knowledge, self-discipline, and prudent family life restrain the increase of births from its almost infinite "power of multiplication." "Subsistence and employment in England have never increased more rapidly than in the last forty years, but every census since 1821 showed a small proportional increase of population since that of the period preceding; and the produce of French agriculture and industry is increasing in a progressive ratio, while the population exhibits, in every quinquennial census, a smaller proportion of births to the population."[66] The wealth of nations and individuals may thus be expected to show slow but steady increase, as for forty years they have:

Production is not a fixed but an increasing thing. When not kept back by bad institutions, or a low state of the arts of life, the produce of industry has usually tended to increase; stimulated not only by the desire of the producers to augment their means of consumption, but by the increasing number of the consumers.[67]

Production and employment are limited by capital. What are the causes of an increase of capital?

Since all capital is the product of saving, that is, of abstinence from present consumption for the sake of a future good, the increase of capital must depend upon two things—the amount of the fund from which saving can be made, and the strength of the dispositions which prompt to it.[68]

It is crucial to observe that the latter depends on specific moral virtues. Professor Laughlin notes the vast funds available for capital from even small savers, by observing that in the United States in 1882–1883, some 2,876,438 persons had deposited in savings banks just over one billion dollars with an average of $356 per depositor.[69] This figure shows what *was* saved; it does not show the entire pool that *might have been* saved. The *will* to save is measured by this difference. What motivates saving? First is the incentive of increase. Yet even with the same profit as inducement, inclinations differ in different persons and communities. "All accumulation involves the sacrifice of a present for the sake of a future good."[70]

This is the fundamental motive underlying the effective desire of accumulation, and is far more important than any other. It is, in short, the test of civilization. In order to induce the laboring-classes to improve their condition and save capital, it is absolutely necessary to excite in them (by education or religion) a belief in a future gain greater than the present sacrifice. It is, to be sure, the whole problem of creating character, and belongs to sociology and ethics rather than to political economy.[71]

The national pool of capital comes from the entire citizenry, from the many poor and middle class as well as from the few rich.

Social conditions also matter. The predictability of law and order, a secure society, and trust in institutions and officials; the experience which a community has of life and its vicissitudes; cultural attitudes toward present and future—all these affect saving. Even industrious peoples, like the Chinese, Mill notes, do not seem to be as concerned with the long term as with the short.[72] Indians on the St. Lawrence and in Peru are different yet again.[73]

It is extraordinary that what R. H. Tawney would later describe as "the acquisitive instinct" is described by Mill in terms of self-sacrifice and of creativity. Mill, it is true, preferred a stationary economy to a dynamic, growing one; in this he differed from Adam Smith, who believed the poor of all nations depended upon dynamic economic development. But Mill was wiser than Tawney, for he saw that acquisitiveness may lead to hoarding as well as to investing. Acquisitiveness is pre-capitalist, not capitalist. Mere hoarding or consumption in the present is, for Mill, morally inferior to provident investment in the future. Professor Laughlin notes: "The disturbed condition of the country in France, owing to wars, leads the thrifty to hoard instead of depositing their savings." This note follows Mill's observation:

There are many circumstances which, in England, give a peculiar force to the accumulating propensity. The long exemption of the country from the ravages of war and the far earlier period than elsewhere at which property was secure from military violence or arbitrary spoliation have produced a long-standing and hereditary confidence in the safety of funds when trusted out of the owner's hands, which in most other countries is of much more recent origin, and less firmly established.[74]

Even personal moral virtue, then, depends upon the social achievement of a favorable investment climate. Mill adds further astute observations upon social class:

The geographical causes which have made industry rather than war the natural source of power and importance to Great Britain [and the United States] have turned an unusual proportion of the most enterprising and energetic characters into the direction of manufactures and commerce; into supplying their wants and gratifying their ambition by producing and saving, rather than by appropriating what has been produced and saved. Much also depended on the better political institutions of this country, which, by the scope they have allowed to individual freedom of action, have encouraged personal activity and self-reliance, while, by the liberty they confer of association and combination, they facilitate industrial enterprise on a large scale.[75]

The central point remains: So far as increases in saving are concerned, "production is susceptible of an increase without any assignable bounds."[76] The ultimate wealth producible upon this planet is not in sight. So far as natural law may yet be known, the full wealth embodied in Creation is yet to be tapped. Thus ends Book I on production.

## 3. DISTRIBUTION AND OTHER ISSUES

Even in his twenties, when he had met Saint-Simon in France, John Stuart Mill was attracted by humanistic ideals of community and equality. He did not find such ideals at variance with the thought and practice of liberalism; his concern was with what would actually work in bringing about a good society. Some of the highlights from the remainder of *Principles of Political Economy* bring this out clearly, particularly Mill's views on property, wages and the future of the laboring classes, profits, and international trade.

Mill introduces his views on property with a judgment that, in his view, marks his greatest contribution to political economy: an affirmation that *distribution is less a matter of science than of morals*. To be sure, every arrangement has inescapable costs; human liberty is constrained by real-world effects. Still, he defends the domain of liberty:

The laws and conditions of the Production of Wealth partake of the character of physical truths. There is nothing optional or arbitrary in them. It is not so with the Distribution of Wealth. That is a matter of human institution solely. The things once there, mankind, individually or collectively, can do with them as they like. They can place them at the disposal of whomsoever they please, and on whatever terms. The Distribution of Wealth depends on the laws and customs of society. The rules by which it is determined are what the opinions and feelings of the ruling portion of the community make them, and are very different in different ages and countries; and might be still more different, if mankind so chose. We have here to consider, not the causes, but the consequences, of the rules according to which wealth may be distributed.[77]

The "primary and fundamental" institution of distribution is private property.

1. PROPERTY.

The institution of private property is virtually universal, Mill notes, but its main historical purpose was "to repress violence and terminate quarrels." Thus emphasis naturally fell on first occupancy. In order to get away from the actual origin of private property in European history, however, Mill switches the subject to "social philosophy" as it might be applied to "a body of colonists occupying for the first time an uninhabited country." Two choices are then possible: private property or socialism. In the first case, hereditary injustices would not be involved and schemes of compensation for "the injuries of nature" and for "the less robust members of the community" might put all on the same par. "But the division, once made, would not again be interfered with; individuals would be left to their own exertions and to the ordinary chances for making an advantageous use of what was assigned them."[78] In the case of socialism, elected magistrates would apportion the produce, either on the strict principle of absolute equality (communism) or on some other principle, or "supposed principle," of justice or general expediency, such that private property would be owned not by individuals but by "communities, or associations, or of the government" (socialism).[79]

Mill then takes up some classic objections to communism and socialism and, noting the "real difficulty" to which they point, shows that other factors, like the force of community opinion, might compensate for them. It may be, for example, that each person "would be incessantly occupied in evading his fair share of the work," or that "selfish intemperance" would lead to an explosion of population. But maybe not. A more serious difficulty is "who is to judge" whom to assign to what labor, given the infinite inequalities both among seemingly similar tasks and among seemingly similar persons.

But, to make the comparison applicable, we must compare communism at its best with the *regime* of individual property, not as it is, but as it might be made. The laws of property have never yet conformed to the principles on which the justification of private property rests. They have made property of things which never ought to be property, and absolute property where only a qualified property ought to exist. Private property, in every defense made of it, is supposed to mean the guarantee to individuals of the fruits of their own labor and abstinence.[80]

To judge private property at its best, Mill proposes that it be rectified to exemplify its fundamental principle "of proportion between remuneration and exertion." In addition, all systems, liberal or communist or socialist alike, depend on two further principles, without which "the condition of the mass of mankind" cannot be "other than degraded and miserable": universal education and a due limitation of population. With such reforms "there could be no poverty, even under the present social condition." Socialism, therefore, is by no means the sole refuge. The question of socialism is "a mere question of comparative advantages, which futurity must determine."

We are too ignorant either of what individual agency in its best form, or socialism in its best form, can accomplish, to be qualified to decide which of the two will be the ultimate form of human society. . . . If a conjecture may be hazarded, the decision will probably depend mainly on one consideration, viz., which of the two systems is consistent with the greatest amount of human liberty and spontaneity. It is yet to be ascertained whether the communistic scheme would be consistent with that multiform development of human nature, those manifold unlikenesses, that diversity of tastes and talents, and variety of intellectual points of view, which not only form a great part of the interest of human life, but, by bringing intellects into stimulating collision and by presenting to each innumerable notions that he would not have conceived of himself, are the mainspring of mental and moral progression.[81]

Mill next treats of the socialist criticisms of liberal institutions, and finds them "open to the charge of exaggeration." The ordinary wages of labor and the range of consumption open to workers, the facts show, are increasing, not decreasing. Further, "socialists generally, and even the most enlightened of them, have a very imperfect and one-sided notion of the operation of competition. They see half its effects, and overlook the other half. They forget that competition is a cause of high prices and values as well as of low; that the buyers of labor and of commodities compete with one another as well as the sellers."[82]

Similarly, socialists misapprehend the proportion of the production of industry shared by all and the proportion of profit.

When, for instance, a capitalist invests £20,000 in his business, and draws from it an income of (suppose) £2,000 a year, the common impression is as if he were the beneficial owner both of the £20,000 and of the £2,000, while the laborers own nothing but their wages. The truth, however, is that he only obtains the £2,000 on condition of applying no part of the £20,000 to his own use. He has the legal control over it, and might squander it if he chose, but if he did he would not have the £2,000 a year also. For all personal purposes they have the capital and he has but the profits, which it only yields to him on condition that the capital itself is employed in satisfying not his own wants, but those of laborers. Even of his own share a small part only belongs to him as the owner of capital. The portion of the produce which falls to capital merely as capital is measured by the interest of money, since that is all that the owner of capital obtains when he contributes to production nothing except the capital itself.[83]

In conclusion, Mill judges that the socialists "have a case for trial, and some of them may eventually establish their claims to preference over the existing order of things, but that they are at present workable only by the *elite* of mankind, and have yet to prove their power of training mankind at large to the share of improvement which they presuppose."[84]

Finally, Mill states his own views on the right to private property, which he by no means sees as absolute.

The institution of property, when limited to its essential elements, consists in the recognition, in each person, of a right to the exclusive disposal of what he or she have produced by their own exertions, or received either by gift or by fair agreement, without force or fraud, from those who produced it. The foundation of the whole is, the right of producers to what they themselves have produced. Nothing is implied in property but the right of each to his (or her) own faculties, to what he can produce by them, and to whatever he can get for them in a fair market: together with his right to give this to any other person if he chooses, and the right of that other to receive and enjoy it.[85]

Mill adds that the right of a bequest, or gift after death, forms part of the idea of private property, but that the right of inheritance does not. He agrees with Bentham that when there are no heirs, and in intestacy, property should escheat to the state.[86]

When it comes to land, Mill looks to whether or not the owner actually improves the land or not. "Whenever, in any country, the proprietor, generally speaking, ceases to be the improver, political economy has nothing to say in defense of private property, as there established."[87]

The essential principle of property being to assure to all persons what they have produced by their labor and accumulated by their abstinence, this principle cannot apply to what is not the produce of labor, the raw material of the earth.... It would be the height of injustice, to let the gift of nature be engrossed by individuals.[88]

Since some writers think that liberal thought insists upon absolute property rights, Mill's further comments deserve much emphasis:

When the "sacredness of property" is talked of, it should always be remembered that any such sacredness does not belong in the same degree to landed property. No man made the land. It is the original inheritance of the whole species. Its appropriation is wholly a question of general expediency. When private property in land is not expedient, it is unjust.... Even in the case of cultivated land, a man whom, though only one among millions, the law permits to hold thousands of acres as his single share, is not entitled to think that all this is given to him to use and abuse, and deal with as if it concerned nobody but himself. . . . The rents or profits which he can obtain for it are at his sole disposal; but with regard to the land, in everything which he does with it, and in everything which he abstains from doing, he is morally bound, and should, whenever the case admits, be legally compelled to make his interest and pleasure consistent with the public good.[89]

## 2. WAGES

Mill's entire theory of wages is too complex for easy summary. But some of his notions do bear on Catholic social thought, particularly his concern to find "Remedies for Low Wages," a subject to which he devotes many pages. Throughout, Mill stresses the role of custom, tradition, and human will, observing how in the real world these affect the abstract ruminations of political economists about competition.[90]

Two factors determine wages, he points out, the size of the wage-fund available and the size of the laboring population. From the total wealth of a nation, its outside capital limits, the people actually devote a smaller sum to savings invested in production. If we imagine these relations as two circles, one within the other, the second is always smaller, how much so depending on "the character of the people" and their will to produce new wealth. Of the smaller circle, some investment goes into fixed capital (buildings, instruments) and some into raw materials; the rest goes into "the wage fund." This, in turn, must be divided among laborers. The two limiting constraints, then, are the size of the wage-fund and the size of the laboring force. No two industries have the same divisions as between fixed capital, raw materials, and laboring force; nor, typically, do any two firms within the same industry.[91]

The simplest way "to provide that workmen shall have *reasonable* wages and the capitalist *reasonable* profits [emphasis his]," Mill observes, is either that a minimum wage be fixed in law or that a board of trade, or other council of employers and employees, reach agreement, "the ground of decision being, not the state of the labor market, but natural equity."[92] Mill is willing to grant "that by one or other of these contrivances wages could be kept above the point to which they would be brought by competition."[93] But he hastens to add that competition oftens keeps wages *up*. Shortages of labor, notably in certain branches of employment, frequently do so. There is a further difficulty. "Popular sentiment looks upon it as a duty of the rich, or of the state, to find employment for all the poor."[94] But this entails compulsion to save and to invest in job-creating production. If this had to be imposed on one generation only, Mill sees no problem. But, then, population is likely to rise until "taxation for the support of the poor would engross the whole income of the country."

It would be possible for the state to guarantee employment at ample wages to all who are born. But if it does this, it is bound in self-protection, and for the sake of every purpose for which government exists, to provide that no person shall be born without its consent. To give profusely to the people, whether under the name of charity or of employment, without placing them under such influences that prudential motives shall act powerfully upon them, is to lavish the means of benefiting mankind without attaining the object.[95]

In a later chapter, Mill distinguishes wages from "the cost of labor." To say the first is to look from the side of the laborer, the second to look from the side of the investor. Ironically, wages are often highest where the cost of labor is lowest; in America, Mill points out, great productivity on the part of labor wins both high wages and low costs of labor. Similarly, low wages are compatible with high costs of labor, where labor is inefficient.[96] Furthermore, Mill sees that the cost of profits also enters into the cost of production, since at every step the profit of previous contributors to the process must be paid. Besides labor, he writes,

There is also capital; and this being the result of abstinence, the produce, or its value, must be sufficient to remunerate, not only all the labor required, but the abstinence of all the persons by whom the remuneration of the different classes of laborers was advanced. The return from abstinence is Profit. And profit, we have also seen, is not exclusively the surplus remaining to the capitalist after he has been compensated for his outlay, but forms, in most cases, no unimportant part of the outlay itself. The flax-spinner, part of whose expenses consists of the purchase of flax and of machinery, has had to pay, in their price, not only the wages of the labor by which the flax was grown and the machinery made, but the profits of the owner, the flax-dresser, the miner, the iron-founder, and the machine-maker.[97]

The best device of all for remedying low wages, in fact, turns out to be the promotion of ownership on the part of labor. The ownership of land is constantly benefited by a rise in national wealth. When laborers share in ownership, even of a home or a small plot of land, they "grow rich while they sleep."[98]

In turning his attention to "The Probable Futurity of the Laboring Classes," Mill observes that the essence of a modern society lies in cooperation, and tries to imagine devices by which the cooperation of labor can be expanded in the processes of production, distribution, industrial partnership, and credit unions (people's banks). His aim, in a sense, is a sort of universal, shared capitalism. He observes the extent to which workers in the United States share in the ownership of land and homes, the growth of cooperatives and credit unions on the Continent, and encourages further experiment in such directions. The ideals of cooperation and sharing do not belong solely to socialists; they are, as well, liberal ideals.

En route to these conclusions, Mill makes several fascinating observations. Ironically, one fruit of liberal progress is literacy, a certain rising affluence, and concern for justice. Correspondingly, "There has probably never been a time when more attention has been called to the material and social conditions of the working class than in the last few years."[99] The newspapers, beginning to reach all classes, carry "a more explicit knowledge of the working classes than ever before."[100] There are many admitted injustices and wrongs, and "new forces" need to be applied "to raise the laborer out of his dependence on other classes in the community."[101]

While dependency is the key, Mill often observes the benefits which have accrued to labor through higher wages and a larger range of accessible goods during the first fifty years of liberalism. Professor Laughlin is able to cite the inaugural address of Mr. Giffen, the President of the London Statistical Society in 1883:

> While the money wages have increased as we have seen, the hours of labor have diminished. It is difficult to estimate what the extent of this diminution has been, but collecting one or two scattered notices I should be inclined to say very nearly 20 per cent. There has been at least this reduction in the textile, engineering, and house-building trades. The workman gets from 50 to 100 per cent more money for 20 per cent less work; in round figures he has gained from 70 to 120 per cent in fifty years in money return. It is just possible, of course, that the workman may do as much, or nearly as much, in the shorter period as he did in his longer hours. Still, there is the positive gain in his being less time at his task, which many of the classes still tugging lengthily day by day at the oar would appreciate.[102]

One appreciates these words more clearly from the following tables. The first shows the average rise in wages cited by Giffen, prices being about the same. The second table is more dramatic. It shows the rise in the *consumption* of food per person by the total population of Britain in 1840 and in 1841.

These figures are all the more remarkable when one recalls that the population of Britain nearly doubled (from 16.5 million to 30 million) during the span of these improvements. Mill held it as principle that population growth would prevent improvement in the condition of the working class, since every gain in wages and goods would then be divided among larger numbers. Nonetheless, when one takes into account the doubling of population, the actual condition of the British working class did not, as Giffen says, improve between 70 and 120 percent, but twice that. In other words, the wealth of Britain distributed to the laboring classes at least quadrupled within fifty years. (It was to do the same during the next fifty years.) While Giffen's figures have been questioned by later scholars, they show that even before the writing of *Rerum Novarum* in 1891 evidence already existed of the benefits to which Pius XI gave testimony in the quotation given at the head of this chapter.

### TABLE 3: RISE IN WAGES IN BRITAIN (1833–83)[103]

| Occupation | Place | Wages fifty years ago, per week | Wages present time, per week | Increase or decrease, amount percent |
|---|---|---|---|---|
| | | s.d. | s. d. | s. d. |
| Carpenters . . . . . . . . . . . | Manchester . . | 24 0 | 34 0 | 10 0 (+) 42 |
| " . . . . . . . . . . . . | Glasgow . . . . . | 14 0 | 26 0 | 12 0 (+) 85 |
| Bricklayers . . . . . . . . . . . | Manchester . . | 24 0 | 36 0 | 12 0 (+) 50 |
| " . . . . . . . . . . . | Glasgow . . . . . | 15 0 | 27 0 | 12 0 (+) 80 |
| Masons . . . . . . . . . . . . . . | Manchester . . | 24 0 | 29 10 | 5 10 (+) 24 |
| " . . . . . . . . . . . . | Glasgow . . . . . | 14 0 | 23 8 | 9 8 (+) 69 |
| Miners (daily wage) . . . . | Staffordshire . | 2 8 | 4 0 | 1 4 (+) 50 |
| Pattern-weavers . . . . . . . | Huddersfield . | 16 0 | 25 0 | 9 0 (+) 55 |
| Wool-scourers . . . . . . . . | " | 17 0 | 22 0 | 5 0 (+) 30 |
| Mule-spinners . . . . . . . . | " | 25 6 | 30 0 | 4 6 (+) 20 |
| Weavers . . . . . . . . . . . . . | " | 12 0 | 26 0 | 14 0 (+) 115 |
| Warpers and beamers . . | " | 17 0 | 27 0 | 10 0 (+) 58 |
| Winders and rellers . . . . | " | 6 0 | 11 0 | 5 0 (+) 83 |
| Weavers (men) . . . . . . . . | Bradford . . . . | 8 3 | 20 6 | 12 3 (+) 150 |
| Reeling and warping . . . | " . . . . . | 7 9 | 15 6 | 7 9 (+) 100 |
| Spinning (children) . . . . | " . . . . . | 4 5 | 11 6 | 7 1 (+) 160 |

### TABLE 4: ANNUAL CONSUMPTION OF FOOD PER PERSON IN BRITAIN (1840, 1881)[104]

| Articles | | 1840 | 1881 |
|---|---|---|---|
| Bacon and hams . . . . . . . . . . . . . . . . . | Pounds | 0.01 | 13.93 |
| Butter . . . . . . . . . . . . . . . . . . . . . . . . | " | 1.05 | 6.36 |
| Cheese . . . . . . . . . . . . . . . . . . . . . . . . . | " | 0.92 | 5.77 |
| Currants and raisins . . . . . . . . . . . . . | " | 1.45 | 4.34 |
| Eggs . . . . . . . . . . . . . . . . . . . . . . . . . . | No. | 3.63 | 21.65 |
| Potatoes . . . . . . . . . . . . . . . . . . . . . . . | Pounds | 0.01 | 12.85 |
| Rice . . . . . . . . . . . . . . . . . . . . . . . . . | " | 0.90 | 16.32 |
| Cocoa . . . . . . . . . . . . . . . . . . . . . . . . | " | 0.08 | 0.31 |
| Coffee . . . . . . . . . . . . . . . . . . . . . . . | " | 1.08 | 0.89 |
| Corn, wheat, and wheat-flour . . . . . . . | " | 42.47 | 216.92 |
| Raw sugar . . . . . . . . . . . . . . . . . . . . . . | " | 15.20 | 58.92 |
| Refined sugar . . . . . . . . . . . . . . . . . . | " | Nil. | 8.44 |
| Tea . . . . . . . . . . . . . . . . . . . . . . . . . . . . | " | 1.22 | 4.58 |
| Tobacco . . . . . . . . . . . . . . . . . . . . . . . | " | 0.86 | 1.41 |
| Wine . . . . . . . . . . . . . . . . . . . . . . . . | Gallons | 0.25 | 0.45 |
| Spirits . . . . . . . . . . . . . . . . . . . . . . . . | " | 0.97 | 1.08 |
| Malt . . . . . . . . . . . . . . . . . . . . . . . . . | Bushels | 1.59 | 1.91 |

It was thus not unreasonable for Mill to look forward to steady improvement in the condition of the laboring class. Professor Laughlin, abridging Mill's argument, gives many examples of cooperatives in distribution, production, and banking, beginning from the Rochdale cooperative in Britain, begun in 1844, and drawing on Holyoake's *History of Co-operation in England* (2 vols., 1879). He examines the struggle in Germany between Schultze-Delitsch and Lassalle, the one urging self-help, the other state-help. The workers' associations begun by the former numbered 961 in 1865, and twice that many in 1877, with more than one million members, owning $40 million of capital, with $100 million on loan, and doing a business of $550 million.[105] These were the associations opposed by Bishop von Ketteler who, nonetheless, sponsored a rival program.

### 3. PROFITS

Since some Catholic writers (although not von Ketteler or Pesch) have difficulty understanding the role of profit, it may be worth summarizing a few of Mill's principles on this theme. In his view, when a saver gains by forbearance from consuming his capital for his own uses, and allows it to be consumed by productive laborers for their own uses, his recompense for this abstinence is called profit. Typically, there are three reasons why profit is earned. First, in an era of productive investment, money has a time value; thus a borrower properly pays interest to recompense the original saver for not using or investing the money himself. Second, since productive investment is generally more risky than a mere loan, the investor "exposes his capital to some, and in many cases, to very great, danger of partial or total loss. For this danger he must be compensated, otherwise he will not incur it." Third, the superintendence of a productive enterprise "requires great assiduity, and often no ordinary skill," which must also be compensated. The mere investment of capital, without direct superintendence (payment for which is actually a species of wage for managerial labor), requires profit solely for the first two functions.[106]

If there is no recompense for the abstinence, risk, and exertion implied in the conversion of wealth into capital, there is not likely to be much productive investment. In that case, the wealthy will merely consume their substance upon their own interests. The social utility of profit is to afford a motive for abstinence from consumption and for productive investment. Such a use of wealth is far more useful to the poor—and to the nation—than the mere consumption of the wealthy. The "comparative value placed, in the given society, upon the present and the future" will determine the strength of abstinence and creativity.

Further, profit depends very much on the individual.

[It] varies very greatly from individual to individual, and can scarcely be in any two cases the same. It depends on the knowledge, talents, economy, and energy of the capitalist himself, or of the agents whom he employs; on the accidents of personal connection; and even on chance. Hardly any two dealers in the same trade, even if their commodities are equally good and equally cheap, carry on their business at the same expense, or turn over their capital in the same time. That equal capitals give equal profits, as a general maxim of trade, would be as false as that equal age or size gives equal bodily strength, or that equal reading or experience gives equal knowledge. The effect depends as much upon twenty other things as upon the single cause specified.[107]

Finally, whereas Ricardo argued that the rate of profit varies with the rate of *wages,* Mill shows that it varies with the *cost of labor.*[108] From Ricardo, Lassalle, and Marx one could deduce "the iron law of wages and profits"; not so from Mill. For a skilled, trustworthy, and productive workforce can simultaneously be paid unprecedented high wages and still keep the cost of labor low, by the sheer productivity and quality of their work. It does not follow that from high wages low profits flow; nor that high profit must keep wages low. Between wages and profits, inventive and productive intellect intervenes. The era of liberalism has not witnessed the "immiseration" of the workers, but rather their *embourgeoisement.* The "iron law" was made of putty.

### 4. INTERNATIONAL TRADE

Pre-liberal thinking about international trade followed the zero-sum model of mercantilism: Nation $X$ can gain only if nation $Y$ loses. In actual practice, international trade is of mutual benefit, for reasons which appear not at first glance but on reflection. Labor and capital cannot easily move from place to place, even though in modern times their movement is more rapid than ever before. As a consequence, profit is not everywhere the same. If it were the same, there would be no difference between international and domestic trade. Three obstacles to mobility create the conditions which make "international" trade different: geographical distance; difference in political institutions; difference in language, religion, and social customs, i.e., in forms of civilization.[109]

What makes international trade attractive is not a difference in the *absolute,* but in the *comparative,* cost of production. Suppose that Sweden and Britain both produce cotton and iron, but that Britain's efficiency allows her to produce cotton at half the Swedish cost and iron at three-quarters the Swedish cost. It would then be to Britain's benefit to procure iron from Sweden in exchange for cotton. For Britain, the profit in selling cotton is twice as large as the loss in buying iron. For Sweden, obtaining cotton at the same price as if it had been made in Sweden, but without the expense of labor and capital, is also a bargain. The *comparative* cost is the difference in Britain between the cost of producing cotton and the cost of producing iron.

International trade also allows countries to obtain what they could otherwise not obtain at all; but that is a benefit only in a superficial sense. The deeper benefit is a more efficient employment of productive

forces in each participating nation. If two countries each tried to produce for itself what it now imports from the other, the labor and capital
of each would be less productive than when each produces for the other
the goods in which its labor is comparatively more efficient. "The labor
and capital which have been expended in rendering Holland habitable
would have produced a much greater return if transported to America
or Ireland. . . . But nations do not, at least in modern times, emigrate en
masse," and thus labor and capital remaining at home in any nation are
most productive if they produce "the things in which it lies under the
least disadvantage."[110] Cultures have special aptitudes; localities enjoy
special advantages from nature; populations have diverse energies and
inclinations. International differences can be turned to assets.

Common opinion holds that the advantage to international trade is
"finding markets," the exports; but this is only the propaganda of "the
selling class" and a "surviving relic of the Mercantile Theory," which
saw in selling the only way to make money. But money is not wealth.
Moreover, the notion that foreign trade is an outlet for surplus produce
cannot be true, for it supposes that "a country is under some kind of
necessity" to produce in sheer waste, and this is ridiculous. When
domestic supply is too large, production stops.[111] The only reason for
further production would be for comparative advantage in the imports
received in foreign trade. But this fact shows clearly that "the only direct
advantage of foreign commerce consists in the imports."[112] For a nation
imports goods which it could not so cheaply produce itself. From this
circumstance, labor and capital are saved from inefficient use, and consumers save on expenses. "Commerce is virtually a mode of cheapening
production; and in all such cases the consumer is the person ultimately
benefited."[113] Lower prices especially raise the standard of living of the
laboring class and the poor. The economic advantage of foreign trade,
then, lies in imports.

But Mill holds that the intellectual and moral advantages of international trade are also "benefits of a high order." These are of four kinds.
First, international trade fertilizes innovation and invention, since the
expansion of markets causes a search for improvements in production.
Second, the opening of foreign trade awakens populations formerly
slumbering in ignorance of what might be done with their own natural
resources or with their own capacities for organization. It also stimu-
lates ambition and forethought for a future different from the present.
Third,

It is hardly possible to overrate the value, in the present low state of human
improvement, of placing human beings in contact with persons dissimilar to
themselves, and with modes of thought and action unlike those with which they
are familiar. Commerce is now, what war once was, the principal source of this
contact. Such communication has always been, and is peculiarly in the present
age, one of the primary sources of progress.[114]

Finally, commerce heightens the ethical character of international relations. The ethical revolution it works is unprecedented. Commerce is mutual, voluntary, and pacific. It is one of the few activities in which all parties benefit by the satisfaction of each. Thus

Commerce first taught nations to see with goodwill the wealth and prosperity of one another. Before, the patriot, unless sufficiently advanced in culture to feel the world his country, wished all countries weak, poor, and ill-governed but his own: he now sees in their wealth and progress a direct source of wealth and progress to his own country. It is commerce which is rapidly rendering war obsolete, by strengthening and multiplying the personal interests which are in natural opposition to it. And it may be said without exaggeration that the great extent and rapid increase of international trade, in being the principal guarantee of the peace of the world, is the great permanent security for the uninterrupted progress of the ideas, the institutions, and the character of the human race.[115]

The liberal vision may be faulted for many inadequacies. But its moral nobility stands clear, all the more so for lacking excessive moral pretension. It seeks to create an interdependent world founded on moral progress, law, mutual consent and mutual satisfaction, and constant improvement in the life of the very poor. More than any rival theory, it has fulfilled, where its writ runs, what it promises. It does not put itself forward as a substitute for religion. Of itself, it is not a threat to religion.

Had John Stuart Mill been a Catholic, his thought would perhaps have inspired the popes and theologians more than it did. Indeed, Mill seems to have been very much ignored, even when the liberal cause he stood for was supportedly being criticized. Many of the criticisms launched by von Ketteler, Pesch, and even Pius XI did not hit the heart of liberal social thought. Mill was neither so materialist nor so individualist as papal thought has imagined liberals to be. His arguments are typically practical, relying upon a moral as well as a merely economic assessment of consequences. Although the language of the Catholic tradition is not native to him, he supplies his own alternative to virtually every Catholic principle of social justice. One can fault Mill at many points, but his intentions, his spirit, and (by and large) the consequences of following his "principles" are indisputably humane, both in themselves and by comparison with existing alternatives.

# CHAPTER 6

# From Politics to Economics: Leo XIII and Pius XI

It is not surprising that the spirit of revolutionary change, which has long been predominant in the nations of the world, should have passed beyond politics and made its influence felt in the cognate field of practical economy.

—LEO XIII, *Rerum Novarum*[1]

## 1. RERUM NOVARUM

From politics to economics: the above opening sentence of Leo XIII's encyclical on "The Condition of Labor" (1891) reflects a tide in the ideas of the French, the British and the Americans since the term "political economy" first appeared in 1615.[2] In earlier centuries theologians and popes had written of politics, regimes, monarchs, and princes. The idea that humans could gain understanding and control over *economics* arose much later. The term "political economy" achieved its classic formulation in 1776, when Adam Smith, who saw it as a branch of "moral philosophy," published his *Inquiry into the Nature and Causes of the Wealth of Nations.* By the time the pope's encyclical appeared, Hamilton, Jay, and Madison had long since written *The Federalist,* and Hamilton his *Report on Manufactures.* Abraham Lincoln, who as president had addressed the Congress of the United States on "the priority of labor," had been dead for nearly thirty years, and John Stuart Mill—who exemplified the turn of mind suggested by the Pontiff—had been dead for nearly twenty.

There is no reference in the Pontiff's letter to "liberalism" or even to democracy. Leo XIII was not yet ready to lend the support of the Catholic church to the democratic idea or to its bills of political and civil rights. There are no direct references to Britain or to the United States, although there seems to be allusion (as Nell-Breuning suggests) to *The Wealth of Nations.*[3] The aim of *Rerum Novarum* is to "refute false teaching."[4] It is, further, "to define the relative rights and the mutual duties of the wealthy and of the poor, of capital and labor."[5] And it is also to find "some remedy . . . for the misery and wretchedness which press so heavily at this moment on the large majority of the very poor."[6]

Immediately, the pope lunges into a refutation of socialism, followed by a ringing philosophical defense of private property. Socialism is founded on the false teaching that, "by transferring property from private persons to the community, the present evil state of things will be set to rights, because each citizen will then have his equal share of whatever there is to enjoy."[7] In the view of Leo XIII, "the present evil state of things" must be set right, although not in the socialist way.

Leo XIII grounds his defense of the right to private property—which, unlike Mill, he calls "sacred"[8]—in the human subject, in the human capacity to choose, in the human capacity for providence, and in the "very reason and motive" of a man's remunerative labor.[9] He rests his teaching on that of St. Thomas Aquinas. His views are not identical to, but they are at least analogous to, those of John Stuart Mill. In one sense, Mill's principles are much more demanding than the pope's; for Mill roots the right to property in the service to the common good provided by the owner who *improves* the property, whereas the Pope roots it in the human need to have material means by which to express human choice and human providence for the future. The aim of both, however, is to assert that property imposes responsibilities as well as rights.

A major principle for Leo XIII is that social classes are not by nature or by history hostile to one another, but as harmonious as those of the members of one single body.[10] The rich and the poor "require one another: capital cannot do without labor nor labor without capital."[11] To set moral limits on the uses of property, to elicit mutual harmony between social classes, and to respect the dignity of each human person seems to the pope tantamount to a renovation of the social order.

For Leo XIII, this renovation could not, morally, be socialist. *"The main tenet of Socialism, the community of goods, must be utterly rejected."*[12] Further, the socialist conception of equality must also be rejected:

Let it be laid down, in the first place, that humanity must remain as it is. It is impossible to reduce human society to a level. The *Socialists* may do their utmost, but all striving against nature is vain. There naturally exists among mankind innumerable differences of the most important kind; people differ in capability, in diligence, in health, and in strength; and unequal fortune is a necessary result of inequality in condition. Such inequality is far from being disadvantageous either to individuals or to the community; social and public life can only go on by the help of various kinds of capacity and the playing of many parts, and each man, as a rule, chooses the part which peculiarly suits his case.[13]

There is a clear asymmetry in Leo XIII's address to economic issues. The capitalists are correct in principle; but they must reform their institutional practices. The socialists are in error in moral principle. In judging socialism, Leo XIII is far more apodictic than John Stuart Mill. The pope does not need to see the results of experiments conducted on false principles.

On the other hand, societies committed to the right to private property have urgent reforms to carry out: in the strengthening of labor unions and cooperative associations of many kinds; in paying a just wage; in seeing to the welfare of women and children; in respecting the dignity, health, and spiritual life of workers on the job. Human beings must be treated as human beings, not as objects, instruments, chattel, or slaves.[14] The state must respect the prior rights of families; intermediary associations must not only be given liberty to act but strengthened in their actions.[15] By judging liberal societies in the light of their professed ideals, the pope strengthens all those reformers, activists, and experimenters who have tried to come to the assistance of the laboring classes.[16] While defending the right to property, Leo XIII is chiefly concerned to correct the imbalance which gives to the wealthy too much power. He comes chiefly to the assistance of labor and the poor, who are too weak and too defenseless.[17]

In pleading for cooperation between all social classes, Leo XIII alludes to *The Wealth of Nations*, voicing a judgment that has echoes of Adam Smith on the role of labor: "Indeed, their cooperation in this respect is so important that it may truly be said that it is only by the labor of the working man that States grow rich."[18] This sentiment, which dates from Adam Smith, as Joseph Schumpeter comments in his *History of Economic Analysis*,[19] is shared by all persons who feel dismay at disparities of wealth. Uncritically, Smith himself used similar rhetoric, although his actual economic analysis did not show that all value is added by labor alone. As we have seen, the pope's claim that wealth is created only by labor aroused great controversy, since by 1891 socialists had claimed it as their own. From this they concluded that, since *only* labor generates wealth, all wealth should belong to labor. We saw in our discussion of Mill's views upon the matter, and later economic analysis has shown, that the creation of wealth results from several factors in addition to "the workers," understood as a class.

On the whole, Leo XIII's brief treatise of barely thirty pages is irenic, balanced, and eloquent. It strengthened many forces of reform. Most of all, perhaps, it marked a recovery of Catholic intellect and self-confidence; and it demonstrated, once again, that Catholic faith is not for the sacristy only, but for incarnation in the economic and political realm. The letter admirably met the pope's initial purposes: it refuted false teachings; it defined mutual duties of capital and labor; and it encouraged remedies to contemporaneous social evils.

## 2. QUADRAGESIMO ANNO

Forty years later, Pius XI (1922–1939) commemorated the anniversary of *Rerum Novarum* with a letter issued in the depth of the Depression, but before the full fury of illiberal Fascism was to be unleashed upon Europe. In this letter, there is rather more anger and ideological passion than in Leo XIII. For the first time, the word "liberal" appears, always pejoratively. From the very first paragraphs, Pius XI insists that Catholic teaching owes nothing to liberalism or to socialism. It is with Pius XI that the idea of Catholic social thought as a "third way" is made official.

The writing of *Quadragesimo Anno* is a story in itself. Pius XI asked the Jesuit General to request that one of the German Jesuits, who were taking part in regular meetings on the social question as the "Winter-haven group," be asked to prepare a draft in total secrecy and without consultation with others. The Jesuit General appointed Oswald von Nell-Breuning, S.J., to the task. Father von Nell-Breuning, a student of Heinrich Pesch, was then forty years old. He taught at Frankfurt-am-Main and specialized in social thought and economics. Among his seminar associates were Gustav Gundlach, S.J., and the layman Goetz Briefs. Father von Nell-Breuning also wrote a line-by-line commentary on the encyclical just after it appeared, on which we shall draw in what follows.

The years 1930–1931 were not happy years in Germany. The fury of the Depression had burst relentlessly on a defeated nation heavily in debt, weakly governed, and suffering under indescribable inflation. Belief in the existing social order was rapidly unraveling. Attacking liberalism as decadent, Adolph Hitler was soon to complete his meteoric rise toward power. Mussolini's Fascism already held sway in Italy. The anti-liberal ideology of Mussolini's new state was being trumpeted in articles, speeches, and announcements; Mussolini, indeed, coined the word "totalitarian." This is the context in which Pius XI's assault upon liberalism was launched. He turns his attention to "the changes which this capitalistic economic order has undergone since the days of Leo XIII." It is not capitalism as such which he attacks; he expresses a certain nostalgia for the older capitalism. But he is bitter about its newest deformations and his charges are severe:

In the first place, then, it is patent that in our days not alone is wealth accumulated, but immense power and despotic economic domination is concentrated in the hands of a few, and that those few are frequently not the owners, but only the trustees and directors of invested funds, who administer them at their good pleasure.

This power becomes particularly irresistible when exercised by those who, because they hold and control money, are able also to govern credit and determine its allotment, for that reason supplying so to speak, the life-blood to the entire economic body, and grasping, as it were, in their hands the very soul of the economy, so that no one dare breathe against their will.

This accumulation of power, a characteristic note of the modern economic order, is a natural result of unrestrained free competition which permits the survival of those only who are the strongest. This often means those who fight most relentlessly, who pay least heed to the dictates of conscience.

This concentration of power has led to a threefold struggle for domination. First, there is the struggle for dictatorship in the economic sphere itself; then, the fierce battle to acquire control of the State, so that its resources and authority may be abused in the economic struggles. Finally, the clash between States themselves. . . .

Unbridled ambition for domination has succeeded the desire for gain; the whole economic life became hard, cruel and relentless in a ghastly measure. Furthermore, the intermingling and scandalous confusing of the duties and offices of civil authority and of the economy has produced grave evils, not the least of which has been a downgrading of the majesty of the State. The State which should be the supreme arbiter, ruling in queenly fashion far above all party contention, intent only upon justice and the common good, has become instead a slave, bound over to the service of human passion and greed. As regards the relations of nations among themselves, a double stream has issued forth from this one fountainhead; on the one hand, economic "nationalism" or even economic "imperialism"; on the other, a no less noxious and detestable "internationalism" or "international imperialism" in financial affairs, which holds that where a man's fortune is, there is his country.[20]

The tone of these remarks is altogether different from Leo XIII's. Pius XI says in his opening paragraphs that Leo XIII "boldly attacked and overthrew the idols of liberalism," yet Leo XIII never mentioned liberalism, nor said anything in essential contradiction to it. Moreover, as one ponders the charges listed above one wonders whether they describe Germany—Italy was already a National Socialist state—or Poland or France or Britain or Spain or the United States. Theodore Roosevelt had long since attacked "the trusts." The pope had allies in the liberal world whom he does not seem to have recognized.

Where Pius XI most departs from Leo XIII, in any event, is in the ferocity of his attack upon liberalism. The key to this assault lies in his judgment upon individualism. "With holy gravity and a severity of judgment quite striking," von Nell-Breuning comments on the opening paragraphs, "he rejects Individualism. We can well say that from here on to the very end of the encyclical there runs a scarlet thread of relentless pursuit into the last, most secret fastnesses of the liberalist and individualist spirit."[21]

There is some reason for Father von Nell-Breuning to feel vindicated by this encyclical; it placed the ideas of his old and dear teacher, Heinrich Pesch, at the center of Catholic thought. He takes pride in pointing out that "Quadragesimo Anno has finally and definitely established, theologically canonized, so to speak, social justice. Now it is our duty thoroughly to study this concept—the spiritual foundation and supporting pillar of Christian solidarity, as it is called by Heinrich Pesch." Pesch called his philosophy "solidarism," von Nell-Breuning adds, "and it is this type of thought which in general is accepted by the Encyclical."[22] Father von Nell-Breuning would be inhuman not to be pleased that the philosophy of his teacher was singled out by the pope to represent the pope's own view of authoritative Catholic teaching. He often comes back to this theme in his commentary.[23]

Some events in Germany contemporaneous with the Encyclical seemed to confirm von Nell-Breuning in the truth of the pope's diagnosis, whose tone von Nell-Breuning finds justly severe. On May 11, 1931, the *Oesterreiche Creditanstalt* collapsed; on July 13, 1931, the *Danatbank* went bankrupt; later, the Kreuger concerns fell apart and Ivan Kreuger committed suicide.[24] These examples tend to confirm von Nell-Breuning's preoccupation. The stock-market crash of 1929 in the United States and bank foreclosures in many other countries were also part of the context.

For what had occurred since 1891, both von Nell-Breuning and the pope thought, was a fundamental shift within the capitalist system. Productive enterprises and market-disciplined *homo oeconomicus* had given way to great empires of finance and credit and to a new type of "man of economic violence who creates markets according to his will, and forces his law upon them."[25]

*Quadragesimo Anno* takes pains to defend the moral integrity of the capitalist system as a system. "It is clear then that the system as such is not to be condemned. Surely it is not vicious of its very nature . . ."[26] The system is not properly ordered; and there are abuses within it. "Here," von Nell-Breuning comments, "the object is to characterize a *fault of the system* which maims our modern capitalistic economy, and for the removal of which we must strive."[27]

To the extent that the descriptions of social reality supplied by Pius XI were true, one cannot fault him either on principle or in tone. Yet von Nell-Breuning appends to his discussion a Report of the Treasury of Great Britain, dated March 11, 1918, urging governmental action to prevent the concentration of banking power in "a very few preponderant combinations."[28] This note suggests that liberal institutions had been looking to their own self-reform more than a decade before the Pontiff wrote. The ferocity of his language in attacking liberalism seems, in this sense, not quite fair.

Furthermore, in constantly assaulting individualism, the pope cites no specific authors or theories. Father von Nell-Breuning describes liberalism as "the perversion of man's freedom," as socialism is "the perversion of man's social nature."[29] This supposed symmetry serves his purpose of portraying solidarism as a middle way.

Yet it would not be so easy for von Nell-Breuning to ascribe, say, to John Stuart Mill, or Abraham Lincoln, or Theodore Roosevelt, or Alfred Marshall all the evils he wished to ascribe to liberalism. That the solidarists diagnosed liberalism correctly is not at all clear. Nor is it clear, on the other hand, that solidarism is not fraught with errors of its own. Its depreciation of the individual, for example, left it rather vulnerable to the mysticisms and coercions of group life, "primordial" feelings, and mass psychology. Its caricatures of liberalism strengthened the fascists in their propaganda against liberalism and on behalf of corporatism. Father von Nell-Breuning, in particular, is given to describing the individual mainly as a center of selfishness, disorder, and domination. Almost never does he see the individual as a resource of conscience, justice, and charity.

Moreover, Anglo-American individualism must be understood within a dramatically different set of institutions, ethos, and cultural history than German or French or Italian individualism. George Santayana in *The German Mind,* for example, shows how German philosophy from Kant through Fichte to Nietzsche makes a certain false egotism the very center of consciousness.[30] In assaulting liberalism and individualism, it is not clear whether von Nell-Breuning was venting a certain Germanic revulsion against British culture, whose tempering institutions he did not understand, or whether his revulsion is actually directed against *German* liberalism and *German* individualism—indeed, against an unspecified anti-Catholic, anti-traditional force in Germany.

In any case, an American reader who reads both *Quadragesimo Anno* and von Nell-Breuning's commentary feels a lack of subtlety in certain formulations. This uneasiness does not extend to matters of principle. It arises precisely in the *descriptive* passages and in those passages which, as von Nell-Breuning imagines, engage in "relentless pursuit into the last, most secret fastnesses of the liberalist and individualist spirit."[31] British and American liberals have not been secret about their beliefs. Some of the books they have written stand among the classics of the world. To diagnose the errors of a liberal like John Stuart Mill, a much more refined analysis would be required. Mill has a strong social sense, a profound concern for the laboring class, an explicit respect for the social dimension of property, a strong commitment to mutuality as between capital and labor, and a sharp awareness of the social and moral context within which political economy must be placed. His liberalism paralleled many of the doctrines of solidarism, without some of the latter's defects.

Nonetheless, both *Rerum Novarum* and *Quadragesimo Anno* were, for their time, farseeing and influential documents. In not a few states, legislation was inspired by them. They have had a significant and, on the whole, beneficent impact upon real affairs. By this very fact, however, they reduced the space available to a "solidarist" middle way. In proportion as nations which are democratic in polity and capitalist in economy have institutionalized many of the papal principles, they have come to exemplify, rather than to serve as contrasts to, Catholic social thought. Compared to 1891 or 1931, for example, the German social market economy of 1984 is far closer to the principles Leo XIII and Pius XI laid down.

Indeed, since the miraculous recovery of Europe after World War II,

Catholic social thought has considerably altered its focus. It would be foolish for it to be concerned with the "immiseration" of the working class; its worry nowadays is, rather, their too-complacent affluence. Thus post-war popes have turned more and more of their attention to the situation of the poor of nations distant from Rome and beyond the circle of economically successful nations. Ironically, some of the poor nations of the world have modeled themselves on Catholic social thought. In such nations, Catholic social thought has not been notably effective in stimulating economic growth or in building the cultural and political institutions necessary to sustain respect for human rights. The *doctrine* is correct, although incomplete, but the teaching on *institutions* is uncertain.

### 3. SOLIDARISM AND CORPORATISM

There are two contributions Pius XI made in *Quadragesimo Anno*. The first was the introduction of the term "social justice" as the foundational term of Catholic social thought. The second was the sketch of the "corporative ideal," by which Pius XI, following Heinrich Pesch, hoped to overcome the so-called division between social classes. Since a full discussion of both these points is given by Jean-Yves Calvez, S.J., and Jacques Perrin, S.J., in *The Church and Social Justice* (chapters VI and XIX), my remarks, relying on that work, may be brief.[32]

"Social justice" is not a term honored by tradition. Leo XIII did not use it. The traditional term Leo XIII implicitly relied upon was the concept of justice familiar since St. Thomas Aquinas, *justitia legalis:* that is, the "higher law" rooted in human nature by which all "positive laws" made by states are measured for adequacy. It was Leo XIII's intent to show that questions of political economy are not *merely* pragmatic, at the beck and call of human will. Economic systems must be assessed in the light of moral philosophy, social philosophy, and natural law. One may always ask of economic arrangements: Are they just? Do they properly respect the dignity of human persons and communities? Are they appropriate for human beings, in their special dignity? Incidentally, it was precisely through raising this question about the *socialist* vision of human nature that Leo XIII first used the term "justice."[33]

The difficulty for German scholars was that in the battle over the meaning of law which developed under Bismarck, the Thomistic concept *justitia legalis* tended to be construed, in German, as equivalent to its opposite, viz., positive law, the will of the state. Seeking an equivalent notion, after several attempts, Heinrich Pesch experimented with "social justice." He intended this concept to call attention both to the social nature of human life, beyond questions of person-to-person or individual ethic, and to the "higher law" beyond positive law. His student, von Nell-Breuning, supplied the new concept suited to Pius XI's needs. For

Pius XI wished to show that action in the social order is not commanded solely by charity, or by the attraction of an ideal, but by *justice:* that is, by claims inherent in human dignity. Some social arrangements, he wished to hold, are incompatible with human dignity.

This insight is basic to the liberal tradition of "natural right" and "the bill of rights." And, as Jacques Maritain and others were later to show, it is actually in keeping with classic Thomistic notions of the person and the common good. For a long time, however, the popes, beginning in the struggles of Pius VII against Napoleon and his successors against the "rights" claimed in the French Revolution, stiffened their spines against liberalism. They understood liberalism chiefly through their experience with turmoil in France and Italy, as E. E. Y. Hales makes clear in *Revolution and Papacy.*[34]

Although Pius XI attacked "individualism" again and again, he did not set forth a Catholic alternative; a vision, say, of "personalism" or "the integrity of the human subject." Until Pope John XXIII, official Catholic teaching was so opposed to individualism that it was cautious in asserting the rights of individual human persons. One sees a distinctly negative bias against the individual in von Ketteler, Pesch, and von Nell-Breuning; it is present also in Pius XI. In this respect, the so-called "middle way" remains undeveloped in Pius XI.

Solidarism makes two claims about the liberal social order. The first is that it is not focused on the common good, but allows each person to pursue his or her own ends. The second is that liberalism focuses upon the atomic individual, overlooking "natural" social organisms. These two claims (and the counterpositions that solidarism puts in their place) are subject to their own weaknesses.

Father von Nell-Breuning brings to light one of them when he observes, in his commentary, that many of the people of Europe are neither Catholic nor committed to Christian revelation; therefore, in addressing them, Pope Pius XI could not speak solely in the language of Catholic faith but chose, instead, "only natural truths and logical reasoning." The pope uses Scripture merely for illustration and to show that nature and revelation are not in contradiction; his argument never rests on premises open only to believing Catholics. "If the social order is determined by the truths of revelation accepted only by believing Christians, or perhaps even only by us Catholics, then certainly the undertaking is futile from the start."[35]

But it is of the very nature of political and economic life that the judgments pertaining to them are based on practical reason, on prudence, not solely on principle. Therefore no two persons are likely to have precisely the same judgment about what constitutes the common good. Catholic theologians and the pope may form a prudential judgment about the common good, but this judgment will not necessarily be the same as that formed by others (and not only non-Catholics). Hence, while solidarists may claim to have a vision of the common good superior to that of liberals, the mere declaration that they have such a vision will not necessarily convince others. A great many empirical, contingent, and merely probable judgments are necessarily included within any such vision, on each of which persons of good will may properly disagree.

Thus the solidarist claim that there *is* a common good does not establish that solidarists are in possession of concrete knowledge about it. Nor does this mere claim establish *how* the common good is to be identified, or which among alternative means and institutional procedures are more likely to attain it.

On the other hand, the *liberal* vision is also a vision of the common good, but the liberal *method* for identifying it and working toward it is considerably different from the solidarist method. As part of their medieval inheritance, Catholics tend to believe that a common vision is best enunciated by a public authority and suffused throughout the society from *above*. By contrast, the liberal method is to multiply the number of active intelligences at the base of society, to maintain free and open discussion, and to arrive at consensus through democratic methods. Similarly, in economic matters, the liberal view is that the constraints inherent in economic activity oblige individual intelligent agents to be guided by the needs and desires of others. Thus economic activities impose by their very nature a coordinating, cooperative tendency. No one intelligent agent needs to have a single vision of the whole in order to discern the specific steps he or she must take in order to adjust to the common flow, in all its variety and sub-departments. Yet a certain other-directedness is absolutely essential to success.

Those who think about economic activities in either the traditionalist or in the socialist vein (the two coincide in remarkable ways) ridicule the phrase (used only twice by Adam Smith in more than a thousand pages) "the invisible hand." Of course, there is no invisible hand. The phrase is a metaphor ("as if by an invisible hand"[36]). Its point is that commerce depends on each participant meeting the needs of others to mutual satisfaction. The centripetal tendencies of markets are, therefore, very powerful. This fact helps to explain how the method of permitting maximal liberties to individual agents does not end in anarchy; on the contrary, societies which practice it tend to produce the most orderly, efficient, and cooperative societies known to history. Furthermore, in such societies, political and moral-cultural institutions properly address needs and aims not attended to by the institutions of the market.

To be sure, liberal methods work best within cultures in which individuals have already appropriated the habits of respect for law, consideration for others, a spirit of compromise and pragmatic adjustment, and a willingness to discipline the self against mere self-will and self-indulgence. Typically, young persons in liberal societies rebel against the pressures of order and conformity inherent in liberal practices. Typically, too, cultures which place great emphasis upon individual independence and unbending pride—cultures like those of Italy and Spain, for example—generate an entirely different social ethos. In such cultures, law is imagined to be a constraint upon liberty which it is rather heroic to flout. Each individual follows the internalized exemplar of the Medici princes, doing so far as they can what they please despite the law. In Italy, one hears often that "Mussolini made the trains run on time." He did so by threatening the death sentence. The ethos within which law must be supported by coercion is quite different from the ethos within which law is regarded as the friend, protector, and vehicle of liberty. Watching the contrasting behavior of Englishmen and Italians at a crowded bus stop illustrates quite well the cultural embodiments of liberty and law, the individual and the community.

Thus a concept like "individualism" may be embodied in cultures so different from one another that the lived meaning of the same term is radically diverse. The proper meaning of such terms cannot be grasped solely in the abstract; their proper meaning is the sense internalized within cultures.

As for Germany—so influential on modern Catholic social thought—one observes immediately the contrast between Catholic and Protestant Germany. Bavaria and Prussia embody two quite different internalizations of sociality and individual discipline. In addition, German culture is significantly different from British or American culture, on the one hand, and from Latin culture, on the other.[37] In a clear sense, "solidarism" is an articulation of a German understanding of the relation of the individual and social life. An American in Germany senses immediately an unfamiliar ethos. Ordinary Germans seem far more inner-directed than Americans. One senses almost tangibly the differences between Kant and Mill; between the internalized autonomous will and the more other-directed moral sentiments. On the other hand, the boisterous togetherness of Germans singing, dancing, and eating (during a dinner cruise on the Rhine, for example) affords an altogether different sense of community from that of an English tea room. Moreover, the social discipline of Germans at work (or as a fighting force) contrasts quite vividly with that of the British or the Americans.

In the writings of solidarists, one feels the German *Catholic* experience of individual and social life.

Finally, the solidarist claim that occupational and vocational groups spring from a "natural" social instinct seems far too like an echo of the medieval guilds and the ancient village *Gemeinschaft* to carry conviction outside of Germany. On this point, indeed, Goetz Briefs, even before his migration to America, disagreed most strongly with the solidarists.[38] Bishop von Ketteler, Pesch, and von Nell-Breuning wished to cure what they thought of as the excessive mobility, atomism, and individualism of modern life. In the economic order, they sought to do this by finding social institutions that would retain as much as possible of the ancient organic connectedness between individuals. Deeply affected by the homogeneity and comprehensiveness within the life of the ancient guilds, they tried to discern some modern equivalent. They set out to imagine the modern political economy as, first, a single corporate organism in itself and, second, a sub-set of "natural" vocational organisms within it: associations of manufacturers, traders, lawyers, doctors, journalists, farmers, and the like. Owners, managers and workers would be represented within each vocational group; the main idea would be to cut across class divisions. Such associations, in their view, would function as organisms rather more total than labor unions, as holistic social microcosms, within which as many aspects of community life as possible would be incorporated. In a sense, these associations would create, as it were, social canopies; they would be modern variants of ancient village life. Within them, individuals would not only work but maintain, as well, a common cultural, religious, and recreational life.[39]

It is not for a North American to pronounce upon the suitability of this model for Germany. But, clearly, the strenuous effort needed to construct such social organisms suggests that they are far from being natural. They depend for their success upon a remarkable homogeneity of spiritual and cultural life. They are organisms whose real purpose— and only hope of success—is to keep alive ancient traditions. The difficulty in doing so in modern conditions promotes a fierce antagonism toward whatever would undermine traditional values. This appears to be the source of the passion directed against liberalism, whose preferred models of association, social life, and internalized social values are quite different.

Contrary to the accusations of the solidarists, moreover, both British and American life maintain powerful social vitalities, although these are quite different in inspiration and in expression from German social life. As early as 1832, Alexis de Tocqueville observed the spirit of association and cooperation which characterized life in the United States.[40] It still does. Americans are "joiners." Typically, they not only work a forty-hour week—and with a remarkable spirit of friendliness, teamwork, and informal camaraderie—but also spend many hours each week attending meetings and social functions. Social life in Britain and America, however, appears to be rooted less in primordial connections and traditions of shared purpose and more in voluntariness. This difference does not make Americans less gregarious, open, accessible, or more socially obdurate and impenetrable; on the contrary, Americans exhibit a social spirit, a range of social virtues, and an instinct for sociality which compares quite favorably with that of the Germans.

In a word, it is not accurate to claim that liberal societies destroy social connections between individuals, which more traditional societies cause to flower. The vitalities of social life in the two types of society are quite different; but neither the one nor the other seems to practice a lesser form of social virtue.

It should not be forgotten that the rise of Fascism in Italy, Germany, and France during the generation 1925–1945 traded very heavily upon an attack on "bourgeois" liberalism and "decadent" individualism. It appealed quite strongly to the primordial social bonds between individuals, to ancient traditions that preceded Christianity, to fatherland, blood, and land. It promised a new, explicitly social discipline. Against this rhetorical onslaught, solidarism was ill-defended.

Furthermore, of all continents, Latin America most self-consciously and energetically tried to realize the "corporative" ideal to which Pius XI pointed in the closing pages of *Quadragesimo Anno*. A full study of corporatism in Latin America would take us too far afield.[41] Suffice it to say that Latin American writers, Catholic and non-Catholic, experienced the model of Anglo-American liberalism as alien. In this, they were much like the German solidarists, to whose ideas (not least through the Jesuits) they eagerly repaired. Trying to create organic societies, they experimented with forms of governance that would institutionalize the vocational orders, through representation of the peasants, industrial workers, managers, lawyers, journalists, government officials, etc. But organic and corporative models generate serious and recurrent flaws. They do not well instruct their participants in the arts of compromise, incremental reform, and pragmatic consensus. They are open to veto from multiple quarters. They afford a social structure too easily captured by dominant elements. They do little to inspire economic growth, flexibility, and invention. They have a marked bias toward protecting every traditional interest. Far from upholding a vision of the common good acceptable to all, they create manifold opportunities for the most powerful groups simply to enforce their own vision of the common good.

Thus the vision of the solidarists, noble in principle, fails to solve the practical problem of how to produce social, economic, and cultural progress. Its fundamental aim is to protect as much of the traditional form of life as possible. In this respect, it is not a transformative vision but a highly conservative one.

Finally, although the solidarists claim that it is liberal societies which will in the end lead to the triumph of socialism,[42] it is exactly the solidarists societies which, in practice, generate the most powerful socialist and communist parties. Germany, France, Italy, Spain, Latin America, the Philippines, and other solidarist cultures seem especially vulnerable. There seem to be two reasons for this. The solidarist assault upon liberal values and liberal institutions parallels the socialist and communist assault. Here, for example, is how a rabidly anti-capitalist, romantically socialist writer in contemporary France employs the solidarist imagination "in the direction of socialism":

Here we may hope that in their traditions of village community or popular solidarity, their wisdom of life, and their philosophical and religious traditions, some of the peoples who are today crushed may be able to invent a new art of producing, living, working, and deciding which will bring to light what the young people of so many countries understood in 1968: the absurd and slimy bloatedness of modern capitalist society.[43]

Second, solidarist values, even though traditionalist, anti-socialist, and anti-communist, cannot be protected or maintained by solidarist institutions. Solidarist institutions are inherently weak and are easy prey to determined revolutionaries.

Solidarist ways of thinking are analogous to socialist ways of thinking. Both have roots in agrarian habits of thought. Both undervalue the creativity of managers, inventors, and persons of commerce. Both undervalue the creativity of the individual. Both too easily imagine that the individual is an inherent enemy of the collective. Although solidarism praises mediating structures, associations, and the principle of subsidiarity (according to which no larger social body ought to do what a smaller social body can do for itself), it fails to grasp the indispensable role of liberal institutions in limiting the power of the state. Under solidarism, the state is limited by doctrine, but not by institutional checks and balances, and thus too easily turns to dictatorship, oligarchy, and strong-man rule from above—in the name, even, of solidarist values.

The problems inherent in the solidarist—or, as Pius XI prefers, corporative—model for society become apparent in the pope's own words. In order to prevent hostility between capital and labor, the pope wishes to commend a new social and juridical order, based upon newly formed organic groups. He envisages the market "as an arena where the two armies are locked in combat."

There cannot be question of any perfect cure, except this opposition be done away with, and well ordered members of the social body come into being: "functional groups," namely, binding men together not according to the position they occupy in the labor market, but according to the diverse functions which they exercise in society. For as nature induces those who dwell in close proximity to unite into municipalities, so those who practice the same trade or profession, economic or otherwise, constitute as it were fellowships or bodies. These groupings, autonomous in character, are considered by many to be, if not essential to civil society, at least a natural accompaniment thereof.[44]

The pope alludes here to the solidarist position. Without showing how this vision can be made to work, Pius XI then relies upon extraordinary foresight and public-spiritedness on the part of leaders:

Order, as the angelic Doctor well defines, is unity arising from the apt arrangement of a plurality of objects; hence, true and genuine social order demands various members of society, joined together by a common bond. Such a bond of union is provided on the one hand by the common effort of employers and employees of one and the same "group" joining forces to produce goods or give service; on the other hand, by the common good which all "groups" should unite to promote, each in its own sphere, with friendly harmony. Now this union will become powerful and efficacious in proportion to the fidelity with which the individuals and the "groups" strive to discharge their professional duties and to excel in them.[45]

Next, the pope sees in "recent times" a new experiment in "syndical and corporative organization," which he commends. The model for this seems to be Spain, Italy, and Latin America, although the pope does not say so as he outlines the idea:

The State here grants legal recognition to the syndicate or union, and thereby confers on it some of the features of a monopoly, for in virtues of this recognition, it alone can represent respectively workingmen and employers, and it alone can conclude labor contracts and labor agreements. Affiliation to the syndicate is optional for everyone; but in this sense only can the syndical organization be said to be free, since the contribution to the union and other special taxes are obligatory for all who belong to a given branch, whether workingmen or employers, and the labor contracts drawn up by the legal syndicate are likewise obligatory. True, it has been authoritatively declared that the juridically established syndicate does not preclude the existence of trade or professional associations not recognized in law.

The corporations are composed of representatives of the unions of workingmen and employers of the same trade or profession, and as genuine and exclusive instruments and institutions of the State they direct and co-ordinate the activities of the syndicates in all matters of common interest.

Strikes and lock-outs are forbidden. If the contending parties cannot come to an agreement, public authority intervenes.

Little reflection is required to perceive advantages in the institution thus summarily described: peaceful collaboration of the classes, repression of socialist organizations and efforts, the moderating authority of a special ministry.[46]

Pius XI himself sees a potential problem. It was clearly evident in Mussolini's Italy:

We feel bound to add that to Our knowledge there are some who fear that the State is substituting itself in the place of private initiative, instead of limiting itself to necesssary and sufficient help and assistance. It is feared that the new syndical and corporative order possesses an excessively bureaucratic and political character, and that, notwithstanding the general advantages referred to above, it risks serving particular political aims rather than contributing to the restoration of social order and the improvement of the same.[47]

Against this fear, the pope appeals to no institutional corrective. To "attain this last named lofty purpose," he writes, "there is need before and above all else of the blessing of God, and, in the second place, of the cooperation of all men of good will." He asks Catholics of professional competence, steeped in the principles of Catholic social thought, to make this system work.[47]

The liberal tradition has, at this point, a more profound awareness of the sinfulness, unreliability, and limited vision of individual persons than the pope here witnesses. "In God we trust," the American liberal tradition embosses on US coins; but the operational meaning of that phrase is "Not in men." That is, *institutional* checks and balances must be set in place even against "men of good will."

The history of corporative and syndicalist models since 1931 does not seem to have fulfilled Pius XI's lofty hopes. Solidarism had failed to offer him an articulated set of institutions by which to effect its noble purposes without terrible abuses of authority. How to prevent abuses by authority has been the Achilles' heel of Catholic social thought in the modern era. It is to solve this problem that liberal institutions have, by trial and error, been arrived at.

## 4. WORLD WAR II

Five years after Pius XI published *Quadragesimo Anno*, Benito Mussolini invaded Ethiopia and Adolf Hitler seized the Rhineland. Shortly thereafter, Hitler marched into Austria and Czechoslovakia. After signing the Molotov-Ribbentrop accords, Hitler and Stalin brutally assaulted Poland in 1939. The war of the Axis powers against liberal civilization had begun. Hitler boasted that his Third Reich, smashing decadent liberal societies, would last a thousand years.

Until Pearl Harbor, isolationist voices dominated US politics. Peace advocates marched on US campuses and a resurgent pacifism was strong in Protestant churches. Virtually alone, Reinhold Niebuhr and a small band of colleagues on February 10, 1941, launched a new journal, *Christianity and Crisis*, in whose lead editorial he wrote:

The inconceivable has happened. We are witnessing the first effective revolution against Christian civilization since the days of Constantine.

The tragic irony of the hour is that so many of the men in America whom this revolution against Christian civilization most concerns seem to be least aware of its implications. The freedom of these men to speak and write depends upon the existence of a certain type of civilization. Yet they talk and act as if they believed that, whoever wins, religion-as-usual like business-as-usual will be the order of the day in America after the war. The fact is that if Hitler carries out his declared designs there is not going to be any religion-as-usual, at least as far as Christians are concerned.[49]

Just before the invasion of Poland, Pius XII, one of the most scholarly and multifaceted popes in history, succeeded Pius XI. During the war, Pius XII tried to define the stake the Catholic world had in the reconstruction that might follow the successful defeat of National Socialism and Japanese Imperial power. In a long series of messages on virtually every subject of social concern, he defended the dignity of the human person against collectivist barbarism, and proclaimed political, economic, and personal liberties. He envisaged societies emerging from the terrors of oppression to build new institutions of freedom with justice. His tone was often quite traditional. Yet the dire necessities of the hour obliged him to sound clear notes of praise for liberty which had been only cautiously voiced by the popes since the French Revolution.

It would require too long a digression to summarize the social thought of Pius XII, extensive and complex as it was. He became a champion of the Christian Democratic parties of the post-war era, for the first time bringing Catholic social thought decisively to the side of democracy. Don Luigi Sturzo, the Italian priest and political scientist obliged by earlier popes to go into exile to the United States, became under Pius XII the founder of Christian Democracy in Italy.[50] Aminatore Fanfani wrote *Catholicism, Protestantism and Capitalism*[51] and Guido Gonella, who paid for it in a Fascist jail, wrote *The Papacy and World Peace,* a primer of reconstruction.[52] Great Catholic laymen, Konrad Adenauer, Charles de Gaulle, Robert Schuman, and Alcide de Gasperi, prepared to rebuild their nations on a new moral basis.

The destruction of so many nations of Europe and Asia created a worldwide hunger for new institutions of political economy, worthy of human dignity. The Catholic philosopher Jacques Maritain, who had written brilliantly during the darkest hours of World War II on the ideals of democracy which the Catholic church ought to embrace, became the French ambassador to the Vatican, one of the architects of the Universal Declaration of Human Rights, and one of the founders of UNESCO. John Courtney Murray, S.J., propounded a Catholic natural law basis for institutions of religious liberty. John A. Ryan of the Catholic University of America, a sometime advisor to President Franklin Delano Roosevelt, had prepared brilliant arguments in favor of a liberal economy committed to freedom with justice. Such works prepared the basis for Catholic social thought after World War II.[53]

The experience of corporate fascism brought words like "corporatism" and "solidarism" into disrepute. Mistrust of the powers of the coercive state reinvigorated the liberal ideal of the limited and the democratic state. Moreover, the succession of "economic miracles" achieved by Japan, West Germany, and other nations under a combination of "liberal" and "social market" economic principles revived the reputation of democratic polities combined with market economies and spiritually pluralistic cultures. For many persons, older ideological rigidities had been softened by the rigors of war and the grim necessities of rebuilding on the ruins. Many could scarcely forget the hunger and the cold of the winters of 1945 and 1946, just after the war. Led by such diverse writers as John Dewey in America and Wilhelm Roepke (*The Humane Economy*)[54] in Europe, many liberals conceded legitimacy to a "social contract" including the provisions of social welfare to the needy. Many socialists, especially the Social Democrats, conceded the advantages of private property, differential incentives, and market mechanisms. The gap between democratic socialists and democratic capitalists considerably narrowed. The former tended to favor initiatives of the political system, the latter initiatives of the economic and moral-cultural systems. The somewhat misleading phrase, "mixed economies" came into use.

At the same time, the more doctrinaire socialists and the more activist liberals turned their doctrinal disputes loose in the Third World (as it came soon enough to be called). The chief difference between them lay in this: the liberals were mainly businessmen or practitioners, and the socialists were mainly intellectuals. The growth of international trade and industry made the world, as the apt word now puts it, quite visibly "interdependent." Many intellectuals put socialist analysis to the service of showing how the poverty of the poor nations, at least of those which made less progress than others (since all made some), was caused by the growth of the rich nations. As an *economic* theory, socialism was largely defeated in the First World, while becoming coercive in the Second World, and attractive to elites in the Third World.

It was in such a maelstrom of conflicting currents that Pope John XXIII suddenly and without warning summoned the Second Vatican Council, calling more than two thousand Catholic bishops from all around the world to four years of meetings every autumn in Rome (1962–1965).[55] The Catholic church discovered its universal character. The problems of the First World seemed to be less a matter of political economy than of spiritual renewal. One could scarcely talk of the "immiseration" of the workers of Europe or North America as the post-war "economic miracles" unfolded. Accordingly, Catholic social teaching turned to the political economy of development.

To put matters a little too simply, Pope John XXIII stressed the *political* part of political economy, bringing the liberal human rights tradition into official Catholic teaching. Following him, Pope Paul VI, eager to address "the development of peoples" began to stress the *economic* part. In the euphoria of the "*aggiornamento*," everything seemed easy. A sly emphasis on "visions" and even a recommendation of "utopian thinking" slipped into Catholic social thought during this interim. There was rather less attention to what actually works. Why were some Third World countries of "the periphery" economically successful, while others were faltering? Why did the nations of the East Asian rim, so desperately poor just a short time ago, overleap some nations far more highly favored by nature? The decade that lasted from about 1965 until about 1975 is to be remembered for its enthusiasm. As we shall see, it marked a new era in Catholic social thought.

# CHAPTER 7

# The Development of Nations: John XXIII and Paul VI

> He who has a talent, let him take care that he hides it not; he who has abundance, let him arouse himself to mercy and to generosity; he who has skill in managing affairs, let him make a special effort to share the use and utility thereof with his neighbor.
>
> —ST. GREGORY THE GREAT (cited in *Rerum Novarum*, 19 and *Mater et Magistra*, 119)

To enter the world of Pope John XXIII is, for persons educated by liberal institutions, a tremendous joy. For here one finds clear and explicit support for the conceptions of human rights (and duties) embodied in liberal institutions. The two great contributions to Catholic social thought made by John XXIII are his encyclicals *Mater et Magistra* (1961) and *Pacem in Terris* (1963).

The first assesses the social progress made by humankind in recent generations, welcomes it, and expresses its main contributions in terms of classic Catholic concepts. Long sections of this document bring conceptions of basic human rights into official Catholic discourse more clearly than ever before. Treatment is also reserved for the problems of development in the Third World. The point of view taken by "good Pope John" is generous, positive, encouraging. He does not so much blame faults as blow gently on faint embers of goodness, as when, in talking of the need for aid from the developed to the underdeveloped nations, he says he is "consoled" by how much is already being done.[1]

In reading Pope John XXIII, one can hardly forget that he was a peasant, with the robust common sense and stalwart optimism of one who knew the resilience of the spring which follows every winter. Early in the 1960s, too, a sense of hope swept the entire world. The devastation of World War II was being forgotten in new "economic miracles." The ideals of democracy and development were young and bright. This most surprising pope seized the hour, abruptly summoning all the world's bishops to Rome for the Second Vatican Council, opening the church to the world, inaugurating an era of uncommon hopefulness.

## 1. "THE PRIORITY OF INDIVIDUAL MEN"

Pope John opens *Mater et Magistra* by making his own the three "fundamental principles of Leo XIII." First, "work, inasmuch as it is an expression of the human person, can by no means be regarded as a mere commodity." For work is the means of all human livelihood for the vast majority of persons. It is the basic human activity. Second, "private property, including that of productive goods, is a natural right possessed by all, which the state may by no means suppress." But this right, flowing from the *social* character of human nature, requires property owners to take into account the welfare of others. Third, there is a natural right for individuals "to enter corporately into associations, whether of workers only or of workers and management."[2]

For John XXIII, these are the fundamentals: work, private property, the right of free association. On them "a healthy socioeconomic order can be built." Both "unregulated competition which so-called *liberals* espouse," he adds, "or the class struggle in the *Marxist sense, are utterly opposed to Christian teaching and also to the very nature of man."[3] The pope thinks of "the so-called liberals" as amoral. He seems to hold that the Catholic understanding of the human person and human social nature is the true liberal understanding.

The pope's own liberal understanding becomes very clear as he develops the thought of Leo XIII in his own way:

Precautionary activities of public authorities in the economic field, although widespread and penetrating, should be such that they not only avoid restricting the freedom of private citizens, but also increase it, so long as the basic rights of each individual person are preserved inviolate. Included among these is the right and duty of each individual normally to provide the necessities of life for himself and his dependents. This implies that whatever be the economic system, it allow and facilitate for every individual the opportunity to engage in productive activity.[4]

This is a marvelous passage in three ways. It strictly limits the state. It empowers individuals and insists on their self-reliance. It establishes the relation of individual liberty to productive activity.

Furthermore, the pope clearly shows the basis of his argument in actual practice (or, as the Marxists like to say, *praxis):*

Experience, in fact, shows that where private initiative of individuals is lacking, political tyranny prevails. Moreover, much stagnation occurs in various sectors of the economy, and hence all sorts of consumer goods and services, closely connected with needs of the body and more especially of the spirit, are in short supply. Beyond doubt, the attainment of such goods and services provides remarkable opportunity and stimulus for individuals to exercise initiative and industry.[5]

The pope comments on the remarkable "multiplication of social relationships" in our liberal era. It is not an era of isolated individuals only, but of a growing number of dependencies and interrelations, which bring "numerous services and advantages."

It makes possible, in fact, the satisfaction of many personal rights, especially those of economic and social life; these relate, for example, to the minimum necessities of human life, to health services, to the broadening and deepening of elementary education, to a more fitting training in skills, to housing, to labor, to suitable leisure and recreation. . . . individuals are enabled to take part in human events on a world-wide scale.[6]

Here the pope offers a beautiful notion of the *common good:* "the sum total of those conditions of social living, whereby men are enabled more fully and more readily to achieve their own perfection."[7]

From this it follows that the "national wealth" of any people is not assessed so much from the gross national product, or from per capita income, "as from the distribution of goods according to norms of justice, so that everyone in the community can develop and perfect himself."[8] This is the norm of equal opportunity.

A very important text comes a little later. It marks a new stage in Catholic social thought emphasizing the importance of *production* as never before:

Justice is to be observed not merely in the distribution of wealth, but also in regard to the conditions under which men engage in productive activity. There is, in fact, an innate need of human nature requiring that men engaged in productive activity have an opportunity to assume responsibility and to perfect themselves by their efforts.[9]

With this text, Pope John XXIII moves from the classic emphasis on distributive justice to what might be called "productive justice." Further, he sees the link between liberty, personal responsibility, self-realization, and productive activity. He could not be clearer. Society is not an anthill or a beehive. The very next paragraph adds:

Consequently, if the organization and structure of economic life be such that the human dignity of workers is compromised, or their sense of responsibility is weakened, or their freedom of action is removed, then we judge such an economic order to be unjust, even though it produces a vast amount of goods, whose distribution conforms to the norms of justice and equity.[10]

The pope grasps, too, the importance of a broad economic base of "small and medium-sized holdings in agriculture, in the arts and crafts, in commerce and industry." He encourages "cooperatives" and asks that "enteprises of the family type" be especially safeguarded and fostered. New conditions keep arising from science and technology, he notes, and from "changing consumer needs and preferences."[11] Flexibility and adaptation, creatively effected by the craftsmen themselves, must be allowed for.

In recent years, ownership has become separated from management, and a new type of professional has greater esteem for income from labor than from ownership. This is, the pope says, "an advance in civilization," for it shows the high spiritual value of labor and the instrumental character of capital goods.[12] Nonetheless, the right to private property is "permanently valid."

Indeed, it is rooted in the very nature of things, whereby we learn that individual men are prior to civil society, and hence, that civil society is to be directed toward man as its end. Indeed, the right of private individuals to act freely in economic affairs is recognized in vain, unless they are at the same time given an opportunity of freely selecting and using things necessary for the exercise of this right. Moreover, experience and history testify that where political regimes do not allow to private individuals the possession also of productive goods, the exercise of human liberty is violated or completely destroyed in matters of primary importance. Thus it becomes clear that in the right of property, the exercise of liberty finds both a safeguard and a stimulus.[13]

There follows the text from which I have drawn the title for this book:

This explains the fact that socio-political groups and associations which endeavor to reconcile freedom with justice within society, and which until recently did not uphold the right of private property in productive goods, have now, enlightened by the course of social events, modified their views and are disposed actually to approve this right.[14]

Pope John urges higher wages for workers, to enable them "to save more readily and hence to achieve some property status of their own."[15]

Tirelessly, Pope John calls for cooperation, collaboration, mutual concern, generosity of heart. A brilliant text concludes this section. Today the activity of the state grows ever broader, but neither by right nor by its own capacity can it displace the social responsibility of private property or meet all the needs that humans must meet.

Wherefore, there is always wide scope for humane action by private citizens and for Christian charity. Finally, it is evident that in stimulating efforts relating to spiritual welfare, the work done by individual men or by private civic groups has more value than what is done by public authorities.[16]

Turning to international development, the pope sees clearly that "many nations with varied endowments have not made identical progress in their economic and social affairs."[17] Those which have made more progress, he gladly notes, should help and are helping those which have made less. He urges the more powerful nations to take care "that citizens in less developed countries—in giving attention to economic and social affairs, as well as to cultural matters—feel themselves to be the ones chiefly responsible for their own progress. For a citizen has a sense of his own dignity when he contributes the major share to progress in his own affairs."[18] Avoidance of dependency—put positively, self-reliance—is crucial to human dignity. The principle of self-reliance, both for persons and for nations, here begins to become ever more prominent in Catholic social thought.[19]

Hence, those also who rely on their own resources and initiative should contribute as best they can to the equitable adjustment of economic life in their own community. Nay, more, those in authority should favor and help private enterprise in accordance with the *principle of subsidiarity,* in order to allow private citizens themselves to accomplish as much as is feasible.[20]

The developed must help the underdeveloped, the rich the poor. But the causes of poverty and hunger lie "in the primitive state of the economy." To remedy this, instruction in skills is necessary, whereby the poor may "acquire the capital wherewith to promote economic growth by ways and means adapted to our times." He notes the help already rendered by international councils, states, private enterprises, banks, and "the great universities of more developed countries." Private citizens already "make loans to these countries that they may initiate various programs calculated to increase production. We gladly take this opportunity to give due praise for such generous activity."[21] The pope urges more such activity.

When a nation makes progress in science, technology, and economic life, there is no doubt that "a great contribution is made to civilization." These, of course, are not the highest goods, only instruments for pursuing such goods.[22] Moreover, even these instruments rest upon the fecundity of God's mind and the human mind:

God in His goodness and wisdom has, on the one hand, provided nature with almost inexhaustible productive capacity; and, on the other hand, has endowed man with such ingenuity that, by using suitable means, he can apply nature's resources to the needs and requirements of existence.... Moreover, the advances hitherto made in science and technology give almost limitless promise for the future in this matter.[23]

Near the end of this letter, John XXIII comes to a startling cardinal principle of Catholic social thought "for all time valid."

The cardinal point of this teaching is that *individual men are necessarily the foundation, cause, and end of all social institutions.* We are referring to human beings, insofar as they are *social by nature,* and raised to an order of existence that transcends and subdues nature.[24]

The first sentence sounds like the cardinal principle of liberalism. The second takes care to place it in the context of human social and transcendent nature. The cardinal tenet of liberalism is not so much denied as subsumed within a social and transcendent framework. The pope self-consciously alludes to his own synthetic effort: "these principles are in accord with the nature of things and the changed conditions of man's social life, and with the special genius of our day. Moreover, these norms can be approved by all."[25]

Nearly all of them, in fact, have been codified in the Universal Declaration of Human Rights accepted by the United Nations in 1948. Quite fittingly then, fifteen years after that Declaration, in his second great letter, *Pacem in Terris,* Pope John XXIII brings virtually every one of these principles, many of them borrowed almost directly from the US Bill of Rights, into the universal patrimony of the church.

## 2. AT LAST, THE BILL OF RIGHTS

Part I of the new encyclical, acclaimed throughout the world for its tone of openness and mutual collaboration, reads almost like a commentary upon one basic human right after another. The very first principle, the foundation of the others, entered history through the US Declaration of Independence. But it is far from being dissonant with the Roman Catholic view of the human person, inherited from the Gospels and from the systematic reflection of such persons as St. Thomas Aquinas.[26]

Any human society, if it is to be well-ordered and productive, must lay down as a foundation this principle, namely, that every human being is a person, that is, his nature is endowed with intelligence and free will. By virtue of this, he has rights and duties of his own, flowing directly and simultaneously from his very nature. These rights are therefore universal, inviolable and inalienable.[27]

So well known are these materials, in fact, that it would be tedious merely to enumerate the rights cogently organized by the pope: the right to life, liberty of conscience, the right to set up a family (with equal rights and duties for man and woman), the "natural right to free initiative in the economic field and the right to work," the right to humane working conditions and a living wage, the right of assembly and association, and the rest. Every fundamental human right imposes a corresponding obligation, so duties, too, are listed. The role of "a great variety of intermediate groups and bodies" in making liberty effective is stressed.[28]

Our age, the pope says, has three characteristics: the working classes have gradually gained ground in economic, political, and cultural life; more rapidly in nations with a Christian tradition than in others, women are now taking part in public life; finally, "the modern world, as compared with the recent past, has taken on an entirely new appearance in the field of social and political life. For since all peoples have either achieved, or are on the way to achieving, independence, there will soon no longer exist a world divided into peoples who rule others and peoples who are subject to others."[29] As Pope John sees history, it is drawing humans to realize their interdependence, the necessity of truth, the blessings of liberty, the mutual benefits of justice, and the scope for charity.[30] Having begun in materialism, modern history is revealing the inner springs of human nature.

Human dignity, for example, requires that individuals have a right to "choose who are to rule the state, to decide the form of government, and to determine both the way in which authority is to be exercised and its limits." Knowing the diverse circumstances of the world of 1963, the pope knows that democracy cannot be imposed by *fiat,* but he takes care to add: "It is thus clear that the doctrine we have set forth is fully consonant with any truly democratic regime."[31]

Thus is a liberal institution given long-delayed papal approval with crystal clarity. Another shortly follows. The duty of the state is to empower individuals and their intermediate institutions.[32]

For this principle must always be retained: that state activity in the economic field, no matter what its breadth or depth may be, ought not to be exercised in such a way as to curtail an individual's freedom of personal initiative. Rather it should work to expand that freedom as much as possible by the effective protection of the essential personal rights of each and every individual.[33]

In the next paragraphs, Pope John also commends the separation of powers: the legislative, the judicial, and the executive, which he describes as "in keeping with the innate demands of human nature."[34] The "paramount task" assigned to government officials, he says, is that of "recognizing, respecting, reconciling, protecting and promoting the rights and duties of citizens."[35]

The unity of all human beings in one human family has always existed, but far-reaching changes in modern life make human interdependence both visible to all and exigent. No nation now lives, nor can live, in isolation.[36] This situation needs some objective expression in worldwide institutions. But any public authority of the world community "must have as its fundamental objective the recognition, respect, safeguarding and promotion of the rights of the human person."[37]

This emphasis upon the individual person is also liberal. It establishes a criterion for international institutions that collectivist societies, which treat the individual as a means, cannot meet. Characteristically, Pope John avoids polemic.

In the last, pastoral part of *Pacem in Terris,* Pope John encourages Catholics to be open, courteous, and cooperative in practical ventures even with those with whom, in philosophy or in principle, they may disagree. This attitude of openness created a sensation at the time. The Italian Christian Democratic Party was then attempting an *aperatura a sinistra,* an opening to the left, in alliance with parties to the left. The United States and the USSR were about to enter the age of "detente." The ecumenical movement was flowering in precedent-shattering ways. The air was full of hope—and alarm. The story went round: "Today even Satan must be addressed as a separated brother."

Pope John XXIII drew an important distinction between "philosophical teachings" and "historical movements," arguing that while the former often remain the same, the latter are often subject to healthy adaptations containing "elements that are positive and deserving of approval."[38] He reserved to ecclesiastical authority the right to judge concrete cases of such practical alliances.[39] But, using such distinctions, many Catholics felt newly free to take part in "Christian-Marxist" dialogues, to collaborate with popular fronts, and to borrow from "Marxist analysis" in practice even while rejecting "Marxism as a philosophy of life."

Without passing judgment on subsequent developments of this sort, particularly in the Third World, let us note that the same principle was in fact being applied by Pope John XXIII regarding liberal institutions. Without accepting liberalism as a *philosophical* position, he borrowed concept after concept from liberal *institutional* life. The foundational principle of Marxism is not the dignity and rights of the individual person. This is the foundational principle which suffuses liberal institutions.

Yet one theme does nag an American liberal, tutored by Reinhold Niebuhr, in reading Pope John XXIII. He is such a *good* man. Almost never does he describe human sinfulness or human evil. He writes with placidity and rationality, with generosity and optimism, seeing the best possibilities in everything. The determination to ward off the worst evils is not so clearly visible. Yet Pope John was no utopian. In *Mater et Magistra,* he warns against the pretext of seeking the best while neglecting the doable good.[40] In *Pacem in Terris*, he warns that "the law of life" is "to proceed gradually." He even admits, at one place, a basic datum of liberal realism, that "there is rooted in each man an instinctive and immoderate love of his own interests."[41] But from this he only concludes, at that place, that "it is difficult at times to discern the demands of justice in a given situation." Still, his treatment of the practical necessity for liberal institutions, against the tyranny of the state, may perhaps show that his own sense of evil, even though kept as it were behind-the-scenes, was operative in his judgments.

Pope John XXIII will long be remembered as "good Pope John." On the record, he embraced the essence of the liberal institutions of human rights and of economic development far more closely than any of his predecessors.

## 3. "THE WORLD IS SICK": PAUL VI

When, quite suddenly, John XXIII died while the Second Vatican Council he had summoned was still in session, Paul VI was crowned Pope on June 29, 1963. A man as thin, wiry, anxious, and melancholy as Pope John had been large, placid, full of good humor and wit, Paul VI had been well-prepared for the papacy. He had been a protege of Pius XII, had served in the Vatican secretariat of state, and had won a considerable reputation as a modern, urban pastor as the Archbishop Cardinal of Milan.

Yet the world of his own social thought—expressed in *Populorum Progressio* in 1967 and *Octogesima Adveniens* in 1971—is quite different from that of John XXIII. The fundamental principles do not shift. But Paul VI's tone wavers between pessimism and utopian hope, while his interpretation of contemporary reality becomes more dour. Paul VI is closer to Pius XI than to John XXIII. In some ways, his thought interrupts the steady realism which flows from John XXIII to John Paul II today.

Coming just four years after *Pacem in Terris, Populorum Progressio* appears to have been prepared by an entirely new team of social thinkers.[42] A note of doom, even of accusatory bitterness, and of defensiveness about the achievements of the Christian West makes its appearance. The horizon of *Populorum Progressio* is no longer that of Europe, but of the developing world. This horizon is not new, since John XXIII had first opened it up; but a sense of guilt intrudes.

Moreover, the document lacks a certain humility. While praising the work of Catholic missionaries throughout the world, Paul VI is rather defensive about mistakes some of them may have made in imposing Western cultural models. But in making development his chief subject, he never once considers the papacy's long hostility to notions of progress and development. Nor does he give credit to those nations, cultures, and philosophical movements that set development in motion. In a sense, *Populorum Progressio* is a sustained effort to come abreast of the revolutionary tide that Adam Smith's *Inquiry into the Nature and the Causes of the Wealth of Nations* had set in motion in 1776. It was Smith, after all, who first glimpsed the possibilities of an interdependent world and of world development, a vision of all nations peacefully united through law and productive commerce. Smith himself was a Christian-Deist, a humanist, and so were many who set to realizing his vision.

Three features of *Populorum Progressio* mark Paul VI's departure from the tone established by John XXIII. First comes the shocking sentiment: "The world is sick" (para. 66). Second comes the suggestion that the poor nations of the world will rise up in rage against the developed nations. To be sure, Paul VI quickly counsels against revolution and even utopian hopes; but he seems to imagine an almost causal relation between the development of some and the underdevelopment of others. Third comes the appeal for new forms of world government. Paul VI's logic at this point is abstract; it does not take into account the political ideals of the Soviet Union, its satellites, China, and other powers whose stated visions of justice and peace are extremely far from the vision of human rights and development sketched by John XXIII in *Pacem in Terris*.

Paul VI's attitude toward liberalism, which he mentions explicitly or implicitly several times, remains ambivalent. Each explicit mention bristles with hostility; yet the implicit allusions call attention to humane achievements within liberal societies, urging that these be applied within the developing nations. Consider, first, the hostile references.

After defending private property and free commerce as rights, although subordinated to claims of justice and charity,[43] Paul VI distinguishes industrialization from liberalism. He praises the introduction of industry as necessary for economic growth and human progress and as a sign of human development; he bids humans through persistent work and creative intelligence to unlock nature's secrets. He praises a growing taste for research and discovery, the ability to take risks, "boldness in enterprises," generosity, and a sense of responsibility. These seem to be ideals underlying liberal institutions.

Immediately, however, Paul VI lashes out quite negatively:

But it is unfortunate that on these new conditions of society a system has been constructed which considers profit as the key motive for economic progress, competition as the supreme law of economics, and private ownership of the means of production as an absolute right that has no limits and carries no corresponding social obligation. This unchecked liberalism leads to dictatorship rightly denounced by Pius XI as producing "the international imperialism of money." One cannot condemn such abuses too strongly by solemnly recalling once again that the economy is at the service of man. But if it is true that a type of capitalism has been the source of excessive suffering, injustices and fratricidal conflicts whose effects still persist, it would also be wrong to attribute to industrialization itself evils that belong to the woeful system which accompanied it. On the contrary one must recognise in all justice the irreplaceable contribution made by the organisation of labour and of industry to what development has accomplished.[44]

Yet this "woeful system" must be compared to its historical alternatives, both in the nineteenth and in the twentieth centuries. The three terms which Paul VI singles out—*profit, competition,* and *property as an absolute right*—demand considerably more reflection than this encyclical offers. Is not profit another name for economic progress? A system producing no new wealth is either stagnant or declining. Is not competition better than state monopoly? Is not a universe of relatively self-reliant (although interdependent) states better than "international imperialism"? Did not John Locke, Adam Smith, and John Stuart Mill—and a host of other liberal thinkers—justify private property through its service to the common good, and, therefore, as a *relative* right? Has not the history of liberal institutions in liberal societies been a history of growing checks upon the economic system, both through effective political reforms (such as the welfare state) and through free and critical moral-cultural institutions? Paul VI seems to assume that "liberalism" means only and solely a radical individualism, materialism, and Darwinian struggle.

Still later, in a passage on equity in trade relations, Paul VI asserts that the highly industrialized nations mostly export manufactured goods, while countries with less developed economies have only food, fibers, and other raw materials to sell.[45] Even in 1967, such an assertion was true more of an earlier age than of recent times. Canada, the United States, Australia, and even the European common market nations export huge quantities of foods, fibers, coal, timber, and other raw materials.[46] More frequently in the 1980s than in 1967, manufactured goods of many sorts (textiles, shoes, steel, electronic goods) are being produced in developing nations, threatening basic industries in the industrialized countries. Overlooking these realities, Paul VI rushed on again to condemn "liberalism":

In other words, the rule of free trade, taken by itself, is no longer able to govern international relations. Its advantages are certainly evident when the parties involved are not affected by any excessive inequalities of economic power: it is an incentive to progress and a reward for effort. That is why industrially developed countries see in it a law of justice. But the situation is no longer the same when economic conditions differ too widely from country to country: prices which are "freely" set in the market can produce unfair results. One must recognise that it is the fundamental principle of liberalism, as the rule for commercial exchange, which is questioned here.[47]

In actual fact, however, what Paul VI seems to be demanding is drastically modified. On the one hand, he asks the industrialized nations not to *abandon* free trade but, rather, to desist from the *protectionism* which keeps from their markets the goods produced more cheaply in the developing world.[48] On the other hand, he recognizes that liberal societies have already made adjustments within their own economies to maintain a sort of progressive equilibrium. Thus he adds immediately:

Moreover, this has been understood by the developed nations themselves, which are striving, by means of appropriate measures, to re-establish within their own economies a balance, which competition, if left to itself, tends to compromise. Thus it happens that these nations often support their agriculture at the price of sacrifices imposed on economically more favoured sectors. Similarly, to maintain the commercial relations which are developing among themselves, especially within a common market, the financial, fiscal, and social policy of these nations tries to restore comparable opportunities to competing industries which are not equally prospering.[49]

Paul VI is, therefore, clearly *not* in favor of abolishing the institution of the competitive market. Instead, he appeals to solutions already practiced within liberal societies.

What holds for a national economy or among developed countries is valid also in commercial relations between rich nations and poor nations. Without abolishing the competitive market, it should be kept within the limits which make it just and moral, and therefore human. In trade between developed and underdeveloped economies, conditions are too disparate and the degrees of genuine freedom available too unequal. In order that international trade be human and moral, social justice requires that it restore to the participants a certain equality of opportunity.[50]

He sees this as a long-term objective, to be reached through international agreements.[51]

In another passage, Paul VI again praises the practice of liberal citizens within their own societies, such as:

... industrialists, merchants, leaders or representatives of larger enterprises. It happens that they are not lacking in social sensitivity in their own country; why then do they return to the inhuman principles of individualism when they operate in less developed countries? Their advantaged situation should on the contrary move them to become the initiators of social progress and of human advancement in the area where their business calls them.[52]

*"Development,"* Paul VI announces toward the end of this document, *"is the new name for peace."*[53] This is exactly the point made by Adam Smith, who believed that all nations would make progress against poverty once the three great activist classes of the pre-modern world began to yield place. The military would bring neither development nor peace; neither would the aristocracy; neither would the clergy. Although universally disdained for their manners and their breeding, economic activists in the fields of commerce and industry would bring about the interdependence of the world, development, and peace. Economic activities have certain peculiar characteristics. They depend upon long-term contracts, and therefore require a stable body of law. They prosper in peacetime, and therefore inspire long-range interests in peace and stability. They advance by mutual collaboration and invention, across all lines of class, nationality, religion, or race, and therefore merit the name of "commerce," the very symbol of civilized, mutual, and voluntary interaction. Economic activities create an interdependent world.

Paul VI, like Leo XIII, is worried, of course, that unequal strength in the market leads to outcomes that are not always fair: "if the positions of the contracting parties are too unequal, the consent of the parties does not suffice to guarantee the justice of their contract, and the rule of free agreement remains subservient to the demands of the natural law. ... Freedom of trade is fair only if it is subject to the demands of social justice."[54] The "law of free competition," he believes, "too often creates an economic dictatorship."[55] Paul VI couches this criticism in the language of abstract law and logic, which he mixes with the language of fact. Logically, the opposite to "economic dictatorship" would seem to be "free competition." The appearance in the world of fact ("too often") of monopoly or economic dictatorship would constitute a violation of that law. For if an underdeveloped nation has several different competitors to whom to sell its goods, that would be better than having but one. This line of thought, in fact, has led recent Vatican theoreticians on international trade to argue that the less developed nations need to open up new market possibilities by trading with each other, not solely with the industrialized nations. The principle seems to be that the more varied the competition, the better.

Furthermore, Paul VI overlooks an important characteristic of trade among nations. When trading partners are unequal, one much more highly developed than the other, it typically happens that the *less* developed nation benefits far more from the trade than does the *more* developed. For the more developed nation, the goods traded are typically marginal; for the less developed, they introduce substantial benefits. Thus, actions which are relatively insignificant to the former may have a sometimes devastating, sometimes disproportionately beneficial, impact on the less developed. Concern to avoid harmful effects would certainly be humane and commendable on the part of the stronger party. What cannot be concluded, however, is that trade should be halted. On the contrary, trade typically helps the weaker party far more than the stronger. It was in this way that, after the devastation of World War II, the rapid resumption of international trade so swiftly raised Japan and Western Europe to levels virtually equal to that of the United States, which was at first by far the stronger partner. That *both* parties should benefit mutually is, of course, not only a better outcome for moral law but also for long-term economic law.

The animus which Paul VI displays against liberalism as an ideology is greatly modified, therefore, by both the empirical assertions and the logic of his own argument.

In a famous article, "Ecclesiastical Economics is Envy Exalted," P. T. Bauer holds, as a secular reader might, that *Populorum Progressio* and *Octogesima Adveniens* "are not theological, doctrinal or philosophical statements reaffirming Christian beliefs. . . . They are political statements based on bogus arguments."[56] He accuses them of being a catch-all of contemporary conventional wisdom among elites in the field of development. In my own view, Bauer is too harsh; he especially errs in regarding the basic principle from which Paul VI argues—that creation belongs to all human beings—as a false principle. As we have seen, it is on precisely this principle that John Locke, Adam Smith, and John Stuart Mill (as well as St. Thomas Aquinas) have relied in *defending* the right to private property. Bauer should have seen this, for he himself makes powerful use of the point that the vast majority of arable lands upon this earth lie still undeveloped, and that nature itself adds very little to human wealth except what human activity produces from it.[57] The liberal tradition, like the Catholic tradition, grounds the natural right to the private ownership of property on the *development* which private owners produce, thus adding to the common good.

The principle that the earth belongs to all humans is essential to the right to private property. In this respect, Paul VI is correct and Bauer wrong. Nonetheless, an objective reader—Catholic or not—must concede that a great many of Paul VI's assertions are either about empirical fact (e.g., current "terms of trade") or about the causes of development and the methods most likely to lead to it. On such matters, papal teaching draws less upon its own theological authority than upon the opinions of secualr experts. In addition, an objective reader must also note that Paul VI inquires very little into the actual history of development in various countries. He ignores the impact of cultural factors upon economic progress. The Japanese, for example, have very few natural resources; the tiny islands of that nation are nearly 100 percent energy-dependent. Yet tiny Japan, population 118 million, produces 10 percent of the gross world product.

What ethos and which virtues must a nation develop if it wishes to achieve humane economic progress, both in production and in distribution? Paul VI is strangely silent about this predominantly moral and spiritual matter. Although he often mentions ethnic cultures, he does not observe any of the substantial cultural differences which seem to lead some peoples to remarkable human progress, as he defines it, and others not.[58] On these points the work of P. T. Bauer is more solid.

Finally, an objective reader—Catholic or not—cannot fail to note that Paul VI sets forth as methods to achieve development the following: higher taxation in richer nations, to be redistributed by their political authorities to local political authorities in the developing world; opening of the markets of the developed world to cheaper goods from the less developed countries, without protectionism; comprehensive economic planning led by local governmental authorities, although respecting the liberties of individuals and intermediate bodies; international agreements about prices and production; a world body charged with political and judicial powers. Such methods represent alternatives of political economy based upon secular, not theological, premises. If the specific methods recommended by the pope were to fail, such failure would not compromise Catholic doctrine. They would injure only the pope's reputation for practical judgment. Much depends, then, on the practical wisdom of Paul VI in comprehending the best secular policies to attain the goals to which he points. As Paul VI himself states in *Octogesima Adveniens,* "One must recognize a legitimate variety of possible options. The same Christian faith can lead to different commitments."[59]

There is one particular text of *Populorum Progressio* which especially awakened Bauer's ire.

We must repeat once more that the superfluous wealth of rich countries should be placed at the service of poor nations. The rule which up to now held good for the benefit of those nearest to us, must today be applied to all the needy of this world. Besides, the rich will be the first to benefit as a result. Otherwise their continued greed will certainly call down upon them the judgement of God and the wrath of the poor, with consequences no one can foretell.[60]

Bauer believes that this sentiment contains two confusions. Paul VI seems to hold that the poverty of the lesser-developed countries (LDCs) is caused by the wealth of the developed countries, but this empirical proposition is not sustainable. In addition, the pope seems to say that the envy of the poor is justified. Bauer finds this immoral.

In fact, I believe, Paul VI is trying to make a less stringent claim, albeit in highly inflamed language. His claim is that the more developed, even if their progress has been justly arrived at, ought to help the poor because of bonds of solidarity. It is in their interest to do so.

This claim is true. At the end of World War II, the United States alone produced more than half—53 percent—of the gross world product. Through its assistance to Japan and Germany (and the rest of Europe), assistance which Winston Churchill termed the most generous action of any nation towards its defeated foes in history, the United States has seen its proportion of the gross world product fall to 23 percent. The economic progress of Western Europe, Japan, and virtually all other nations since World War II, has not hurt the United States. On the contrary, it has been in the interest of the United States. Similarly, the growth of many other new centers of economic progress —on the East Asian rim, in Latin America, in Africa, and throughout the world—is in the interest of the United States. The spread of democratic institutions and of free economies able to sustain economic development creatively and inventively creates for the United States a more sympathetic world, closer to its own ideals.

In certain key areas, *Populorum Progressio* is an ambivalent and vaguely phrased document, uncertain which institutions of political economy it actually means to commend. *Octogesima Adveniens*, issued four years later, achieves a better balance.

## 4. EIGHTY YEARS AFTER

In 1971, eighty years after *Rerum Novarum*, Paul VI more squarely placed his thought on development in the papal mainstream. Like Pius XI and John XXIII, he was compelled to note the vast social progress made by liberal societies since 1891. Indeed, it would have been more gracious of him to have said so more openly. Never in the history of the North Atlantic community had so many lived so long, in such good health, and in more intense participation in so many free activities of politics, culture, and economic life. The distance traversed between 1891 and 1971 was immense.

The church, Paul VI says, "travels forward with humanity and shares its lot in the setting of history." He notes the wide diversity in which Christians around the world find themselves.

In the face of such widely varying situations it is difficult for us to utter a unified message and to put forward a solution which has universal validity. Such is not our ambition, nor is it our mission. It is up to the Christian communities to analyze with objectivity the situation which is proper to their own country. . . .[61]

But the principal fact to be addressed is that "the social question has become worldwide."[62] After surveying the vast scope of change around the world—the decline of agrarian and the swift rise of urban ways of life, in particular—the pope turns to new "aspirations and currents of ideas." Whereas previous popes had often thought *against* the times, Paul VI tries to think *with* them, singling out two new currents much in the air: aspirations to equality and participation.

Here a note of realism breaks in. "Without a renewed education in solidarity, an overemphasis of equality can give rise to an individualism in which each one claims his own rights without wishing to be answerable for the common good."[63] Then comes an odd section on "The Political Society." Equality and participation, Paul VI begins, promote "a democratic type of society." Yet of all the various models proposed, "none of them gives complete satisfaction, and the search goes on between ideological and pragmatic tendencies."[64] Political activity, he goes on, "should be the projection of a plan of society." But neither the State nor political parties should impose an ideology; "cultural and religious groupings" should, in freedom, develop "those ultimate convictions on the nature, origin and end of man and society."[65] This seems to be a liberal principle separating the institutions of the moral and cultural system from the political system.

Later, Paul VI comes back to the "Christian Meaning of Political Activity," saying that economic activity is necessary and good, but subject to a "radical limitation." He asserts that "each man feels that in the social and economic field, both national and international, the ultimate decision rests with political power."[66] This, however, is clearly not true in religious, scientific, intellectual, or artistic matters. Some do not believe that it is true in economic matters. To be sure, in most societies, only the State has police and military powers; it holds a monopoly on the sanctions of force. But its rights to intervene elsewhere are severely limited. Sure enough, the next paragraph observes that the state respects "the legitimate liberties of individuals, families and subsidiary groups," and "acts within the limits of its competence." But does it? Did most states in 1971 do so? These sentences are not accurate descriptions. Again: The State "always intervenes with care for justice and with devotion to the common good . . ." This is not a realistic description of the abuses typical of states, their rulers, their bureaucracies, their police forces. It suggests no feeling for the harm States can do, and have done, to economic development; no recognition of their widespread abuses of human rights; no Niebuhrianism at all. Clearly, Catholic tradition holds that political society is good by nature, but also that, like all things human, it is corrupted by human sinfulness. In this sense, this portion of the social thought of Paul VI is not liberal; it almost never adverts to the corruptions characteristic of governments everywhere, but perhaps especially in Third World countries today, their stupendous economic errors, their greed. The only sins it sees are those of economic institutions. It does not see how necessary it is, if sustained and widespread economic progress is to occur, for economic decisions to be free of political domination.

One can agree, of course, that "ultimate decision rests with political power," in matters, for example, like selling high technology to the Soviet Union. (The so-called neo-conservatives in the United States hold strongly to the principle that, in foreign policy, political institutions are prior to economic institutions.) Yet if political decisions dominate economic decisions in every sphere, the power of political elites will be served to the detriment of economic progress and the common good. Paul VI is plainly not clear about the relation he would commend between political and economic power. Insofar as he wishes to defend the rights of religion and of individuals and their intermediate groups from unlimited state power, he is a liberal: "An attitude of encroachment which would tend to set up politics as an absolute value would bring serious danger."[67] Insofar as he encourages unchecked political power in the economic sphere, he is not.

Paul VI holds that the Christian "cannot adhere to the Marxist ideology, to its atheistic materialism, to its dialectic of violence, and to the way it absorbs individual freedom in the collectivity."[68] At the same time, urging some caution, Paul VI does allow Christians to yield to "the attraction" some of them feel today for "socialist currents," idealizing socialism in terms of "a will for justice, solidarity and equality." He even gives three long paragraphs to the "Historical Evolution of Marxism," seeming at least to allow Christians to follow it in "its more attenuated forms . . . as a scientific activity, as a rigorous method of examining social and political reality, and as the rational link, tested by history, between theoretical knowledge and the practice of revolutionary transformation."[69] The next paragraph warns that it would be "illusory and dangerous" to forget that Marxist analysis is tightly linked to "the practices of class struggle" and a "totalitarian and violent society."[70] But his high praise of Marxist scientific rigor "tested by history" may invite Christians to forget this link. It is also praise poorly deserved: Marxism has been thoroughly discredited as a science, even by Marxists.

Paired with his rejection of Marxism, Paul VI says a Christian may not adhere, either, "to the liberal ideology which believes it exalts individual freedom by withdrawing it from every limitation, by stimulating it through exclusive seeking of interest and power, and by considering social solidarities as more or less automatic consequences of individual initiatives, not as an aim and a major criterion of the value of the social organization."[71] He later adds one full paragraph defining "The Liberal Ideology," just after his description of the evolution of Marxism.

On another side, we are witnessing a renewal of the liberal ideology. This current asserts itself both in the name of economic efficiency, and for the defense of the individual against the increasingly overwhelming hold of organizations, and as a reaction against the totalitarian tendencies of political powers. Certainly, personal initiative must be maintained and developed. But do not Christians who take this path tend to idealize liberalism in their turn, making it a proclamation in favour of freedom? They would like a new model, more adapted to present-day conditions, while easily forgetting that at the very root of philosophical liberalism is an erroneous affirmation of the autonomy of the individual in his activity, his motivation and the exercise of his liberty. Hence, the liberal ideology likewise calls for careful discernment on their part.[72]

Such a critique seems to me aimed at writers like Ayn Rand. It falls very wide of the mark in describing Adam Smith, James Madison, Abraham Lincoln, John Stuart Mill, or even such contemporaries as Hayek, Friedman, Samuelson, and Galbraith. It misses entirely the genius of liberal institutions.

In the ideological combat between Marxism and liberalism, is Paul VI really so neutral as he sounds? To be sure, the Church wishes to stand above all ideologies. Its own role and mission are for all times and all cultures. They are not reducible to contemporary ways of thinking. What sort of guidance to the developing world does Paul VI offer, however, when he dares not criticize the "attentuated" Marxism and vague socialism which are the *lingua franca* of intellectual elites? Does he fear to challenge them?

There is a simple test. Paul VI, like John XXIII, holds the dignity of the individual human person to be the fundamental criterion of the good society. Each person, made in the image of God, is the ground of inalienable rights. No Marxist or collectivist society can offer appropriate protection for such a person. Neither do most traditional societies. Among the 160 regimes now incarnated on this planet, which twenty or thirty nations best protect human rights? All are liberal societies.

Consider economic development. Among the 160 existing regimes, which twenty or thirty nations best nourish the creativity and invention, the individual liberty and voluntary teamwork, which alone lead to economic progress? Some forty years ago, Japan ranked below several nations in Latin America; its workmanship had one of the lowest of reputations. Liberal institutions have helped to propel it in meteoric fashion.

More than Paul VI recognizes, so determined is he to use the term *liberalism* with disdain, his own commitments to human rights and to economic development commit him to liberal institutions. His attacks on liberal ideology are a red herring.

## 5. THE PEACE AND JUSTICE ESTABLISHMENT

Yet Paul VI's two encyclicals cannot be understood in a vacuum. In 1963, when he had become pope, he introduced a new theme into the Vatican Council: "The Church Speaks to the Contemporary World." He guided through the Council its statement on religious liberty. In 1969, 1971, and 1974, he assigned a synod composed of representatives of the world's bishops a study of social justice in the world. In 1967 he established a new office in the Vatican, the Commission on Justice and Peace, to study problems of world development. Most of its members were caught up in the enthusiasm of *"aggiornamento"*, so much so that a chronicler of that period and one of its participants, the good and serious American, Father Joseph Gremillion, uses "the *aggiornamento* church" and *"aggiornamento* theology" to mark an entirely new era in church history.

The word *aggiornamento* came into usage when Pope John XXIII, asked why he had without warning called an Ecumenical Council, an event of a century, said with twinkling eyes: "to bring the Church up to today." His image suggested that the Church had been static, conservative, behind the times. Few disputed that. Then, in the first flush of worldwide headlines and renewed secular influence, won by the character of John XXIII, by *Pacem in Terris*, and by widespread acclamation of the "progressiveness" of Vatican Two (1961–1965), the first staffers of the Justice and Peace Commission believed that henceforth they would never again be behind events, they would take the lead. They would recognize where the world was going before the world did. They would lead the way into the future. "Reading the signs of the times" became their preoccupation. "Hope," "the future," and "utopia" became their buzzwords. Quickly they learned about the United Nations, and took its work on food, population, and world peace as harbingers of a new world order, beyond the nation-state (harking back to the era before the Peace of Westphalia, *before* the nation-state).

Moreover, remembering a time when as churchmen they had been looked down upon as reactionary and out of touch, they began to settle old scores. Whereas liberal scientific and technological elites had for generations described the Catholic clergy as unenlightened, *aggiornamento* theology permitted the same clergymen to take possession of the moral high ground. Citing pollution, the "limits to growth," the protests of the counterculture, the Cold War, the threat of nuclear weapons and the arms race, and the multiplying populations of the poor Third World, the *aggiornamento* theologians turned the tables. Father Gremillion's rather heady history of the era, written during 1974–

1975 and published in 1976, reveals the psychological circumstances of the hour with uncanny power.

Father Gremillion describes how secular humanists had long criticized Catholic social teaching for its emphasis upon the seemingly static concept of natural law. Gremillion cites the embarrassment felt by Cardinal Maurice Roy of Canada in 1973 even in using the phrase "natural law":

This concept seems too "essentialist" to the people of our time, who challenge, as being a relic of Greek philosophy, the term "Natural Law," which they consider anachronistic, conservative and defensive. They object further that the expression was defined arbitrarily and once and for all in a subjective and Western manner, and is therefore one-sided and lacking in any moral authority for the universal conscience.[73]

Instead of displaying self-confidence in its own traditions, the *aggiornamento* church became suddenly embarrasssed by seeming "Western," and it replaced its ancient compass with a new one. The ancient one had been the tradition of intellectual inquiry, the *philosophia perennis*, which Walter Lippmann had seen as the soul of liberal societies.[74] The new compass became "consciousness-raising" or "conscientization." Gremillion writes:

We see here the rhetoric as well as the conviction that dominated the rest of the sixties: Men all over the world—claiming their rights in the socioeconomic order—increasingly conscious of their dignity—making claims on the political level—a new awareness prompting them to claim a share in the public administration—women conscious of their human dignity.

This whole process of growing consciousness by peoples and groups now deeply influences the Church. The aggiornamento documents acknowledge and accept the growing "conscientization" of the Church itself by the movement for human dignity in the world. . . . Still it took centuries of experience *by and in the world* to awaken the Church to this dignity of man from which arises religious freedom. That is why *Gaudium et Spes*, with its conciliar teaching of human dignity, offers hope that current Catholic concern for man and his future will endure and increase. By listening more attentively to the real world in which it now willingly finds itself, the Church might at least keep up with the continuing creation of God and of man in this-world.[75]

Where does this lead? Gremillion again:

The conscious claim for human dignity and rights generated in turn another level of conscientization: that their realization is blocked in most countries by existing power structures; that these unjust institutions—economic and political, educational and cultural, military and media—intertwine and reinforce each other; that a small power elite, through inheritance or recruitment, dominates the nation; and that these oppressive national structures combine to forge a transnational system of injustice.[76]

In this vein, Gremillion writes, Paul VI in 1968 visited Medellin, Colombia, for the conference of the Latin American bishops, and encouraged them to attack "systems and structures which cover up and favor grave and oppressive inequalities."[77] The bishops of Latin America criticized dominant elites within their own countries, but with even more gusto *external* neocolonialism . . . international monopolies and international imperialism of money."[78] Cardinal Roy, the President of the Justice and Peace Commission, raised the decibel level at the United Nations in 1970:

We have now a world economy in which *all* the positions of strength, all the wealth, all the investment, all the commercial services and above all, the whole crucial apparatus of research are concentrated in the small elite of nations which have already achieved modernization.[79]

He further urged a world tax on richer peoples to be distributed to the poor and asked that

. . . a fundamental reconsideration of the planet's resource use and management be undertaken so that the increasingly irrational levels of extravagance, waste and pollution of the "high consumption societies" should not jeopardize the poorer nations' hopes of development and humanity's ultimate hopes of survival.[80]

Situations of injustice had become so blatant, Gremillion writes, that Paul VI declared in 1971 that "many people are reaching the point of questioning the very model of society. . . . The need is felt to pass from economics to politics."[81]

By October, 1971, representative bishops from around the world, gathering in Synod, "scrutinizing the 'signs of the times' and seeking to detect the meaning of emerging history," spoke as if they were a UN Third World Committee. They discerned:

The serious injustices which are building around the world of men a network of domination, oppression and abuses which stifle freedom and which keep the greater part of humanity from sharing in the building up and the enjoyment of a more just and more fraternal world. . . . the unequal distribution which places decisions concerning three quarters of income, investment and trade in the hands of one third of the human race, namely the more highly developed part.[82]

How easily, one wants to say, Catholic clergymen have passed from right to left, without ever pausing to cherish liberal institutions. Father Gremillion describes the way Third World leftists view the current world situation. "The aggiornamento documents," he adds, "agree with the fundamental position of the South."[83] It is remarkable that even the Americans and Canadians seem to relish this attack upon "dominant elites." A clue to this feeling may be unwittingly revealed by Father Gremillion. He writes sarcastically:

The Wasp nationality, naturalized citizens (non-Anglo names are sometimes prominent) and blue-blood natives alike, is still at it—a bit bloodied now by Vietnam; a bit buffaloed by Soviet arms supremacy; a bit befuddled because ethnics, Blacks, Chicanos, and their Third World relatives are biting back. The Wasps are more than a bit aghast at Arab and Iranian national effrontery, uniting again as they did 1,200 years ago against superior Europeans. They threaten the Wasp modern way-of-waste, so completely opposed to the Puritan austerity which empowered and polarized the American pioneers. And they interfere, worse still, with the monetary system and multinational corporation, twin tools of the world business boom since World War II, tempered too in the blest triangle of Harvard, Wall Street, and Washington.[84]

In actual fact, the description of the world situation as it appears to the Vatican Justice and Peace Commission seems not very different from the way it appears to Marxist thought. Dominant elites hold the multitudes within the vise of an "unjust world system," which in practice "is principally a Western creation. Its chief managers and beneficiaries are North America, Western Europe and Japan."[85] Although Paul VI and the clergymen of Justice and Peace counsel patience and peaceful methods, others who embrace their analysis may be understandably less dispassionate and considerably less scrupulous.

The Catholic church under Paul VI attempted to do two things at once. It wished to protect the human rights of individuals, families, and intermediate institutions as Marxism does not desire to do. But some in it also wished to accept the Marxist analysis of economic imperialism, and to claim that dominant elites had become rich through oppressing others and were unconscionable beneficiaries of the misery of others. Such heady brew is unstable. Its fruit is the schizophrenia felt most acutely in Catholic nations, between terrified defenders of the status quo on one side and righteous revolutionaries on the other.[86] Its fundamental defect is its dependence upon the empirically flawed "theory of dependency" and its failure to grasp how wealth is actually created. Justice and Peace, the name Paul VI chose for his commission, illustrates the problem. Justice and Peace—but not freedom. In a stagnant society, one can have justice and peace. One can have justice and peace, of a sort, even in a totalitarian society. Yet, justice and peace are not, even on the premises put forward by John XXIII and Paul VI, sufficient ideals for Catholic social thought. Justice and peace alone will not lead to economic development or protect human rights. Until Justice and Peace becomes *Freedom,* Justice and Peace, Catholic social thought cannot in practice achieve the ends it has set for itself.

Moreover, Paul VI's flirtation with Marxist analysis and his disdain for the ideology of liberalism have unleashed a mischievous dualism in the Catholic world. His successors have already had to cope with clergy and laity more confused about Marxist revolution than before his pontificate. The blood of the pope's dear friend, Premier Aldo Moro of Italy, was shed by terrorist groups, among whom were former activist Catholics. In Nicaragua, former Catholics committed to an analysis of the world very like Paul VI's own, booed and hissed his successor, Pope John Paul II. And even the Justice and Peace Commission would have to remark that, given international terrorism which has reached even to an attempt on the life of John Paul II, if a new *Pacem in Terris* were issued, it would have to be called *Bellum in Terris*.

The fifteen years from 1963 to 1978 must be regarded as an enthusiastic, optimistic, and unself-critical period in Catholic social thought.

# CHAPTER 8

# Creation Theology: Pope John Paul II

Labor is prior to, and independent of, capital. Capital is only the fruit of labor, and could never have existed if labor had not first existed. Labor is the superior of capital, and deserves much the higher consideration. Capital has its rights, which are as worthy of protection as any other rights. Nor is it denied that there is, and probably always will be, a relation between labor and capital, producing mutual benefits.

—ABRAHAM LINCOLN, 1861[1]

Many anti-American cartoons abroad depict Uncle Sam brandishing a dollar as a symbol of American civilization. There is more ignorance than malice in this platitude. As a matter of fact, it is not money, it is work which holds sway over American civilization.... American civilization thus lays stress on the dignity of work and the fecundity of work transforming matter and nature.

—JACQUES MARITAIN *Reflections on America*

On May 13, 1981, on his way to give a homily in preparation for his delivery later that week of a ninetieth-anniversary encyclical commemorating *Rerum Novarum*, Pope John Paul II was gunned down by the bullets of an international terrorist using Bulgarian assistance and allegedly with Soviet approval.[2] Had John Paul II not lived, one wonders whether his encyclical, *Laborem Exercens*, would have ever been officially delivered, as it eventually was, later that year.

The theme of "solidarity" is an old one in Catholic social thought, but John Paul II gives it a new clarity. His is a personalist version of "solidarity," which he contrasts with the "organic connectedness" claimed by Marxism. Leo XIII knew Marxism only as an idea. Pius XI knew it as a cruel experiment far away in Russia, its terror (in 1931) still in its early phases. But Pope John Paul II spent virtually his entire adult life under Marxist socialism. He clarifies the meaning of "solidarity" by emphasizing the primacy of the individual human *subject*. Here he draws upon some of the most impressive resources of recent Western philosophical thought, the traditions of phenomenology and existential-ism (which owe so much to the experiences of American pragmatism and individualism, and especially to William James[3]).

In focusing on the individual human *subject*, Pope John Paul II places the tradition of Bishop von Ketteler, Pesch, and previous popes on clearer, fresher ground. Thereby he establishes the basis for a new theory of human action and human personality—the subject matter of his own earlier philosophical works.[4] This new material provides the basis for a *critical* theology of economics. Through it, John Paul II shifts the point of view of Catholic social thought away from "liberation" and toward "creation."

Quite brilliantly weaving together the traditions drawn on by Leo XIII and Pius XI with the new philosophies and unprecedented experi-ences of the twentieth century, Pope John Paul II has chosen to high-light "perhaps more than has been done before—the fact that human work is a key, probably the essential key, to the whole social question."[5] He has also squarely rooted the "elements for a spirituality of work" in the biblical category of co-creation, highlighting the crucial role played by *invention* and *discovery* in the human vocation "to subdue the earth." In short, Pope John Paul II has illustrated a remarkably "American" way of approaching the nature and the destiny of man, the role of capital and labor, private property and community. *Laborem Exercens* is oriented toward the future.

## 1. MAN AS THE SUBJECT OF WORK

Animals do not work, only man works, the pope asserts. Work bears "the mark of a person operating within a community."[6] Work has an interior dimension of spirit and intentionality, of intellect and will, and a social dimension. "Man is the image of God partly through the mandate received from his creator to subdue, to dominate, the earth. In carrying out this mandate, man, every human being, reflects the very action of the Creator of the universe." Again: "The expression 'subdue the earth' has an immense range. It means all the resources that the earth (and indirect-ly the visible world) contains and which, through the conscious activity of man, can be discovered and used for his ends." Thus the pope imag-ines that the Creator has hidden many resources in his creation, which it is the task of humans to discover through conscious labor. He envisages "future phases of development, which are perhaps already to some ex-tent beginning to take shape, though for the most part they are still almost unknown to man and hidden from him."[7]

In technology the pope sees "that ally of work which human thought has produced," "the fruit of the work of the human intellect and a historical confirmation of man's dominion over nature."[8] Yet technology can also become man's enemy, and so the pope turns to the *subject* of work, the human person.

"It is always man who is the purpose of the work, whatever work it is that is done by man—even if the common scale of values rates it as the merest 'service,' as the most monotonous, even the most alienating work."[9] Anyone who has worked in any field knows the toil and suffering always involved in it—the teacher grading papers, the dentist probing mouths, the digger in a gravel pit, the miner, the preacher, the political leader. The pope quotes from Ecclesiastes (2:11): "Then I considered all that my hands had done and the toil I had spent in doing it," and he adds: "There is no one on earth who could not apply these words to himself."[10] In short, the pope wishes to place the consideration of work upon the plane of human dignity, beyond all considerations of a merely material or merely economic nature. Work is made for man, not man for work—as Jesus had earlier said even of the sabbath.

From the beginning of the industrial age, the pope asserts, "various trends of materialistic and economistic thought" posed a danger to this Christian understanding.[11] The pope's view of this matter has a lineage that goes back to the inversion Karl Marx made of Ricardo's discussions of labor. (This issue is a lively one in Poland's intellectual debates between Catholic and Marxist thinkers; it was clearly articulated by Polish delegates to a conference in Rome two months after *Laborem Exercens* appeared.)[12] According to Marx, Ricardo viewed labor only as a commodity and treats it in a materialistic way. Marx maintained Ricardo's materialism, and thus made labor an instrument of class struggle. Polish Catholic thought rejects both Marx and Ricardo, in the name of Christian Personalism. Here is how Pope John Paul II frames the issue:

For certain supporters of such ideas, work was understood and treated as a sort of "merchandise" that the worker—especially the industrial worker—sells to the employer, who at the same time is the possessor of the capital, that is to say, of all the working tools and means that make production possible. This way of looking at work was wide-spread especially in the first half of the 19th century. Since then explicit expressions of this sort have almost disappeared and have given way to more human ways of thinking about work and evaluating it.[13]

The pope opposes any situations, Marxist or capitalist, in which

man is treated as an instrument of production, whereas he—he alone, independent of the work he does—ought to be treated as the effective subject of work and its true maker and creator. Precisely this reversal of order, whatever the program or name under which it occurs, should rightly be called "capitalism"—in the sense more fully explained below. Everybody knows that capitalism has a definite historical meaning as a system, an economic and social system, opposed to "socialism" or "communism." But . . . it should be recognized that the error of early capitalism can be repeated wherever man is in a way treated on the same level as the whole complex of the material means of production, as an instrument and not in accordance with the true dignity of his work—that is to say, where he is not treated as subject and maker, and for this very reason as the true purpose of the whole process of production.[14]

In accepting the Marxist view of early capitalism and, in particular, in accepting as a *definition* of capitalism the reversal of right order, the pope seems to have committed a historical injustice. This point may be sharply illustrated by the conflict between slave labor and free labor in the United States in the mid-nineteenth century. To assert, as the pope does, that under capitalism free labor is regarded as "merchandise" goes too far. Merchandise can be bought; it is not hired. The hired laborer retains an independence and a dignity lacking both to the peasants and serfs of central Europe and to slaves in America. The hired laborer accepts a contract for a time, for his own purposes. An especially good illustration of this reality appears in Abraham Lincoln's address at the Wisconsin State fair in 1859.

In these Free States, a large majority are neither hirers nor hired. Men, with their families—wives, sons and daughters—work for themselves, on their farms, in their houses and in their shops, taking the whole product to themselves, and asking no favors of capital on the one hand, nor of hirelings or slaves on the other . . . there is not, of necessity, any such thing as the free hired laborer being fixed to that condition for life. There is demonstration for saying this. Many independent men, in this assembly, doubtless a few years ago were hired laborers. And their case is almost if not quite the general rule.

The prudent, penniless beginner in the world, labors for wages awhile, saves a surplus with which to buy tools or land, for himself; then labors on his own account another while, and at length hires another new beginner to help him. This, say its advocates, is free labor—the just and generous, and prosperous system, which opens the way for all—gives hope to all, and energy, and progress, and improvement of condition to all. If any continue through life in the condition of the hired laborer, it is not the fault of the system, but because of either a dependent nature which prefers it, or improvidence, folly, or singular misfortune.[15]

In Lincoln's experience, free labor is different from slavery or serfdom. The free laborer retains his dignity and his liberty. He feels the undercurrent of upward mobility. He does not always move with this current (Lincoln's letters to his own unambitious, dependent brother attest poignantly to those who take no advantage of their opportunities).[16] In a word, it is emphatically *not* the case that capitalism can be *defined* as a reversal of the subjective dimension of work, in which the hired laborer is treated merely as an instrument of production. Such a reversal is a sin against capitalism, not its inward dynamic. There are many texts in Adam Smith, particularly in his reflections on the reasons why colonies prosper,[17] in Alexander Hamilton's "Report on Manufactures,"[18] and in other central documents of democratic capitalism which take, in effect, the same view of the *moral* question as does Pope John Paul II.

## 2. THE PRIORITY OF LABOR OVER CAPITAL

Pope John Paul II goes on to "recall a principle that has always been taught by the church: the principle of the priority of labor over capital."[19] In the process of production, "labor is always a primary efficient cause, while capital, the whole collection of means of production, remains a mere instrument or instrumental cause." This very idea, which the pope describes as "an evident truth that emerges from the whole of man's historical experience," was also expressed in Lincoln's First Annual Message to Congress, on December 3, 1861:

Labor is prior to, and independent of, capital. Capital is only the fruit of labor, and could never have existed if labor had not first existed. Labor is the superior of capital, and deserves much the higher consideration. Capital has its rights, which are as worthy of protection as any other rights. Nor is it denied that there is, and probably always will be, a relation between labor and capital, producing mutual benefits. The error is in assuming that the whole labor of community exists within that relation.[20]

Lincoln attached a very great importance to the principle of free labor and its superiority to capital. He himself had worked as a hired laborer. He valued the system of liberty, political and economic. He saw its importance for the entire human race:

This is the just, and generous, and prosperous system, which opens the way to all—gives hope to all, and consequent energy, and progress, and improvement of condition to all. No men living are more worthy to be trusted than those who toil up from poverty—none less inclined to take, or touch, aught which they have not honestly earned. Let them beware of surrendering a political power which they already possess, and which, if surrendered, will surely be used to close the door of advancement against such as they, and to fix new disabilities and burdens upon them, till all of liberty shall be lost. . . . The struggle of to-day, is not altogether for to-day—it is for a vast future also. With a reliance on Providence, all the more firm and earnest, let us proceed in the great task which events have devolved upon us.[21]

On the priority of labor over capital, both Abraham Lincoln and Pope John Paul II share the same principle, and expect from it common fruitfulness.

## 3. THE MEANING OF CAPITAL

If the definition which Pope John Paul II gives capitalism is derogatory, the definition he gives to capital is severely limited. He writes: "Everything contained in the concept of capital in the strict sense is only a collection of things."[22] "Man alone is a person," the pope adds. He includes in this "collection of things" both "the natural resources placed at man's disposal, but also the whole collection of means by which man appropriates natural resources and transforms them in accordance with his needs (and thus in a sense humanizes them). . . ." One might argue that the pope's definition of capital is too narrow, since it excludes the *persons* whose investments in the discovery and transformation of natural resources, and in the means of production, go beyond the mere self-centered indulgence in material luxuries such as have characterized the wealthy aristocracy of most cultures at most times. Still, Pope John Paul II actually uses this narrow definition to creative effect. His central intention is to show that both capital and labor are centered in the same purpose: the primacy of man.

Thus, for the pope, "capital cannot be separated from labor; in no way can labor be opposed to capital or capital to labor, and still less can the people behind these concepts be opposed to each other.[23] "A labor system can be right"—that is, "intrinsically true and also morally legitimate"—"if in its very basis it overcomes the opposition between labor and capital . . ." He continues: "Opposition between labor and capital does not spring from the structure of the production process or from the structure of the economic process." This is a remarkably *anti*-Marxist view. In general, the pope goes on, the economic process "demonstrates that labor and what we are accustomed to call capital are intermingled; it shows that they are inseparably linked."

The pope attributes the break between capital and labor, as though both were two impersonal forces, to the error of considering human labor solely according to its economic purpose. He calls this error "economism" and he likens it to materialism, that is, a belief in the primacy or superiority of the material over the personal and the spiritual. Still, although dialectical materialism pursued this line of thought rigorously, "economism influenced this non-humanistic way of stating the issue before the materialist philosophical system did."

Here perhaps, the pope fails to note that, as a scientific discipline, economics necessarily abstracts from the full tissue of humanistic discourse in order to concentrate upon one aspect of reality only, under its own proper formal light. This is true of any science. The error would lie, then, not in the science itself, or in legitimate abstraction, but in employing such a science as if it were a full vision of human life. In this sense, economism is to economics what scientism is to science.

The pope implicitly recognizes this point, noting shrewdly that "the antinomy between labor and capital . . . did not originate merely in the philosophy and economic theories of the 18th century; rather it originated in the whole of the economic and social practice of that time, the time of the birth and rapid development of industrialization . . . " Too much attention went to the means, the creation of wealth, too little to the end: man himself. "It was this practical error that struck a blow first and foremost against human labor, against the working man . . . " He then notes that this "same error, which is now part of history and which was connected with the period of primitive capitalism and liberalism" can nevertheless be repeated whenever similar premises recur.

From the point of view of democratic capitalism, one can have few objections to the pope's argument. Abraham Lincoln justified the capitalist system on similar grounds. It is, however, a little odd to think of labor in subjective, personalist terms, without thinking of capital in equally humanistic terms. The use to which wealth is put by human beings does have large moral consequences for entire societies. If the wealthy live in luxury and spend their money solely for their own amusement, they create a certain atmosphere throughout the body politic. At the end of the eighteenth century, Adam Smith directed attention to those cities in Europe which lived off the luxury of courts and governments.[24] In all cases, the citizenry of such places, depending on moneys so spent, lived in considerable indolence and dissipation. In those relatively few cities, however, in which the wealthy were beginning to invest in commerce and industry, rather more admirable habits of life were visible among the citizenry.

In short, it makes a *moral* difference whether the wealthy simply consume their wealth or save and invest it. Capital, too, has its subjective, moral, and humanistic dimension. Indeed, some humanists today speak of the habits and skills appropriated by individuals or peoples as a form of "human capital," a sort of natural resource developed to its potential. Unlike material possessions, internalized skills are inalienable; once acquired, they are part of a person forever.

## 4. OWNERSHIP

The pope seems to concede this point, for he hastens to add that in speaking of labor and capital he does not mean to be dealing with abstract concepts or "impersonal forces."[25] "Behind both concepts there are people, living, actual people: On the one side are those who do the work without being the owners of the means of production, and on the other side those who act as entrepreneurs and who own these means or represent the owners." The pope takes his stand alongside *Rerum Novarum* and *Mater et Magistra* on "the right to private property even when it is a question of the means of production."

This Catholic principle, he notes, "diverges radically from the program of collectivism as proclaimed by Marxism and put into practice in various countries in the decades following the time of Leo XIII's encyclical." He then adds: "At the same time it differs [he does not say *radically*] from the program of capitalism practiced by liberalism and by the political systems inspired by it."

No pope has ever lived within the system of capitalism, liberalism, and democracy; characteristically, the popes since Pius IX have denounced "liberalism." So it is instructive to inquire in which exact way

Pope John Paul II believes the Catholic principle differs from democratic capitalism today. "In the latter case," he writes, "the difference consists in the way the right to ownership is understood." His description of this precise difference, however, seems not to be historically correct. In the actual practice of democratic capitalism, whether in the United States, Japan, West Germany, Sweden, or other nations which might so be described (respecting private property and markets in their economic systems, democracy and rights in their political systems, and liberal pluralism in their cultural systems), his concerns about the ordering of private property to the common good are already observed in a multitude of institutional ways.

Christian tradition, the pope writes, has never upheld private property as an "absolute and untouchable" right. The means of production, he continues, "cannot be possessed against labor, they cannot even be possessed for possession's sake, because the only legitimate title to their possession . . . is that they should serve labor and thus by serving labor that they should make possible the achievement of the first principle of this order, namely, the universal destination of goods and the right to common use of them." He concludes, then, that "one cannot exclude the socialization, in suitable conditions, of certain means of production." Such "socialization," presumably, has already occurred in virtually all advanced economies, through thick and complex bodies of commercial law and regulations. Other forms of "socialization" have also occurred directly through the relative nationalization of industries like transport, utilities, and the like, and through joint stock ownership, the pension plans of workers, and other devices.

"From this point of view," the pope writes, "the position of 'rigid' capitalism continues to remain unacceptable, namely the position that defends the exclusive right to private ownership of the means of production as an untouchable 'dogma' of economic life. The principle of respect for work demands that this right should undergo a constructive revision both in theory and in practice."[26] But the pope here seems not to see the harmony between his own theory of property and that of John Stuart Mill. And property law in the United States, for example, has undergone tremendous revolutions in the last fifty years, owing to the complexity of patents, innovations, revolutions in production, and the like. Indeed, the pope himself notes that in speaking of the labor which now modifies the patrimony of a nation's capital, he must include "not only so-called manual labor but also the many forms of intellectual work, including white-collar work and management."[27] This is an important point. For today the ownership of great corporations tends to be broadly dispersed, not least through pension plans, and even corporate management has a relationship to ownership more like that of labor than like that of the owner-manager of an earlier era.

"In the light of the above," the pope adds, "many proposals put forward by experts in Catholic social teaching" have been put into practice: "proposals for joint ownership of the means of work, sharing by the workers in the management and/or profits of businesses, so-called shareholding by labor, etc." Recognition "of the proper position of labor and the worker in the production process demands various adaptations in the sphere of the right to ownership of the means of production."

The pope, therefore, demands "continual revision" of " 'rigid' capitalism." But he hastens to add that "these many deeply desired reforms cannot be achieved by an *a priori* elimination of private ownership of the means of production. For it must be noted that merely taking these means of production (capital) out of the hands of their private owners is not enough to ensure their satisfactory socialization." He then attacks the new class of managers under collectivist systems, "claiming for itself a monopoly of the administration and disposal of the means of production and not refraining from offending basic human rights."

Further on, the pope calls for "associating labor with the ownership of capital, as far as possible," a point we have treated in chapter three. The pope also calls for "producing a wide range of intermediate bodies with economic, social and cultural purposes." Here the emphasis on mediating structures and the associative principle strikes very close to the heart and genius of American life, as described by Tocqueville and many since.

Finally, the pope summarizes his "personalist" argument. "Labor is in a sense inseparable from capital," and the worker "wishes to be able to take part in the very work process as a sharer in responsibility and creativity."[28]. He does not wish to be caught "in a system of excessive bureaucratic centralization, which makes the worker feel that he is just a cog in a huge machine moved from above . . ." for "man's work concerns not only the economy but also, and especially, personal values." This is "the principal reason in favor of private ownership of the means of production." For the personalist argument holds that "the human person can preserve his awareness of working 'for himself.' " Private property is the secret both to personalism and to creativity.

## 5. INVENTION AND DISCOVERY

By choosing the biblical category of creation as his fundamental metaphor for the social order, Pope John Paul II goes beyond "liberation theology" to something rather deeper and more promising. "Since work in its subjective aspect is always a personal action, an *actus personae*, it follows that the whole person, body and spirit, participates in it, whether it is manual or intellectual work."[29] Being faithful to his own person, the human being "shares by his work in the activity of the Creator." Moreover, he "develop[s] that activity and perfects it as he advances further and further in the discovery of the resources and values contained in the whole creation."[30]

The Creator, in Pope John Paul II's vision, has hidden within creation untold riches, resources, and possibilities which it is the vocation of humans to discover and to realize, for the common good of all. He places great emphasis, therefore, upon invention and discovery. This is the golden thread he sees down the epochs of history, as humans through their labor discover more and more of the Creator's secrets and bring them to human use. It is through such discovery that man "subdues the earth":

Man dominates the earth by the very fact of domesticating animals, rearing them and obtaining from them the food and clothing he needs, and by the fact of being able to extract various natural resources from the earth and the seas. But man "subdues the earth" much more when he begins to cultivate it and then to transform its products, adapting them to his own use. Thus agriculture constitutes through human work a primary field of economic activity and an indispensable factor of production.[31]

This passage tempts me once again to return to the vision of Abraham Lincoln, who commended a similar message to the good people of Wisconsin in 1859, calling upon them, in effect, to be what Pope John Paul II asks us to be: co-creators with God.

No other human occupation opens so wide a field for the profitable and agreeable combination of labor with cultivated thought, as agriculture. I know of nothing so pleasant to the mind, as the discovery of anything which is at once new and valuable—nothing which so lightens and sweetens toil, as the hopeful pursuit of such discovery. And how vast, and how varied a field is agriculture, for such discovery. The mind, already trained to thought, in the country school, or higher school, cannot fail to find there an exhaustless source of profitable enjoyment. Every blade of grass is a study; and to produce two, where there was but one, is both a profit and a pleasure. And not grass alone; but soils, seeds, and seasons—hedges, ditches, and fences, draining, droughts, and irrigation—plowing, hoeing, and harrowing—reaping, mowing, and threshing—saving crops, pests of crops, diseases of crops, and what will prevent or cure them—implements, utensils, and machines, their relative merits, and [how] to improve them—hogs, horses, and cattle—sheep, goats, and poultry—trees, shrubs, fruits, plants, and flowers—the thousand things of which these are specimens—each a world of study within itself.[32]

## 6. CREATION THEOLOGY

One of the most interesting features of *Laborem Exercens* is that both the right and the left have acclaimed it. Writing in the *Ecumenist*, Gregory Baum says that "Catholics who have followed the recent shift to the left in Church teaching and have therefore acquired socialist sympathies are delighted with the encyclical and understand it as a confirmation of the direction in which they have moved."[33] Simultaneously, under the editorship of Philip Lawler, the Heritage Foundation published four highly respectful and sympathetic lectures on the encyclical, in which the lecturers also found their views confirmed.[34] Baum reads the encyclical for its "extended, critical and creative dialogue with Marxism." The Heritage lecturers believe that it confirms the basic principles and practices of liberal capitalist democracies which they as Catholic scholars have come to cherish.

In some sense, both these readings seem correct. Pope John Paul II came to intellectual maturity fighting against a pervasive Marxist catechetics. His own writings record the intellectual battles he has fought to express contemporary Catholic values against the domination of Marxism. There is ample evidence in this encyclical of this continued opposition. To call the pope's dealings with Marxism "dialogue" is euphemistic. Yet it is clearly true that his own thought has been shaped more by the living experience of Marxism than by the living experience of liberal capitalist democracies.

There is one decisive feature in Pope John Paul II's encyclical, however, which seems to tip the balance. Whereas Gregory Baum stresses those aspects of the encyclical which encourage "collectivism" (the pope actually uses the word "socialization") and "planning," the greatest single stress of the encyclical falls upon the human person, the *subject* of human labor. This concept comes closer than any other in the tradition of papal documents to emphasizing, although in a traditional Catholic context, the role of the *individual*. As we have seen, it is this stress which gives Pope John Paul II a new "personalist" defense of the traditional Catholic teaching on private property. This emphasis also correlates strongly with Vatican Council II's teachings on religious liberty and individual conscience.

For over a century, the popes have spoken of the Anglo-American philosophical and cultural tradition in almost exclusively pejorative terms. "Liberalism" has been scorned. So also has "individualism." To be sure, there are elements in this Anglo-American tradition widely criticized by many besides the popes. Anglo-American scholars as diverse as John Dewey, William James, and Josiah Royce have written powerfully and beautifully about community, in ways that make connections both to the traditions of Thomism and to those of European phenomenology, existentialism, and personalism.[35] In condemning "liberalism" and "individualism," the popes have, on the one hand, been less than specific regarding authors and doctrines; on the other, they have not always expressed clearly the ways in which the church itself has adopted certain liberal values (like religious liberty, the "open church," *aggiornamiento,* and others) as its own. Finally, if there are some notions of liberalism and individualism to be rejected, Catholics nourished by a liberal and individualistic culture have a right to expect some clarity about a specifically *Catholic* form of liberalism and individualism. It is not likely that everything about liberalism is to be condemned. Nor is it likely that every form of individualism must be condemned.

Indeed, without a strong theory of individual responsibility, how could one defend liberty of conscience? Or respect dissent? Or endorse solitude, hermitage, the interior life, personal vocation, or other traditional Catholic forms of nourishing brave and strong individuals? Again, not all forms of community are healthy or consistent with Catholicism. Familism of certain kinds, for example, has injured many traditional Catholic cultures by imposing upon individual family members constraints which damage conscience. "He who loves father or mother . . . and he who loves son or daughter more than me is not worthy of me" (Matthew 10:37). Mere conformity, mindless "group think," emotionally crippling cliques, and partisanship of various sorts can easily corrupt genuine Catholic community. In any truly admirable form of Catholic community, built upon the ideal of charity, there is an exquisite interplay between the twin values of the inimitable person and the common good.[36]

Indeed, concepts like "individualism" and "community" are realized in practice quite differently in different Catholic cultures. Contrasts between Catholic Ireland and Catholic Italy, Catholic Austria and Catholic Argentina, Catholic Spain and Catholic Poland, might easily be drawn, more perhaps in the sphere of actual living than in the sphere of speculative theory.

Furthermore, the experience of those two polarities—the person and the community—seems to be rather different for different generations even within the living memory of present-day families. I believe my own great-grandparents in Slovakia, a region quite close to that in which Pope John Paul II's family has its roots, were stronger, bolder, more ornery individuals—while living within rather closed village communities—than any of their descendants in succeeding generations. In the course of family history, in our case as in millions of others, it seems that great changes have taken place precisely around these two polar realities. From generation to generation, the liberties and hopes of individuals have changed, and so has the character of the communities in which they live. I, for one, would not judge all these changes as negative, nor all as positive. In all these various circumstances, our families have been nourished by the Eucharist and by Catholic faith in its many dimensions.

The task which lies ahead for Catholic theology, therefore, is to give more consideration to subtler conceptions of the person and the community. These realities differ in different historical eras and different cultural locations. It is possible that the life-forms of Catholic clergy and religious have changed less than those of Catholic lay persons. In any case, good theology ought to touch the ground it covers. In this respect, much is yet to be learned about the specific life-forms of personhood and community in Anglo-American cultures. These cultures are perhaps less known to sophisticated theology than any other.

Without question, economic relationships affect the life-forms of personhood and community. But economic relationships do not exhaust the texture of our lives. We live within various political institutions, too, as well as within various cultural institutions (family, church, neighborhood, intellectual networks, and the rest). A pluralistic society invites us to choose among many possible life-forms. Some change their vocations more than once, in order to experience new horizons. Some change their political commitments. Some experience dramatic religious changes. In a free and open society, it is not easy to generalize about the inner life of individuals. Furthermore, a society with a vast variety of commercial, industrial, and nonprofit enterprises generates ever new activities for the human mind. No single person can possibly learn the techniques and processes of all the complex fields which touch contemporary life.

The Catholic lay person has experienced a tremendous explosion in human creativity during the past two hundred years. Virtually all the innovations and inventions of this sudden historic outburst of creativity spring from democratic capitalist lands. Such societies have been designed precisely to stimulate individual and corporate creativity. Jacques Serban-Schreiber observed in *The American Challenge* (1968) that social organization aiming at innovation is the genius of America and that Europe would have to learn it—and now, both Europe and Japan have done so.[37] Sometimes one hears the argument that modern creativity was not caused by a capitalist economy, but by technology. Yet under which economic arrangements are technological breakthroughs nourished and promoted? The British Royal Society long awarded prizes for scientific and practical inventions. More significant, the law of patents protected inventors and their royalties as copyright laws protected authors.[38] Financial incentives justified years of expense and sacrifice in practical research. Native intelligence comes alive under such a system. A system that bases itself upon human creativity reaps many rewards.

Man the maker—*homo faber*—is not entirely determined by forces outside himself. His own capacities for self-reflection, invention, and innovation constitute in him the *imago Dei:* The image of God the Creator. The human person acts in a self-planned, creative, intelligent way. He makes his own decisions about himself. This is the radical theology Pope John Paul II propounds. It is in sharing in the creativity of the Creator that the human subject fulfills his vocation. It is in using his own creative talents that the human person follows "the will of the Creator that work should enable man to achieve that 'dominion' in the visible world that is proper to him."[39] In this vocation, the human person gains "dominion" over every force of mere determinism. The human person is *not* entirely the creature of nature and of society, but is capable of dissent, of heroism, of fidelity to his own individual calling. That same human person expresses the will of God in self-realization.[40] This is a profound theory of individualism—perhaps better to be called personalism (in the spirit in which Jacques Maritain distinguishes between the person and the individual).[41]

The creation theology of Pope John Paul II is clearly different from recent liberation theology, although its aims for peace, justice, and liberty remain the same. Creation theology differs from liberation theology, first, in rejecting the thesis of class struggle; second, in justifying capital as the material embodiment of human labor down the ages, while stressing the priority of labor; third, in rejecting the primacy of the contrast between oppression and liberation, in favor of the contrast between the absence and the presence of creativity; fourth, in emphasizing the strict connection between the human person as the subject of labor and his right to the fruits of his labor, including the right of ownership; fifth, in highlighting the danger of nationalization, collectivization, and socialization in which a "new class" of government administration comes to power, "claiming for itself a monopoly of the administration and disposal of the means of production and not refraining even from offending basic human rights"[42]; sixth, in interpreting the meaning of "socialization" more exactly than ever before, so as to preserve in it respect for the individual human person and his rights to private property:

We can speak of socializing only when the subject character of society is ensured, that is to say, when on the basis of his work each person is fully entitled to consider himself a part owner of the great workbench at which he is working with everyone else.[43]

As means to this end, the pope recommends several techniques not only entirely compatible with democratic capitalist practice, but already beyond the experimental stage. In particular, he emphasizes "associating labor with the ownership of capital, as far as possible" and "producing a wide range of intermediate bodies with economic, social, and cultural purposes."[44] The latter is an invitation to the associative principle which Tocqueville found so striking in American life,[45] the "mediating structures" about which Peter Berger and Richard John Neuhaus have written persuasively.[46] The former is practiced—but not nearly as broadly as it ought to be—not only in the rapidly growing employee stock ownership plans (ESOPs), but also in pension fund investments, profit-sharing plans, and corporative worker-ownership.[47]

The pope adds in an important paragraph:

The person who works desires not only due remuneration for his work; he also wishes that within the production process provision be made for him to be able to know that in his work, even on something that is owned in common, he is working "for himself." . . . In the mind of St. Thomas Aquinas, this is the principal reason in favor of private ownership of the means of production. While we accept that for certain well-founded reasons exceptions can be made to the principle of private ownership—in our own time we even see that the system of "socialized ownership" has been introduced—nevertheless the personalist argument still holds good both on the level of principles and on the practical level. If it is to be rational and fruitful, any socialization of the means of production must take this argument into consideration. Every effort must be made to ensure that in this kind of system also the human person can preserve his awareness of working "for himself."[48]

Finally, creation theology aims actually to *improve* the lot of the poor. In this way, it overcomes a nagging difficulty in liberation theology, which rhetorically announces an "option for the poor" without in any way conceiving of an economic system creative enough actually to raise up the economic standing of the poor. In rejecting an economic theory based entirely upon "growth," a theory lacking due emphasis upon the need to *distribute* the fruits of growth, liberation theology is on solid ground. But by depending upon tried-and-failed socialist experiments in economics during the past forty years, liberation theology offers the poor a stone. "The economic system and the production process benefit precisely when these personal values are respected," the pope writes, when "the human person can preserve his awareness of working 'for himself.' "[49]

The human person is a creator and nowhere more so than in his daily economic tasks. Entire economies must become creative. Subsistence living is no longer enough. In virtually every nation of the world, huge tracts of arable land now go uncultivated. There is virtually no nation which could not be self-reliant in agriculture.[50] Yet a great many nations are not able now to feed themselves. This lack cannot fairly be ascribed to nature or to nature's God. It must be ascribed to national *systems* of political economy. Nations like India have shown during the past decade how formerly food-dependent nations can, by making systemic changes (especially in incentive structures) and by popular use of agricultural science, move not only to self-reliance in foodstuffs but even to the exportation of foods.[51] In a word, the possibilities of human creativity must be tapped.

The Creator did not treat all nations equally in their natural endowments. Culture differs from culture. Each person is incarnated in a particular setting of nature and a particular national history, "the great society to which man belongs on the basis of particular cultural and historical links." Each national culture "is not only the great 'educator' of every man, even though an indirect one (because each individual absorbs within the family the contents and values that go to make up the culture of a given nation); it is also a great historical and social incarnation of the work of all generations."[52] Yet in each of these national locations, in each of these historical cultures, the human person is made in the image of God. Each has the vocation to work and to create. Creation theology does not set person against person, class against class, nation against nation. It calls forth the human capacity to create a new world, *novus ordo seclorum* (to use the traditional American phrase in a way which transcends its parochial limits).

As a pioneer in the creativity which every nation of the world may express, the United States has a special role to play in the task of development in which the world is now engaged. Some experts estimate that 800 million persons on this planet are living in abject hunger. Yet just 200 years ago, the entire population of the earth—mostly living lives which might be aptly described as "solitary, poor, nasty, brutish, and short"—also numbered 800 million. It is the tremendous creativity of modern work which has allowed the population of the earth to rise to 4.6 billion persons, some 3.6 billion of whom have escaped the most abject poverty. The task before us, a task demanding all the creativity we possess, is to improve the lot of our poorest brothers and sisters. That is our "option for the poor." Pope John Paul II calls us to it, not in the mode of resentment and hostility, in the fashion of worldly ideologies, but in the mode of a theology of creation, in faith and in love. His is authentic Christian teaching, rooted both in centuries of reflection upon the Word of God and in reflection upon the experience of our time. It, too, is a theology of *praxis:* of what works for the human person in his subjectivity, and for "the economic system itself and the production process." What works is social organization for personal creativity. A society so constructed reflects the image of the Blessed Trinity, the Creator of all things, Lord of history, Spirit brooding over dark creation.

# Part III

# ETHOS, VIRTUES, AND INSTITUTIONS: THE FUTURE DEVELOPMENT OF CATHOLIC SOCIAL THOUGHT

What then ... is an "ethic" which by definition makes a theme of the ethical? And what is an ethicist? We can begin more easily by saying what, in any case, an ethic and an ethicist cannot be. An ethic cannot be a book in which there is set out how everything in the world actually ought to be but unfortunately is not, and an ethicist cannot be a man who always knows better than others what is to be done and how it is to be done.

—DIETRICH BONHOEFFER, *Ethics*

The degree of well-being which society enjoys today would be unthinkable without the dynamic figure of the businessman, whose function consists of organizing human labor and the means of production so as to give rise to the goods and services necessary for the prosperity and progress of the community.

—JOHN PAUL II, address in Milan, June 1983

# Catholic Social Thought in the Future: Toward a Theology of Commerce and Industry

No sketch of the commercial republic should neglect to stress that, as a model both for a national polity and for the entire trading world, it tended to ignore or transcend the conventional divisions within nations and among them. Its eighteenth-century proponents could realistically urge men to consider their larger interdependence without expecting (or even desiring) the neglect of national interest and identity, for commerce, properly understood and reasonably conducted, would serve both man and citizen. Commerce inclined men to consider one another primarily as demanders and suppliers, to consider the world as constituting "but a single state, of which all the [particular] societies are members." Commerce was preeminently traffic in movable things that have little if any identification with a particular state of the kind real property necessarily has. In what Adam Smith called "the great mercantile republic"—by which he meant all producers and traders of movables—the owners and employers of capital stock were properly citizens of the world and "not necessarily attached to any particular country." What began as a simple recognition of our separate and common needs would end in a complex, ever-changing interdependence. Even as each labored intently to satisfy his own wants, men would become commercial cousins, cool fellow-citizens of a universal republic. . . . The contrast with and opposition to the Christian and Greek worlds could hardly have been greater.

—RALPH LERNER in *Liberation South, Liberation North*

What will Catholic social thought look like on the hundredth anniversary of *Rerum Novarum* in 1991? Or in 2001? It has undergone many rapid developments in recent years. It is certain, having learned from experience, to develop further.

## 1. THE POLITICAL ECONOMY OF DEVELOPMENT

Its most pressing need is to move from general principles of "social justice" to an image of the *institutions* most likely to make the observance of these principles regular and routine. A concrete image of the institutions of the future is always necessary in political philosophy, because the latter is an exercise in practical intellect and is ordered toward action. Action must have a concrete goal, formed first in active imagination. Such an exercise, in fact, was first undertaken by the Catholic philosopher Jacques Maritain, the true architect of the modern Catholic tradition of human rights and democracy, in *Integral Humanism*.[1]

Maritain distinguished between practical reasoning that is *practical-practical*, concerned with what to do now, and that which is *practical-ideal*, concerned with the concrete imagining of what might practically be done during a lifetime.[2] Both sorts of reasoning are the opposite of utopian thinking. But reasoning about the *practical-ideal* does share with utopian thinking a concern to imagine the future. It differs from utopian thinking (which is, literally, "no place") in limiting itself to a future which is practicable, that is, a goal which practical steps begun today might, with luck, actually achieve, due account being taken of known obstacles and unforeseen evil contingencies.

Because practical reasoning is ordered to action, and because action is ordered to concrete goals, practical reasoning depends heavily upon the exercise of the practical imagination. But to imagine is always to be concrete and thus to foreclose other possibilities.

It is true that Catholic social thought is, and must be, universal and transcendent. It cannot be locked into one stage only of historical development. It cannot endorse a set of institutions that work well in certain cultures but which, for various reasons, would not work for others. Nonetheless, Christianity is an incarnate and historical religion, devoted to working within the real texture of concrete history. Provisionally, it must choose this, not that, discerning as best it can the institutions of the moment that meet its tests of practical wisdom. It will always demand yet more of these institutions than any such institutions can deliver. In this sense, it works always as yeast in dough; its principles are dynamic and never in this world to be fully at rest.

Thus any institutions which Catholic social thought might imagine as its practical ideal must meet one particularly severe criterion. They must be reformable from within. That is, they must be inherently dynamic, open not only to the criticism of Catholic and humanistic conscience from within, but also to practical steps toward further reform. They must also be subject to the remedies always needed by human institutions, if the latter are to resist natural tendencies toward sin, error, and decline. "Politics," Peguy said, "always begins in mysticism; mysticism always ends in politics." A practical ideal leads to programs and institutions, which never fully realize that ideal and which always generate their own sources of decline. It is difficult to achieve social progress in history; it is even harder to maintain it. Asked as he strode from the Constitutional Convention what had been achieved for the people, Benjamin Franklin told the inquiring Mrs. Powell, "A republic, *if you can keep it.*"

As we have learned, Catholic social thought has at long last settled on the fundamental principle of the dignity of the individual human person. It has incorporated into itself the liberal institutions of human rights. Following Maritain, it has distinguished the *person* from the *individual,* and it has emphasized the social dimension of human personality inherent in the *common good.* To speak of the individual is to look, merely externally, as it were, at the individual as a member of a group; to speak of the person is to emphasize the internal liberties and responsibilities of his or her free intellect and will. Further, it has recognized, again following Maritain, the distinction between *society* and the *state.* The organs of government, or even of political parties, are not the only social organs for defining or for realizing the common good. There are many other social agencies, from the family to voluntary associations, from the free press and universities to the churches, which contribute to full and free social life. From the fact of a social obligation, one cannot conclude that the *state* must fulfill it; these social agencies, most of them voluntary, capable of social action, are more in accord with human liberty. Finally, Catholic social teaching has recognized both the fact and the social benefits of pluralism, even with respect to conceptions of human nature and destiny at variance with its own.

In a sense, Jacques Maritain is the great genius of modern Catholic social thought, at least in the political order. It was his achievement to think through the basic concepts inherent in the most worthy liberal institutions, those of human rights particularly, and to reformulate them in the language of the *philosophia perennis,* the language of Aristotle and Aquinas, which has so long been the central patrimony of Catholic intellectual life. In doing so, Maritain blazed the path which John XXIII so brilliantly summarized in his treatise on human rights in the first part of *Pacem in Terris.*

John Courtney Murray, S.J., (1904–1967) made another important contribution. Indebted to Maritain, Murray thought through the inarticulate premises of American institutions of religious liberty. It was given to him later, in person at the Second Vatican Council, to make them accessible to the universal Church. Murray's work was crucial in Vatican II's great Declaration of Religious Liberty, guided through the Council by Paul VI. Murray recognized that there were three sets of premises essential to the argument. One set was theological, another philosophical, and the third political or institutional. His stress upon this last set of premises is an original and enduring contribution.

Theological premises were needed to clarify the relation between liberty of personal conscience in the free assent of faith and the theological obligations both of persons and of communities to seek God and to follow truth. Philosophical premises were needed to achieve concepts of the person, society, state, the common good, pluralism, dialogue, and the rest. Political or institutional premises were needed to show how conflicting values and purposes would actually be met in practice. For it is not enough to have correct theological and philosophical premises and to argue logically. It is also necessary to show how, institutionally, all rights and values are respected, in due proportion, through the routines and regularities of ordinary practice. The design of such institutions requires a special order of practical wisdom, beyond a capacity for correct theological and philosophical argument.

This is the new frontier of Catholic social thought. To have achieved clear theological and philosophical conceptions and principles for social questions is a great achievement, many decades in the making. To grasp the sorts of institutional designs which will make the achievement of such principles routine and regular in the working of human institutions is a further—and indispensable—task.

Murray is also important for another reason. He grasped more clearly than most the often overlooked insight of St. Thomas that the social order is grounded in civil conversation. Since human beings are creatures of insight and choice, their proper mode of forming societies is different from that of other animals. A human social order rests upon a consensus of practical reason. A social order which appeals to something less than intellectual conviction and voluntary commitment violates the nature of men and women. Human beings achieve such practical consensus only through reasoned dialogue, conducting themselves with civility, exchanging points of view and arguments until reasoned agreement is attained.

To be sure, on many matters, civilized persons must agree to disagree. But social policy cannot go forward until there is at least a sufficient consensus on matters of practice, even when each party to the consensus might yield consent for theoretical reasons quite different from those of others. If social life demanded uniformity of theoretical reasons, it could seldom be truly free and rooted in conscience. Happily, a consensus on practical matters is more easily reached. The maintaining of a civil conversation is, therefore, the essence of a free and democratic society worthy of human beings.

Catholic social thought based on such principles, it is clear, cannot be fully realized within any and all institutional structures. To be sure, the Word of the Gospels applies within any and all types of institutions. But not every type of institution incarnates the full implications of the vision of human beings expressed in the Gospels. In an important sense, no imaginable institutions within history—always, as the Gospels teach, a history of sin, error, and contingency—reflect the fullness of the Gospels. All will be flawed. Thus the institutions of this world must always be designed for human beings who are frail, who often err, and who sometimes willfully choose evil. It is not Christian to design institutions in the expectation that any human being will be always faithful to the Gospels.

While Catholic social thought, therefore, can never be bound to the *status quo,* it also can never yield to the sort of perfectionism or utopianism which assumes that any human being will act always wisely, justly, and in charity. While such virtues must be encouraged in season and out, and even always applied as the standard which, with God's grace, human beings are bound to meet, Catholic social thought may not design institutions in the expectation that such virtuous living may normally be counted upon. To live as a saint is a heroic act. Further, even saints often sin, often err, and still more often lack political wisdom. Catholic social thought, therefore, is limited to designing institutions which afford checks and balances, as well as means of redress against the predictable frequency of human sinfulness.

Finally, if human beings are to live in civil conversation, it follows that the economic base of society must everywhere be raised up from its immemorial levels of poverty, illiteracy, ignorance, apathy, and bare subsistence (or less). Human persons are embodied; their common good, even the good of civil conversation, has as its precondition a sufficient material base. Many societies both of yesterday and of today have never provided such a material base to all their citizens. Therefore Catholic social thought, which developed first (in Aquinas) with respect to *political* philosophy, has in modern times had to attend to *economic* questions. Until human beings learned how to produce wealth in a regular and sustained way, there was no practical possibility of eliminating this world's almost universal poverty, illiteracy, disease, and ignorance. In the year 1800 there were only 800 million persons on this planet, and the average age at death hovered at nineteen or twenty. In France Victor Hugo had described *les misérables,* but travelers from Europe who visited other continents found poverty and other ills far worse than in their own experience. As John XXIII observed in 1963, not all parts of the world have developed equally or at an equal rate.

Adam Smith—whose work is, alas, much disdained and seldom studied in Catholic circles—was the main discoverer of the causes of wealth, and the first to conceive of universal development and universal interdependence. The drafters of the US Declaration of Independence observed truly that "all experience has shewn that mankind are more disposed to suffer, while evils are sufferable, than to right themselves by abolishing the forms to which they are accustomed." Today, however, everyone speaks of the "awakening" of the whole world to new possibilities of development.

An objective observer must, therefore, recognize that the term "development" has itself appeared at a relatively late moment in history. So also has the initial breakthrough which grounds that term in historical fact. Imagine a chart on which every people and culture of the world is listed, a chart which is organized in a graph illustrating the decades in one dimension, and the achievement by each of these peoples and cultures in the various measures of development (infant mortality, longevity, nutrition, literacy, education, and the rest) in another dimension. Such a chart reveals instantly that development is like a course through history along which peoples and cultures move at various rates. If one further imagines ours as the Age of Development, still incomplete, one can see how far the peoples and cultures of the world have come and how far they have yet to go. If, by supposition, one dates the beginning of Development at about A.D. 1800, and imagines that certain standards constituting the full development of all will be met, say, by 2050, the Age of Development will then span 250 years. If that is plausible, we have now reached the three-quarter mark. The declaration by the United Nations of the First and the Second Decades of Development (1960–1980) implies some such temporal map.

It is clear enough that the production of a material base sufficient to feed, clothe, house, educate, and employ the nearly 5 billion persons which the world will shortly be supporting remains an immense and unprecedented human task. It is a task which the plural moral, religious, and humanistic traditions of the human race impose upon us.

Catholic social thought has need, therefore, not only of political wisdom, as evidenced in its recent full embrace of the concepts and institutions of human rights, but also of economic wisdom. How is new wealth to be produced in a sustainable and progressive way? How are the capacities of individuals to invent and to create everywhere to be unleashed? What sorts of economic institutions give best promise of meeting human needs swiftly, efficiently, and universally?

To their credit, thinkers of the left have been among the first to confront the universal problem of poverty and need. Their own current bias, derived from Marxism, is to neglect the creative task of producing new wealth, while identifying the maldistribution of current wealth as the *cause* of poverty. A harsh version of this theory fosters the excitation (conscientization) of envy and class struggle. Milder versions invoke the "theory of dependency," which holds that the rich nations are the cause of the poverty of the poor nations. Dependency theory, first advanced in the 1960s, has not held up well to empirical analysis. It fails to explain both why some recently poor nations (such as Japan) have made rapid progress and why some nations highly favored in nature both in mineral and in agricultural resources do relatively poorly. It fails, too, to explain why some minority cultures, even when discriminated against, do well even within poor nations. Most of all, however, dependency theory fails to diagnose the potential causes of wealth within poor nations and to offer practical proposals for producing greater wealth.

There is, of course, some truth in dependency theory, if only its suggestion that one effect of the rapid worldwide spread of industry and commerce since World War II is to have made the world, as Adam Smith foresaw, economically interdependent. The exigent needs of the poor make an undeniable claim upon the rest of us.

But what sort of claim? What would actually work? The goal of any efforts in this area is to overcome poverty. This necessarily means producing and distributing new wealth, since no one desires to *increase* the dependency of LDCs by making them permanent wards of other nations. Catholic social thought is firm on the point of national self-reliance.[3] There are, therefore, two parts to this question. What can citizens of the more highly developed nations do to assist the LDCs in their own quest for self-reliance? And what should the LDCs do in order to attain economic self-reliance?

The first question is easy to answer in brief, if cryptic, form. Citizens from the developed world must do everything possible to help the less fortunate. This includes, above all, creative practical thinking, for the key to wealth is the human mind. It also includes practical assistance—not through money alone—on a scale not yet seen. Dozens of practical suggestions have been made by scores of commissions and study groups. Every suggestion has also been criticized by others, often of different philosophical views, on the grounds that it won't work, is insufficient, or is counterproductive. But no method of assistance can be expected to carry a guarantee or to be beyond criticism. One can, therefore, reply in the short locution: "Do *everything* possible, keep your eye on what works, and persevere." There is plenty of room for a diversity of methods. There is no end to what needs to be done. And we should not patronize the poor, as if what has worked for ourselves and others cannot work for them; we ourselves are the children of poverty. For the moment, I leave a discussion of particular strategies until later.

The fundamental question is the second one, how to attain self-reliance. For no amount of aid will make up for a deficiency of indigenous institutions in the recipient nation. And even if no external aid were forthcoming, each poor nation would be only as vital as its own institutions. The principle of self-reliance applies at both these extremes and in all the (more likely) circumstances in between. But what should poor nations do? What institutions should they try to build?

There is no question here of trying to imagine one set of institutions equally suitable to every culture. On the other hand, most poor nations must confess that their existing institutions leave them poorer than they would like to be. The desire for development is a desire for institutional change. What changes should poor nations undertake?

Since much depends upon the ethos of each culture (even among minority cultures within nations), we must treat different cultural groups differently. Since there are only 160 nations, we could treat each individually; the list would not be much more complex than the periodic table of individual chemicals. Yet many nations share a similar culture. It is already widely accepted that Western European nations, Australia, Canada, Israel, and the United States, even in their diversity, share a common ethos, and that the Soviet bloc nations live under a regime which attempts to achieve all possible uniformity. Similarly, it is illuminating to link together the nations guided by the Islamic ethos. The nations of South America also share the ethos of a distinctive family of cultures, as do those of Central America and the Caribbean. The nations of the East Asia rim share an ethos which has various diverse roots in the Confucian ethic of family, hard work, the ardent pursuit of education, and immense social discipline. In this respect, Japan, the recognized leader of the region, shares much with South Korea, Taiwan, Singapore, Malaysia, and Hong Kong. The vast population of China represents yet another ethos, an unstable blend of Confucianism and Marxism. The largest democracy in the world, India, shares a distinctive ethos, blending many religious cultures, chiefly Hindu, with British institutions and Fabian ideals. The nations of black Africa, rich in natural resources, represent yet another family of nations sharing many family resemblances.

Looked at in this way, the diversity of the modern world is not overwhelming. Cultural ties link many diverse nations in nine or ten sets of ethical and institutional families.

Of these cultural groupings in the developing world, the Catholic Church has special ties to certain nations in every part of the world, but especially to the nations of Latin America. For purposes of discussion, therefore, we might wisely focus attention upon what Catholic social thought ought in the future to be teaching the peoples of Latin America. What changes ought Latin American peoples to undertake, in order to ease the sufferings of the poor?

Latin America is a region of immense geographical and cultural diversity. Yet virtually all its nations share Latin culture, languages, and Catholic faith. The continent is rich in natural resources of many kinds. Every nation among them has sufficient arable land and a sufficiently favorable climate to be able to feed itself. If Latin Americans shared the ethos, the virtues, and the institutions of the Japanese, they would assuredly be among the economic leaders of the world. The secrets of producing wealth do not seem to be altogether obscure. One may learn from those who have mastered them. In the Japanese case, this is particularly helpful, since in 1950 Japan ranked lower in economic development than several nations of Latin America.[4]

To a remarkable degree, the secrets of producing wealth are spiritual. A very great deal depends upon insights, attitudes, psychological disciplines, habits of social cooperation, a capacity for organization, a passion for literacy and education, and a spirit of invention, creativity, and economic activism. Minorities which share such spiritual qualities typically demonstrate economic advancement even in the midst of majority populations still suffering considerable poverty.[5] The *cause* of the wealth of nations is chiefly the human spirit, focused in a creative and productive way.[6]

There is much Catholic social thought can do in diagnosing, analyzing, and teaching the requisite spiritual attitudes. Paul VI was correct to warn developing nations that they should not surrender their traditional virtues and ethos lightly, in order to imitate such vices as excessive individualism, cupidity, materialism, or superficial consumerism.[7] But *these* are not the causes of wealth. On the contrary, they are vices which corrupt and undermine economic growth. Furthermore, as widely different cultures such as those of Japan, Costa Rica, and Jordan show, the road to sustained economic growth is not univocal. Cultural diversity flourishes under conditions of democracy and a modern capitalist economy. It is true, nonetheless, that entrance upon the stage of international communications and trade does play a certain role in bringing cultures together, in allowing them to learn from and to become closer to other cultures, and to create at least the beginnings of a diverse but unified world culture.

Individuals must, of course, *choose* the ethos through which they express their humanity. Cultural diversity is the seedbed of creativity, in the sense that a broad range of alternative points of view increases the probabilities of flexible and creative response to world trends. The corollary to this proposition, however, is that some peoples will do better in certain activities than other peoples do, in accordance with the attitudes, habits, and practices nourished in the ethos of each. As one ethos differs from another, so will the pattern of actions likely to spring from it. Thus, in choosing an ethos, each people also chooses its place in the unequal pattern of national achievements. Some peoples highly favored by nature do not make use of their advantages as well as other peoples less favored, and succeed less well in achieving economic growth. What peoples *cannot* do is choose one ethos and then complain of the disadvantages within which it constrains them. Who wills the end must also will the means.

Observing the differential savings rates of diverse peoples in the middle of the nineteenth century, John Stuart Mill noted that *culture* plays a decisive role in the willingness of individuals, aggregated in nations, to forego consumption in order to save, accumulate capital, and invest in the future. Some peoples of equal economic product save far more from present consumption than others do.[8] Some live for today—*carpe diem*, as the ancient proverb put it—while others invest in the future. Over time, the latter are bound to acquire economic advantages.

What orients one culture more to the present, another more to the future; one to consumption, the other to savings?* It is, in part, a difference in spiritual attitude. But this, too, is affected by social institutions, by cultural habits, by the example of others, and by the presence or absence of stable political conditions. Paul VI blames those wealthy persons in the LDCs who do not invest in the future of their own nations, but send their savings abroad.[9] This is an astute point. On the other hand, the depredations committed upon domestic economies by successions of dictators of various ideologies, rampant inflation, threats of confiscation, recurrent devaluations, and other *institutional* hazards combine to make ethical practices such as the pope favors seem not to be wise but foolhardy. There are many ideologies about the proper role of government. Yet objective analysts can agree that governments which do not at the very least provide long-range stability in the rules and regulations of economic life profoundly penalize the providence of individuals and families.

In such intercultural comparisons, there are many puzzles. Latin America possesses vast stretches of unclaimed arable land. Yet even on the land made productive over generations, few if any Latin American nations during the nineteenth century turned their agricultural wealth into capital, investing it in the future. By contrast, the small farms of Great Britain were habitually capitalized—that is, gains were prudently saved and invested in commerce and industry—so that from a much lower agricultural base Great Britain built up a store of capital in the generations preceding the nineteenth century, on which the subsequent Industrial Revolution was based. Why did this not happen in the early history of Latin America? Perhaps the Catholic ethos, which seemed then to oppose capital formation and investment, played some role. If not, what did?

Thus it seems useful for the future development of Catholic social thought to ask itself about its own role in generating an ethos, a set of appropriate virtues, and those institutions which are favorable to economic progress. *These are fundamentally spiritual values.* They fall entirely within the mission of the Church.

## 2. THE SPIRIT OF ECONOMIC PROGRESS

> Though the ordinary work of society remained to be done by ordinary men, the commercial republic promised these citizens literally a new birth of freedom and invested them with a new sense of self-esteem. For now, as these men collectively and for the first time assumed decisive political and social significance, they found their aspirations raised, their energies stirred and directed, their capacities enlarged. They

---

*I do not mean to imply that savings are the sole source of new capital. Profit-making economic activities also generate new capital. More often overlooked, an intelligent use of credit—then invested in profit-making activities—also generates new capital.

would move forward with confidence, believing that "one Man of tolerable Abilities may work great Changes, and accomplish great Affairs among Mankind" if only he brought the proper method and diligence to his task. They would move forward with no apology to those who might view their concerns as "trifling Matters not worth minding or relating," for a "seemingly low" or trivial matter, when recurring frequently, gained "Weight and Consequence." They would act on the belief that "Human Felicity is produc'd not so much by great Pieces of good Fortune that seldom happen, as by little Advantages that occur every Day." Thus, in promoting their private affairs and tending to their public business—however slight or narrow—they could look forward to physical gratification, enhanced social standing, and the satisfaction of performing an acknowledged public service. Even their notions of what *is* their business grew; they would come to take a selfish interest in the public weal.

—RALPH LERNER in *Liberation South, Liberation North*

Reflecting on his experience in the United States more than 150 years ago, the French Catholic writer Alexis de Tocqueville jotted two columns on a page of his notebook. Over one he wrote "religion" and over the other "a commercial people." Under the latter, he wrote: "egoism, cupidity, and pride." Under the former, he wrote: "Religion creates a barrier, it is a brake."[10] His vision may be said to be one proper to an aristocrat. It dramatically misperceives the spirit of economic life. Consider solely the fact that the Protestant reformers accused the Catholic religion precisely of egoism, cupidity, and pride. It is a kindergarten notion to believe that "a commercial people" is more given to such perennial vices than "religion." All around the world, even as Toqueville wrote, the leaders of religion had amassed massive landholdings and held entire nations under oppressive taxes.

A close examination by Catholic social thinkers of the institutional restraints within a commercial republic is long overdue. The first imperative of a society committed to economic progress is to convert wealth to capital, consumption to savings, miserly hoarding to investment in the future. Far from being immoral or even amoral, such a conversion is an act of self-denial and the acceptance of responsibility for the future. It instructs those who would follow such a pattern in self-discipline, frugality, forethought, and a venturing spirit. For such reasons, Max Weber held that what is most distinctive about the new order of economic progress is spiritual. He may have been too narrow in calling that spirit "Protestant" or even "Calvinist," since the Japanese, for example, are not typically either; he was trying to stress its "inner-worldly" character, its practicality. Weber was correct in perceiving that the new event in world history is a revolution of the spirit, an altered sense of the human vocation and religious obligation. Its aim is to eliminate poverty in all nations.

Further, the counterintuitive discovery that a relatively free market is a better *social* device than the statist economies of the age of mercantilism is itself of considerable spiritual importance. Proponents and critics alike have typically misdiagnosed it. Some proponents argue that the virtue of the market system is that it frees the intellect and the will of the individual; that it, therefore, empowers individuals in the realm of free choice; and that it binds individuals together in voluntary, rational, mutual contracts of agreement. Critics charge that the market is a device for encouraging excessive individualism; that it leads to anarchy; and that, untrammeled and unchecked, it hurts the weak to the benefit of the strong. The crucial point missed by both proponents and critics is that markets are *social* institutions, bringing multitudes of individuals together and obliging them to attend to aggregated patterns of choice.

In an important sense, markets *socialize* individuals, obliging them to be other-regarding. Further, markets are *impersonal,* blind to a person's race, creed, nationality, or social class. This is why many minorities, discriminated against in politics, education, and other fields, find liberty and success in markets. The goals served by markets are social, not personal; that is why markets do not, unless distorted by extraneous elements (which hinder their own operation), regard a person's individual characteristics in their essential exchange functions.

As Giovanni Sartori has observed, the fundamental paradox of market and Marxist systems has been ignored.[11] The fundamental Marxist proposition purports to regard *individuals in their individuality*—"From each according to his abilities, to each according to his needs." But the fundamental proposition of markets regards the common good: "The free market actually achieves the public good better than a statist economy." The market is indifferent to individuality, since it aggregates multitudes of choices in the impersonal factor of price; whereas through the collective will of the leadership, Marxism purports to attend to individuality. This paradox deserves public recognition.

Yet markets cannot function well in societies which do not meet certain preconditions. Three cultural deficiencies are especially noteworthy. Where peoples live close to subsistence and self-sufficiency, with relatively few goods or services to exchange, and with few means of transport to or communication with other sources of goods and services, markets are otiose. Second, market behavior requires that information costs be met. A literate, well-informed population can use markets far more beneficially than a population ignorant of the differences among preferred goods and services. Thus active markets are typically the result of higher levels of literacy and sophistication, except in those matters (such as foodstuffs and implements) well known to purchasers whatever their level of informational skills. Third, market behavior requires purchasing power. In some regions of the world, many live so close to subsistence that their entrance into markets is relatively infrequent. As a counterexample, however, the historical record shows many evidences of very poor persons (sometimes large proportions of an entire minority group) beginning in primitive markets with almost no purchasing power, and yet through that institution significantly and rapidly "bettering their condition."[12]

Catholic social thought has seldom or never examined commercial activities as a type of human work. Most papal references to labor seem to take as their informing image the industrial laborer, the artisan, or the peasant farmer. They fail to envisage the hundreds of millions of the world's Catholics who work in small businesses of their own. They ignore the barbers and beauticians, the tobacco shop owners, the storekeepers, the electrical contractors, the plumbing and heating firms, the bakery owners, the butchers, the restaurateurs, the publishers of ethnic newspapers, the rug merchants, the cabinetmakers, the owners of jewelry stores, the managers of fast-food restaurants, the ice cream vendors, the auto mechanics, the proprietors of hardware stores and appliance shops, the tailors, the makers of ecclesiastical candles, the lacemakers, and multitudes of others. If not a majority, a great bulk of the world's Catholics earn their living through the activities of commerce.

As Montaigne foresaw, furthermore, commercial activities temper the classic religious temper—prone to intolerance, righteousness, enthusiasm, and fanaticism—in ways that even religion must come to respect. Commerce requires attention to small losses and small gains; teaches care, discipline, frugality, clear accounting, providential forethought, and respect for regular reckonings; instructs in courtesy, friendliness, openness, and tolerance; softens the barbaric instincts and commands attention to manners; teaches fidelity to contracts, honesty in daily dealings, and concern for one's moral reputation. These qualities are, of course, ridiculed by artists and aristocrats, the passionate and the wild of heart. The regularity of commercial life establishes a regimen of asceticism. The romantic, therefore, heap disdain on the "petty bourgeoisie," the "small souls of shopkeepers," and over the historical arch of commerce they hang the sign CAVEAT EMPTOR. These satiric thrusts illuminate the ideal of commerce whose abuses they mock. "The petty bourgeois," one may hear at an academic cocktail party, "is a man who in dealing with others thinks mostly of himself, and in thinking of himself thinks mostly about the opinion of others." As a witticism, it is not bad. Regarding the ideals of courtesy, service, and reliability which set the moral standards for the bourgeoisie, it is not informative. Persons of commerce sell the books which make fun of them. They seldom write books of their own about the customers with whom they must deal, including their critics.

Persons of commerce have much at stake in the rule of law, in a sound currency and predictable governmental administration, in available credit, in conditions of peace and prosperity, and in a broad public spirit of cooperation and amity. Commerce is the name for free, mutual, and voluntary exchange among peoples. It is the normal activity by which interdependence is realized and the common good of all served.

It is an activity typically more unifying than politics, nationalism, religion, or conquest. Its nature is social, as is its function and as are the virtues it inculcates.

Many less-developed countries suffer under elites whose conspicuous consumption, cupidity, corruption, and indifference to their own populations are legendary. Typically, in such countries, commerce is neither well-established nor broadly based. Lacking a large middle class engaged in commercial activities, such nations typically exhibit an immense gap between the few wealthy and the many who are dismally poor. The absence of a thick and complex commercial life makes upward social mobility for the poor improbable.

Without a broadly based commercial class, the achievement of democracy is difficult and fragile. Contrariwise, wherever the commercial class grows in breadth and independence, its members typically chafe under rule by military dictatorships, organize political parties, and clamor for democratic institutions. A large commercial base is a necessary but not sufficient condition for the literacy, independence, and active citizenship on which democracy depends. It is no accident that the democracies of Western Europe, Australia, Canada, Israel, the United States, Japan, and Costa Rica rest upon a broad social base in commercial life.

Finally, commerce is the major institution both of invention and of bringing new inventions speedily to the service of peoples. One of the major (and most overlooked) institutions of our age is the law of trademarks and patents. This law nourishes creative intellect in industry and commerce by supplying the protection of royalties in reward for the often long and expensive search for new and better products or services. Yet even good ideas, if left to sit in unread papers in libraries, would never be brought to the service of peoples apart from commercial institutions eager to invest in bringing new products speedily to market. Many foolish and wasteful ideas, of course, are also brought to market, just as poor books vastly outnumber worthy ones. In the life of commerce as in the life of the mind, liberty to create, matched to social protection of the royalties accruing, brings much that is shoddy; but the good fruits justify liberty.

If one visits a tiny poor nation like Bangladesh, one is struck by the absolute necessity of commercial development. Although small in area, this poor nation is immensely fertile, fed by the delta of the Ganges and blessed with sun and rain. Since 1945, however, its population has grown from 39 million to 99 million. What to outsiders might seem like a "population explosion" seems to the Bengali a happy thing: their children are living. For the population of the land is growing, not because parents are having more children than they used to; on the contrary, most are having fewer. The average age of death of the Bengali has climbed from about nineteen in 1945 to just over fifty-five.

Bangladesh can no longer survive on agriculture alone; the land cannot be subdivided further. The only hope of millions is an expansion of industrial and commercial activities. Bangladesh will need to begin making for its own internal use light bulbs, refrigerators, stoves, bicycles, water pumps, and all the other objects of daily life, not only to afford its people basic decencies, but also to supply productive employment to its workforce. Self-sufficiency in food, while not yet attained, is not out of the question, since the land is so fertile and the growing seasons so many. Food-processing plants would help to preserve abundant harvests and to supply exports to lands whose growing seasons are less favored.

The Bengali are an able, amiable, hardworking, and aspiring people. Until late at night the streets of Dacca resound with construction and commercial activity. Many Bengali who are illiterate can recite the Koran by heart, and many shops and huts display a large portrait of the national poet, Tagore. The Bengali are a people of the word, even among those who are not literate. They need assistance in capital, management, and techniques of organization. Recognizing their own limits, they are willing and eager to have others come to teach and to help.

Such examples may be multiplied the world over. The creation of the hundreds of millions of new jobs the world will need in the next twenty years for the unemployed and the underemployed is a heroic challenge. It cannot be met by agriculture alone. Its fulfillment depends, disproportionately, upon a swift infusion of local commercial and industrial activism. Capital, of course, is in immensely short supply. Regulations and tax laws inhibit economic activism. In some cases, the ethos which would inspire economic activism, although natural to the human race, is inhibited by contrary customs. In other cases, the virtues of economic activism are not only not taught, but treated with disdain by elites of government, the arts, and religion. Commerce is regarded as parasitical, unworthy, and crass. Aristocratic, feudal, military, and religious traditions often oppose it. Public institutions inhibit and penalize it. Must Catholic social thought do likewise?

Economic activism is no less a part of co-creation, of sharing in the work of the Creator in bringing creation to its further completion, than political activism. The theology of liberation offers the world of the poor far less hope than the theology of creation. Political activism produces far fewer goods and services than economic activism, and it is surely not desirable that the state become the chief employer of its people. Catholic social thought has so far failed to recognize sufficiently the *economic* part of political economy, particularly in its spiritual and creative dimensions.

Finally, every poor nation ought to have as its first priority the feeding of its own people. As Nobel Prize winner Norman Borlaug has often said, every nation on this planet has sufficient arable land to feed its own people. There is hunger in the world, not because of God and not because of the niggardliness of nature, but chiefly because of government policies. Many governments set limits to food prices. This shortsighted policy obliges farmers to endure the hard work of farming at a financial loss. The obvious result is that farmers cut back on production. When India, long predicted to be a scene of bitter famine by 1984, removed its own price controls on food, farmers suddenly found new strips of unused land to farm. Food production rose and the increasing supply kept prices down. Farmers began to prosper. India has become a net exporter of food.

The world of the poor nations is far from realizing its own immense creative potential. More than a hundred national experiments in political economy have been tried by the new nations since 1945. Most have bitterly disappointed the dreams of their founders. Most were based on the mildly socialist (and intuitively attractive) premise that the best way to achieve economic development is through government planning. Yet no panel of experts, however bright, can plausibly make economic decisions for millions of their fellow citizens. What seems intuitively sound does not work in practice. The source of economic wisdom does not lie in the State, nor in expert planners; it lies in the millions of aspiring economic decision-makers, in the people, whose multitude of personal decisions, in the aggregate, add up to more intelligence than that possessed by any bureaucracy of planners. Unleashing the creative energies of the people is the single most important key, not only to respect for their individual human dignity, but to economic progress as well. The task in many nations is to stress the potential of every individual, and to strengthen each individual institutionally. It is an immense—but liberating—task.

The preconditions for that happy outcome are, as we have seen, many. A number of those preconditions fall directly in the realm of the human spirit: a favorable ethos; appropriate virtues; and favorable institutions. Catholic social thought, especially with respect to predominantly Catholic nations like those of Latin America, Poland, the Philippines, and elsewhere, is in a position to give leadership to the human spirit in these matters. Given the achievement of such things, there is much that the peoples of the developed world can offer by way of ideas, capital, and personal and organizational assistance of every sort. Without them, dependency can only grow.

But there is, of course, a rival theory. Paul VI seemed cautiously to license it in *Populorum Progressio* and *Octogesima Adveniens,* and in its earliest years the Pontifical Commission Justice and Peace seemed also to surrender to its enthusiasms. That view is that the poor world is poor because of the oppression of the rich nations. Thus the road to economic progress and the protection of human rights to be followed by the poor nations is that called, generically, "liberation theology." Typically, such theology rejects Marxism. Yet, also typically, it employs "Marxist analysis." In the place of "class struggle," it puts "liberation from oppression." How has liberation theology worked in practice?

# CHAPTER 10

# Liberation Theology in Practice

> Salvation and justice are not to be found in revolution but in evolution through concord. Violence has always achieved only destruction, not construction; the kindling of passions, not their pacification; the accumulation of hate and ruin, not the reconciliation of the contending parties. And it has reduced parties to the difficult task of rebuilding, after sad experience, on the ruins of discord.
>
> —JOHN XXIII *Pacem in Terris*, 162

> To our requests for specific information about the working of the new industrial order the Socialists, as a rule, answer in terms of prophesied results. They leave us in the dark concerning the causes by which wonderful results are to be produced.
>
> —JOHN A. RYAN *Distributive Justice*

There are by now probably more good accounts of liberation theology than there are examples of it.[1] For, as typically happens, only a very few theologians—in this case, led by Gustavo Gutierrez and Juan Luis Segundo—do the lion's share of the innovation; most of the rest is commentary. I will not summarize that teaching further. My aim here is to respond to it.

The underlying intention of liberation theology is to lift up the poor. The means for doing so is, first, to overturn institutions that keep them from being free participants in social decisions and that bind them to malnutrition, unemployment, disease, ignorance, and fear; and, second, to construct new institutions which will accomplish the opposite. This is a noble intention. It inspired Adam Smith to conduct his thousand-page *Inquiry into the Nature and Causes of the Wealth of Nations* (1776). It is the animating intention of all democratic capitalist societies. Its basic themes were first enunciated for our generation by Franklin Delano Roosevelt in 1941 in his famous speech on the "Four Freedoms," and by Harry S Truman after World War II.[2]

The difficulty with liberation theology is not its underlying intention. Rather, the difficulty arises from its *praxis*. Liberation theology, biblical realism (Reinhold Niebuhr, Jacques Maritain), and American pragmatism (William James, John Dewey, Sidney Hook) all agree that theory is not sufficiently tested solely by its conceptual clarity and logical consistency, but also by its practical consequences. Liberation theology certainly places considerable emphasis on the superiority of *praxis* to both *theoria* and *orthodoxy*. Even in its own terms, therefore, liberation theology must be judged by its praxis.

I wish to leave to one side an important theoretical objection to liberation theology. Some theologians believe that it so alters the meaning of "the poor" and "the oppressed," and the meaning of "salvation," "redemption," and "liberation," that it is not conceptually consistent (except by intention) with Christian theology; i.e., it is a kind of gnostic heresy. While I believe that there is merit in that charge, it is not the charge on which I would now rest most weight. For our present purposes, let us suppose that the scheme of action proposed by liberation theology *is* consistent with the teaching of the Jewish and the Christian scriptures about the promises held out by God to "the poor" and "the oppressed."

The two most insistent *practical* claims of liberation theology are the following: first, that its basic insights are validated by the "expressed conscience" of "the poor," testifying to one another in their *comunidades de base;* second, that liberation theology offers a *praxis* which flows from the consciences so expressed.

What sort of intellectual warrant should be given to public opinion, even if it is the public opinion of "the poor" and "the oppressed"? Even supposing that that public opinion has been rigorously gathered—a supposition nowhere verified in the literature of liberation theology— what reason is there for believing that it is not ideologically tainted? Extensive survey data are available for Latin America. Such surveys show that public opinion in various Latin American nations, especially among the peasants and the workers, is quite complex and seldom that of the liberation theologians.

It is one thing to claim that the poor ought to be heard. Of course they should. "The cry of the poor" may, further, even be said to be relatively privileged as a theological source, as compared with the testimony of the few wealthy or the fledgling middle class, not so much on the basis of truth or accuracy (which remain to be assessed) as on two other bases. First, one may suppose (although it is by no means certain) that theologians and other intellectuals who read books, give lectures, and appear on radio and television are more likely to be sympathetic to the rich and to the bourgeoisie, and, therefore, need to encourage one another incessantly to compensate by paying more attention to the poor. I believe that, in fact, this supposition is incorrect; in our generation, the "war on poverty" is major news everywhere, and few targets are easier to attack in print than "the rich" and "the middle class." Still, for argument's sake, let us grant the supposition. Second, one may suppose that the poor, who suffer various painful disabilities just because they are poor, are likely to voice real grievances. Their suffering should be eased. And their legitimate grievances should be rectified.

But it is sometimes also claimed, at least implicitly, that what the poor say is *ipso facto* true, and that the "analysis" of the situation given by the poor is *ipso facto* a true analysis. For this claim there is not the slightest shred of evidence.

What the poor cry out deserves to be sympathetically heard. It does not, however, suffice to still critical and practical inquiry. The poor may have things wrong. Their opinions are not necessarily God's, nor do they necessarily carry the warrant of truth.

For one thing, no more than others do the poor speak with one voice. Not all are Catholics. Not all are democrats. Not all are Marxists. The opinions of the poor are complex, multiple, various. The opinions of the poor deserve the same weight as those of any other social class and must, like them, meet tests independent of subjective desire. If the poor, for example, overwhelmingly supported Hitler, that would not make them—or Hitler—correct. If the Islamic poor overwhelmingly endorsed the annihilation of the Israeli people, that would not make them correct. If the Hindu and Islamic poor engaged in fratricidal bloodletting, that would not endow their activities with binding moral imperatives. If the poor of Latin America were to be entranced by a contemporary equivalent of Mussolini, that would not justify their every opinion and action.

*Comunidades de base* may be seen as a contemporary parallel to the voluntary associations in every social class which Tocqueville discerned in North America in 1832.[3] North Americans typically form small local communities, committees, study groups, and action groups in profusion. Each has some wisdom to contribute to the common good. None has intellectual warrant to dominate all others, not even if it were a majority formed around moral principles: a "moral majority."

Liberation theology seeks intellectual prestige by claiming to represent the voice of the poor. Whether liberation theologians actually do speak for a majority of the poor, however, is far from certain; and, even if they did, majoritarian opinion is by no means a warrant for truth. The truthfulness of liberation theology is not, and cannot be, established by basking in the prestige conferred upon the poor by Jewish-Christian culture. An "option for the poor" is entirely admirable; but the US Statue of Liberty expresses it, too. There remain many conflicting social philosophies which claim to lift up the "huddled masses, yearning to breathe free." The issue as to which does the better job of lifting up the poor is not settled by the claim to be speaking for the poor, but by actual achievement.

We come, then, to the other claim of liberation theology, that *praxis* is to be the decisive point of critical judgment. Very well, then. How is liberation theology to be assessed, on the testimony of its *praxis*?

Some good things must be said. Many persons inspired by liberation theology have diagnosed the abuses of tyrants (such as Somoza) and heroically given their lives in overturning them. Liberation theology has its martyrs. But not all martyrs, even in the revolt against Somoza, were inspired by liberation theology. Furthermore, several of the most vocal leaders among the liberation theologians in Nicaragua—Ernesto Cardenal, Miguel d'Escoto, and others—have been accused of betraying Nicaragua to a new oppression, that of a Marxist-Leninist clique held in power and ideologically held in line by Cuban and Soviet financing, military power, and secret police. The outcome is still doubtful. What cannot be denied is that the cause of liberation theology has already been wounded, perhaps mortally, by the *praxis* of liberation theologians among the Sandinist ruling class. Its moral correctness is at least not indisputable.

On a more general level, one of the most striking things about the writing of liberation theologians is its abstractness. Far from being descriptive, concrete, and practical, it is intricately speculative, ideological, and academic. Words like "praxis," "action," and "revolution" convey intellectual excitement. But one can read volume after volume of liberation theology without learning anything concrete about the economics, politics, or histories of the specific countries in which they are written. One learns from them almost nothing about the differences between Costa Rica and Nicaragua, or between Peru and Argentina. The teeming variety of the thirteen remarkably different nations of South America—so different again from the nations of Central America—is nowhere reflected. How can such abstruse books be credited with leading to *praxis?* Liberation theology, to date, is speculative; not practical.

On the other hand—to go back to an earlier point—what the *comunidades de base* often do, as opposed to what speculative theologians write about them, is what in North America we would call "social organizing." In the peasant cultures of Latin America and elsewhere, individuals are often tied by "organic" links to extended families and neighbors, but in the face of the larger world they have often seemed to be slumbering, passive, unorganized. By contrast, there is today a kind of "great awakening." The humble are often organizing themselves to dig a well, or to make legitimate demands upon local authorities for running water, pavement, or sanitation. *Praxis* of this type is highly commendable. The virture of social justice consists specifically in persons organizing themselves socially to redress injustice or to create new justice in down-to-earth, attainable ways. This aspect of liberation theology commands esteem; it could easily be translated into categories of thought familiar to North Americans. Exponents of liberation theology have, alas, often preferred to seem adversarial rather than collaborative.

One of the claims made by liberation theologians of Latin America, for example, is "dependence" on the United States, its multinational companies, and its military might. This subject is treated rhetorically, as if North Americans must simply agree with such claims. That cannot be conceded, however, until specific accusations are set forth, with their supporting evidence. For the historical economic performance of Latin America relative to that of North America, the United States is innocent until proven guilty.

No doubt, the United States has often *been* guilty. But the most sweeping claims do not seem to hold up. What does dependency theory explain? It purports to explain why Latin America is poor. But it offers Latin America no theory about development of wealth, which might help the region tap into its tremendous natural potential. It does not explain why the nations of Southeast Asia, less favored by nature and in the face of greater odds, have actually achieved greater development. It expresses resentment (however, in some cases, justified), but does not offer creative ways by which Latin America may do better in the future. It is a theory about poverty, which hardly needs explanation, rather than a theory for creating new wealth, which does.

For almost as many generations as the United States has been independent of Great Britain, Latin American nations have been independent of Spain and Portugal. One may concede that British institutions have been proved historically more favorable to the development of democracy, institutions of human rights, and economic creativity than Spanish or Portuguese traditions. Indeed, in the generations since independence, some Latin American nations seem to have prospered better than their "mother" countries, Spain and Portugal. Yet some Latin Americans, not only of the left, do not blame their current circumstances on Latin institutions, but rather upon the United States. This seems odd. For, until World War II, trade between North and South America was disproportionately small, as compared with trade between either and Europe. The decisive fact seems to be that most Latin nations remained predominantly statist and agrarian in their economies, rather than liberal, industrial and commercial. Most resisted the *liberalismo* of the British and the Americans, as uncongenial to the Latin ethos and offensive to its more aristocratic and (some thought) morally superior traditions.

Latin American literature is full of abuse for the alleged individualism, crassness, and materialism of Anglo-American commercial culture. The Latins prefer the aristocratic mode. Moreover, Latin America first encountered *liberalismo* in its French version, laicist, anti-clerical, materialist, and utopian. They met liberalism in Rousseau, not in Locke and natural law.

In natural resources, furthermore, Latin America is not inferior to North America. Some experts believe that Brazil alone (which is larger than the entire United States, Alaska aside) has natural resources greater than those of any nation on earth. If economic prosperity depended upon natural resources, Latin America would be wealthy, indeed.

Latin American theologians virtually never offer economic evidence for their assertions. Their argument seems to be *a priori:* "It is in the nature of capitalism to exploit; the United States is capitalist; QED." They seem to assume that North American corporations are not only inherently rapacious but clamoring to enter Latin American markets. During recent years, however, the process has been exactly in the opposite direction. Even regional giants like the United Fruit Company have been discouraged in Latin American markets, and have retrenched and diversified elsewhere. No US firm, for example, now maintains more than 10 percent of its gross investments in the Central America-Caribbean region. (Admittedly, this is the region in which the U.S. has sinned the most.)

In 1983 US citizens had a total of $883 billion invested overseas (foreign citizens had investments totaling $663 billion in the United States).[4] Three-quarters of this overseas investment is in Europe, Japan, Canada, and Mexico. Of the remainder, a larger part (about 16 percent of the total) is in Latin America, the rest in Asia and Africa. Each year, the American economy has a gross national product of more than $3 trillion. One can see instantly that the size of total US investment in Latin America is less than 1 percent of the annual US gross national product. Were all of Latin America closed to US investment, or even trade, the adjustment in the United States would be significant, but hardly major. "Dependency" seems an odd word for such a modest relationship, and not only from the US side. For even supposing that Latin America did not trade with North America at all (as with few exceptions it hardly did until World War II), but only with Europe, Asia, and Africa, its economic status would not be fundamentally altered.

Among economists, and especially among Marxists, dependency theory had a vogue in the 1960s. The case has not proved to be demonstrable; most have abandoned or seriously modified it. It is the sort of case that must be supported by evidence, not merely asserted. Liberation theology rises or falls with such evidence from *praxis.*

The case of Japan is particularly nettling for liberation theology. Its cities leveled in 1945, its capital base exhausted, its labor force horribly shrunken by vast losses of life from a decade of brutal warfare in China and throughout the Pacific, its reputation for quality of workmanship one of the poorest in the world, its experience with democracy virtually nonexistent, its dependence on the United States for several years virtually total, Japan has risen to be an economic power greater than all of Latin America together. Its poor have been uplifted. Its citizens enjoy liberties unprecedented in their long and noble history. Their island home, except for a climate favorable to agriculture, is one of the poorest lands of the earth in physical resources. The Japanese have demonstrated beyond a doubt that the secret to creating wealth lies in the human spirit: in wit, invention, concentration on the future, discipline, and cooperation.

The Japanese refuse to think of themselves as "victims" or "oppressed." Such self-images are passive, breed hopelessness, and throw the burden of decisive action upon distant others. The Japanese have instead thought of themselves as masters of their own destiny, as creators, and they set out to achieve what they have within a single generation brilliantly achieved, winning in peace what they could not win through war: preeminence as a peaceful, productive, commercial power.

The example of Japan is important for another reason. Seeking excuses for the relatively poor performance of Latin America (although, since 1945, Latin America has achieved spectacular rates of growth in literacy, education, technological sophistication, and both agricultural and industrial output),[5] liberation theologians tend now to rely upon the claim that "the terms of international trade" keep them poor. This accusation usually has three parts.

1. Massive unemployment in Latin America means that, even when there are advances in productivity in Latin American industry, these advances are passed along only to a relative few in the industrial workforce. It is alleged, accordingly, that wages are not forced to rise with increases in productivity as they would under conditions of full employment.

2. Some 80 percent of the exports of Latin America are of primary goods—such a coffee, cocoa, bananas, copper, and bauxite—and prices for these goods (most of which are easily replaced by substitutes) have been in decline for two decades. So Latin Americans fall farther and farther behind in paying international debts and in standards of living.

3. Most of the world's effective demand is concentrated in the hands of the citizens of the twenty-nine affluent nations of the world, so export industries in Latin America must concentrate upon production for that demand rather than upon producing goods for the needy in Latin America.[6]

These are plausible charges. To the extent they are true, they deserve serious attention. Still, the second and the third points obscure the truly important matter: the key to economic development in Latin America is a rapid and steady increase in the manufacturing sector, both to compensate for weaknesses in the market for single-crop commodities and to increase employment. Some of this manufacturing must be for export, to pay for foreign exchange.[7]

Thus the second objection says that demand for primary goods is falling, a serious matter since primary goods (chiefly agricultural) constitute the vast majority of exports. The third says that even though the export of manufactures is quite small, it would be wrong to raise it for export to the affluent. One asks: What manufactured goods do affluent Americans now purchase from Latin American producers? It is not easy to think of Latin American brand names in autos, electrical appliances, television, electronics, or any other products aimed at the affluent, as one thinks of brand names from Holland, Germany, Britain and Japan. The manufactured goods which flood US markets from Third World countries, indeed, appear to be those aimed at the *less* affluent shopper: cheaper leather goods, shoes, shirts, and other textiles.

Most of all, these objections beg fundamental economic questions. Quite apart from manufacturing for export, Latin American nations benefit internally by every new job they create in the manufacturing sector *aimed at their own populations*. First, this reduces their need for imports. Second, it helps solve the problem of unemployment facing every agrarian society, since work on the land simply cannot offer sufficient employment at current levels of population growth. Third, the growing millions of Latin Americans need all sorts of goods and services: schools, clinics, clothing, and appliances. Refrigerators, for example, are not luxuries when children require fresh milk and other foods; electric lamps are not luxuries for students. The huge domestic markets of Latin America provide ample opportunities for the growth of a highly successful industrial and commercial system. The Japanese have shown how quickly an economy can be transformed; the skills to do so are independent of race and culture and may be learned. The capital accumulation possible in such markets would also reduce the need for external investment from abroad.

It may be true that advances in productivity in Latin American industry are not broadly shared with the industrial labor force in the form of higher wages. That is an empirical point for economists to verify or to falsify. Yet it would be surprising if wages in manufacturing were not higher than other wages; in Latin America, they surely are. Moreover, the abundance of cheap labor gives Latin American manufacturers competitive advantages over producers who have more highly paid labor forces elsewhere. It is not impossible to turn disadvantages of one sort into advantages of another sort.

It should be noted, moreover, that the preponderance of US exports in recent years has shifted to primary goods such as foodstuffs, timber, and coal. It is no longer true that the United States only imports primary goods, while exporting manufactured goods.[8] Third World nations are producing a growing share of the manufactured goods traded in the developed world, while importing many primary goods. In this shift, the countries of East Asia, however, have been progressing faster than Latin America.[9]

One of the interesting features of international trade is that, more often than not, the *weaker* party benefits proportionately more by trade than the wealthier party. This may seem counterintuitive, but upon reflection the reason is apparent. To the wealthier party, gains from trade with poorer nations are typically marginal; substitutes are easily available; the terms of trade are not so immensely significant. Thus Japan and Western Europe, even when broken by World War II, swiftly became full competitors of the at first much stronger US economy. From producing 53 percent of the world's gross product in 1945, the US share has shrunk to 23 percent. In this way, the weak grow stronger, not so much by taking away from the stronger (the US economy is not weaker in 1983 than it was in 1945), as by more rapid internal expansion.

In considering per capita incomes, it is an arithmetical law that the "gap" between the richer and the poorer nations will increase, under ordinary conditions, *even when the lot of the poor within them is rising*. Consider a poor nation whose per capita income is $700 per year, while that of the top twenty most developed nations is over $9000 per year. If, year by year, the poorer country manages an almost impossible 10 percent annual increase in per capita income, while the wealthier countries expand by a sluggish one percent each year, the *absolute* gap grows ever wider. At the end of the first year, per capita income rises in the poorer country to $770, while that in the developed country rises to $9090: the earlier gap was $8300, the later one $8320. The poor are doing better; the wealthier nations, even in sluggish times, widen the gap.

The scandal of economic inequalities between nations is not the *gap* between them. That is a red herring. The scandal is that so many nations are not generating such economic activism as continually raises the lot of their poor. This is not a result of a "gap"; it is its cause.

The most urgent moral imperative is to raise the living standards of the poor. This goal is conceptually quite different from the proposal that all incomes in all nations should be equalized. Those who focus upon the inevitable fact of "the widening gap" do mischief, for two reasons. The first reason is their reliance upon an arithmetical law, whose practical significance for changing the lot of the poor is nil. The second reason is their neglect of the important and humane issue, about which a great deal can actually be done: raising the income and living standards of the poor. Attention to the incentives of production does far more in practice toward accomplishing this task then a self-destroying emphasis upon distribution. The moral focus ought not to be upon a vain effort to "narrow the gap," but upon empowering the creativity of the poor by freeing them for their inherent productivity.

A second law has to do with the "take-off" point. Until the very poor rise above a certain level of annual income—which some economists put at about $1000 per annum, but others somewhat higher—they have very little effective buying power and cannot purchase even what they need. Manufacturers, therefore, cannot sell to them, even though, in one sense, the needy represent a huge potential market. Among other reasons, this point induced Henry Ford to raise wages in his factories to a then unprecedented $5 per day so that, he said, workers could buy the cars they built. The higher wages, spreading to other industries, led to a larger effective market; the larger market generated both new jobs and thus still larger markets; the price of Ford autos fell from $800 to $200. At one point, nations are caught in a vicious circle; needs are great but demand and supply don't mesh. At some threshold point, the circle becomes beneficent, when demand and supply propel each other forward. Getting Latin Americans out of the vicious and into the beneficent part of the curve is critical.

In summary, liberation theology seems to fail the very test on which it places so much stress: the test of *praxis*. The "option for the poor" *is* the correct option. Everything depends, however, upon the next institutional step. If your intention is to create new wealth and to generate a highly mobile society, of great upward mobility for all and of rotating mobility among elites (as new elites constantly replace the old), the secrets for doing so are now well established. The most vital experiments today, even in the socialist world, concern various forms of return to private ownership, to incentives, and to markets. This is true in the USSR, in China, in Yugoslavia, in Hungary, and throughout the socialist world.[10] The gate to the creation of wealth is narrow and the way strait; not every method passes the test of praxis.

What most hinders liberation theology is a Latin tradition, many generations old, of blaming outsiders, while exempting oneself from responsibility for one's own future. The current form of this tradition is to aspire to the benefits of capitalism while refusing to recognize the moral validity of its requisite habits and institutions; of invention, forethought, saving, investing, punctuality, workmanship, and the like. This is perhaps an ethnic bias, at root, based upon disdain for Anglo-American (and Japanese) culture.

Cardinal Arns was once heard to say that it was not for the Church to say that capitalism or socialism is better; only, in his eyes, capitalism seems morally inferior, since each farmer must be allowed *to own his own land and to keep his profits for himself*. That is what the Cardinal calls socialism. But is it not a basic principle of capitalism? If liberation theology is for what works, it will one day discover that Marxism-Leninism is incompatible not only with the generation of broad, popular prosperity, but also with the practice of democracy. For only democracy guarantees associations of persons the power to defend their own human rights institutionally and with effect. In practice, private ownership, differential incentives, markets, and institutions of sustained economic invention and creativity seem to be necessary (if not sufficient) conditions for a practical, functioning democracy. This is because, without private ownership, citizens and their families have no substantial independence from the state. And when the presses are owned by the state, freedom of the press also languishes.

An objection often raised is that many nations in Latin America are already capitalist, but are not democratic; so capitalism and democracy do not necessarily go together. To this, the first response, as above, is that capitalism is a necessary but not a sufficient condition for democracy. The more important response is that Latin American states are not capitalist. It is true that most Latin American nations have markets and respect private property; but virtually all pre-capitalist societies did, too. In fact, Latin American economies remain pre-capitalist in their neglect of free markets, in favor of the sort of neo-mercantilism in which markets are disproportionately controlled by the state. Some describe Latin economies, not as democratic capitalism, but as state capitalism; typically, the state controls half or more of the economy. Second, agriculture, rather than industry or commerce, tends to dominate the economy; and a landed aristocracy, a pre-capitalist class, tends to set its agenda. Third, the commercial class is relatively small and the ethos of commerce is typically disdained. Fourth, the middle class, itself relatively small, is dominated by professional classes in law, government, journalism, medicine, and literary-academic life. Fifth, commercial and industrial skills in invention, entrepreneurship, management, marketing, and other practical domains are neither widespread nor highly prized. In a word, those sociological and ethical components are lacking which (a) give capitalism its special spirit and dynamism, and (b) make its practical habits of mind a suitable base for democratic practices. (By way of confirmation, it seems to be true that Costa Rica is both the most democratic and the most capitalist of Latin American nations.)[11]

To be specific, democratic institutions depend on the growth of a large and stable middle class. The ownership of property must be broad and, in opportunity, universal. Sociologically, this means the widest possible promotion of small businesses and productive enterprises; even the major corporations, for example, could do more than they are doing to include their workers in the role of ownership as well as of labor. Ethically, it means the diffusion of those ideals and habits which encourage prudence, frugality, savings, investment, risk-taking, invention, and entrepreneurship. It means an emphasis upon economic, rather than solely upon political, activism. It means a wise use of credit for productive, profit-making activities especially on the part of the poor. For neither revolutions nor political parties produce goods and services; these are the creations of economic activists.

Far from there being a correlation between dictatorship and a free market, the former long antedates the latter in modern history. What the free market is free *from* is state control. Inevitably, dictators are in practice destroyers of free markets. In Chile, the unilateral pegging of the exchange rate under the dictatorship of Pinochet has been immensely destructive of Chile's small-business sector. Under military dictatorships in Argentina and Peru, the state came to dominate those two economies in ways unprecedented in recent times.

It is the tragedy of liberation theology that it has been born in a part of the world in which democracy has long been fragile, not least because its underlying base in a free, inventive, and creative economy has been sadly lacking. The tradition of Catholic social thought seems also to be, in part, responsible for this gap in social *praxis*. For this tradition does not yet teach or promote the ethos on which a free economy is based: saving, investment, entrepreneurship, invention, and the virtues of commercial and industrial life. Its own traditional predispositions are agrarian (as in G. K. Chesterton's "distributism"). That may help to explain why Catholic cultures—from Southern Europe to South America, from Poland to the Philippines—lag behind other nations in the processes of economic development and stable democratic governance. Liberation theology, alas, intensifies the weakest features of the tradition. It offers, in practice, not so much a cure as a predictable decline, both in economic development and in personal and social liberty.

The prognosis for Catholic countries of the Third World is far less good than that for countries shaped by Confucius. It makes me sad to say this, since nothing in Catholicism makes such outcomes inevitable, except current unnecessary weaknesses in theological reflection. There are several things we could do. One is to study the cultural preconditions of economic growth. Which virtues and what sort of ethos need to be present in society, if economic development is to occur? Another is to study the cultural preconditions of democracy. Are the traditional Christian virtues sufficient as a base for democratic living, or do some new virtues need also to be learned? What sorts of institutions need to be established? Do not the practices of social cooperation, social trust, and social activism need to be developed, in place of apathy and familism?

Theologians have an obligation to think ahead for the church, experimenting with new ideas about institutions, which may one day form the practical basis for Catholic social thought, as it develops in the future. Liberation theologians deserve credit for challenging us to think more seriously about the problems of such nations as those of Latin America. To pay them the compliment of serious attention, we must not merely assent to every word they write, but, rather, in a spirit of camaraderie, give them vigorous argument where argument seems called for. North America, too, has its own tradition of liberation theology, having welcomed millions of "the wretched refuse" of the earth to a new nation, "conceived in liberty and dedicated to the proposition that all men are created equal." We must be as faithful to our own experience as the liberation theologians are to theirs. Only from the clash of argument may we together envisage a new future for the poor of this hemisphere and the world.

Especially in Latin nations, our North American ideals are badly comprehended. So it is doubly worth examining them. Is "possessive individualism" really our ideal? Of course not! Our sins may be as scarlet, but some of our ideals, neglected even in our own theories, are most visible in practice.

# CHAPTER 11

# The Communitarian Individual in American Practice

The political associations which exist in the United States are only a single feature in the midst of the immense assemblage of associations in that country. Americans of all ages, all conditions, and all dispositions, constantly form associations. They have not only commercial and manufacturing companies, in which all take part, but associations of a thousand other kinds—religious, moral, serious, futile, extensive or restricted, enormous or diminutive. The Americans make associations to give entertainments, to found establishments for education, to build inns, to construct churches, to diffuse books, to send missionaries to the antipodes; and in this manner they found hospitals, prisons, and schools. If it be proposed to advance some truth, or to foster some feeling by the encouragement of a great example, they form a society. Wherever, at the head of some new undertaking, you see the Government in France, or a man of rank in England, in the United States you will be sure to find an association.... A government can no more be competent to keep alive and to renew the circulation of opinions and feelings amongst a great people, than to manage all the speculations of productive industry. No sooner does a government attempt to go beyond its political sphere and to enter upon this new track, than it exercises, even unintentionally, an insupportable tyranny; for a government can only dictate strict rules, the opinions which it favours are rigidly enforced, and it is never easy to discriminate between its advice and its commands.... Governments therefore should not be the only active powers.... Amongst the laws which rule human societies there is one which seems to be more precise and clear than all others. If men are to remain civilized, or to become so, the art of associating together must grow and improve, in the same ratio in which the equality of conditions is increased.

—ALEXIS DE TOCQUEVILLE *Democracy in America*

Latin Americans overlook the actual practice of liberal institutions, which are far more communitarian than they imagine. True, some liberal thinkers are excessively individualistic (*Looking Out For Number One!*), and there are strains of excessive individualism in American life, as there were in the Italian Renaissance and among the *conquistadores* of Latin America. Yet the actual texture of daily organizational life in the

United States has a communitarian side seldom brought to consciousness. Catholic social thought has so far missed this important reality. This may be understandable, since even many Americans have not made themselves conscious of the communitarian temper of American daily life. In recent years, however, the inadequacies of both our major political parties is forcing such consciousness to the surface.

For a new public policy is emerging in the United States. Both parties are in the grip of necessities larger than their prior intellectual conceptions. It is by no means clear which party will better succeed in grasping the new necessities and successfully mastering them. Neither can wholly return to the outdated and unworkable habits of the recent past.

Succinctly stated, the emergent public policy begins by facing squarely the existence of recalcitrant social problems, and by recognizing that tried-and-true Republican conceptions of "trusting the individual" are as insufficient as the hoary Democratic conceptions of "leaving it to the state." The public policy thinking of Republicans is becoming less individualist, more social. The public policy thinking of Democrats is becoming less statist, more willing to look to social agencies other than government.

The meeting place of these two trends, which questions of cost and humaneness make virtually inevitable, lies in the concept of mediating structures. Since this concept depends on two assumptions about the actual character of the American social system, we must reflect on the personality type actually promoted by the American system and on the character of that system itself. Ethics begins in politics, Aristotle warns us; the *ethos* is shaped by the *polis*.

## 1. TWO ASSUMPTIONS

Two common misunderstandings about the United States, often shared by Americans themselves, are that we are a nation of individualists, weak and fractured in our communities, and that ours is a "free enterprise" economy, which at best offers a pale imitation of the "mixed" social democratic economies of Great Britain and West Germany.

The emergent public philosophy is based on quite different assumptions. Two of these may be succinctly stated: (1) The secret to the psychology of Americans is that they are neither individualists nor collectivists; their strong suit is association, and they freely organize themselves, cooperate, and work together. (2) The social system of the United States is constituted of three independent, yet interdependent, systems of institutions, organized along different axes and even different values: a political system, an economic system, a moral-cultural system.

This second assumption needs some explaining. In actual practice, each of the three systems which constitute our social system plays an important role in strengthening and restraining the other two. In particular, the political system has as one of its central tasks to "promote the general welfare." Its role in promoting and regulating commerce and industry, and in empowering associations of citizens, is critical. The role of the economic system in fulfilling the material aspirations of all citizens, in teaching them crucial virtues, and in freeing them for aesthetic, religious, and moral pursuits, is indispensable to the legitimation of the political system.

The American system is neither a statist nor a laissez-faire system. From the beginning, the state has undertaken tasks essential to the promotion of commerce and industry, but in a special American spirit. For the most part, the state has not tried to *control* or *manage* economic activities. Rather, it has actively provided indispensable infrastructures and preconditions which the economic system can scarcely provide for itself.

This, then, gives rise to the central question in American political economy: How, in practice, ought the American political system to address itself to the notable American capacities for free association and the building up of mediating institutions? Individualism alone is not sufficient, and it is not in the American grain. Free enterprise alone is not sufficient. Neither is an omni-activist state.

## 2. ASSOCIATIVE COMMUNITY

Frequently, in discussions of community, scholars accept as their primary model a form of life, either that of family kinship or that of the agricultural village, characteristic of pre-modern societies. This model enables them to speak of "the breakdown of community." For it is clearly true that in a post-modern society earlier forms of community are fractured and opened up. It does not so clearly follow, however, that the earlier ideal of community represents the highest form, or that all other forms ought to be measured by it.

One of the founding images of the American sense of community lies in such documents as "the Mayflower Compact." A hallowed literary and liturgical tradition employs the image of God's covenant with his freely chosen people and their acceptance thereof as the original model for this idea. The Jewish and Christian God first loves humans, and then is loved freely in response. The ideal of community between God and humans, based upon free election on both sides, came in this way to inform the classic American ideal of human community.

Compared to the traditional societies of "The Old World," it is no doubt true that the communities of "The New World" experienced conditions of uprooting, mobility, and voluntariness of a unique sort. Immigrants had to "break" from their communities or origin, in order to build new communities in a new land. But they *did*, in almost all cases, build communities, not only on the frontier, but in city neighborhoods. True enough, the at first distinctively American experience of emphasizing the right of each individual to pursue personal happiness led to a new exhilaration on the part of individuals, who in large numbers were taught to depart from the bosom of their families to "make their way in the world." Perhaps because ancient communal ties were so strong, great symbolic energies had to be unleashed to encourage young persons to "break" from their homes and to "strike out on their own." Thus the cowboy, even the gangster, the outsider, the loner, the "Marlboro man," became powerful and distinctively American symbols.

This symbol of the lonely individual was embodied often enough in reality to be credible. Still, this symbol tells only a small part of the American experience. Apart from myth, the American individualist is remarkably communitarian. Few cultures in the world, I think, promote in their young as many habits of cooperation, sympathy, teamwork, organization, and other social virtues as the American. Tocqueville already noticed this trait in 1835, a trait, perhaps, required by the necessities of settling a new continent. Nearly all tasks were too large for one man or family alone. Cooperation was indispensable to survival. The associative ethos of Judaism and Christianity reinforced its importance. Is there an American village or city without its annual "Brotherhood" awards?

In fraternity and association, Americans were not violating an ethos, but fulfilling it, and not only for physical, but also for psychical survival. American philosophers like Josiah Royce and John Dewey are preeminent among philosophers of the world in their astute and detailed reflections on the centrality of community to human life.

The American ideal of community, however, has never been collectivist or state-centered or all-encompassing. If, on the one side, Americans are not individualists, neither do they admire total belonging to one institution alone. There is not one overarching religion to which all subscribe. Although the English language and the heritage of British political institutions have given the nation the backbone of its common culture, there is no strictly enforced particular ethnic or cultural horizon, and the common culture itself is shaped by the continuing contributions of many cultures. The continental size of the United States makes for disparate regional interests, experiences, and perceptions. The promotion of commerce and industry further divided the nation into diverse and competing values and interests. The number of associations many citizens belong to is quite staggering. Organizations as diverse as the Veterans of Foreign Wars, the Lions Club, Parent-Teacher Associations, the Boy Scouts, the Girl Scouts, athletic leagues, and all the multitude of voluntary associations embraced under the United Way and all the committees, organizations, and activities promoted by a multitude of churches, keep many Americans almost as busy attending meetings after school or work as they are during the work week.

Between individualism and collectivism, there is a third way. Between the individualist and the collectivist, there is the communitarian individual. The American way of overcoming individualism is not through an all-consuming attachment to the state or any other collective, but through the building up of many diverse associations and communities. It is not an American ideal to be self-enclosed, indifferent to others, hostile, or cold. Even such volumes as *Looking Out for Number One* and *Assertiveness Training* have as their premise that learning such things is against the ordinary grain.

Given their social skills, Americans are in a position, in addressing social needs, to go beyond individualism and beyond statism. Given the mutual respect of the economic system and the political system, each with its own strengths and weaknesses, Americans are in a position to maintain an activist government—yet without establishing government as the chief agency for managing and administering vast social programs. A swollen government must be taught to divest itself of as many activities involving its own managerial administration as possible. Simultaneously, it must catalyze other social agencies and offer them the support to perform the necessary tasks better and more efficiently.

The American principle is to empower individuals through local agencies to achieve their own independence. In many cases, government must do the empowering. Without government, many important social energies cannot be released. Thus the American ideal of political economy depends upon the wisdom and undergirding strength of an activist government, which must remove impediments, lend assistance, and through positive actions release the manifold energies of the private sector. A do-nothing political system would fail "to promote the general welfare." A do-everything political system smothers it. Finding the techniques that actually empower citizens is at the heart of wise political economy.

## 3. POLITICAL ECONOMY

In his speeches on world development, President Reagan has had opportunity to preach for others what has worked for Americans: "the magic of the market," liberty, inventiveness, enterprise. Less noticed have been his further remarks on the role of the American political system in promoting development:

Free people build free markets that ignite dynamic development for everyone and that's the key, but that's not all. Something else helped us create these unparalleled opportunities for growth and personal fulfillment. A strong sense of cooperation, free association among individuals, rooted in institutions of family, church, school, press and voluntary groups of every kind. Government too played an important role. It helped eradicate slavery and other forms of discrimination. It opened up the frontier through actions like the Homestead Act and rural electrification. And it helped provide a sense of security for those who, through no fault of their own, could not support themselves.

Government and private enterprise complement each other. They have, they can and they must continue to co-exist and cooperate. But we must always ask: Is government working to liberate and empower the individual? Is it creating incentives for people to produce, save, invest and profit from legitimate risks and honest toil? Is it encouraging all of us to reach for the stars? Or does it seek to compel, demand and coerce people into submission and dependence?[1]

The distinctively American conception of political economy is not that of a free economic system alone, nor that of an omnicompetent state. In the American model—more fully realized in practice than in abstract theory—the political system is distinguished from the economic system, but is interdependent with it in many ways. Utility companies represent a form of semi-private, semi-public business. Some corporations—port authorities, the Tennessee Valley Authority, the Postal Service and many others—have a uniquely public character, while yet being somewhat insulated from direct day-to-day control by the political system. Furthermore, without governmental regulation, competition would lack the common rules without which a fair game cannot be played. To list all the ways in which the political system modifies, supports, and regulates private industries of extremely diverse sorts would take us too far afield. But it is important to notice that, in practice, the relations between the American political system and its dynamic economic system in its own baffling diversity are extremely complex.

Even in the pages of *The Federalist*, Madison and Hamilton properly understood that one of the chief tasks of political leadership is to create conditions for a flourishing and diverse economy. Correspondingly, one of the chief tasks of business leadership is to nourish the sorts of prosperity, economic progress, fairness, and sense of community which are essential to a democratic polity. Neither politics alone nor economics alone is sufficient. Democratic capitalism is neither socialist nor laissez-faire in its conceptions. It is a form of *political economy*, a set of coordinate, not subordinating, systems. At one extreme, the state does not attempt to absorb into itself and utterly to subordinate to itself the entire economy. At the other extreme, no business or industry is without political responsibilities expressed by sanction of law, by custom, and by self-restraint.

It is difficult to draw exact lines in any purely theoretical way marking off the precise limits of the political system and of the economic system. Yet industry by industry, case by case, adjudication of rights and responsibilities is constant. Errors at either extreme are relatively easy to spot, even if partisans at the extremes may strenuously argue their positions. What cannot be denied is that, equally, the political system and the economic system each has its integrity and assigned turf, even as particular cases and the general proportions of the playing field are passionately debated.

It is common to describe the American system as a "mixed" system, neither purely capitalist nor purely socialist. Parallel to the expression "political economy," I prefer to describe it as "democratic capitalism." The ideal of democratic capitalism is not that of a purely independent free enterprise system or laissez-faire; nor is it the ideal of democratic socialism. Democratic capitalism is not a halfway house, nor a "mix," between socialism and laissez-faire. It is, in its own right, a quite distinctive ideal.

There is a tendency in democratic socialist thought to grant the state, or at least the political system, ultimate and final power over the economic system. There is a tendency in libertarian or laissez-faire thought to subordinate the state to the economic system, and the social texture of actual life to the solitary individual. By contrast, the ideal of democratic capitalism is that of two coordinate systems, in some respects independent of each other and in some respects interdependent, but neither subordinate to the other.

There is one set of problems, which, perhaps more than any other, has since about 1955 tipped the American system closer to the socialist ideal. These are the problems of "the safety net," gathered under the rubric of "the welfare state." Typically, faced with a social problem, one set of critics has turned to the individual, while another set has turned to a state agency. From social security programs to aid for families with dependent children, from assistance for the handicapped to unemployment compensation, the argument almost always has been settled by increments of state activism. For social problems are, of their nature, beyond the capacity of solitary individuals. Does it follow, however, that they are best addressed directly and in a managerial way by the state?

## 4. THE ROLE OF MEDIATING STRUCTURES

Undeniably, a large society faces problems that may overwhelm solitary individuals. Undeniably, the solutions to social problems must also be social. It does not follow that the state is the only, or the most effective, or the cheapest, or the most sensitive and affect-laden social agency. Besides the state, there are many other social agencies, some already existing, and some perhaps yet to be imagined.

The dimensions of the sudden growth in the social welfare sector of the federal budget are spectacular. In 1955 federal entitlement payments to individuals stood at approximately $20 billion or 21 percent of the federal budget. By 1970 these sums had grown to approximately

$70 billion or 31.8 percent. By 1980 they had grown again to $270 billion or 46 percent. Projections for 1984 come to just over $400 billion or 52.7 percent of the budget, and no end to uncontrolled escalation is in sight.[2]

Many entitlement payments do not, of course, go only to the poor. All retired senior citizens are entitled, for example, to the social security payments they have been conscientiously foregoing during their working years. Still, when $400 billion has been spent to eliminate poverty during 1984 alone, citizens may well ask why eliminating poverty costs so much. Are cheaper, more effective methods not available?

Suppose, for example, that one accepts an extreme estimate of 34 million Americans who would, without transfer payments, be living below the official poverty line for a non-farm family of four, $9862 per year. How much ought it to cost, in strict mathematical terms, to see to it that all poor persons received cash sufficient to bring them above this line? For the sake of simplicity, let us divide the number of poor individuals into household units of four each. That makes 8.5 million poor households. To transfer cash payments of $10,000 to each such household directly would cost about $85 billion ($10,000 × 8.5 million households). Poverty—in this strictly mathematical sense—could be eliminated at a fraction of what is currently being expended. The actual "poverty shortfall" in 1982—the gap between what the poor actually earned and the amount needed to bring all over the poverty line—was $45 billion.

It is by no means clear, then, that current federal strategies for eliminating poverty follow the most direct, effective, and cost-efficient path.

There is, indeed, a certain contradiction in much recent thinking about the elimination of poverty. On the one hand, poverty is most easily described in monetary terms: so many dollars for a non-farm family of four. On the other hand, government entitlement payments are chiefly designed to meet specific *crises* in which individuals may be involved. Thus there are programs for medical assistance; for food stamps; for families with dependent children; for rent supplements; and for many other specific cash and non-cash transfer payments. Each of these programs has its own criteria, paperwork, administrative apparatus, and self-policing functions. Two problems here arise. First, measuring the non-cash benefits, especially medical care, is extremely difficult. Second, the methods employed by all the many administrative agencies are, cumulatively, far more costly than direct cash payments to the poor. Given the cash themselves, the poor might better select—and with far less dependency—their own priorities.

The social problems of poverty are clear enough. So also are the responsibilities of *society* to meet these problems. Two arguments have so far been addressed, however, against choosing *the federal government* as the agency through which to meet those needs. One is the constant escalation of costs. The other, related, concerns the efficiency of government as a practical agency. The factor of cost imposes the reality principle. It is the second factor, however, which gives rise to the search for other agencies besides those of government to meet the necessary tasks.

Everyone agrees that a good society ought to provide a "safety net" for its less fortunate citizens. Programs for direct cash transfers to the poor—a guaranteed annual income—have more than once been proposed in the Congress. This direct approach has so far failed of adoption.

Another idea has, therefore, come under consideration. If direct cash transfers through some form of guaranteed annual income are not adopted, and if the strategy of multiple governmental agencies to meet multiple specific crises gives rise to uncontrollable costs, are there not other social agencies which might properly meet undeniable social needs? There are, in any society, many other social agencies besides the state. Because these social agencies mediate between the individual and the state, and mitigate the vulnerability of individuals left to themselves, such agencies have come to be known as "mediating" or "mitigating" institutions. Among them are the churches, schools, unions, fraternals, neighborhood organizations, and other voluntary associations of every sort.

The question then arises: What is the federal government doing to empower—or to emasculate—such mediating structures? This danger of emasculation was foreseen by Tocqueville:

Above this race of men stands an immense and tutelary power, which takes upon itself alone to secure their gratifications and to watch over their fate. That power is absolute, minute, regular, provident, and mild. It would be like the authority of a parent if, like that authority, its object was to prepare men for manhood; but it seeks, on the contrary, to keep them in perpetual childhood: it is well content that the people should rejoice, provided they think of nothing but rejoicing. For their happiness such a government willingly labors, but it chooses to be the sole agent and the only arbiter of that happiness; it provides for their security, foresees and supplies their necessities, facilitates their pleasures, manages their principal concerns, directs their industry, regulates the descent of property, and subdivides their inheritances: what remains, but to spare them all the care of thinking and all the trouble of living? . . . the supreme power then . . . covers the surface of society with a network of small complicated rules, minute and uniform, through which the most original minds and the most energetic characters cannot penetrate, to rise above the crowd. The will of man is not shattered, but softened, bent, and guided; men are seldom forced by it to act, but they are constantly restrained from acting. Such a power does not destroy, but it prevents existence; it does not tyrannize, but it compresses, enervates, extinguishes, and stupefies a people, till each nation is reduced to nothing better than a flock of timid and industrious animals, of which the government is the shepherd.[3]

Is it not possible that social needs can be met more efficiently, more cheaply, more effectively, and with greater affect through social agencies in the private sector? Might not costs to government be reduced if the government used its own funds to strengthen these non-governmental organizations, rather than to attempt to meet all social problems itself?

In the pragmatic context of American life, such programs are liable to begin piecemeal, as small experiments. No grand architecture is yet in place, even though the basic conception seems to be gaining adherents. Let us simply list, then, some examples of how this new approach would work.

1. Consider a family with a retarded child. If the child is hospitalized in a governmentally funded hospital (and in some cases this may be necessary), the costs may run to $30,000 or more per child per year. If, on the other hand, the family would be willing to care for the child at home, then either a cash transfer or a tax credit of, say, $2000 per year might so empower it. Invested over ten years, such funds might pay for special facilities in the home such as muscular exercisers or other therapeutic devices. The savings to the government would seem to be great. The affectivity generated by family care might, for all concerned, and however costly in human terms, be priceless. Furthermore, in at least some instances, individual churches or other groups have sponsored programs for the retarded and the handicapped in their localities. At a fraction of the costs of total institutionalization, such programs have been able to provide a daily environment, sometimes including income-producing work suitable to those involved, of remarkable human quality. Such churches or other local agencies might well require some federal subsidy to meet their costs. Even if such a subsidy reached as high as $4000 per year per handicapped person, it would be far less than the cost of total institutionalization.

2. A bill before the Senate Labor and Human Resources Committee allowed taxpayers the choice of a tax credit or a deduction for each household that includes a dependent person who is at least sixty-five years old. This bill encourages families to maintain their care for grandparents and other elderly relatives. It also gives the elderly the satisfaction of contributing a significant share to family income through the tax credit or deduction. Not all the elderly would be covered by such a provison, but a significant number would be. To the profound human value of a multigenerational household would also be added an empowering incentive. (Not to be neglected is a source of at least some child care for fortunate families.)

3. Another bill would exempt from taxation certain trusts established for the benefit of elderly parents or handicapped relatives, and would provide a deduction for contributions to such trusts. While not univer-

sally applicable, this possibility might relieve pressures on social security for at least some millions of retired persons.

4. Another bill would allow corporations, large or small, to deduct all contributions made to a joint employee-employer day care facility. A variation of this provision was enacted in the Economic Recovery Act of 1981.

5. The Economic Recovery Act of 1981 also permits working spouses to invest the first $2000 of earnings in a tax-exempt Individual Retirement Account (IRA). Accumulating over a working lifetime at compound interest, such a fund would provide a substantial sum (easily $100,000 or more) available at retirement. This provision has two important social effects. Since over half of all married couples now have two incomes, a great many households may be stimulated to add substantial sums, tax-free to them, to the national pool of investment capital. Savings will thus be encouraged. Furthermore, sole reliance upon social security payments will be reduced. Both spouses will be accumulating substantial retirement accounts.

6. In every community, rural and urban, there are private associations or networks involved in feeding the elderly, in developing supervised activities for teenagers, and the like. In times of stress, it has been found, individuals in trouble turn first and most often to these personal, local networks for assistance. Last of all do they turn to governmental agencies. Furthermore, they report higher rates of satisfaction when they turn to persons already known to them among their neighbors, in their churches, and in fraternals with which they are affiliated.[4] A measure of governmental subsidy to such local networks and associations, already in place and functioning with natural emotional ties of many sorts, would seem to offer an effective use of such funds. Costs would seem to be far less than for governmental duplication of local capacities.

7. Two decades ago, teenage unemployment among whites was higher than among blacks. Currently, the figures for teenage unemployment among blacks is considerably higher. The figure is often announced in percentages: "Forty Percent (or Fifty Percent) Black Youth Unemployment." In hard numbers, however, the scale of the problem is more readily apparent. Fluctuating monthly, the figures from the Department of Labor tally just under 400,000 black youths unemployed.[5] Considered simplistically, at the minimum wage of approximately $6000 per year, the total financial cost of employing all 400,000 of these young persons comes to $2.4 billion annually. It does not seem beyond the reach of Americans to invent ways for making at least part of the required wage costs available through local institutions, which might put such youngsters to productive work.

Missing has been the link between work to be done and the unemployed who wish to do it. The fastest growing sector in the U.S. economy has been the service sector and the many small businesses that are mushrooming in it. Many such businesses are uniquely suited to young employees. Eighty percent of all new jobs in the United States are supplied by small businesses.[6] I do not have in mind the precise mechanism that would expedite the hiring of larger numbers of currently unemployed black youths. Yet appropriate tax credits or deductions to small businesses precisely for such employees seem likely to increase their numbers substantially. Combined with a reduction of paperwork so onerous for small business, and especially with respect to a work force that is demographically and vocationally quite volatile and temporary in its commitments (many are either in school or in those various forms of transition common to late adolescence), incentives designed for this purpose would seem promising.

Institutions such as churches, libraries, and voluntary organizations should be drawn directly into the task of designing employment for teenagers. Adult guidance seems even more important for *attitudinal* training than for training in specific job skills. The technical question is how to empower such institutions to furnish sound employment, of which most of them, involving labor-intensive work, are much in need. The problems of the CETA programs, which attempted to do something like this, but with a very heavy governmental overlay, are well-known. The amount of moneys spent seem disproportionate to the actual number of employees put to work and to the amount of wages actually paid. The philosophy of CETA, significantly, involved a high degree of governmental management. A philosophy which placed greater reliance upon local mediating structures, while drawing upon governmental resources as a catalyst, would entail a technically different design.

The involvement of many citizens in meeting local needs is a good to be desired. How can the government stimulate, and financially catalyze, such involvement? Instead of thinking of the state as the agency of first and full responsibility, can we learn to think of it as an empowering agency—neither administering nor doing so many tasks, but helping to stimulate other social agencies to do them?

One suggestion that may have some merit is offered by Stephen Roman and Eugen Loebl in their stimulating book, *The Responsible Society*.[7] Self-consciously, they try to conceive of government as a catalyzing rather than as a managerial agent. One device they recommend is that the government create a fund for certain types of socially necessary activities, from which private institutions may borrow at greatly reduced interest rates. (Such programs are already in operation for agricultural purposes.) As the institutions repay these loans, the fund is replenished. The burden falls upon the institutions to make such employment as they offer financially productive. Imagine, for example, that a local church or benevolent organization would borrow from this fund sufficient capital to employ ten youngsters as plasterers, painters, carpenters, and repairmen, under supervision and at something above the minimum wage, in the repair and restoration of local housing. In many neighborhoods, there is visible work to be done, and some in the community would be willing to pay at least modest sums to have it done. It is likely that local enterprises might succeed where governmental agencies have not, and at lower public costs.

Another suggestion is to turn more seriously to the churches of America. There is virtually no local community, no village, without its church. Most of these churches are already involved in social action of various sorts. It is said that the churches cannot undertake to meet vast and expensive social problems alone. They cannot collect sufficient funds. They do not have all the necessary forms of expertise. They cannot properly manage functions which are not properly their own. No one, of course, thinks of the churches as the only, or even as the primary, social agencies of the land. Yet they are a critical resource, drawing upon the ideals and energies of more than 100 million Americans. How might we arrange our national address to social necessities so as to make it possible for the churches to extend their activities more efficiently and further than they already have, and to do so better, and with greater affectivity, than government can? The present generation of ecumenism and cooperation, bridging many ancient sectarian chasms, offers a fresh opportunity to the nation. Habits of cooperation nourished now for some twenty years place these institutions in a new light in American society. Things before impossible now seem, at least, possible. Can we not take advantage of the moment?

Centripetal, nationalizing forces are strong in America today. But what these great national forces cannot produce is a public policy tailored to the human scale, an intelligent and flexible and nuanced grasp of local realities. Local people know local characteristics best, even though all simultaneously feel the pressures of national images, ideals, and purposes. The republic is not where it was twenty years ago. New things are possible. One universal public policy for a nation of continental size, of tremendously varied climates, economic bases, and local cultures, carries within it the seed of local abuse and local ridicule. By contrast, a public policy rooted in local communities, but catalyzed and assisted in its necessities by a vigilant national administration, more closely fits the texture of today's reality. National government alone cannot manage a national community.[8]

The ideal of democratic capitalism is to bring the three independent, interdependent systems—the political system, the economic system, the moral-cultural system—into harmonious collaboration. Moral-cultural institutions such as the churches, the schools, families, and the press cannot meet our social problems alone. Economic institutions such as the great corporations, the unions, and small businesses cannot meet them alone. Political institutions such as the agencies of government cannot meet them alone. If it was an earlier error to rely solely upon individuals, and a later error to rely too much upon the state, self-knowledge suggests a new approach to public policy through empowering other social agencies besides the state. Adopting it step by step and pragmatically, sorting out what works from what does not work, we may with this approach carry the American experiment forward in ways at once original and also consistent with its founding ideal.

Such a conception of social policy has international implications, to which we now return.

# CHAPTER 12

# International Economics

The social question is now worldwide.
—PAUL VI *Octogesima Adveniens*, 5

If there is to be social justice in this world, *institutions* of social justice must be built. Since the foundation of social justice is the dignity of the individual person, its first principle is freedom, in which that dignity resides. Such freedom means, as John XXIII declared, the right to life. It also means the right to liberty. And it means the freedom to choose one's own destiny, the right to the pursuit of happiness: the right to choose the meaning of life, so declaring one's own identity before God and humankind.

The Pontifical Commission charged with the problems of development is called "Justice and Peace." Over the years, this Pontifical Commission has prepared several studies of its own, in addition to its reprints of papal teaching. One in particular, *International Economics: Interdependence and Dialogue*, prepared by Paul Steidl-Meier, S.J., of the Gregorian University in Rome, condenses views widely shared in the Third World.[1] Thus, in considering his text, we shall actually be addressing a way of interpreting reality into which many Catholics have slowly been drifting, without intense and probing discussion. Open disagreement on these topics is precisely what we do not find, but we should find, in an "open church."

Father Steidl-Meier holds that "the ideal of progress sums up the spirit of the Enlightenment." He cites Robert Nisbet's *History of the Idea of Progress* for this view, but that seems to be an error. For to do so would be to render the idea of progress entirely secular, whereas its roots actually lie in the Jewish and Christian conception of history as a story, in which Jews and Christians are held responsible for changing history and for realizing within it some approximation of the Kingdom of God. Although a teacher of Nisbet's younger days, J. B. Bury, inclined toward the more secular view, Nisbet himself finds it untenable:

What is the future of the idea of progress in the West? Any answer to that question requires answer to a prior question: what is the future of Judeo-Christianity in the West? For if there is one generalization that can be made confidently about the history of the idea of progress, it is that throughout its history the idea has been closely linked with, has depended upon, religion or upon intellectual constructs derived from religion.

Even during the Enlightenment, a few Condorcets excepted, the idea of progress continued to be closely and deeply united with Christianity, as the important works of Lessing, Kant, Herder, Priestley, and others emphasize. It is much the same in the nineteenth century. For every Marx among prophets of progress, dozens lived and wrote who made Christianity or some religious substitute for Christianity the cornerstone of faith in progress.... Even Mill, apparent atheist through much of his life, came in his final years to declare the indispensability of Christianity to both progress and order.... In sum, it is evident beyond reasonable challenge that from Hesiod to Toynbee, Schweitzer, and Teilhard de Chardin the relationship between religion and the concept of progress has been organic in character.[2]

Steidl-Meier next asserts that the notion of progress "clearly affirms the work of life on this earth and the possibility of the perfectibility of human nature."[3] On the latter point, the perfectibility of humankind, the Anglo-American Enlightenment was in substantial disagreement with the Continental Enlightenment.[4] The premises of both democracy and capitalism, as understood in the Anglo-American tradition are based on the *fact* of human fallibility and sinfulness. Humans, James Madison observed in *The Federalist,* are neither beasts nor angels.[5] It would be a colossal mistake, such thinkers believed, to base hopes for social structures upon a belief in human perfectibility; progress, yes, but never total conversion.

Father Steidl-Meier further believes that the modern ideal of progress "is found in the power of human reason and science" and that it is "precisely in the application of science through economic and technological growth that the development of future potential" is realized.[6] He attributes to the Enlightenment "tremendous optimism" in "science and technology" and in "institutions of freedom guided by the light of reason." Again, this seems not to be entirely accurate. The market, as we have seen, is not a rationalistic, scientific device, planned by technological experts. On the contrary, it is a social invention for empowering all individuals at every level of life. Indeed, it gives the many poor more economic power, and greater social mobility, than any other system. Moreover, democratic freedoms do not rest so much on scientific reason as on that sort of practical reason which is intermixed with sentiments, passions, and interests. It is guided less by a single dominant reason than by the free interchange of ideas, and by the checks and balances of power-diffusing institutions.

"The notion of progress," Steidl-Meier argues, "implicitly asserts the superiority of European culture and Western civilization."[7] But John Locke, Adam Smith, James Madison, and Thomas Jefferson believed that their ideas, admittedly learned in large measure from Judaism and Christianity, were part of the universal inheritance of humankind. The rights they claimed are given to all humans by the Creator and are not limited solely to Europeans or Western civilization. In 1948 the entire United Nations embraced them as universal.

Steidl-Meier holds that socialism and capitalism are the "two dominant paradigms" of the modern world. He believes they both "espouse a materialistic approach to political economic affairs." It is, of course, obvious that socialism (in its Marxist form) is atheistic and despises religion as the opiate of the people. Yet Steidl-Meier believes that "non-atheistic forms of socialism" and "most forms of capitalism" are also "materialist."

This is seen in two ways. First there is a reversal of priorities. People so emphasize the value of this life on earth that they put riches, status and self-interest ahead of solidarity and commitment. The second way is more subtle for in their interpretations of social reality they remove whatever religion there is from the realm of political economy to the private, inaccessible sphere of inner worldly consciousness. The result is curiously the same as the atheist denial of religion, for in no case should religion be mixed up with either politics or business. Thus in "modern" thought politics and economics are not religious issues, either because there is no authentic religion or because it is privatized.[8]

These assertions need serious qualification. Jesus himself complained that most people put "riches, status, and self-interest" ahead of the life of the spirit. Neither democratic socialism nor democratic capitalism teach any such preference as a doctrine. On the contrary, both of them appeal emphatically to spiritual values, including those of solidarity and commitment, of which there are many tangible evidences in Western Europe, the United States, and elsewhere. Democratic capitalism, in particular, nourishes and depends upon vital and independent moral-cultural institutions. The universities, the press, the churches, and countless activist organizations of considerable spiritual force are *not* merely "privatized" in Western societies.

Perhaps Father Steidl-Meier is confusing the confessional state, which publicly establishes religion, with the pluralistic state, which while not relegating religion to a solely inward, private sphere does, nonetheless, renounce the right to command the consciences of all. Religion in pluralist societies is not *official;* but it is and remains *public.* It is by no means confined solely to inwardness. The practice of the Vatican in its own public teaching on politics and economics shows that this is so.

Father Steidl-Meier's assertions about there being "no authentic religion" or only a "privatized" religion will seem astonishing even to fundamentalist Protestants in the United States, who might be supposed to insist upon the religion of individual conscience, the separation of church and state, and the transcendent claims of religion *beyond* those of politics and business. Neither Billy Graham nor Jerry Falwell may fairly be described as leading a merely private Christian life. The public role of religion in free societies today is not what it was in traditional feudal societies. But neither is religion as "privatized" as some sociologists of the 1960–1970 era claimed.

Father Steidl-Meier sees clearly that socialist collectivism is incompatible with a democracy which respects the dignity of individuals. But his view of liberalism is faulty:

Liberalism focuses upon the primacy of the individual; it accords primary importance to individual liberty and accepts as valid the principles of self-interest and mutual self-interest (the social contract entered into freely).[9]

It is more accurate to regard self-interest as a *fact*, however regrettable, than as a *principle*. John XXIII called attention to this fact, as the Gospels often do. Furthermore, as we saw in Chapter 1, economists in particular use the term self-interest in a way quite different from theologians. Theologians have in mind self-love, concupiscence, pride, and selfishness. Economists do not deny the frequency of such characteristics, but they do not mean by "self-interest" anything quite so narrow. From their perspective, even the noblest of motivations pursued by the self—including self-sacrifice, holiness, scholarly or artistic pursuit of "ends in themselves" such as truth and beauty—are "interests." For them, but not for theologians, the term is general and universal; it designates *whatever* human beings freely choose.

Yet there is a way of speaking of "self-interest rightly understood" as a principle. So Alexis de Tocqueville spoke of it:

The principle of interest rightly understood is not a lofty one, but it is clear and sure. It does not aim at mighty objects, but it attains without excessive exertion all those at which it aims. As it lies within the reach of all capacities, every one can without difficulty apprehend and retain it. By its admirable conformity to human weaknesses, it easily obtains great dominion; nor is that dominion precarious, since the principle checks one personal interest by another, and uses, to direct the passions, the very same instrument which excites them.

The principle of interest rightly understood produces no great acts of self-sacrifice, but it suggests daily small acts of self-denial. By itself it cannot suffice to make a man virtuous, but it disciplines a number of citizens in habits of regularity, temperance, moderation, foresight, self-command; and, if it does not lead men straight to virtue by the will, it gradually draws them in that direction by their habits....

I am not afraid to say, that the principle of interest rightly understood appears to me the best suited of all philosophical theories to the wants of the men of our time, and that I regard it as their chief remaining security against themselves. Towards it, therefore, the minds of the moralists of our age should turn; even should they judge it to be incomplete, it must nevertheless be adopted as necessary.[10]

Steidl-Meier next argues that these two paradigms, capitalism and socialism, diverge on their vision of the economy.

Both attempt to be scientific and rational. Liberal democracy does so in terms of the market which accords maximum scope to private initiative and individual liberty. There are, of course, conditions for fair market practices; in fact, the maintenance of such conditions is the primary role of government. In the scenario of market rationalism it is supposed that both individual development and the development of society will occur if the fair conditions of individual liberty and the social contract are maintained; supply and demand will equalize themselves in the free play of market forces and optimal resource use will be assured.[11]

There is a sense, of course, in which liberals hold that markets, checked by both the democratic polity and the humane values of moral-cultural institutions (including the free press, the universities, and the churches), are "rational." They do not hold them to be "scientific." A clear distinction must be made between the directive (*dirigiste*) use of the words "scientific" and "rational" and the diagnostic use. Economics as a professional discipline is not like physics. Like the other social sciences, it is a species of practical wisdom. Economists try to *understand* markets. They do not claim to be able to *direct* them scientifically and rationally. They are able to detect recurrent events, and even schemes of recurrent events expressed as "laws"; they are also able to assign, within limits, schemes of "probabilities" for certain events or recurrences of events. On the whole, practicing economists are quite humble about the limits of their present understanding and their capacities for prediction. Their usual diagnoses of current events or predictions of probable future events are typically modest. They are more likely to propose their own interpretations as *reasonable* or *prudent,* citing supporting evidence and historical precedent. A very good example of this tendency is Herbert Stein's account of national economic policies in the United States from 1932–1982, *Presidential Economics.*[12] The claim of liberalism is not that markets are "scientific" but that behavior in markets is intelligible and open to intelligent agents, few of whom are economists.

Steidl-Meier finds that both paradigms, socialist and capitalist, possess "inner logical coherence with seemingly total explanatory power." Both, he says, ascribe failures of events to fit their own "ideal scheme of things" to "dysfunctions," such as "market imperfections" or "class enemies."[13] But this is to imagine that socialist and liberal views of the economy are symmetrical. They are not. Socialism is a holistic vision, in which political, economic, and moral-cultural power is concentrated in a single set of principles and in a single central authority. Liberal societies separate the powers of the political system, the economic system, and the moral-cultural system, diffusing the centers of decision-making within each of them, and respecting the choices of every individual. Catholic social teaching, moreover, is not as symmetrical in its assessment of the two as Steidl-Meier suggests.

Father Steidl-Meier, launching upon an analysis of "contemporary crises," ignores a vacuum at the center of his argument. He pretends to a position which is Olympian, outside any and all institutional frameworks. From that institutional vacuum, he discerns three contemporary crises: growing numbers of the absolutely poor in developing countries; growing numbers of the relatively poor and the unemployed; and growing national deficits and "stagflation" (no real growth combined with inflation). Many, he concludes, are losing faith in world systems. Existing levels of organization are not adequate to the crises.

It is plain that Steidl-Meier himself has lost faith in both capitalism and socialism. He speaks of "the jungle of liberal capitalism" and "the zoo of collective socialism."[14] He thinks of the Church as "a persuasion group," its power to affect policy "limited" but "real." The Church asks, "What is happening to our neighbors?" in international economics, and "How is God speaking to us in this network of social relations?" Political and economic development is a "fundamentally religious" issue. To it the Church brings "a profoundly communitarian ethic."

Yet a "communitarian ethic" can be expressed only through institutions of political economy. An incarnational Church cannot be anti-institutional. Father Steidl-Meier seems to go out of his way to accept the socialist critique of liberal capitalism. In his analysis of the three contemporary crises, while rejecting socialist outcomes, he consistently follows socialist analysis, omitting important points. He goes even farther out of his way to misinterpret the communitarian ethic of liberal societies, making them seem more materialistic, more individualistic, and more self-centered than they are. He wishes to assume a seemingly neutral, detached point of view. He explicitly dissociates himself from Western civilization.

On one important matter, Father Steidl-Meier injects a crucial note of realism. Nearly every nation, he observes, possesses "both the natural and the human resources to be self-sufficient in food." Yet often productivity is far below sufficiency, for lack of "capital, management, and technology." The developing countries are desperately short of capital and "face severe constraints in building" it up.

Financial capital investment is an indispensable key to economic growth, for it leads to new productive capacity and, in so doing, creates jobs for workers, as well as generating the production of goods and services to meet the needs of the population. The most serious problem facing developing countries today is to amass an investible surplus of financial capital.[15]

There are only three main ways to accumulate capital, Father Steidl-Meier correctly observes: "To earn it and save it; to borrow it; to be given it. Each way has a price."

When a large part of the population lives at bare subsistence, "they do not save, they do not constitute a strong market for domestic goods, they cannot pay much in taxes, and they surely do not make up a market for financial instruments such as stocks and bonds." The vicious circle of population growth tends "to consume whatever growth takes place."[16] What can be done?

Bilateral aid from the richer countries often comes with political costs. Private foreign investment introduces transnational corporations, whose own set of priorities may "introduce unfavorable patterns of resource use." Exports of raw materials tend to be at low and unstable price levels, and exports of manufactured goods face increasingly severe trade barriers. When poor nations turn to borrowing, finally, they face staggering levels of debt, which they do not produce enough to pay off.[17]

This picture is bleak. Yet Father Steidl-Meier holds that "the means to solve the problem" are available, but "the political will to resolve the outstanding issues is lacking."[18] For Steidl-Meier, the problem is organizational. Decisions today are made by management elites. It is difficult even to obtain basic information on trade, finance, and development.

But we do know that significant numbers of poor countries selling raw materials, for instance, channel their funds through holding companies in Switzerland where they are protected by secrecy. What is not clear is how much of the new income, credit and aid destined for poor countries ever reaches those countries or is used for anything else than aggrandizing the positions of the already privileged elites.[19]

Here Steidl-Meier confronts the basic importance of an underlying moral ethos. For a political economy to function effectively, it must "be as free from corruption as possible. This is not a small problem."[20]

At this point, Father Steidl-Meier seems to be less neutral, in fact, than he earlier affected to be. His prescription is that of a political economy which is both based on markets and checked by political and moral-cultural institutions:

There are two broad paths which may be followed: 1) the market path which, by definition, must be based upon economic incentives and 2) planning, regulations and agreements which, to be effective, must be based on political economic sanctions (rewards and penalties). Clearly, both of those measures as I have stated them appeal to self-interest and mutual self-interest. It would be cynical to exclude generosity, altruism, and sacrifice for others, but it is not something which can be counted on as automatically forthcoming over the long term. While such attitudes should be fostered and associated measures even legislated it cannot be assumed that corporations and governments or the body politic do or will behave in such a way.[21]

Further, his description of the ills of planned economies is forthright:

Goods are produced for which no real market exists or the market carries few advantages. Production facilities may be set in place, but the supply of raw materials may not arive due to a poor transport system. Goods may spoil due to a lack of warehouses, losses may occur because decisions were based on partial or faulty information. Good managers and qualified skilled workers are often in short supply. The list of honest problems and errors can be almost infinitely extended on the basis of case histories.[22]

More than one suspects, and here as well, Catholic social thought appeals again and again to liberal institutions, including private property, markets, essential governmental regulation, and joint public-private efforts in education, health, and in the necessary upbuilding of infrastructural needs like pure water, roads, airports, energy sources and the like. Emphasis is placed on national self-reliance, on the principle of subsidiarity which empowers local social forces beyond the state, and citizen participation.

Finally, Steidl-Meier urges less developed countries to diversify their production; to diversify their trading partners; and to diversify both production and trade with other LDCs, so as not to rely excessively on the developed world. World government spending, Steidl-Meier adds, will have to be reduced. But the *costs* of this belt-tightening must not be borne only by the poor, in the loss of social services. Budget cuts should be made in arms, not medicare and food, and "if more taxes are needed, it might be well to begin with those who have the ability to pay rather than squeezing them out of the poor."[23]

What is lacking in this short and useful conspectus is attention to how wealth is actually produced, beginning with broad masses of persons at the bottom of society. It is flatly wrong to believe that wealth trickles down. On the contrary, it percolates up. When price controls were removed from products in India, production soared. The new production kept food prices low. The capital which launched Great Britain into the Industrial Revolution was first earned on its farms. The capital which made the United States a leading economic power flowed first from the rich production of its farms. The creation of wealth starts from below, and proceeds by way of invention, practicality, and a host of small improvements quite close to immediate production, where "the rubber hits the road."

What is to be done? Freeing local agriculture from farm price controls, encouraging self-reliance in food supply, is the very first step toward development. It starts at the bottom. It is profoundly affected by governmental policies. In the United States, it was government that passed the Homestead Act, liberating American agriculture from the pattern of large estates inherited from the Holy Roman Empire; that established great land-grant universities, on the principle that the main cause of wealth is intellect; that supported the rural Extension Service, which brought scientific information, techniques, and assistance to every rural area; that built the great dams for irrigation and power; that passed the Rural Electrification bill; that created the interstate highways and, earlier, the great canals and waterways; that has established price supports, farm credit bureaus, and other indispensable devices. It is not contrary to the liberal ideal for governments to "promote the general welfare" and to "empower people."

Most of all, it is crucial for LDCs to promote invention and practical improvement in every sphere. For this, no institution is as important as a government patent office, encouraging inventors by protecting their inventions (a critical form of private property of the human spirit) and giving them the incentive of time-limited patents. All peoples possess an inventive streak and a practical turn of mind. Incentives for developing this vast reservoir of wealth are crucial to economic development. The production of wealth starts with tinkerers and inventors on the farm and on the factory floor. Nothing is so essential to a nation as the creative spirit of its people.

But this spirit must be stirred. It cannot be allowed merely to slumber. It should not be repressed. Governments that smother the inventiveness of their peoples injure human dignity and punish themselves.

Finally, the LDCs must learn—and teach—the spirit of commerce and industry. Nowhere in the world is agriculture alone sufficient. The large transnational corporations, or even the large domestic corporations now springing up throughout the LDCs, are not the backbone of a self-reliant, growing, democratic economy. For this, a multitude of small businesses must spring up. Far too much attention is given to large organizations and complex bureaucracies. The economic genius of a people resides in its small family businesses. Throughout most of the LDCs, bicycles are an effective means of transport. Bicycles can be manufactured in small shops. So it is with most domestic tools, implements, and furnishings. Yet small businesses, like agriculture, are very sensitive to governmental policies, such as taxation, regulation, credit, the stability of currency, and the like. It is wise to tax small businesses lightly and to encourage their formation by every possible device of government.

Typically, the governments of LDCs are staffed by university graduates, political activists, and others accustomed to working in large, risk-free institutions. They have typically been taught to disdain the "bourgeoisie," "shopkeepers," and "business." They often refer to such persons as "middlemen" or "parasites," and view them chiefly as targets fat for taxation. Often, family entrepreneurs are poor, without formal education, and successful chiefly by dint of their capacity to capitalize on the labor of other family members. Political activists typically show little understanding of such economic activists. All this must change if the national agenda is truly economic creativity.

For economic creativity is another word for development. Its springs

lie in the human spirit, made in the image of the Creator. Its evangelical image lies in the carpenter shop that nourished Jesus of Nazareth
for thirty years. The air it breathes is freedom. The wealth it stores up,
transmuted into capital investment, is the stuff from which eventual
distribution for the too young, the too old, the weak, and the sick is
made available. Every person who launches a new enterprise successfully removes self and family from the rolls of the needy, and typically
becomes the employer of still others. There are "vicious circles" in
LDCs. The creation of small enterprises is a "beneficent circle," beginning at the humble bottom of society, spreading slowly outwards in ever
wider ripples, until the whole body of an LDC is no longer poor but
proudly self-reliant.

Given economic self-reliance, neither literacy nor democracy can be
far behind. Self-reliant citizens want to govern themselves. They insist
upon governing themselves. Their hearts and their habits, not parchment barriers, are the true protection of human rights. A poor nation
like Bangladesh, a nation of 99 million persons, needs at least seven
million small commercial, industrial, and service businesses. So it is with
every other nation, if freedom with justice is ever to be institutionalized
on earth, in political economies worthy of human dignity.

Catholic social thought has yet to discover the practical secrets of the
human spirit which infuse liberal institutions, but the course we have
followed shows clearly enough that this discovery lies just around the
next turn, just over the crest, along the road so arduously followed. For
the Catholic commitment to the dignity of each individual person now
demands as its institutional expression a full panoply of liberal institutions: in the polity, in the economy, and in the domain of conscience,
ethos, virtues, ideas, and information.

Which direction will Catholic social thought follow in the future?
Some Catholic thinkers are likely to experiment further with Marxism,
until disillusioned, as so many millions have been, by experience. But
the logic of Catholic social thought has, through trial and error, already
set in place the basic liberal benchmarks: the dignity of the human
person, the interdependence of all peoples, the economic development
of all nations, institutions of human rights, the communitarian personality, and the vocation of each human being to become a co-creator with
God in unlocking the secrets so lovingly hidden in nature by nature's
God. The task before Catholic social thought is to identify the institutions through which these ideals, common to Judaism, Christianity, and
liberalism, become routinized in this poor world of sinful but aspiring
humankind.

# CHAPTER 13

# Pope of Liberty, Pope of Creativity: John Paul II

No encyclical of John Paul II's has stirred as much international controversy as "Concern for Social Reality," *Sollicitudo Rei Socialis*. Although the text did not appear until the end of February 1988, it was backdated by 51 days so as to be dated in 1987 (30 December), in time to mark at least the year of Paul VI's encyclical, *Populorum Progressio* (26 March 1967). Nearly a year late, Pope John Paul II's encyclical shows clear signs of representing in its drafting several different factions. Yet it also shows many signs of the Pope's vivid experience under Marxist regimes and of his own personal phraseology.

The "creation theology" so brilliantly established in John Paul II's *Laborem Exercens* (15 September 1981) once again supplies the basic architecture of the new letter. This foundation in the dynamic of Genesis firmly places papal social thought in the narrative line of the Anglo-American experiment in political economy. In that tradition modern institutions of economic, political, and cultural development first entered into history.

The American experiment, in particular, springs from, and is inconceivable apart from, two biblical narratives, Creation and Exodus.[1] The design of the American *ordo* cannot be understood apart from a practical acceptance of the Jewish-Christian doctrine that from sinful persons sinful structures come. Any workable *ordo*, therefore, must include checks and balances against man's sinful tendencies. On the seal of the United States the image of a pyramid reminds Americans, who wandered across the desolate ocean from the comforts of Europe to a New Eden, that they had been preceded by the people of Israel, who wandered in the desert from the fleshpots of Egypt toward the Promised Land. Above this symbol is the invocation of the Creator who cares for particulars and singulars: "*Annuit Coeptis*: [Providence] smiled on our beginnings." The new order is designed to be a "system of natural liberty," fitted to the nature of free persons, capable of governing themselves through reflection and choice.[2]

"The God Who gave us life," Thomas Jefferson wrote, appealing to Genesis, "gave us liberty."[3] And in the Declaration of Independence of 4 July, 1776, the revolutionary Continental Congress announced:

> We hold these truths to be self-evident: that all men are created equal, that they are endowed by their Creator with certain unalienable rights, that among these are life, liberty, and the pursuit of happiness. That to secure these rights, governments are instituted among men, deriving their just powers from the consent of the governed.

George Weigel, whose survey of the long Catholic tradition of political thought, *Tranquillitas Ordinis*, has already established itself as a classic of our time, has elsewhere treated of the strong steps forward Pope John Paul II has taken in *Sollicitudo* concerning the importance of liberal democratic institutions to the fulfillment of Catholic moral theology.[4] My task in this chapter is to analyze the fresh steps *Sollicitudo* has taken in identifying the *economic* institutions necessary to such fulfillment.

## Four Classic Principles

The four classic principles of Catholic teaching about the good and realistic society on which *Sollicitudo Rei Socialis* draws can be briefly stated:

1. A good and realistic human society must take account of the role of original sin and of persistent actual sins of commission and omission, which mark every stage of human development until the Second Coming. Because sinful humans cannot create sinless structures, realism precludes dreams of utopia. Every actual human institution is marked by sins that spring from the human heart.

2. As the root of sin lies in human liberty, so also does the dignity of free men and women. Dignity springs from liberty. It arises from the human capacity for *reflection* and *choice*, a capacity that imprints within every human being the "image of God, the Creator," and endows every person with the unalienable rights inherent in such liberty.[5]

3. As God the Creator is One, so is the human race one. The human race is social, even familial (one family of the One God). Every person is by vocation committed to advancing the common good of all. The goods of creation are destined for all, and the work of all is necessary to bring creation to fruition.

4.      In order to secure human rights, governments are necessarily formed among humans. They must be rooted in the participation and consent of all the people; the people are sovereign. A corollary of this vision is the "principle of subsidiarity."6 Governments are necessary both for securing human rights (restraining the sinfulness of one human regarding others) and for achieving the common good through respecting the dignity of every person. Yet, unable to escape the universal fact of sin, government is simultaneously both an agent of the common good and a threat to the common good. Government, therefore, must be limited. The state is a *subsidium*, a help, and not an end in itself. To protect the dignity of the person and the free associations through which the social nature of humans is normally expressed, the state is expressly forbidden to do those things that persons and their free associations can do for themselves. It is empowered to come to their assistance (subsidium) only in those matters in which its powers are necessary for the common good. The state in Catholic teaching is a *limited* state. It loses legitimacy if it violates the human liberty and dignity it is formed to serve. Human persons are not made for the state, but the state for persons.

Each of these fundamental principles of Catholic social teaching is, in fact, embodied in such founding documents of the United States as the Declaration of Independence, the Constitution, the *Federalist*, and other classics of the American tradition. Like the American framers, Pope John Paul II–and, in general, the Catholic natural law tradition favored by modern popes since Leo XIII–goes back to Genesis and its universalist vision of all humanity as one. The American framers appealed to no specifically *American* rights, only to *human* rights belonging to every human everywhere. That is why they spoke of a New Order "of the Ages," wrote of the system of natural liberty (not merely of "American" liberty), looked to unalienable rights endowed in humans "by their Creator," and dared to entrust their fate to the care of Providence. Their experiment tested certain propositions for all humankind, not solely for themselves.

Moreover, in appealing to "liberty," the American framers did not mean *any* liberty, such as egoism or licentiousness,7 but rather–as Pope John Paul II noted in Miami in the autumn of 1987–"ordered liberty."8 A classic American hymn defines such ordered liberty simply: "Confirm thy soul in self-control, Thy liberty in law." The Statue of Liberty, a gift to America from France's liberal party in 1886, invokes a similar lesson: The Lady holds the light of Reason aloft in one hand, against the darkness, and in the other holds a tablet of the law (marked "MDCCLXXVI" as if to recall "We hold these truths . . .").

Many of the texts in *Sollicitudo Rei Socialis* come closer to expressing this vision–dear in one version to Catholic social teaching, and in another to the classical American tradition–than any prior document of any pope. You will not find such consonance in Leo XIII, Pius XI, or Paul VI. Only in the "Christmas

Messages" of Pius XII during the dark days of the struggle against Nazi totalitarianism,[9] and in John XXIII's *Pacem in Terris*, are there approximations.[10] More clearly than his predecessors, John Paul II has defined the *institutional structures* that best secure a Jewish-Christian vision of human rights and the dignity of the person. In sum, John Paul II's first contribution in *Sollicitudo* lies in his especially acute sense of the role of certain specific institutions in protecting basic human rights. His second lies in making central to his thought the most universal of starting places, the story of Creation in Genesis.

### Progress Beyond *Populorum Progressio*

In order to make John Paul II's theoretical and institutional advances plainer, we do well to look again at the encyclical whose anniversary he is celebrating. *Populorum Progressio* was issued fifteen months after the conclusion of the Second Vatican Council. At the Council, the great panorama of Catholic bishops of all races from what was then just beginning to be called "The Third World" came for the first time into the full view of the fascinated public. (Compare the 700 bishops at Vatican I in 1870 to the 2,200 at Vatican II in 1961). Heretofore, "Catholic Social Teaching" had been centrally addressed to the problems of industrialization, and especially to the workers of Europe.[11] The Church and its terminology were Eurocentric, and America was largely out of focus, dim on the periphery. Such terms as "liberal" were employed in the sense that they had acquired on the European Continent: anti-Catholic, radically anti-religious, atheistic, and materialistic. Although "Manchester liberals" were occasionally mentioned (by Pius XI, for example), this reference appears to have been derived from a group of German economists who used that name.[12]

Between 1947 and Vatican II, meanwhile, Europe had already experienced the "European miracle" of swift political and economic recovery through the combination of democratic institutions and a modified capitalism which the Germans call the "social market economy." But during the Council, the attention of the Church was jolted by the comparative economic stagnation of Latin America, Africa, and Asia. This is the problem that Paul VI addressed in *Populorum Progressio*. He had become the first "pilgrim pope," and had been deeply impressed, as he notes, by what he had seen on his worldwide trips.[13]

Consider the situation when Paul VI wrote that encyclical in 1967. The capital stock of Japan had been all but levelled in World War II, an unnecessary war into which unchecked war lords had led a great nation. By 1967, Japan had already recovered dramatically; but it was still far from being the economic giant that it was to become during the next twenty years. In 1967, South Korea was far poorer than any nation in Latin America, and Taiwan, Hong Kong, and Singapore still ranked among very poor developing nations. In 1965, life expectancy in Latin America as a whole was 57 years; in Africa, 42 years; and in Asia 44 years. (By 1985, these crucial numbers would advance to 64, 51 years, and 52 years, respectively.)[14] Seeing the misery, even as populations were beginning the experience advances in hygiene and health, Paul VI began with a lapidary phrase: For him, the "principal fact" of 1967 was that "the social question has become world-wide"[4].

Thus did Pope Paul VI bring the Catholic Church face-to-face with the reality that Adam Smith had been the first to articulate in 1776: the possibility, and therefore the moral duty, that all the nations of the world could break out from the age-old prison that poverty had imposed upon the human race, through a systematic inquiry into the nature and causes of the wealth of nations. (Leo XIII had already alluded to *The Wealth of Nations* in *Rerum Novarum* in 1891.)[15] Nearly thirty years earlier, by contrast, Pope Pius IX had issued his *Syllabus of Errors*, hurling at Continental liberalism such anathemas as: "The Roman Pontiff can and ought to reconcile himself to, and agree with, progress, liberalism and recent civilization."[16] Against development, the Church seemed then to have shut its door. Leo XIII opened it by more than a crack. But Paul VI, following Vatican II, was now willing to walk through it, saying in one of the most famous lines of *Populorum Progressio*: "Development is the new name for peace" [87].

Literally, of course, this statement is not true. The pursuit of justice is more often like a flaming sword. New standards of health and medicine mean bulging populations. Pre-modern institutions strain under modern dynamisms. Economic, political, and cultural development impose a new set of moral obligations. Most of all, once the secrets of how to create wealth in a systematic fashion have been discerned, then poverty is no longer morally acceptable. Given the suffering imposed by the ancient prison of poverty, the *new moral obligation is development*. Morally, if we can lift the siege of immemorial poverty by creating new wealth on a worldwide basis, among all peoples, we must do so. No national leader can any longer say: "My people are a poor people; and we intend to keep them that way." Development, in sum, is a new moral obligation. Turmoil, not peace, is the first result, although not the hoped for and ultimate result.

Thus, Adam Smith launched a process that would inspire the entire world to undertake a three-hundred-year journey toward developing the wealth of every nation. Obviously, not every people would choose to proceed at the same pace. Indeed, the burden of Smith's argument was that many of the experiments in "the Colonies" (soon to become the United States) were in advance of those of Great Britain. He argued that Great Britain should learn from these experiments, and break the stranglehold of state mercantilism that was keeping Britons far poorer than they ought to be. In this long historical process, he thought, one nation should learn from another. The new art of "political economy," of which Smith is justly called the founder, was in his mind empirical, rooted in experience, corrigible by trial and error. He himself ransacked the world (much of his book is about practices in what we would today call the "Third World") for examples and lessons. And he by no means thought that development should be economic solely. He was a moral philosopher by training, of an unusually empirical bent, and shared a Protestant Christian sense of "moral sentiments" and communitarian values.[17]

This vein in Anglo-American thought is made more explicit by Paul VI: "Development cannot be limited to mere economic growth" [14]. Pope Paul VI cites *The Conditions of Economic Progress* by the lay Catholic economist Colin Clark of Australia (a nation in the South that early developed far beyond Third World status), and quotes directly from Father Lebret's work on the dynamic of human development:

> We do not believe in separating the economic from the human, nor development from the civilizations in which it exists. What we hold important is man, each man and each group of men, and we even include the whole of humanity.[18]

This was Adam Smith's point in addressing all nations.

"Increased possession is not the ultimate goal of nations," Paul VI writes, "nor of individuals. All growth is ambivalent" [19]. Adam Smith and the other pioneers in the new science of political economics hoped to provide new ways of discerning in advance some of the consequences of various courses of action. Theirs, they accepted, was only a "dismal science" of means and probable consequences. It would have to be employed in the light of moral criteria supplied by sources beyond themselves. Quite self-consciously, the first political economists of Anglo-American background conceived of their discipline as a handmaiden of morals and ethics.[19]

"All social action involves a doctrine," Paul VI writes. He does not say this only to separate his own vision of development from those "based upon a materialistic and atheistic philosophy . . . which [does not] respect . . . human freedom and dignity" [39]. He says it, expressly, in order to promote "a new humanism." Here Paul VI specifically footnotes Jacques Maritain's *Integral Humanism*. In a later book, Maritain wrote that his vision of a humanistic future is best approximated by the example of the United States, a country whose institutions he had learned to love during, and after, his wartime exile.[20]

Some commentators think that Paul VI has words about property that liberals find hard to swallow. For example: "Private property does not constitute for anyone an absolute and unconditioned right;" and again, "The right to property must never be exercised to the detriment of the common good" [23]. But compare those sentences to John Locke:

> . . . labor being the unquestionable property of the laborer, no man but he can have a right to what that is once joined to, *at least where there is enough, and as good left in common for others*.[21]

And to John Stuart Mill:

The justification, in an economical point of view, of property in land . . . . [is] only valid, in so far as the proprietor of land is its improver. Whenever, in any country, the proprietor, generally speaking, ceases to be the improver, political economy has nothing to say in defense of landed property, as there established . . . .

When the "sacredness of property" is talked of, it should always be remembered, that any such sacredness does not belong in the same degree to landed property. No man made the land. It is the original inheritance of the whole species. Its appropriation is wholly a question of general expediency. When private property in land is not expedient, it is unjust.22

For Adam Smith, "the cause of the wealth of nations" is intelligence, research, and discovery, combined with a will to explore new horizons and to take risks. The source of wealth, in short, is human creativity. Paul VI clearly understands this, for he writes [25]:

By persistent work and use of his intelligence man gradually wrests nature's secrets from her and finds a better application for her riches. As his self-mastery increases, he develops a taste for research and discovery, an ability to take a calculated risk, boldness in enterprise, generosity in what he does and a sense of responsibility.

But, then, in his famous paragraph 26, Paul VI defines what he calls "unchecked liberalism," which Pius XI in 1931 had denounced as "the international imperialism of money." That year was the slough of the Depression, and Hitler was on his way to seizing power in Germany. Many "liberal" nations were soon to fall under Axis control, and the others, especially Britain, were mortally threatened. Notwithstanding the later liberation of Europe, and notwithstanding the "miraculous" development of Europe after World War II, Paul VI then defines "unchecked liberalism" in terms that no liberal society of 1967 actually embodied. He means by "unchecked liberalism" a system

which considers profit as the key motive for economic progress, competition as the supreme law of economics, and private ownership of the means of production as an absolute right that has no limits and carries no corresponding social obligation.

One year before Leo XIII wrote *Rerum Novarum*, economic historian Stephen T. Worland notes, the Sherman Anti-Trust Act (not to mention social legislation since) made this definition inapplicable to realities in the United States.23 In the light of universal sin, liberalism like everything else is properly given check.

Another famous sentence opens paragraph 66: "The world is sick." Its illness, says the Pope, lies chiefly in "the lack of brotherhood among individuals and peoples." A moment later, he calls upon Western "industrialists, merchants, leaders or representatives of large enterprises." First he commends their virtue at home, then upbraids their vices abroad: "It happens that they are not lacking in social sensitivity in their own country; why then do they return to the inhuman principles of individualism when they operate in less developed countries?" [70] In this and in many other passages, the encyclical overlooks the difference between the systems of developed nations and those of undeveloped nations. Virtue without institutions is seldom sufficient. To support virtue and to restrain vice, well-designed checks and balances are necessary. Individuals can scarcely function in the same way in one set of institutions as in another.

Poorly designed systems quite often frustrate virtuous persons, whereas well-designed institutions make even less virtuous persons function better than they otherwise might. Father Jozef Tischner gives examples from Poland, concerning the frustration of Polish fishermen, who labor at risk to life and limb, only to learn that their catch frequently rots in ill-kept refrigerated warehouses, under the management of incompetent authorities.24 Suppliers of public transport in Lima, Peru, 95 percent of whom are working as "illegals", cannot gain legal incorporation papers, obtain legitimate credit, or qualify for insurance; they must labor uneasily outside the law.25

Consider, too, a virtuous family in Argentina trying to save funds for their children's education as the inflation of 1985 reached more than 100 percent *per month*. Morally, should such a family invest those funds in Argentina? If they do, at that rate of inflation, their children will not be able to afford higher education. If with many others they do not, Argentina will lose its sources of internal investment, and will not be able to develop. Individuals cannot escape the realities of the institutions in which they must live and work.

I wrote in greater detail about *Populorum Progressio* in Chapter 7. The judgment made there seems to me to be confirmed by events. Let us now look at the steps beyond Paul VI taken by John Paul II, especially in economics.

## Creation Theology

*Sollicitudo* is divided into seven parts. Let us highlight important points in each, in turn. In what follows, italics within quotes are those of the official Vatican edition of the encyclical. For the most part, quotations are in the sequence of their appearance. Numbers in brackets indicate the section from which the quotation is taken.

His introduction repeatedly alerts us that, while maintaining continuity with the past, Pope John Paul II intends to say something "new." He grants that *Populorum Progressio* retains its force as "an *appeal to conscience*," but John Paul II wants to extend its impact and bring it to bear upon 1987, not 1967. For time passes "*ever more quickly*" today, "the *configuration of the world* in the course of the last twenty years . . . has undergone notable changes and presents some totally new aspects." John Paul's emphasis is upon the new. *Progressio*, in his view, is dated. Indeed, "the aim of the present *reflection* is to emphasize, through a theological investigation of the present world, the need for a fuller and more nuanced concept of development"[4]. A fuller and more nuanced concept-that is the aim.

In Part II, John Paul II credits Paul VI with three points or originality. In each case except the last, though, John Paul II highly qualifies that originality. First, Paul VI addressed an economic and social problem in a theological, papal way; but Leo XIII, John Paul notes, had already done this in 1891. Second, Paul VI asserted that "the social question is now worldwide"; but "in fact," *Sollicitudo* notes, Pope John XXIII "had already entered into this wider outlook" six years earlier [9]. This is faint praise.

The third point of originality is the one Pope John Paul II develops. He chooses as a summary of *Populorum Progressio*: "Development is the new name for peace," and says that, if this is true, "war and military preparations are the major enemy of the integral development of peoples" [10]. This does not appear to be an empirical claim. No evidence for it is produced, nor are various forms of apparently contradictory evidence addressed. So the words need to be examined closely.

In the war between Iran and Iraq, for example, development *has* been interrupted by awful war. Yet during the two decades from 1947 to 1967 Western Europe and Japan had by a political, economic, and cultural "miracle" leapt far beyond the poverty and misery to which World War II had reduced them. Had they not resisted Soviet expansion, however, could they have done so? Despite the burden of "military preparedness," they had developed far beyond their pre-war state. They also developed far beyond the laggard nations of the Third World, many of whom had escaped the destruction of World War II entirely. To offer another example: despite the heavy burden of military preparedness imposed upon South Korea by the unrelenting bellicosity of its communist neighbor to the North (whose government did not scruple to set off a bomb in Burma to kill as many of the South Korean cabinet as its agents could), South Korea has developed with remarkable rapidity during the years from 1967 to 1987.

Clearly, Pope John Paul II's intention here is not to set forth empirically all the factual materials relating "war and military preparedness" to "development," materials which are almost as various as the nations. His is a more commonsense point. Would it not be morally better if the resources currently going into arms would go into ending poverty worldwide? Would that no arms were necessary! Would that all citizens could be involved in peaceful human commerce and cultural interchange! Would that there were no Berlin Wall separating the two branches of Europe! No doubt, too, the Pope hopes to speed the "liberalization" of the U.S.S.R. along, so that that Wall will come down. (It is noteworthy that in China, the U.S.S.R. and nearly all other places, although not in papal documents, "liberal" has become a positive word. The history of the word "liberal" in Italy may supply clues to the Vatican's special usage.)[26]

In Part III, John Paul II offers his "Survey of the Contemporary World." The "first fact" he notes is that "*the hopes for development*, at that time so lively [1967], today appear very far from being realized." Paul VI had "no illusions," John Paul II says. Elsewhere, though, "there was a *certain* widespread *optimism*" about development. If Paul had no illusions, John Paul admits to "a *rather negative* impression" of "the present situation of the world." He writes: "Without going into an analysis of figures and statistics," it is sufficient to point to the multitudes suffering from "the intolerable burden of poverty" [12-13]. His intention is expressly not analytical, nor even empirical, but rather to come to the moral point.

His "first *negative observation*" concerns "the persistence and often the widening of the *gap*" between the developed and the developing nations. "Gap" is "perhaps not the appropriate word," he notes, since the reality is not "stationary" but has to do with "*the pace of progress*." (Actually, the pace of economic growth is often *higher* in Third World countries. But even when some attain a 10-percent annual growth, versus one-percent in developing nations, this results arithmetically in a wider gap.[27] The Pope recognizes the inadequacy of the word "gap." The point he wishes to make is not the arithmetic one; his point is the prolonged suffering of the poor. Why does it happen? He turns quickly to "*the differences of culture*" and "*value systems*" between the various population groups . . . which help to create distances" [14]. This is an important *economic* point. The habits of people do differ, with enormous economic consequences. Consider the Chinese, a successful subculture wherever they go. Consider the percentage of gross world product that the roughly 120 million Japanese of 1980 produced, compared to that produced by the roughly 120 million Brazilians.[28] Differences of culture and value systems do make an economic difference.

Then come two passages of extraordinary originality in papal teaching. John Paul II speaks first of "a right which is important not only for the individual but for the common good." Yet, "in today's world . . . [this] *right to economic initiative* is often suppressed." This "*right to private initiative*" becomes central to the rest of the document, the linchpin of John Paul II's theological vision of a good economic order. He grounds "the spirit of initiative" in "*the creative subjectivity of the citizen*." (Each citizen is made in the image of the Creator.) Moreover, the Pope sees that this right serves both the *common good* and the human spirit. His primary justification for it is a common good argument. He contrasts respect for it with its suppression, and rests his case on experience.

> Experience shows us that the denial of this right, or its
> limitation in the name of an alleged "equality" of everyone in
> society, diminishes, or in practice absolutely destroys the
> spirit of initiative, that is to say the creative subjectivity of the
> citizen. As a consequence, there arises, not so much a true

equality as a "levelling down." In the place of creative
initiative there appear passivity, dependence and submission
to the bureaucratic apparatus which, as the only "ordering"
and "decision-making" body–if not also the "owner"–of the
entire totality of goods and the means of production, puts
everyone in a position of almost absolute dependence, which
is similar to the traditional dependence of the worker–
proletarian in capitalism. This provokes a sense of frustration
or desperation and predisposes people to opt out of national
life, impelling many to emigrate and also favoring a form of
"psychological" emigration [15].

This passage is a silver spike in the heart of Marxism-Leninism.

The second vital point made by John Paul II in this section redefines
poverty. Deprivation of material goods is bad; but "in today's world there are
many other *forms of poverty*." In some ways, the denial of rights of the spirit is a
worse form of poverty than material deprivation.

The denial or limitation of human rights–as for example the
right to religious freedom, the right to share in the building of
society, the freedom to organize and to form unions, or to take
initiatives in economic matters–do these not impoverish the
human person as much as, if not more than, the deprivation of
material goods? And is development which does not take into
account the full affirmation of these rights really development
on the human level? [15].

This is another silver spike to the heart.

Since 1967, John Paul II judges, "conditions have become *notably worse*."
In this summary judgment, the Pope is obviously discounting certain
achievements, since he mentions elsewhere that some developing nations (India
is one) have become "self-sufficient in food." He could have mentioned, but did
not, that levels of longevity and higher education are advancing strikingly, and
that advances in health and longevity are better indices of development than
many others.[29] Again a number of nations poor in 1967 rank today among the
developed countries (several nations of East Asia among them). Still, he
discerns "various causes" for the "deterioration" he observes. The first is
"undoubtedly grave omissions on the part of developing nations themselves."
The second is that developed nations "have not always, at least in due measure,
felt the duty" to help less affluent countries [16].

In particular, he discerns–without specifics and without citing evidence–
economic, financial and social *mechanisms* which, although they are
manipulated by people, often function almost automatically, thus accentuating
the situation of wealth or some and poverty for the rest."

The Pope turns next to three specific *signs* of "underdevelopment," two of which occur even within the developed countries: the housing shortage; the "shrinking" of sources of employment; and the debt crisis of the Third World [17-19]. Regarding the last, the document produced by the Pontifical Commission for Justice and Peace (27 December 1986),[30] which the Pope cites, has been praised by the editorial writers of the *Wall Street Journal*. The one point the document overlooks is that many nations have borrowed huge sums ($50 billion in the case of South Korea), but used this capital so creatively that they have not only paid interest on it, and returned much of the principal ahead of schedule, but have also made a profit on it. Far from stagnating or declining, such nations have used debt to leap forward. Others, of course, have borrowed the capital of others, but put it to such uncreative use that they cannot now repay it. This is a tragedy, in whose resolution (the Institute of Justice and Peace wisely wrote) all must participate. The lending peoples have been preparing themselves to absorb considerable losses. Capital placed at risk is often, in fact, lost in that way.

Regarding the homeless, the Pope has a good point, widely accepted. Regarding unemployment in the development nations, however, he does not note that Western Europe has lost 2 million net jobs since 1970, whereas the United States during the same period has generated 35 million new jobs. (The U.S. figure gained 500,000 in February 1988 alone, the month in which the encyclical appeared). The U.S. today has a higher proportion of adults over fifteen years of age employed (62 percent) than at any time in its history.[31] In the United States, the "sources of work" are plainly not shrinking. Most of the 35 million jobs were created by small businesses. Indeed, during 1985, some 12,500 new businesses were established during every week, 650,000 per year.[32] The reason for this lies in the Pope's often-repeated principle: the right to private economic initiative. In Europe, by contrast, the obstacles young persons encounter in trying to start new businesses are formidable. European governments have chosen security for those already employed, and their economies have stagnated accordingly.[33] The United States has chosen the right to private economic initiative, and has thereby experienced the longest period of steady economic growth in its history.

In sections 20-23, the encyclical argues that another cause of deterioration in the developing nations is the military rivalry between the Eastern and Western blocs. (Elsewhere, Peter Berger discusses this theme from an empirical point of view.)[34] The Pope claims to be offering a factual "Survey of the Contemporary World." Such a factual survey has no more authority than the facts warrant. Regarding the "parallelism" between East and West that the Polish pope surprisingly alleges, I make the following brief comments:

1.   These paragraphs must be read in the light of the body of the Pope's earlier work.

2.   The actual *praxis* of East and West must be evaluated in the light of the *moral criteria* the Pope proposes for the good society. Every one of these criteria reflects basic principles of Western, but not Eastern, societies.

3.   Twenty-five million Americans (one in ten) have roots in the lands under the domination of the U.S.S.R. They know well that their lands of origin do not have the same voluntary relation to the Warsaw Pact that Western nations have to NATO. They know through family experience the moral and empirical differencs between life in the East and life in the West.

4.   "Moral equivalence" (a phrase not used by the Pope) is flatly rejected by both the left and the right in the United States.[35] It is common Western practice to *criticize* both West and East, although everyone knows that the act of criticism has very different consequences in each.

5.   Evidence to support the claims in sections 20-23 is lacking. The lack of historical detail embodied in these passages has puzzled the Pope's admirers and made many who have normally been hostile to him gleeful. Further comments follow in section 6, below.

It seems that the Pope is so eager to have the Wall between East and West come down, and the suffocating Iron Curtain removed, that he has permitted himself a certain rhetorical excess, in order to achieve a more liberal, open, and free international society, shaped by Western ideas of respect for such basic rights as religious liberty and the right to private economic initiative. His aim is noble. These passages, indeed, recall Alexander Solzhenitsyn's Harvard address, "A World Split Apart," in which, however, the prophetic novelist in criticizing both sides was more careful than the encyclical to avoid claims of moral parallelism.[36]

"The *demographic problem*," the Pope observes, cuts both ways. Some nations do suffer "difficulties" from growing populations. But "the northern hemisphere" is suffering from a "*drop in the birthrate*," which is already having severe "repercussions for the aging of the population" [25]. The Pope could here have cited Ben Wattenberg's powerful study, *The Birth Dearth*.[37] Here the Pope could also have made, and did not, a powerful connection between his emphasis on "the image of God" endowed in humans by their Creator and his "right to promote economic initiative." Each new infant is not solely an open mouth, a consumer (lowering the national per capita income by increasing the size of the population), but also has a brain, hands, and heart able to invent and to create far more than he or she will ever consume in life. This fact, indeed, is the very ground of development. The cause of the wealth of nations is the wit [Latin, *caput*] of every single citizen. Many of the most highly developed nations (Japan, Hong Kong, the Netherlands) are among the most densely populated places on earth; many of the less developed (Brazil, for example) are among the least densely populated.

Next the Pope turns to the "*positive aspects*" in the contemporary world, especially "the increased insistence that *human rights should be respected*" [26]. This is a triumph for Western conceptions of human rights as natural, universal, and beyond the claims of states. He also mentions his "*ecological concern.*"[38] Coming from what is one of the most polluted spots on earth, beneath the air inversion over the region of Krakow in Poland, the Pope knows vividly the heavy pollution that heedless and incautious industrialization can wreak upon nature and humankind.

Finally, the Pope also recognizes that certain "Third World" countries, despite the burden of many negative factors, "have succeeded in reaching a *certain self-sufficiency in food*, or a degree of industrialization which makes it possible to survive with dignity and to guarantee sources of employment for the active population" [26]. Since these achievements flow from the Pope's stated moral principles, especially from respect for the right to private economic initiative, we may hope that in a later encyclical the Pope will reflect upon the nature and causes of these success stories, amid his generally negative impressions about the current situation.

## The History of Liberty

Philosophically and theologically, Chapter IV on "Authentic Human Development" is the heart of this encyclical. Here the Pope turns to theology as story. He roots this story in the Creation story of Genesis. He says, "A part of this diverse plan. . . *is our own history*, marked by our personal and collective effort to raise up the human condition." In this great story, the Church plays a role, has "a duty," and urges "all to think about the nature and characteristics of authentic human development" [31]. This last point establishes a large agenda for the future.

Development, the Pope begins, "is *not* a straightforward process, *as it were automatic* and *in itself limitless*." Plainly, "the mere accumulation of goods and services, even for the benefit of the majority, is not enough for the realization of human happiness." In this light, he criticizes "a form of *superdevelopment*, equally inadmissible. . . which consists in an *excessive* availability of every kind of material goods," which "easily makes people slaves of 'possession' and of immediate gratification." This is a theme that many Americans welcome. Most of us are fond of criticizing our own civilization in this respect, and in denouncing with the Pope "the so-called civilization of 'consumption' or 'consumerism,' which involves so much 'throwing away' and 'waste.'" Those who live that way suffer, just as the Pope says, "a *radical dissatisfaction*" [28]. Materialism is not satisfying. Humans do not live by material things alone.

The Pope points out that "having" is necessary for "being." It is wrong that some are "deprived of essential goods" and so "do not succeed in realizing their basic human vocation." Others who have much, caught by "the call of 'having'," do not "really succeed in 'being.'" We must see material goods as "a gift from God." More than that, "the danger of the misuse of material goods and the appearance of artificial needs should in no way hinder the regard we have for the new goods and resources placed at our disposal and the use we make of them." Being made in God's image, we have a special relation to "the *earth* from which God forms man's body, and the breath of life which he breathes into man's nostrils" (cf. Gen. 2:7). Economic development, therefore, is "*necessary*," but not sufficient. It is "*necessary*, . . . since it must supply the greatest possible number of the world's inhabitants with an availability of goods essential for them 'to be.'" This is a nice revision of the Benthamite calculus: "The greatest good for the greatest number." The "notion of development," then, is not only a profane notion, "but the *modern expression* of an essential dimension of man's vocation" [28-30].

"The fact is that man was not created, so to speak, immobile and static" [30]. Humans have a vocation to pursue development. As Romano Guardini used to say, the liturgy is "all creation, redeemed and at prayer." The human vocation is to bring creation to its preordained fruition, to discover, to create. The Pope's Genesis view of the world brings the Catholic church into the world of progress and development—with an acute sense of sin, human fragility, and the need for mercy (the subject of the Pope's second encyclical).39

The Pope is far from being entirely pessimistic. "The story of the human race described by Sacred Scripture is, even after the fall of sin, a story of *constant achievement* . . . today's 'development' is to be seen as a moment of the story which began at creation, a story which is constantly endangered by reason of infidelity to the Creator's will, and especially by the temptation to idolatry." Development is a "*difficult yet noble task*," in which "it is always man who is the protagonist" [30]. One wishes that in a later encyclical, the Pope will humbly admit that many of those who first dreamed of development found the Catholic church (and other churches of their time) rather unsympathetic and undiscerning. For, even explicitly, John Paul II admits to reappropriating their dream, but now within a new horizon: "Here the perspectives widen. The dream of 'unlimited progress' reappears, radically transformed by the new outlook created by Christian faith"[31].

In the *Federalist*, Madison and Hamilton wrote so often in a pessimistic vein of the sinfulness that humans have shown throughout recorded history, that finally in No. 76 Hamilton feels obliged to correct the balance by showing that, nonetheless, humans do often rise above their faults to perform nobly and to secure the common good.40 Similarly, John Paul II, having sounded many "pessimistic" notes, as he admits, turns now to correct the balance.

The Pope cites the "*optimistic vision*" of history and work, that is to say of the *perennial value* of authentic human achievements," often found in the Fathers of the Church. He explicitly commends St. Basil the Great, Theodoret of Cyr, and St. Augustine's *City of God*, Book XIX [31 at n. 58].

The Pope turns again to liberty, stressing that the development of peoples or nations "should also include individual cultural identity and openness to the transcendent. Not even the need for development can be used as an excuse for imposing on others one's own way of life or own religious belief" [32]. This passage offers important support for systems of pluralism and liberty of conscience. He emphasizes that "The *intrinsic connection* between authentic development and respect for human rights once again reveals the *moral character* of development," especially as regards "each individual." Development that does not respect spiritual requirements "will prove unsatisfying and in the end contemptible" [33].

Toward the end, the Pope links *solidarity* and *freedom* in a most important way. (In this volume, I have pointed out that "freedom" is essential to the Catholic concept of social justice–that "justice" and "peace" alone are not enough. The Lay Commission on Catholic Social Thought and the U.S. Economy also stressed that, without "freedom," the concept of "solidarity" may suggest the suppression of dissent, lack of liberty, etc.)[41] He writes: "In order to be genuine, development must be achieved within the framework of solidarity and freedom, without ever sacrificing either of them under whatever pretext" [33].

Finally, in section 34, the Pope turns again to ecology, making three comments: Humans must "take into account *the nature of each being* and of its *mutual connection* in an ordered system." Second, "*natural resources* are limited; some are not, as it is said, *renewable*." Third, the result of industrialization must not be the pollution of the environment [34]. All these are today part of the secular conventional wisdom of the West. The City of Pittsburgh, where I partially grew up, was then one of the nation's most polluted cities, and is now one of the cleanest.

On these points, the Pope is here factually inexact only about "limits" on natural resources. The fundamental natural resource is the human mind.[42] "Resources" are constantly changing, as the mind finds better substitutes for older materials. Fiber optics are replacing copper in lines of communication; plastics and ceramics are replacing steel in many automobile parts; electronic power is replacing mechanical power. For thousands of years oil was not a resource useful to humankind; since 1853, and for a time, it is; and now new substitutes are being sought for it. And so on. The Pope's case about the *moral* and *spiritual* dimension of progress points in fact to the creative power of the human mind, made in the image of God. The human mind was created so that it might discern ever *new* resources, and bring them forth from the ample treasury that the Creator entrusted to humankind. Within this biosphere lie unimagined resources, appropriate to every changing era, not yet discovered.

Pope John Paul's Section V, "A Theological Reading of Modern Problems," expressly goes beyond "an analysis limited exclusively to the economic and political causes of underdevelopment." He looks for "*moral causes.*" He looks to "the behavior of *individuals* considered as *responsible persons.*" He stresses that he is speaking in the context of "political decisions" and "political will" [35]. This gives him an opportunity to repeat his opposition to a cavalier use of the expression "structures of sin" (as in his Apostolic Exhortation *Reconciliatio et Paenitentia*).[43] Structures of sin "are rooted in personal sin, and thus always linked to the *concrete acts* of individuals." He reprints as a footnote the central passage of the Exhortation: "The real responsibility, then, lies with individuals. A situation—or, likewise, an institution, a structure, society itself—is not in itself the subject of moral acts." In other words, no one can escape personal responsibility by blaming "institutions" or "structure." To speak of "sinful structures" is to use a shorthand for the "accumulation and concentration of many *personal sins*" [36 at n. 65].

The Framers of the U.S. Constitution recognized this very concept. Since men are not angels, Madison wrote in *Federalist* 51, government is necessary; but, then, since public officials are not exempted from the burdens of sinfulness, checks and balances are also necessary if the guardians are also to be guarded. Since institutions staffed by sinners can never be sinless; since structures are always sinful because the individuals who operate them are sinful, "ambition must be made to counteract ambition."

> This policy of supplying, by opposite and rival interests, the defect of better motives, might be traced through the whole system of human affairs, private as well as public. We see it particularly displayed in all the subordinate distributions of power, where the constant aim is to divide and arrange the several offices in such a manner as that each may be a check on the other-that the private interest of every individual may be a sentinel over the public rights.

But the obverse is also true. Given the proper checks and balances, citizens may be encouraged to act in a virtuous fashion, concerned for the common good as well as their own. Virtue is indispensable. The idea that institutions can function without virtue is "chimerical."

Next the Pope diagnoses two "very typical" structures opposed to God's will:

> On the one hand, the *all-consuming desire for profit*, and on the other, *the thirst for power*, with the intention of imposing one's will upon others. In order to characterize better each of these attitudes, one can add the expression: "at any price." In other words, we are faced with the absolutizing of human attitudes with all its possible consequences [37].

No one, I think, can deny that such attitudes, wherever they occur, are contrary to the will of God. In societies in which systems are divided, and powers are divided, acts of this sort are also contrary to the civil law. In such societies, moral and political institutions check and balance economic activities. Similarly, the division of powers and a great many other checks and balances within constitutional governments drastically restrict "the thirst for power." In Western countries today, in fact, a more realistic question is whether political power is not too *weak*, too divided by checks and balances, too subject to electoral change. The United States, for example, is often accused by friends and foes of changing directions after each election. No one wishes to do away with checks and balances. Many do wonder, though, how democratic systems can prevail amid current dangers, as Jean-François Revel has written in *Why Democracies Perish*.44

The Pope's reason for introducing these considerations seems to be to show, if I may paraphrase Charles Péguy, that "development is moral or not at all." The path to it is "*long and complex*." For "obstacles to integral development [the very phrase echoes Maritain's *Integral Humanism*] are not only economic but rest on *more profound attitudes* which human beings can make into absolute values" [38]. The Pope, therefore, appeals to responsible persons to use their liberty with virtue. His name for the sum of the virtues needed is "solidarity," in which each is responsible for all, concerned for the common good of all.

> For world peace is inconceivable unless the world's leaders come to recognize that interdependence in itself demands the abandonment of the politics of blocs, the sacrifice of all forms of economic, military or political imperialism, and the transformation of mutual distrust into collaboration. This is precisely the act proper to solidarity among individuals and nations [39].

For the Pope "*solidarity* is understandably a *Christian virtue*" [40]. Even if others may not understand it in the same way, Christians ought to exemplify it before the world. No doubt, that is why many millions hope that the current small steps toward the "liberalization" of the Soviet Union are not a chimera. Not very long ago, after all, the greatest enemies of the Western Allies were Japan and Germany. Under liberalized governments, both those formerly Axis powers have turned their energies to peaceful pursuits, and both have joined the other liberal societies of the West in comity and amity. All hope and pray that a liberalized Soviet Union, having given up its reckless claim to world domination, will also choose the path of development and peace, both internally and externally. The publics of the West would, in such circumstances, be entirely willing to join with the U.S.S.R., as during our lifetimes they have joined with Germany and Japan. That earlier conversion is an earnest of the conversion that yet could come. Not long ago after every Mass Catholics used to pray for "the conversion of Russia," as the Lady of Fatima (to whom the Pope is especially devoted) requested.

Part VI is called "Some Particular Guidelines." "The Church does not have *technical solutions* to offer," John Paul II writes; and it "does not propose economic and political systems or programs." There comes, then, an unbecoming boast, calculated to make non-Catholics wince; the Church is an "expert in humanity" [41]. Most of the important practical "guidelines" briefly mentioned by John Paul II stress the importance of freedom.

First, though, comes a very important clarification of a false interpretation that has plagued Catholic social thought for at least sixty years, a false notion to which I called attention in *Spirit of Democratic Capitalism*.[45] The Pope writes:

> The Church's social doctrine is not a "third way" between liberal capitalism and Marxist collectivism, nor even a possible alternative to other solutions less radically opposed to one another: it is not an ideology, but rather the accurate formulation of the results of a careful reflection on the complex realities of human existence, in society and in the international order, in the light of faith and of the Church's tradition. Its main aim is to interpret these realities, determining their conformity with or divergence from the lines of the Gospel teaching on man and his vocation, a vocation which is at once earthly and transcendent; its aim is thus to guide Christian behavior. It therefore belongs to the field, not of ideology, but of theology and particularly of moral theology [41].

Next, the Pope stresses the "*love of preference* for the poor," and the need for "an international outlook" in embracing "the immense multitudes" of those in need [42].

As a particular guideline, the Pope asserts again that "the right to property is *valid and necessary*, but . . . is 'under a social mortgage,'" and falls under the principle (common to John Locke and John Stuart Mill) that "the goods of this world are *originally meant for all*." For Locke and Mill, the practical question is which *social system* is more likely to develop the goods of creation for the common good? To this query, as we have seen, Pope John Paul II has already answered: a regime respecting "the right to economic initiative." His answer, then, is virtually the same as Locke's and Mill's. But John Paul II carries the point well beyond the question of material poverty:

> Likewise, in this concern for the poor, one must not overlook that special form of poverty which consists in being deprived of fundamental human rights, in particular the right to religious freedom and also the right to freedom of economic initiative [42].

John Paul II has been specifically commended by the *Wall Street Journal* for calling for "the *reform of the international trade system. . .* and a *review of the structure of existing International Organizations*" [43].

Then in section 44, the Pope returns to one of his central and often-repeated themes:

> Development demands above all a spirit of initiative on the part of the countries which need it. Each of them must act in accordance with its own responsibilities, not expecting everything from the more favored countries, and acting in collaboration with others in the same situation. Each must discover and use to the best advantage its own area of freedom. . . . It is important then that as far as possible the developing nations themselves should favor the self-affirmation of each citizen, through access to a wider culture and a free flow of information.

He again points to the nations that "achieved the goal of *food sufficiency*" as a model for all others.

Then come two crucial clarifications of the Pope's moral criteria for the good society: Democratic political institutions are "a *necessary condition and sure guarantee*" of the development of "the whole individual and of all people." Another "essential condition for global *solidarity* is autonomy and free self-determination, also within associations such as "*new regional associations* inspired by criteria of *equality, freedom and participation*" [44-45].

### Freedom, At Last

This long encyclical opens its final chapter with the sentence: "Peoples and individuals aspire to be free." Citing Latin America, the Pope adds: "This approach makes *liberation* the fundamental category and the first principle of action."[46] At last, the Church concerned with Justice and Peace is adding "Freedom" as its "fundamental category" and "first principle." That this is done with reference to Latin America rather than to North America underlines the Vatican's delayed recognition of "ordered liberty" in the North American experience.

In the face of "the *sad experiences* of recent years" and "the mainly *negative picture* of the present moment," the Pope recalls that "The Church has *confidence also in man*, though she knows the evil of which he is capable." For this section [47], there are many parallels in the *Federalist*. Here as elsewhere, North American formulations, developed from Cicero, Aristotle, and other classic sources, and tested under modern conditions, would vindicate the Pope's confidence in democracy and development.

In closing, the Pope writes: "I wish to *appeal* to all men and women without exception." He adds that it is "appropriate to emphasize the *preeminent role* that belongs to the *laity*." In these matters, the laity must take the lead. They must test the cutting-edge hypotheses, gain the self-correcting experience, and "think about the nature and characteristics of authentic human development" [47]. They must, in short, recapitulate Adam Smith's effort, but in a Catholic framework. They must conduct a sustained *Inquiry into the Nature and Causes of the Wealth of Nations*, where wealth means not only material wealth, but also the security of rights, especially rights of religious liberty and pluralism, and a sense of international community (solidarity) based upon respect for autonomy and free association.

"*No temporal achievement*," the Pope concludes, "is to be identified with the Kingdom of God." All such achievements are only partial, anticipatory, "imperfect and temporary." The Pope entrusts to Mary, the Mother of God, his concern for all children in "this *difficult moment* of the modern world" [48-49].

## Moral Parallelism

Let us return, now, to a fuller discussion of the most controversial of the Pope's empirical claims about the present world. There are nine such passages, which journalists referred to as "moral parallelism" or "equidistance" or "moral equivalence." Six of them occur in Part III, "Survey of the Contemporary World" and three are repeated among the descriptive materials in Part V, "A Theological Reading of Modern Problems." The first six are found on six consecutive pages in sections 20-23, and the remaining three in sections 36, 37, and 39.

The main heading under which these texts fall, in the Pope's words, is "the *political* causes of today's situation." The Pope singles out one large generic fact: "Faced with a combination of factors which are undoubtedly complex, we cannot hope to achieve a comprehensive analysis here. However, we cannot ignore a striking fact about the *political* picture since the Second World War." He believes that this fact "has a considerable impact" on development. "I am referring to the *existence of two opposing blocs,* commonly known as the East and West." He adds in a generic euphemism, "Each of the two blocs tends to assimilate or gather around it other countries or groups of countries, to different degrees of adherence or participation" [20]. That the Pope does not intend to speak precisely is clear. Cardinal Lustiger of Paris has noted recently, for example, that there are more bishops for the Ukrainian rite in the United States than in Ukrainia today.[46] Most members of the Soviet bloc do not literally "gather around" the U.S.S.R.; Estonia, Latvia, Lithuania, Poland, Hungary, Czechoslovakia, and many others have been conquered. They have been kept within the East bloc by force, under the explicit terms of the Brezhnev Doctrine.

The Pope judges that the opposition between the blocs is at its depth "*ideological* in nature," on the basis of "two very different visions of man and of his freedom and social role." At this point, he is silent on which vision of freedom he supports, although the rest of the encyclical makes that crystal clear. "It was inevitable," he judges, that this "*ideological opposition* should evolve into a growing *military opposition*." What sort of inevitability he has in mind is not clear. But while trying to bring about change by persuasion, he is perhaps suggesting that such opposition has been freely chosen, and so may be freely altered. Perhaps, though, he is worried that over the next two or three decades the East will come to prevail. In that case, there is not much use in throwing his support to the West. He can only try to keep certain values alive, and to hold aloft certain institutions (democracy, the right to religious liberty, the right to private initiative, etc.) as long-term ideals. Alternatively, he may see both sides as capable of a rapid evolution, and wishes to promote this possibility.

> The question naturally arises: in what way and to what extent
> are these two systems capable of changes and updatings such
> as to favor or promote a true and integral development of
> individuals and peoples in modern society? [21]

He thinks that "at the present time" the danger "of an *open and total* war . . . seems to have receded, yet without completely disappearing."

The Pope judges that "the tension *between East and West*" concerns "two *concepts* of the development of individuals and peoples." Both concepts he describes as "being imperfect and in need of radical correction." The Church, he later writes, offers no "third way" between these two concepts. It does offer "guidelines" that help to form consciences. The "moral criteria" he in fact proposes do not seem to require the same degree of "radical" change in the West that they would require in the East. The inferred parallelism breaks down.

What especially concerns him are the "internal divisions" that this ideological opposition engenders in developing countries, "to the extent in some cases of provoking full civil war." In addition "investments and aid for development are often diverted from their proper purpose and used to sustain conflicts, apart from and in opposition to the interests of the countries that ought to benefit from them." This leads some countries to fear "falling victim to a form of neo-colonialism." The result is that the non-aligned nations affirm "the right of every people to its own identity, independence, and security, as well as a right to share, on a basis of equality and solidarity, in the goods intended for all" [21].

This, the Pope says, is "a clearer picture of the last twenty years." It shows that the conflict between East and West in the North is "an important cause of the retardation or stagnation of the South." Instead of being "*autonomous nations*," the nations of the South "became parts of a machine, cogs on a gigantic wheel." The one example the Pope gives is that "the center of communications" in the North "frequently impose a distorted vision of life and of man" [22]. Americans who have watched "Dynasty" and "Dallas" on overseas television concur with that. But, surely, such distortions—in television shows produced from a clearly left-wing and anti-business point of view—[47] injure the reputation of the United States much more than they cause economic "retardation" or "stagnation" in the South. Perhaps, though, feeding the prejudices of leftists does encourage economic retardation.

The Pope's words in these passages are extremely general. The variety among developing nations is staggering. Brazil is not like Bangladesh, nor is Zaire like Argentina, nor South Korea like North Korea, nor Afghanistan like Nicaragua. It is not easy to be certain which nations and which circumstances he has in mind. Pope John Paul II is describing a very big picture but without detail. Even in describing the two blocs he does not mention obvious differences. He writes:

> Each of the two blocs harbors in its own way a tendency toward *imperialism*, as it is usually called, or towards forms of neo-colonialism: an easy temptation to which they frequently succumb, as history, including recent history, teaches [22].

"Each in its own way"–the difference is not specified. The implication is that the way of the East is not identical to that of the West. Is there a *moral* difference between these two somehow different ways? The Pope does not say.

The Pope blames "an unacceptably exaggerated concern *for security*." He estimates that

> The very needs of an economy stifled by military expenditure and by bureaucracy and intrinsic inefficiency now seem to favor processes which might muitigate the existing opposition and make it easier to begin a fruitful dialogue and genuine collaboration for peace [22].

This passage seems to allude to recent pressures within the U.S.S.R., articulated by General Secretary Gorbachev, where the military budget consumes nearly 20 percent of the GNP. In the West, the defense budget of the U.S. has declined relative to the GNP and to the federal budget since 1960. In 1988, it stands at 6.1 percent.[48] The Pope repeats Paul VI's appeal "that the resources and investments devoted to arms production ought to be used to alleviate the misery of impoverished peoples" [23]. The infusion of new moneys might not accomplish that, however, since as the Pope suggests elsewhere investments in foreign aid are often used corruptly, and are often squandered. Certain sorts of systems strangle development. Aid passed through such systems may not reach the impoverished at all.

John Paul II does make one distinction between the faults of the West and the East. He suggests that "the West gives the impression of abandoning itself to forms of growing and selfish isolation." By contrast, "the East in its turn seems to ignore for questionable reasons its duty to cooperate in the task of alleviating human misery" [23]. Is this brief criticism of faults adequate to reality?

The Pope describes "*the millions of refugees*" as one of the "consequences" of this division in the world, and as a "festering *wound*" [24]. He knows as well as we do that the direction in which the refugees stream is one-way.

The three passages on the two blocs in Part V occur in the section on "structures of sin." In the Eastern bloc, the very concept of personal sin (the source of all structural sin) is denied. In the West, this concept is the foundation of the social system. Sin is the reason for limited government, with divided powers; for an economy of private initiative and its diversity; and for religious liberty and liberty of conscience, in open pluralism. In the light of his analysis of behind certain decisions, apparently inspired only by economics or politics, are real forms of idolatry: of money, ideology, class, technology" [24]. There are comparable observations in the mainstream of Western literature, in which Francis Bacon's "Idols of thought" is a traditional theme. Such classical writers as Madison in politics and Smith in economics make this theme the foundation of their thinking. Democratic and capitalist institutions are rooted in recognition of this capacity for self-delusion. That is why checks and balances are necessary.

On the surface, these nine passages have boosted in the world press the moral standing of the East, and lowered that of the West; to that extent, their net effect upon the world does not promote the moral theology that is the Pope's ultimate aim. Some critics in response have blamed the press. It is true that a close reading of the text does not support the exaggerated focus of the early reports from Rome. Yet those stories did focus, as journalists are trained to do, upon the new encyclical's most surprising and sensational lines.

When one reviews Pope John Paul II's papal utterances as a whole–his frequent praise of U.S. institutions, for example–[49] and when one reviews the underlying moral theology of this encyclical, even the most exposed lines of his argument are more cautious than first reports suggested.

However, a system constituted by democracy, by the exercise of private initiative in economics, and by religious liberty, is *intended* for relentless criticism. That is the principle of its development. A lively mind is the cause, not only of economic wealth, but of human progress in all dimensions. Pope John Paul II has said that the main theme of his papacy is "the primacy of the human spirit." That theme animates this encyclical.

### Conclusion: The Liberal Society

Pope John Paul II is both more pessimistic and more inspired by human possibilities for creativity than was Pope Paul VI. Both of them failed to study the "economic miracles" of the two decades before they wrote–Paul VI the "European miracle" of 1945 to 1967, and Pope John Paul II the "East Asian miracle" of 1967 to 1987. But John Paul II's emphasis on "the right to economic initiative" comes closest to explaining the cause of these miracles. Both popes, rather inexplicably, failed to study thoroughly the causes of success stories.

Pope Paul VI underemphasized the internal capacities for creativity in the poor countries, several of which were to astonish the world with their growth after 1967. And in asking the wealthy nations to share their "superfluous" wealth,[50] Paul VI seemed to beg several crucial questions. Will such shared wealth be used for corrupt purposes, in fruitless ways, and in systems whose internal design is bound to strangle development in its crib? Or will there be systematic internal reforms? John Paul II pays significantly greater attention to these questions, but with far less sharpness of detail than current knowledge warrants.

He also goes beyond Paul VI in five vital ways: in his emphasis on *democracy* as an essential condition for authentic development; in his emphasis on "*the right to economic initiative*," as an essential condition both for meeting the common good and for respecting the creative subjectivity of the person; and in his emphasis upon *religious liberty*, the deprivation of which, he says, is a deprivation worse than material poverty. Fourth, his declaration that Catholic social teaching does *not* offer a "*third way*" clarifies a longstanding misconception. His stress on freedom as the "fundamental category" and "first principle of action" for Catholic social teaching adds to "justice" and "peace" the value indispensable to a freely given faith, *ordered liberty*.

Under Pope John Paul II, Catholic social thought is steadily advancing. Not only did Cardinal Ratzinger's two letters on liberation theology, particularly the second, make available to the Church a usable definition of Christian "liberty."[51] But here in *Sollicitudo Rei Socialis*, John Paul II speaks of "freedom" as a "fundamental category" and "the first principles of action." Whether one regards the political order, the economic order, or the cultural order–the three orders mirrored in the structure of Vatican II's *Gaudium et Spes*–Pope John Paul II comes down on the side of ordered liberty. He stands, fundamentally, as what Americans would call a "liberal," in at least three ways.

Regarding the political order, John Paul asserts that democracy, the rule of law, limited government, and respect for human rights are "essential conditions" of a social order conformable to God's will.

Regarding the economic order, the Pope emphasizes in a new way that "the right of economic initiative" is the fundamental principle of authentic development. This right springs from the image of God that inspires human subjectivity. Through it, humans are endowed by God with an inalienable creativity, which serves the common good of all. By the same token, all of creation is destined for the common good of all. Experience has shown that regimes of private property and private initiative better develop the resources of nature than do collectivist or traditionalist regimes, both of which are statist in different ways and degrees.[52] As a limitation on the power of the state, the right to private initiative is necessary both for personal creativity and for the common good.

Regarding the moral order, the Pope makes religious freedom, pluralism, and the transcendent rights of conscience central to authentic development. The deprivation of such rights is worse than material deprivation. He says no scheme of development can justify imposing one's own faith or religion upon others.

Where these moral criteria of John Paul II are given expression in the institutions of society, such a society would, in the honorific sense, properly be called a "free society."

Thus, despite the clear signs of being the work of a committee; of having been delayed by internal disputes; of displaying sudden insertions and unexplained turns in the argument; of diverse literary styles; and of an organization anything but tightly logical, *Sollicitudo Rei Socialis* does succeed in advancing Catholic social teaching beyond Paul VI in *Populorum Progressio*, and even beyond *Laborem Exercens*. As an "inquiry into the nature and the characteristics of authentic human development," it blazes a rough trail for the future. Later inquiries will no doubt sharpen and deepen its principles yet further and organize them more tightly. At some point, too, papal documents will draw lessons from "success stories," since all the world wishes to learn how to build successful institutions of political liberty, economic creativity, and cultural vitality.

It is not easy being the Pontiff ("bridge") of a universal church. Factions within the church view reality in many quite different horizons. Such factions, pitted against one another in civil argument and in due regard for the lessons of experience, can spur each other to achieve the ultimate good of all. The competition of ideas is as necessary to Catholic social thought as it is to the free society. Those who value the liberal society may rejoice that so many central liberal ideals are slowly gaining acceptance, one by one, in the Church's continuing reflection.

Finally, it would be a real challenge for the Church to conduct an inquiry into the specific economic failures of Catholic nations around the world, such as those of Latin America and, among its successful Confucian neighbors, the Philippines. Are there important gaps in Catholic thought and traditions? Why do some Catholic nations develop so slowly? Why are Catholic peoples so much more vulnerable than Protestants to Communist parties?[53] It would be a real challenge for the Church, during the next decade or so, to concentrate specifically upon economic development in Catholic nations. This would test Catholic methods against alternate methods. It would also fulfill the maxim: Charity begins at home. Were Catholic nations quickly to become world leaders in human development—and in invention in every dimension—the credibility of Catholic social thought would be much enhanced.

## Notes

1. See Russell Kirk, *The Roots of American Order* (LaSalle, Illinois: Open Court, 1974), ch. 2, "The Law and the Prophets."
2. The Continental Congress asked Benjamin Franklin, John Adams, and Thomas Jefferson "to prepare a device for a Seal of the United States of North America." Their design included "Pharaoh sitting in an open Chariot, a Crown on his head and a sword in his hand passing through the divided Waters of the Red Sea in pursuit of the Israelites." U.S., Department of State, *The Seal of the United States: How It was Developed and Adopted* (Washington, D.C.: Department of State, 1892), pp. 5-6. See also Richard S. Patterson and Richardson Douglass, *The Eagle and the Shield: A History of the Great Seal of the United States* (Washington, D.C.: U.S. Government Printing Office, 1976); Leonard Wilson, *The Coat of Arms, Crest and Great Seal of the United States of America* (San Diego, Calif.: By the Author, 1928).
3. Thomas Jefferson, "A Summary View of the Rights of British America, 1774," in Adrienne Koch and William Peden, eds., *The Life and Selected Writings of Thomas Jefferson* (New York: Modern Library, 1972), p. 311.

4.  See George Weigel, *Tranquillitas Ordinis: The President Failure and Future Promise of American Catholic Thought on War and Peace* (New York: Oxford University Press, 1987); and his essay in Kenneth Myers, ed., *Aspiring to Freedom* (Grand Rapids, Michigan: Eerdmans, 1988).

5.  In the first paragraph of the *Federalist*, Alexander Hamilton writes: "It seems to have been reserved to the people of this country, by their conduct and example, to decide the important question, whether societies of men are really capable or not of establishing good government from *reflection* and *choice*, or whether they are forever destined to depend for their political constitutions on *accident* and *force*" (my emphasis).

6.  "It is a fundamental principle of social philosophy, fixed and unchangeable," Pius XI writes, "that one should not withdraw from individuals and commit to the community what they can accomplish by their own enterprise and industry. So, too, it is an injustice and at the same time a grave evil and a disturbance of right order, to transfer to the larger and higher collectivity functions which can be performed and provided for by lesser and subordinate bodies. . . .
    "The more faithfully this principle of 'subsidiarity' is followed and a hierarchical order prevails among the various organizations, the more excellent will be the authority and efficiency of society, and the happier and more prosperous the condition of the commonwealth." *Quadragesimo Anno*, 79-80.

7.  In an 1858 report to the Holy See, Archbishop John Hughes explained how Americans understand liberty: "Liberty, in this Country, has a very clear and specific meaning. It is not understood in Europe, as it is here. Here, it means the vindication of personal rights; the fair support of public laws; the maintenance, at all hazards, of public order, according to those laws; the right to change them when they are found to be absurd or oppressive." John Tracy Ellis, ed., *Documents of American Catholic History* (Milwaukee: Bruce Publishing Co., 1956), pp. 338-9.

8.  "From the beginning of America, freedom was directed to forming a well-ordered society and to promoting its peaceful life. Freedom was channeled to the fullness of human life, to the preservation of human dignity and to the safeguarding of all human rights. An experience in ordered freedom is truly a cherished part of this land." John Paul II, "The Miami Meeting with President Reagan," *Origins*, 24 September 1987, p. 238.

9.  In his Christmas Message of 1944, Pius XII declared that "the democratic form of government appears to many as a postulate of nature imposed by reason itself" because democracy guarantees the citizen the right "to express his own views of the duties and sacrifices that are imposed on him" and the right not to be "compelled to obey without being heard." The peoples of Europe, "taught by bitter experience, . . . are more aggressive in opposing the concentration of dictatorial power that cannot be censured or touched, and call for a system of government more in keeping with the dignity and liberty of the citizens. . . . These multitudes . . . are today firmly convinced . . . that had there been the possibility of censuring and correcting the actions of public authority, the world would not have been dragged into the vortex of a disastrous war, and that to avoid for the future the repetition of such a catastrophe we must vest efficient guarantees in the people itself." See also Guido Gonella, *The Papacy and World Peace* (London: Hollis and Carter, 1945).

10. In *Pacem in Terris*, 8-26, John XXIII gives his own Bill of Rights, which includes the right to life, the right to free inquiry, to worship, to work, to private property, to free association, to emigrate and immigrate, to equal protection of the laws, etc.

11. Joseph Gremillion writes: "Before the aggiornamento, Catholic social teaching addressed itself almost exclusively to the North Atlantic region, the nations that first experienced the Industrial Revolution. Indeed, original reflection on the Gospel, Church, and modern economic power was concentrated within a small oblong diamond whose points reach approximately Paris, Brussels, Munich, and

Milan." "Overview and Prospectus," in Gremillion, ed., *The Gospel of Peace and Justice: Catholic Social Teaching since Pope John* (Maryknoll, New York: Orbis Books, 1976), p. 35.

12.  See my discussion of "The 'Manchester Liberals'" in this volume, ch. 5, pp. 71-87.

13.  "Before We became Pope, two journeys, to Latin America in 1960 and to Africa in 1962, brought Us into direct contact with the acute problems pressing on continents full of life and hope. Then on becoming Father of all We made further journeys to the Holy Land and India, and were able to see and virtually touch the very serious difficulties besetting peoples of long-standing civilizations who are at grips with the problem of development." Pope Paul VI, *Populorum Progressio*, 4.

14.  U.N. Department of International Economic and Social Affairs, *Demographic Indicators of Countries* (New York: United Nations, 1982).

15.  See Oswald von Nell-Breuning, *Reorganization of the Social Economy: The Social Encyclical Developed and Explained* (New York: Bruce Publishing Co., 1936), p. 131.

16.  Quoted in Newman C. Eberhardt, *A Summary of Catholic History*, 2 vols. (St. Louis, Missouri: Herder, 1962), 2:467.

17.  Robert N. Bellah recently wrote that "there is a benign, optimistic, and profoundly moral quality to Adam Smith's notion of the invisible hand that was transformed almost into its opposite in the gloomy amoral scientism of Malthus's iron laws." Smith's defense of the free market, Bellah adds, "was based on his belief in the virtues of the 'system of natural liberty' that it embodied. Yet much as Smith admired the effectiveness of the self-regarding virtues in contributing to a productive economy, he never imagined that they were superior to the other-regarding virtues." Bellah, "The Economics Pastoral, A Year Later," *Commonweal*, 18 December 1987. Gertrude Himmelfarb has influenced Bellah in this area. She writes: "For Smith political economy was not an end in itself but a means to an end, that end being the wealth and well-being, moral and material, of the 'people,' of whom the 'laboring poor' were the largest part." *The Idea of Poverty: England in the Early Industrial Age* (New York: Knopf, 1984), ch. 2, "Adam Smith: Political Economy as Moral Philosophy," p. 63.

18.  *Populorum Progressio*, 14, quoting Louis Lebret, *Dynamique concrète du développement* (Paris: Economie et Humanisme, Les Editions Ouvrières, 1961), p. 28.

19.  Adam Smith subordinates political economy to the prudential judgment of the legislator: "Political economy, considered as a branch of the science of a statesman or legislator, proposes two distinct objects; first, to provide a plentiful revenue or subsistence for the people, or more properly to enable them to provide such a revenue or subsistence for themselves; and secondly, to supply the state or commonwealth with a revenue sufficient for the public services." *An Inquiry into the Nature and Causes of the Wealth of Nations*, ed. R. H. Campbell, A. S. Skinner, and W. B. Todd, eds., 2 vols. (Indianapolis, Indiana: Liberty Classics, 1981), Book IV, "Of Systems of Political Economy," p. 428. John Stuart Mill writes that political economy more directly concerns the production of wealth than its distribution: "The laws and conditions of the production of wealth partake of the character of physical truths." But "it is not so with the distribution of wealth." The "opinions and feelings of mankind" determine the distribution of wealth and are part of "a far larger and more difficult subject of inquiry than political economy." Mill, *Principles of Political Economy*, ed. Sir William Ashley (London: Longmans, Green & Co., 1909; reprint ed., Fairfield, New Jersey: August M. Kelley, 1976), Book II, ch. 1, sec. 1, pp. 199-200.

20.  See *Populorum Progressio*, at no. 44. In 1958, Maritain wrote: "I would like to refer to one of my books, *Humanisme Intégral*, which was published twenty years ago. When I wrote this book, trying to outline a concrete historical ideal suitable to

a new Christian civilization, my perspective was definitely European. I was in no way thinking in American terms, I was thinking especially of France, and of Europe, and of their historical problems, and of the kind of concrete prospective image that might inspire the activity, in the temporal field, of the Catholic youth of my country.

"The curious thing in this connection is that, fond as I may have been of America as soon as I saw her, and probably because of the particular perspective in which *Humanisme Intégral* was written, it took a rather long time for me to become aware of the kind of congeniality which existed between what is going on in this country and a number of views I had expressed in my book.

"Of course the book is concerned with a concrete historical ideal which is far distant from any present reality. Yet, what matters to me is the *direction* of certain essential trends characteristic of American civilization. And from this point of view I may say that *Humanisme Intégral* appears to me now as a book which had, so to speak, an affinity with the American climate by anticipation." Jacques Maritain, *Reflections on America* (New York: Charles Scribner's Sons, 1958), pp. 174-75.

21. John Locke, *Second Treatise*, 26. Locke adds: "The same Law of Nature, that does by this means give us Property, does also *bound* that *Property* too. *God has given us all things richly*, 1 Tim. vi. 17, is the Voice of Reason confirmed by Inspiration. But how far has he given it us? *To enjoy.* As much as any one make use of to any advantage of life before it spoils; so much he may by his labor fix a Property in. Whatever is beyond this, is more than his share, and belongs to others. Nothing was made by God for Man to spoil or destroy." Ibid., 31.

22. Mill, *Principles of Political Economy*, Book II, ch. 2, sec. 6, pp. 231, 233.

23. "Now it is obvious, given the existence of the Sherman Act and the way Section 1 has been enforced, that Pope Paul's definition of liberal capitalism is grossly inaccurate as a description of the U.S. economic system. For the Sherman Act clearly forbids some kinds of profit seeking. And it is certainly not the case that in our system 'private ownership . . . carries no social obligation.' The history of the Sherman Act shows that a business executive who uses his property to form a cartel-who flouts his social obligation by violating Section 1-will be put in jail. There may be somewhere in the world, somewhere in history, economic systems that tolerate the crude individualism stigmatized by Pope Paul VI. But the record shows the U.S. economy is not one of them." Stephen T. Worland, "The Preferential Option for the Poor: An Economist's Perspective," Inaugural Lecture of the William and Virginia Clemens Chair, St. John's University, Collegeville, October 23, 1987 (pamphlet).

24. Father Tischner, reported to be one of the authors of *Sollicitudo*, writes of Poland: "What good does it do when a fisherman exceeds a quota if there is no place to store the excess fish? What good does it do when people build a steel mill if the steel produced in it is more expensive and of poorer quality than the steel available on the open market? This . . . kind of betrayal consists in condemning work to senselessness." *The Spirit of Solidarity*, trans. Marek B. Zaleski and Benjamin Fiore, (New York: Harper & Row, 1984), p. 86.

25. Peruvian novelist Mario Vargas Llosa writes: "In Lima alone, informal commerce (excluding manufacturing) provides work for some 445,000 people. Of the 331 markets in the city, 274 (83 percent) have been constructed by informals. With regard to transport, it is no exaggeration to say that the inhabitants of Lima can move around the city thanks to the informals since, according to the findings of the Institute for Liberty and Democracy, 95 percent of the public transportation system of Lima belongs to them. Informals have invested more than $1 billion in the vehicles and maintenance facilities. . . . Half of the population of Lima lives in homes constructed by informals. Between 1960 and 1984 the state built low income housing at a cost of $173.6 million. In the same period, the informals built homes

for the incredible sum of $8.2 billion (forty-seven times more than the state)."
"Peru's Silent Revolution," *Crisis*, July-August 1987, pp. 4-5, from the introduction
to Hernando de Soto, *El Otro Sendero: La Revolucion Informal* (English translation
forthcoming).

26.  For an extended contrast between Italian liberalism and Anglo-American
liberalism, see E. E. Y. Hales, *Pio Nono (Garden City, New York: Image Books,
1962); see also Hales, *The Church in the Modern World: A Survey from the French
Revolution to the Present* (Garden City, New York: Image Books, 1960). Perhaps
in recognition of this contrast, the Italian text of *Sollicitudo* avoids the word
*liberale*, preferring the pejorative *liberista*; to a materialistic, highly egocentric and
anti-Catholic form of Latin libertarianism. A similar history supplies negative
connotations for "liberal" in Latin America.

27.  Marc Plattner has described the pitfalls of concentrating on the "gap" between
developed and developing nations. For example, according to a World Bank study,
"*despite the unprecedentedly high growth rates of the industrialized countries,
there was a slight narrowing of the relative gap from 1950 to 1975*" (original
emphasis). But, "while the developing countries were succeeding in narrowing the
relative gap during the 1970s, their per capita GNP was growing at a *slower* rate
than it had during the 1960s (when the gap had been widening)." "Thinking about
the 'North-South Gap,'" *This World*, Winter 1984, p. 26.

28.  In 1980, Japan and Brazil contained 2.6 percent and 2.7 percent of the world's
population, respectively. But Japan produced 9 percent of world gross national
product, while Brazil produced only 2 percent. U.S. Central Intelligence Agency,
National Foreign Assessment Center, *Handbook of Economic Statistics*
(Washington, D.C.: U.S. Government Printing Office, 1981), Fig. 1.

29.  See Nick Eberstadt's essay in Peter L. Berger, ed., *Modern Capitalism*, vol. 2:
*Capitalism and Equality in the Third World* (Lanham, Maryland: University Press
of America, 1987).

30.  See Pontifical Commission 'Iustitia et Pax,' *At the Service of the Human
Community: An Ethical Approach to the International Debt Question* (Vatican
City: Vatican Polyglot Press, 1986).

31.  Calculated from *Economic Indicators*, January 1988, p. 11.

32.  National Commission on Jobs and Small Business, "Summary of Meeting of
September 10-11, 1985, Washington, D.C.," (typescript).

33.  Peter Drucker writes: "Big business has been losing jobs since the early '70s. . . .
Nearly all job creation has been in small and medium-sized businesses, and
practically all of it in entrepreneurial and innovative businesses." By contrast,
"there are few signs of entrepreneurial dynamism in Western Europe." "Why
America's Got So Many Jobs," *Wall Street Journal*, 24 January 1984. The late
Arthur F. Burns, former U.S. Ambassador to West Germany, concurred: Largely
due to tax incentives, "the spirit of risk-taking and entrepreneurship therefore
remained alive in the United States. In Massachusetts, for example, which became
a depressed area during the 1950s, entrepreneurially-minded scientists joined
venture capitalists, enterprising commercial bankers, and managerial experts in
establishing and nourishing hundreds of small high-technology firms. Before many
years passed, they succeeded in transforming Massachusetts into one of the most
progressive parts of the American economy. . . .

"There has been no corresponding upsurge of entrepreneurship in Europe. There
are many reasons why the entrepreneurial spirit is less firmly implanted in Europe.
I have already alluded to some of them-the high level of taxation, the regulatory
burdens, the immense power of trade unions, and the increasing share of labor in
national income. . . .

"The institutional limitations on entrepreneurship in Europe are further inhibited
by psychological attitudes. Investors are more fearful of failure and therefore are

less inclined to take risks, and this is a major reason why Western Europe has been so deficient during the past ten to fifteen years in creating new jobs." "The Condition of the World Economy," *The AEI Economist*, June 1986, pp. 3-4.

34. See his essay "Empirical Testings," in Meyers, ed., *Aspiring to Freedom*.

35. See Michael Kinsley, "Dining on Red Herrings," *Curse of the Giant Muffins and Other Washington Maladies* (New York: Summit Books, 1987). Apparently, only the editors of *The New Oxford Review* proclaim moral equivalence (editorial, April 1988).

36. Solzhenitsyn explicitly condemned moral equivalence: "Very well known representatives of your society, such as George Kennan, say: 'We cannot apply moral criteria to politics.' Thus we mix good and evil, right and wrong, and make space for the absolute triumph of absolute evil in the world. Only moral criteria can help the West against communism's well-planned world strategy." "A World Split Apart," in Ronald Berman, ed., *Solzhenitsyn at Harvard* (Washington, D.C.: Ethics and Public Policy Center, 1980), pp. 13-14.

37. See Ben J. Wattenberg, *The Birth Dearth: What Happens When People in Free Countries Don't Have Enough Babies?* (New York: Pharos Books, 1987).

38. For example, the Pope writes that "the direct or indirect result of industrialization is, ever more frequently, the pollution of the environment, with serious consequences for the health of the population." *Sollicitudo Rei Socialis*, 34.

39. See Pope John Paul II, "Dives in Misericordia," *Origins* 11 December 1980.

40. Hamilton writes: "The supposition of universal venality in human nature is little less an error in political reasoning than the supposition of universal rectitude. The institution of delegated power implies that there is a portion of virtue and honor among mankind, which may be a reasonable foundation of confidence." *Federalist* 76.

41. See Lay Commission on Catholic Social Teaching and the U.S. Economy, *Toward the Future* (Lanham, Maryland: University Press of America, 1984); and *Liberty and Justice for All: Report on the Final Draft of the U.S. Catholic Bishops' Pastoral Letter* (Notre Dame, Indiana: Brownson Institute, 1986).

42. See Julian L. Simon, *The Ultimate Resource* (Princeton, New Jersey: Princeton University Press, 1981); Julian L. Simon and Herman Kahn, eds., *The Resourceful Earth: A Response to Global 2000* (London: Basil Blackwell, 1984); Max Singer, *Passage to a Human World* (Indianapolis, Indiana: Hudson Institute, 1987).

43. John Paul II, "Apostolic Exhortation on Reconciliation and Penance," *Origins*, 2 December 1984.

44. See Jean-François Revel, *Why Democracies Perish*, trans. William Byron (Garden City, New York: Doubleday, 1984). See also Luigi Lombardi Vallauri and Gerhard Dilcher, eds., *Christianesimo, Secolarizzazione e Diritto Moderno* (Milan: Giuffre Editore Milano, 1981).

45. "In a sense, by standing outside the historical stream of democratic capitalism, the popes were able to make some legitimate criticisms of abuses and errors within it, and to support many proposals for humane reforms eventually adopted by it. Yet, simultaneously, the remnants both of the medieval world and state mercantilism were crumbling all around them. Resisting socialism and standing outside democratic capitalism, Catholic social teaching laid claim to a certain neutrality-but gradually came to seem suspended in air. Catholic thought began to deal with every sort of regime, traditional and modern, even while its talk of a Catholic 'middle way' seemed empty, since there are, in fact, no existing examples of that middle way. . . .

"For this reason, perhaps, the programs of the 1940s and the 1950s in which Catholic thinkers had invested so much hope for 'the reconstruction of the social order'-Catholic Action, the Young Christian Workers, the Christian Democratic parties-achieved some notable successes but lacked the force of an alternative ideal.

To be anti-communist and anti-socialist, and only halfheartedly committed to democratic capitalism, is to represent not a 'middle way' but a halfway house. Such movements collapsed of their own lack of a serious ideal." Novak, *The Spirit of Democratic Capitalism* (New York: Simon and Schuster, 1982), p. 247.

46. Jean-Marie Lustiger, "Les Defis du catholicisme americain," *Le Monde*, 5 July 1986.

47. See S. Robert Lichter et al., *The Media Elite: America's New Power Brokers* (Bethesda, Maryland: Adler & Adler, 1986). See also Ben Stein, *The View from Sunset Boulevard: America as Brought to You by the People Who Make Television* (New York: Basic Books, 1979).

48. The CIA long estimated Soviet defense spending at 14 percent of GNP; in 1988 these estimates had to be revised to 20 percent, after the Soviets admitted their economy had grown at a much lower rate than earlier assumed.

49. In his first speech upon arriving in the U.S., Pope John Paul II declared: "I come to join you as you celebrate the bicentennial of that great document, the Constitution of the United States of America. I willingly join you in your prayer of thanksgiving to God for the providential way in which the Constitution has served the people of this nation for two centuries: for the union it has formed, the justice it has established, the tranquility and peace it has ensured, the general welfare it has promoted and the blessings of liberty it has secured.

   "I join you also in asking God to inspire you-as Americans who have received so much in freedom and prosperity and human enrichment-to continue to share all this with so many brothers and sisters throughout the other countries of the world who are still waiting and hoping to live according to the standards worthy of the children of God." *Origins*, 24 September 1987, p. 231.

50. "The superfluous wealth of rich countries should be placed at the service of poor nations. The rule which up to now held good for the benefit of those nearest to us, must today be applied to all the needy of this world. Besides, the rich will be the first to benefit as a result." *Populorum Progressio*, 49.

51. See "Instruction on Certain Aspects of the 'Theology of Liberation,'" *Origins*, 13 September 1984: "Instruction on Christian Freedom and Liberation" (Vatican City: Vatican Polyglot Press, 1986). The latter Instruction provides a careful description of Christian liberty (sec. 73): "The supreme commandment of love leads to the full recognition of the dignity of each individual, created in God's image. From this dignity flow natural rights and duties. In the light of the image of God, freedom, which is the essential prerogative of the human person, is manifested in all its depth. Persons are the active and responsible objects of social life.

   "Intimately linked to the *foundation*, which is man's dignity, are the *principle of solidarity* and the *principle of subsidiarity*.

   "By virtue of the first, man with his brothers is obliged to contribute to the common good of society at all its levels. Hence the Church's doctrine is opposed to all the forms of social or political individualism.

   "By virtue of the second, neither the State nor any society must ever substitute itself for the intiative and responsibility of individuals and of intermediate communities at the level on which they can function, nor must they take away the room necessary for their freedom. Hence the Church's social doctrine is opposed to all forms of collectivism."

52. The distinguishing characteristic of a capitalist system is neither private property nor markets nor profit, since all these also appear in pre-capitalist, traditionalist systems (cf. Jerusalem in the biblical era). What a capitalist system adds to traditionalist systems is a social system organized to promote *the creativity of the human mind*. Precisely defined, capitalism is the mind-centered system of universal opportunity. Among the institutions supporting the creativity of the mind are: a system of risk and private initiative; a system of personal choice and personal

incentives; copyright and patent laws "to promote the progress of science and useful arts"; universal education; institutes of higher education and research, such as are embodied in the U.S. Land Grant College Act of 1862; popular institutions making credit available to the poor and the underprivileged; open access to markets through cheap and swift legal incorporation of new businesses; and social reinforcement for a new moral virtue (which in many languages lacks even a proper name), *enterprise* or *personal initiative*. Enterprise is the habit of attentiveness and alertness to new and improved ways of doing or making. See Israel M. Kirzner, *Discovery and the Capitalist Process* (Chicago: University of Chicago Press, 1985); and Novak, *Will It Liberate? Questions About Liberation Theology* (Mahwah, New Jersey: Paulist Press, 1986), ch. 10, "The Constitution of Liberty."

53.   What, James Billington asks, "is the crucial difference between England, America, and Switzerland, where revolutionary traditions did not develop, and France, Italy, and Poland (as well as other Slavic, Germanic, and Latin lands), where they did?

". . . England, America, and Switzerland. . . had previously experienced and *legitimized ideological opposition* to medieval Catholicism. They were, in short, nations in which Protestantism was, if not the dominant creed as in America, at least a venerable and coequal one as in Switzerland. Secondly, each of these nations in different ways had found ways to *institutionalize political opposition* through an effective system of parties." Billington adds: "Much experience in nineteenth-century Europe supports the argument that Protestantism and parliamentarianism provided a kind of alternative equivalent to revolution." *Fire in the Minds of Men: Origins of the Revolutionary Faith* (New York: Basic Books, 1980), pp. 203-4.

# Notes

## Chapter 1. Theology and Economics: The Next Twenty Years

1. For the complete texts, see *The Social Teaching of Wilhelm Emmanuel von Ketteler*, trans. Rupert J. Ederer (Washington, D.C.: University Press of America, 1981), pp. 3–99.

2. See Heinrich Pesch, *Lehrbuch der Nationalökonomie*, 5 vols., rev. ed. (Freiburg im Br.: Herder, 1920–1926); also *Social Order* 1 (April 1951), the entire issue of which was devoted to Pesch's work; Oswald von Nell- Breuning, S.J., *Reorganization of Social Economy* (New York: Bruce Publishing, 1939); Goetz Briefs, *The Proletariat: A Challenge to Western Civilization* (New York: McGraw-Hill, 1937); and the collection of his essays on Catholic social thought in *Review of Social Economy* 41 (December 1983); Franz H. Mueller, "The Church and the Social Question," in Joseph N. Moody and Justus George Lawler, *The Challenge of Mater et Magistra* (New York: Herder and Herder, 1963) and *Heinrich Pesch: Sein Leben und Seine Lehr* (Cologne: Verlag J. P. Bachem, 1980); see also Mueller's eight-part series on liberalism: "The Nineteenth Century Catholic Critique of the Liberal Theory of Freedom of Thought and Utterance," *Social Justice Review*, November 1952–June 1953.

3. Frederick Broderick, *Right Reverend New Dealer: John A. Ryan* (New York: Macmillan, 1963).

4. "Throughout the period, the Catholic Church was on the continent of Europe the object of legislative and administrative attacks from hostile governments and parliaments—in England hostility did not go beyond violent talk about 'Vaticanism'—which is what might have been expected in a predominantly 'liberalistic' world. What could not have been expected is that these attacks everywhere ended in retreat and that they left the Catholic Church stronger than it had been for centuries.... Around 1900 it was a common observation to make that in a Catholic family the old and elderly were laicist and liberal and the youngsters believers and 'clerical.' This is one of the most significant patches of color in our pictures. But for the purposes of this book another fact is of still greater importance. Political Catholicism from the first stood for social reform. I cannot do more than mention the names of de Mun, von Ketteler, von Vogelsand. This concern of the Catholic Church with the conditions of labor was nothing new and only adapted an old tradition to the problems of the epoch. But something that was new developed toward the end of the century, namely, a definite scheme of social organization that, making use of the existing elements of groupwise co-operation, visualized a society—and a state—operating by means of self-governing vocational associations within a framework of ethical precepts. This is the 'corporative' state adumbrated in the encyclical *Quadragesimo Anno* (1931). Since it is a normative program and not a piece of analysis, no more will be said about it in this book. I merely add the name of the man who has done more than any other for this conception of society, Heinrich Pesch, S.J." Joseph A. Schumpeter, *History of Economic Analy-*

*sis*, ed. Elizabeth Boody Schumpeter (New York: Oxford University Press, 1954), pp. 764–765). Schumpeter's footnote adds: "That great man (1854–1926) was not particularly proficient in analytic economics, which is why his treatise, *Lehrbuch der National-ökonomie*, (1905–23) will not be mentioned again though, so far as scholarship is concerned, it has few equals" (p. 765, n. 11).

5. For the texts of *Rerum Novarum* and *Quadragesimo Anno*, see William J. Gibbons, S.J., ed., *Seven Great Encyclicals* (Great Rock, New Jersey: Paulist Press, 1963). For the texts of *Mater et Magistra, Pacem in Terris, Populorum Progressio*, and *Octogesimo Adveniens*, see Joseph Gremillion, S.J., ed., *The Gospel of Peace and Justice* (Maryknoll, New York: Orbis, 1976). For the text of *Laborem Exercens*, see *Origins* 11 (September 24, 1981).

6. Walter Rauschenbush's works were seminal, esp. *Christianizing the Social Order* (New York: Macmillan, 1912) and *A Theology for the Social Gospel* (New York: Macmillan, 1917). For related developments see Martin E. Marty, *Righteous Empire: The Protestant Experience in America* (New York: Dial Press, 1970), Chapter 6; and Bernard Murchland, *The Dream of Christian Socialism: An Essay on Its European Origins* (Washington, D.C.: American Enterprise Institute, 1982), esp. his Selected Bibliography.

7. See the *Festschrift* for Niebuhr, John A. Hutchison, ed., *Christian Faith and Social Action* (New York: Charles Scribner's Sons, 1953). Hutchison's essay, "Two Decades of Social Christianity," provides an excellent short history of the social gospel movement. Among my favorite collections of Niebuhr's essays are *Christianity and Power Politics* (New York: Scribners, 1940) and *Christian Realism and Political Problems* (New York: Scribners, 1953).

8. See esp. Walter Muelder, *Foundations of the Responsible Society* (New York: Abingdon, 1959); *Moral Law in Christian Social Ethics* (New York: The Edwin Mellen Press, 1966); and *The Ethical Edge of Christian Theology: Forty Years of Communitarian Personalism* (New York: The Edwin Mellen Press, 1983). The autobiographical introduction to the latest volume lucidly describes the intellectual currents of the last fifty years. The *Festschrift* for Muelder is Paul Deats, Jr., ed., *Toward A Discipline of Social Ethics: Essays in Honor of Walter George Muelder* (Boston: Boston University Press, 1972).

9. See e.g., Thomas Sieger Derr, "The Economic Thought of the World Council of Churches," *This World* No. 1 (Winter/Spring 1982):20–33.

10. See Ronald J. Sider, *Rich Christians in an Age of Hunger* (Glen Rock, New Jersey: Paulist Press, 1977); David Chilton, *Productive Christians in an Age of Guilt Manipulators* (Tyler, Texas: Institute for Christian Economics, 1981); Gary North, *An Introduction to Christian Economics* (Nutley, New Jersey: Craig Press, 1973); Herbert Schlossberg, *Idols for Destruction* (Nashville: Thomas Nelson, 1983), esp. Chapter 3, "Idols of Mammon"; and Ronald H. Nash, *Social Justice and the Christian Church* (Milford, Michigan: Mott Media, 1983).

11. Mill writes: "Writers on Political Economy profess to teach, or to investigate, the nature of Wealth, and the laws of its production and distribution; including, directly or remotely, the operation of all the causes by which the condition of mankind, or of any society of human beings, in respect to this universal object of human desire, is made prosperous or the reverse." John Stuart Mill, *Principles of Political Economy*, ed. J. Laurence Laughlin (New York: D. Appleton and Co., 1888), p. 47. Commenting on this point, the editor observes: "It will be noticed that political economy does not include ethics, legislation, or the science of government. The results of political economy are offered to the statesman, who reaches a conclusion after weighing them in connection with moral and political considerations" (ibid.).

12. "Thus prudence is cause, root, mother, measure, precept, guide, and prototype of all ethical virtues; it acts in all of them, perfecting them to their true nature; all participate in it, and by virtue of this participation they are virtues." Josef Pieper, *Prudence*, trans. Richard and Clara Winston (New York: Pantheon Books, 1959), p. 20.

13. The pope defines "economism" as the error of "considering human labor solely according to its economic purpose" *Laborem Exercens*, 13.

14. See Erik Erickson, *Identity: Youth and Crisis* (New York: Norton, 1968), pp. 91–107; and *Insight and Responsibility*, (New York: Norton, 1964), Chapter 4.

15. See Leo Moulin, *L'Aventure Européenne* (Brussels: De Tempel, 1972), Chapters 4–7.
16. R. H. Tawney, *The Acquisitive Society* (New York: Harcourt, 1920).
17. Max Weber, *The Protestant Ethic and the Spirit of Capitalism*, trans. Talcott Parsons (New York: Charles Scribner's Sons, 1958), p. 17
18. Weber writes (ibid.; p. 154): "Christian asceticism, at first fleeing from the world into solitude, had already ruled the world which it had renounced from the monastery and through the Church. But it had, on the whole, left the naturally spontaneous character of daily life in the world untouched. Now it strode into the market-place of life, slammed the door of the monastery behind it, and undertook to penetrate just that daily routine of life with its methodicalness, to fashion it into a life in the world, but neither of nor for this world. With what result, we shall try to make clear in the following discussion." See ibid., Chapter 5: "Asceticism and the Spirit of Capitalism."
19. See Mill, *Principles of Political Economy*, Chapter 3: "Of Wealth."
20. Quoted in J. Philip Wogaman, *The Great Economic Debate* (Philadelphia: The Westminster Press, 1977), p. 133. See also Paul Tillich, *The Socialist Decision*, trans. Franklin Sherman (New York: Harper & Row, 1977); and Murchland, *The Dream of Christian Socialism*.
21. Selected primary works of Distributists: Hilaire Belloc, *The Servile State* (1912; reprint ed., Indianapolis: Liberty Classics, 1980). G. K. Chesterton, *Utopia of Usurers* (New York: Boni and Liveright, 1917); and *The Outline of Sanity* (New York: Dodd, Mead, and Co., 1927). Eric Gill, *Money and Morals* (London: Faber & Faber, 1937). Selected secondary sources on Distributism: Jay P. Corrin, *G. K. Chesterton and Hilaire Belloc: The Battle Against Modernity* (Athens, Ohio: Ohio University Press, 1981). Alzina Stone Dale, *The Outline of Sanity: A Life of G. K. Chesterton* (Grand Rapids: William B. Eerdmans Publishing Co., 1982). Edward S. Shapiro, "A Distributist Society," *Catholicism in Crisis*, January 1984. Michael Novak, "Saving Distributism," *The Chesterton Review* 10 (February 1984):13–34.
22. See my discussion of Niebuhr's evolving critique of socialism in *The Spirit of Democratic Capitalism* (New York: Simon and Schuster/American Enterprise Institute, 1982), pp. 315–332.
23. See Broderick's account of the 1914 debate on socialism between Morris Hillquit and John A. Ryan in *Right Reverend New Dealer: John A. Ryan*. For the debate itself see Morris Hillquit and John A. Ryan, *Socialism: Promise or Menace?* (New York: Macmillan, 1914).
24. See Gertrude Himmelfarb, "Introduction," *On Liberty and Liberalism: The Case of John Stuart Mill* (New York: Alfred A. Knopf, 1974). For a further discussion of Mill, see Chapter 5, below.
25. Some of the oversights in traditional Catholic social thought are exhibited by Stuart Gudowitz in "A Christian View of Economic Virtue," *The New Oxford Review* (March 1984). In reply (ibid., June 1984) George Gilder raises some pertinent questions not yet faced by Catholic social thought.

## Chapter 2: Perfect Enemy of Good: Against Utopianism

1. See Friedrich A. Hayek, *The Constitution of Liberty* (Chicago: Henry Regnery, 1960).
2. See "The Traditional Pragmatism" in Michael Novak, *A Time to Build* (New York: Macmillan, 1964), pp. 323–353: "God himself acts not through Reason, as the divine geometer, but through practical wisdom, as the one whose greatest glory is not that he moves everything in necessary, rigid patterns, but that he creates, loves, and respects contingent things in their contingency" (p. 344). Hayek, *The Constitution of Liberty*, acknowledges that the tradition of practical wisdom is common both to the Whigs and to Aquinas, observing that "in some respects Lord Acton was not being altogether paradoxical when he described Thomas Aquinas as the first Whig" (p. 457, n. 4).
3. "The defeat of Mazzini's Roman Republic in 1849 was a check to the political aspirations of Mazzini and Garibaldi, but it was also a (temporary) victory for the Papacy over Mazzini's Religion of the People. Cavour's victory in closing the monasteries was

the prelude to his assuming political sovereignty over the Papal State. Napoleon's planned withdrawal from defending Rome in 1864 provided the occasion for the issue of that notorious religious-political document, the Syllabus of Errors. The Errors of that Syllabus were largely Cavour's, Mazzini's and Napoleon's." E. E. Y. Hales, *Pio Nono* (Garden City, New York: Image Books, 1962), p. 14.

4. "I will nevertheless continue for the moment to describe as liberal the position which I hold and which I believe differs as much from true conservatism as from socialism. Let me say at once, however, that I do so with increasing misgivings, and I shall later have to consider what would be the appropriate name for the party of liberty. The reason for this is not only that the term 'liberal' in the United States is the cause of constant misunderstandings today, but also that in Europe the predominant type of rationalistic liberalism has long been one of the pacemakers of socialism." Hayek, *The Constitution of Liberty*, pp. 397–398.

5. [W]hen a man engages in remunerative labor, the very reason and motive of his work is to obtain property, and to hold it as his own private possession. If one man hires out to another his strength or his industry, he does this for the purpose of receiving in return what is necessary for food and living; he thereby expressly proposes to acquire a full and real right, not only to the remuneration, but also to the disposal of that remuneration as he pleases.... [I]t is precisely in this power of disposal that ownership consists, whether the property be land or movable goods. The *Socialists*, therefore, in endeavoring to transfer the possessions of individuals to the community, strike at the interests of every wage earner, for they deprive him of the liberty of disposing of his wages, and thus of all hope and possibility of increasing his stock and of bettering his condition in life.

"What is of still greater importance, however, is that the remedy they propose is manifestly against justice. For every man has by nature the right to possess property as his own. This is one of the *chief points of distinction* between man and the animal creation." *Rerum Novarum*, 3, 4 and 5 (emphasis in original).

6. "Private ownership . . . is the natural right of man; and to exercise that right, *especially as members of society*, is not only lawful but absolutely necessary. 'It is lawful,' says St. Thomas of Aquin, 'for a man to hold private property; and it is also necessary for the carrying on of human life." *Rerum Novarum*, 19 (emphasis added).

"We have seen that this great labor question cannot be solved except by assuming as a principle that private ownership must be held sacred and inviolable. The law, therefore, should favor ownership, and its policy should be to induce as many people as possible to become owners.

"Many excellent results will follow from this; and first of all, property will certainly become more equitably divided.... If working people can be encouraged to look forward to obtaining a share in the land, the result will be that the gulf between vast wealth and deep poverty will be bridged over, and the two orders will be brought nearer together." *Rerum Novarum*, 35, 36.

7. Leo XIII added other traditional arguments in favor of private property: It is in accordance with civil, natural, and divine law. It is necessary when people prepare for the future. It is needed to provide for one's offspring. See *Rerum Novarum*, 5, 8, 10.

8. *Rerum Novarum*, 10.

9. See B. Sarda, *Revue Catholique*, année xxvi, p. 10.

10. Quoted in Newman C. Eberhardt, *A Summary of Catholic History*, 2 vols. (St. Louis: B. Herder Book Co., 1962), 2:467.

11. Schumpeter offers a brilliant discussion of the various types of liberalism; see Joseph A Schumpeter, *History of Economic Analysis* ed. Elizabeth Boody Schumpeter (New York: Oxford University Press, 1954), pp. 394–395. See also his discussions of individualism, pp. 888–889.

12. See Chapter 1, note 20.

13. "Culture depends for its very existence on leisure, and leisure, in its turn, is not possible unless it has a durable and consequently living link with the *cultus*, with divine worship." Josef Pieper, *Leisure: The Basis of Culture*, trans. Alexander Dru, with an

Introduction by T. S. Eliot (New York: Pantheon Books, 1952), p. 19. Again: "The medieval university stood in the current of *urban* life. This at first glance purely sociological fact had a great deal to do with its intellectual vitality. . . . The pupils of Abelard were an entirely different social type [from those of Anselm]. They were the singers of the *carmina burana,* so to speak; they were itinerants moving from one urban university to the next, freely joining together in 'nations,' terrorizing the citizens of the city and often their professors as well—and so on. The decisive fact about them was their urban stamp, which took the form of a new security, an emphatic independence of feudal lords, a new sense of freedom." Josef Pieper, *Guide to Thomas Aquinas,* trans. Richard and Clara Winston (New York: Pantheon Books, 1962), p. 59 (emphasis in original).

14. See Carlton Hayes, *Political and Cultural History of Modern Europe* (New York: Macmillan, 1936).

15. In his *Summary of Catholic History,* Father Newman C. Eberhardt, C.M., asks his readers to appraise the maxims of laissez-faire from such samples as these: "The natural price of labor is that price which is necessary to enable the laborers to subsist and perpetuate their race without either increase or diminution. . . . There is no means of improving the lot of the worker except by limiting the number of his children. . . . All legislative interference must be pernicious" (Ricardo). "The poverty of the incapable, the distresses that come upon the imprudent, the starvation of the idle, are the decrees of a large, far-seeing benevolence" (Spencer). "The true gospel concerning wealth . . . is that the law of competition is basic to economic society, divine and irrevocable . . . because it ensures the survival of the fittest in every department" (Carnegie). "Godliness is in league with riches. . . . Material prosperity is helping make the national character sweeter, more joyous, more unselfish, more Christlike (Protestant prelate of Massachusetts, Dr. Lawrence)." Eberhardt, 2:402–403, quoting Emmet John Hughes, *The Church and Liberal Society* (Princeton: Princeton University Press, 1944), pp. 157–158, 200.

16. "The break occurred in such a way that labor was separated from capital, as though they were two impersonal forces, two production factors juxtaposed in the same 'economistic' perspective. This way of stating the issue contained a fundamental error, what we can call the error of economism, that of considering human labor solely according to its economic purpose. This fundamental error of thought can and must be called an error of materialism, in that economism directly or indirectly includes a conviction of the primacy and superiority of the material, and directly or indirectly places the spiritual and the personal (man's activities, moral values and such matters) in a position of subordination to material reality." *Laborem Exercens,* 13.

17. See John A Ryan, *A Living Wage* (New York: Macmillan, 1912). *Distributive Justice* (New York: Macmillan, 1916). Also his autobiography, *Social Doctrine in Action* (New York: Harper & Bros., 1941). John Courtney Murray, *We Hold These Truths* (New York: Sheed and Ward, 1960). Major works by Jacques Maritain on Catholic social thought include: *Christianity and Democracy,* trans. Doris C. Anson (New York: Charles Scribner's Sons, 1944). *The Person and the Common Good,* trans. John J. Fitzgerald (New York: Charles Scribner's Sons, 1947). *Man and the State* (New York: Charles Scribner's Sons, 1958). *Reflections on America* (New York: Charles Scribner's Sons, 1958).

18. The best textual analysis I have encountered of papal statements on "social justice"is by William Ferree, S.M., *Introduction to Social Justice* (Dayton, Ohio: Marianist Publications, 1948). Father Ferree stresses "the duty to organize socially" (p. 55); "in Social Justice there is *never any such thing as helplessness"* (p. 47). This little pamphlet, in its simplicity, is quite penetrating.

19. John A. Ryan noted this characteristic in 1916 and quoted from a prominent socialist: "Never has our party told the workingman about a 'State of the future,' never in any way than as a mere utopia. If anybody says: 'I picture to myself society after our programme has been realised, after wage labour has been abolished, and the exploitation of men has ceased, in such and such a manner,—' well and good; ideas are free, and everybody may conceive the Socialist State as he pleases. Whoever believes in it

may do so; whoever does not, need not. These pictures are but dreams, and Social Democracy has never understood them otherwise."

To this position, Ryan replies: "From the viewpoint of all but convinced Socialists, this position is indefensible. We are asked to believe that the collective ownership and operation of the means of production would be more just and beneficial than the present plan of private ownership and operation. Yet the Socialist party refuses to tell us how the scheme would bring about these results; refuses to give us, even in outline, a picture of the machine at work." Ryan, *Distributive Justice*, pp. 152–153. The opening claim is from Morris Hillquit, *Socialism in Theory and Practice* (publishing data not given), p. 107, citing Wilhelm Leibknecht.

20. See the *Nicomachean Ethics*, X, ix, 1179b.

21. Albert Camus, *The Rebel: An Essay on Man in Revolt*, trans. Anthony Bower (New York: Vintage Books, 1956), p. 302.

22. Voegelin lists "six characteristics that, taken together, reveal the nature of the gnostic attitude." The second and most basic one is "the belief that the drawbacks of the [present] situation can be attributed to the fact that the world is intrinsically poorly organized . . . [but] it is likewise possible to assume that the order of being as it is given to us men . . . is good and that it is we human beings who are inadequate. But gnostics are not inclined to discover that human beings in general and they themselves in particular are inadequate. If in a given situation something is not as it should be, then the fault is to be found in the wickedness of the world." The fifth aspect—"the gnostic trait in the narrower sense"—is a "belief that a change in the order of being lies in the realm of human action." The sixth is that "Knowledge—gnosis—of the method of altering being is the cental concern of the gnostic . . . the construction of a formula for self and world salvation." Eric Voegelin, *Science, Politics, and Gnosticism* (Chicago: Henry Regnery, 1968), pp. 86–88. See also Voegelin, *The New Science of Politics* (Chicago: University of Chicago Press, 1952), pp. 107–161.

23. Reinhold Niebuhr, *Moral Man and Immoral Society* (New York: Charles Scribner's Sons, 1932), Chapter 1. A brief conspectus of Niebuhr's approach is found in his Introduction, p. xx: "What is lacking among all these moralists, whether religious or rational, is an understanding of the brutal character of the behavior of all human collectives, and the power of self-interest and collective egoism in all intergroup relations. . . . They do not see that the limitations of the human imagination, the easy subservience of reason to prejudice and passion, and the consequent persistence of irrational egoism, particularly in group behavior, make social conflict an inevitability in human history, probably to its very end."

24. "What then is the crucial difference between England, America, and Switzerland, where revolutionary traditions did not develop, and France, Italy, and Poland (as well as other Slavic, Germanic, and Latin lands), where they did?

"The key difference appears to lie in two common features of the way in which change and opposition developed in England, America, and Switzerland. These were nations that, first of all, had previously experienced and *legitimized ideological opposition* to medieval Catholicism. They were, in short, nations in which Protestantism was, if not the dominant creed as in America, at least a venerable and coequal one as in Switzerland. Secondly, each of these nations in different ways had found ways to *institutionalize political opposition* through an effective system of parties. . . . That opposition, moreover, assumed the disciplined form of a limited number of political parties—usually two major ones." James H. Billington, *Fire in the Minds of Men: Origins of the Revolutionary Faith* (New York: Basic Books, 1980), pp. 203–204, (emphasis in original).

25. The authors of *Pontiff*, always provocative if not always reliable, "learned there are at least two unpublished studies in the Vatican on the question of why so many contemporary terrorists have Catholic backgrounds. One study was commissioned in the aftermath of the Moro murder; the other was produced a year later." Gordon Thomas and Max Morgan-Witts, *Pontiff* (Garden City, New York: Doubleday & Company, 1983), p. 447, n. 1 to Chapter 4.

26. " 'Commerce cures destructive prejudices'; it 'polishes and softens barbaric morals.' In making men more aware of both human variety and sameness, commerce made them less provincial and in a sense more humane. 'The spirit of commerce unites nations.' Driven by their mutual needs, trading partners entered into a symbiosis they could ill afford to wreck by war. They would learn how to subordinate disruptive political interests to those of commerce. Such nations, devoting themselves to a 'commerce of economy,' had, so to speak, a necessity to be faithful; since their object was gain, not conquest, they would be 'pacific from principle.' " Ralph Lerner, "Commerce and Character: The Anglo-American as New-Model Man" in Michael Novak, ed., *Liberation South, Liberation North* (Washington, D.C.: American Enterprise Institute, 1981), p. 36. Internal quotes from Montesquieu, *L'Esprit des lois,* XX, 1, 2, 7, 8.

27. " 'Political economy' made its appearance as early as 1615, in Antoyne de Montcretien's *Traicte de l'oeconomie politique.* The term was introduced into England by William Petty later in that century, and received wide currency with the publication, almost a decade before the *Wealth of Nations,* of James Steuart's *Inquiry into the Principles of Political Oeconomy."* Gertrude Himmelfarb, *The Idea of Poverty: England in the Early Industrial Age* (New York: Alfred A. Knopf, 1984), p. 42. See also the excellent annotated version of John Stuart Mill's *Principles of Political Economy* edited by Sir William Ashley (Fairfield, New Jersey: Augustus M. Kelley, 1976), especially Sir William's introduction.

28. "For [Adam] Smith political economy was not an end in itself but a means to an end, that end being the wealth and well-being, moral and material, of the 'people,' of whom the 'laboring poor' were the largest part. And the poor themselves had a moral status in that economy—not the special moral status they enjoyed in a fixed, hierarchic order, but that which adhered to them as individuals in a free society sharing a common human, which is to say, moral, nature." Himmelfarb, *The Idea of Poverty,* p. 63. The entire chapter on Adam Smith (pp. 42–63) shows how liberalism focused upon eliminating poverty.

29. See E. E. Y. Hales, *Pio Nono,* especially Chapter 7, "Pio Nono *versus* Liberalism," pp. 266–304. See also Hales, "The Condemnation of Liberalism," *Revolution and Papacy: 1769–1846* (London: Eyre & Spottiswoode, 1960), pp. 278–295.

30. Billington, *Fire in the Minds of Men,* p. 307.

31. *Rerum Novarum,* 3.

32. *Quadragesimo Anno,* 120.

33. "Furthermore, [Pius XI in *Quadragesimo Anno*] emphasized that the views of *communists,* as they are called, and of Christians are radically opposed. Nor may Catholics, in any way, give approbation to the teachings of *socialists* who seemingly profess more moderate views. From their basic outlook it follows that, inasmuch as the order of social life is confined to time, it is directed solely to temporal welfare; that since the social relationships of men pertain merely to the production of goods, human liberty is excessively restricted and the true concept of social authority is overlooked." John XXIII, *Mater et Magistra,* 34 (emphases in original). Leo XIII, of course, condemned socialism categorically for several reasons. See note 5 above, and notes 35 and 36 below.

34. "Let it be laid down, in the first place, that humanity must remain as it is. It is impossible to reduce human society to a level. The *Socialists* may do their utmost, but all striving against nature is vain. There naturally exists among mankind innumerable differences of the most important kind; people differ in capability, in diligence, in health, and in strength; and unequal fortune is a necessary result of inequality in condition. Such inequality is far from being disadvantageous either to individuals or to the community; social and public life can only go on by the help of various kinds of capacity and the playing of many parts, and each man, as a rule, chooses the part which peculiarly suits his case." *Rerum Novarum,* 14 (emphasis in original). Again: " . . . if all may justly strive to better their condition, yet neither justice nor the common good allows anyone to seize that which belongs to another, or, under the pretext of *futile and ridiculous equality,* to lay hands on other people's fortunes. It is most true that

by far the larger part of the people who work prefer to improve themselves by honest labor rather than by doing wrong to others. But there are not a few who are imbued with bad principles and are anxious for revolutionary change, and whose great purpose it is to stir up tumult and bring about a policy of violence. The authority of the State should intervene to put restraint upon these disturbers, to save the workmen from their seditious arts, and to protect lawful owners from spoliation." *Rerum Novarum*, 30 (emphasis added).

35. "The idea, then, that the civil government should, at its own discretion, penetrate and pervade the family and the household, is a great and pernicious mistake. . . . Paternal authority can neither be abolished by the State nor absorbed; for it has the same source as human life itself. . . . The Socialists, therefore, in setting aside the parent and introducing the providence of the State, act *against natural justice,* and threaten the very existence of family life. [*Ed.:* This is the first modern papal introduction of the concept later to be expressed as "social justice." See Chapter 6, note 33 below.]

"And such interference is not only unjust, but is quite certain to harass and disturb all classes of citizens, and to subject them to odious and intolerable slavery. It would open the door to envy, to evil speaking, and to quarreling; the sources of wealth would themselves run dry, for no one would have any interest in exerting his talents or his industry; and that ideal equality of which so much is said would, in reality, be the leveling down of all to the same condition of misery and dishonor.

"Thus it is clear *that the main tenet of Socialism, the community of goods, must be utterly rejected;* for it would injure those whom it is intended to benefit, it would be contrary to the natural rights of mankind, and it would introduce confusion, and disorder into the commonwealth. Our first and fundamental principle, therefore, when we undertake to alleviate the condition of the masses, must be the inviolability of private property." *Rerum Novarum*, 11, 12 (emphasis in original). Leo XIII also worried that socialists would use taxation as a means of attacking property rights: "[T]he three important benefits [of private property], however, can only be expected on the condition that a man's means be not drained and exhausted by excessive taxation. The right to possess private property is from nature, not from man; and the State has only the right to regulate its use in the interests of the public good, but by no means to abolish it altogether. The State is, therefore, unjust and cruel, if, in the name of taxation, it deprives the private owner of more than is just." *Rerum Novarum*, 35. Pius XI further argued that socialists sacrificed liberty to materialistic concerns: "Because of the fact that goods are produced more efficiently by a suitable division of labor than by the scattered efforts of individuals, Socialists infer that economic activity, only the material ends of which enter into their thinking, ought of necessity to be carried on socially. Because of this necessity, they hold that men are obliged, with respect to the production of goods, to surrender and subject themselves entirely to society. Indeed, possession of the greatest possible supply of things that serve the advantages of this life is considered of such great importance that the higher goods of man, liberty not excepted, must take a secondary place and even be sacrificed to the demands of the most efficient production of goods. This damage to human dignity, undergone in the 'socialized' process of production, will be easily offset, they say, by the abundance of socially produced goods." *Quadragesimo Anno*, 119.

36. See notes 5–7, above.

37. Irving Kristol, "Socialism: Obituary for an Idea," *Reflections of a Neoconservative* (New York: Basic Books, 1983), p. 114.

## Chapter 3: An Awareness of Sin: The US Catholic Bishops and the US Economy

1. Joseph Gremillion, *The Gospel of Peace and Justice* (Maryknoll, New York: Orbis, 1976), p. 35.

2. John Courtney Murray, *We Hold These Truths* (New York: Sheed and Ward, 1960), esp. Chapters 1, "E Pluribus Unum," 8, "Is It Basket Weaving?" and 9, "Are There

Two or One?" See also John Raymond Traffas, "John Courtney Murray's Theology of Political Right: An Analysis of Murray's Theory of Religious Liberty in Terms of the Teaching of *Dignitatis Humanae*," (unpublished Th.M. thesis, University of Dallas, 1976), pp. 157–160, 171–173.

3. See Herbert Marcuse, "Repressive Tolerance," in *A Critique of Pure Tolerance*, ed. Robert P. Wolff, et. al., (Boston: Beacon, 1969).

4. Murray, *We Hold These Truths*, pp. 157–160, 171–173.

5. "Class may (or may not) find phenomenological expression, but at root it is a mode of self-definition. There are aristocrats in England who are as poor as church mice but are definitely 'upper class.' And there are immigrants to the United States who are also as poor as church mice but are definitely 'middle class' from the moment they set foot here. The very thought that there is someone ('up there?') who knows better than we do what class we are in is as breathtaking in its intellectual presumption as it is sterile for all serious purposes of social research." Irving Kristol, *Reflections of a Neoconservative* (New York: Basic Books, 1983), pp. 199–200. See the whole of Chapter 14, "Some Personal Reflections on Economic Well-Being and Income Distribution."

6. Spencer Rich, " 'Poverty Gap' Put at $45 Billion," *Washington Post*, 19 October 1983, p. A6. Testimonies of Rudolph G. Penner, Director, Congressional Budget Office and Sheldon Danziger of the Institute for Research on Poverty, University of Wisconsin, to the House Ways and Means Committee, 18 October 1983.

7. US Bureau of the Census, Current Population Reports, Series P-60, Number 140, *Money Income and Poverty Status of Families and Persons in the United States: 1982* (Advance Data From the March 1983 Current Population Survey), (Washington, D.C.: US Government Printing Office, 1983), Tables B, 14, 17, 18; Note: persons identified as Hispanic may be of any race.

8. Ibid., table 17.

9. Greg J. Duncan *et al.*, *Years of Poverty, Years of Plenty: The Changing Economic Fortunes of American Workers and Families* (Ann Arbor, Michigan: Institute for Social Research, The University of Michigan, 1984), Chapters 1 and 2.

10. National Center for Education Statistics, *Opening Fall Enrollment*, 1982 (unpublished).

11. See Ken Auletta, *The Underclass* (New York: Random House, 1982).

12. Charles A. Murray, *Safety Nets and the Truly Needy: Rethinking the Truly Needy* (Washington, D.C.: Heritage Foundation, 1982), p. viii.

13. Telephone inquiry, US Department of Commerce, Bureau of the Census, 6 October 1983; figure from unpublished Current Population survey. Half of all poor households received at least $6477 in 1982 as cash; half received less. See US Department of Commerce, Bureau of the Census, *Money Income and Poverty Status of Families and Persons in the United States: 1982*, table 20. See also note 6, above.

14. United States, President, *Public Papers of the U.S. Presidents* (Washington, D.C.: Office of the *Federal Register*, National Archives and Record Service, 1953– ), John F. Kennedy, 1962, pp. 102–103 (emphasis added).

15. *New York Times*, 2 February 1962.

16. US Department of Commerce, Bureau of the Census, *Statistical Abstract of the United States: 1982–83*, table 73.

17. "Prior to 1970, women 15 to 19 years old had less than half of all illegitimate births. By 1975, as a result of decreasing illegitimacy rates at older ages and increasing rates among women 15 to 19 years old, teenage women accounted for more than half of all illegitimate births." US Bureau of the Census, *Perspectives on American Fertility*, Series P-23, No. 70 (July 1978), pp. 40–41. From 1975 to 1979, the number of births to unmarried women aged 15–19 increased by 14 percent, from 222 per 1000 to 253 per 1000. See *Statistical Abstract of the United States: 1982–83*, table 97.

18. Calculated from *Money Income and Poverty Status of Families and Persons in the United States: 1982*, tables 14–15. As a proportion of the total poverty population, female heads of households with their dependent children virtually doubled between 1960 and 1982, climbing from 15 percent to 29 percent. Despite a reduction in the total number of poor children, from 17.3 million in 1960 to 13.1 million in 1982, the

number of poor children in families headed by females increased from 4.1 million to 6.7 million during the same period of time. See ibid., tables 14–15.

19. United States Department of Commerce News, CB 83–127, 22 August 1983.
20. *Money Income and Poverty Status of Families and Persons in the United States: 1982*, tables 1, 14, 17.
21. Ibid., tables 15 and 18.
22. Ibid., table 18.
23. Ibid.
24. National Center for Health Statistics, *Monthly Vital Statistics Report*, Advance Report of Final Natology Statistics, vol. 31, no. 8, (November 30, 1982).
25. Ibid.
26. *Money Income and Poverty Status of Families and Persons in the United States: 1982*, table 15.
27. Ibid.
28. Ibid., table 14.
29. See Gertrude Himmelfarb, "Adam Smith: Political Economy as Moral Philosophy," *The Idea of Poverty: England in the Early Industrial Age* (New York: Alfred A. Knopf, 1984), pp. 42–63; see esp. pp. 52–53.
30. Peter Berger, "Speaking to the Third World," *Commentary*, October 1981, p. 30.
31. Robert Fox, "For the Record," *Washington Post*, 25 January 1984.
32. For data on employment history of women, see *Statistical Abstract of the United States, 1982–83*, table 625, p. 376. Also Jane Seaberry, "Unprecedented Changes Forecast for Population," *Washington Post*, 22 January 1984, p. G7.
33. Peter F. Drucker, "Why America's Got So Many Jobs," *Wall Street Journal*, 24 January 1984, p. 32.
34. United States, Executive Office of the President, Council of Economic Advisors, *Economic Indicators* (April 1984), p. 13.
35. Ibid.
36. Geoffrey H. Moore, "Another 1929," Speech to the Center for International Business Cycle Research, Graduate School of Business, Columbia University, New York, 3 June 1983.
37. Deborah Pisetzner Klein, "Trends in Employment and Unemployment in Families," US Department of Labor, Bureau of Labor Statistics, *Monthly Labor Review* (December 1983), p. 21. See also Elizabeth Waldman, "Labor Force Statistics from a Family Perspective," ibid., pp. 17–18.

## Chapter 4: The Architects of Catholic Social Thought

1. *The Social Teachings of Wilhelm Emmanuel von Ketteler*, trans. Rupert J. Ederer (Washington, D.C.: University Press of America, 1981), p. viii. For other assessments see John A. Ryan and Joseph Husslein, *The Church and Labor* (New York: Macmillan, 1920), pp. 24–54. T. Brauer, *The Catholic Social Movement in Germany* (Oxford: The Catholic Social Guild, 1932), pp. 26–31. Of special note is Francesco S. Nitti's discussion of von Ketteler in Nitti, *Catholic Socialism* (New York: Macmillan, 1908), Chapters 5 and 6 and George Metlake, *Christian Social Reform*, preface by William Cardinal O'Connell (Philadelphia: The Dolphin Press, 1912).
2. Josef Thesing, ed., *Economy and Development* (Mainz: Hase & Koehler Verlag, 1979); hereafter cited as *Economy and Development*.
3. Quoted in George Metlake, *Christian Social Reform* (Philadelphia: Dolphin Press, 1912), p. 5.
4. For a recent discussion of Bismark's attitude toward the clergy, see Edward Crankshaw, *Bismark's* (London: Macmillan, (1981).
5. *The Social Teachings of Ketteler*, pp. vii–viii.
6. Ibid., p. 3. The titles of the sermons are as follows: "The Christian Concept of Private Property Rights," "The Obligation of Christian Charity," "The Christian Concept of Human Freedom," "The Christian Concept of Human Destiny," "The Christian Con-

cept of Marriage and the Family," and "On the Authority of the Catholic Church." For texts, see pp. 5–99.

7. Ibid., pp. 313–314.

8. Ibid., p. 348.

9. Ibid., p. 344.

10. "What would become of our German fatherland if this liberalism, that singlehandedly has laid waste a great neighbor nation, succeeds in penetrating ever more deeply the bosom of our Germany. Even the German army will stop being what it is if the poison of liberalism begins to infect it. Say what you will, the successes of the Prussian and German armies are attributable in large measure to the deep inroads that liberalism has made among our enemies." "Liberalism, Socialism, and Christianity" in *The Social Teachings of Ketteler*, p. 515.

11. The Konrad Adenauer Stiftung has published an excellent set of essays on the difference between liberal economics (of the Anglo-American type, as understood in Germany) and the German "social-market economy." Some of the founders of the concept of "social-market economy" are included. See especially the three essays by Alfred Müller-Armack: "Economy Systems from a Social Point of View," "The Socio-Political Model of the Social Market Economy," and "Thirty Years of Social Market Economy," pp. 95–162, in *Economy and Development*.

12. *The Social Teachings of Ketteler*, p. 349.

13. "The principal characteristic of the pre-war German regime of princes, generals and landowners, the law-professors who endowed it with academic legitimacy, and the Lutheran pastors who gave it moral authority, was illiberalism. This ruling caste hated the West with passionate loathing, both for its liberal ideas and for the gross materialism and lack of spirituality which (in their view) those ideas embodied. They wanted to keep Germany 'pure' of the West. . . . These Easterners drew a fundamental distinction between 'civilization,' which they defined as rootless, cosmopolitan, immoral, un-German, Western, materialistic and radically defiled; and 'culture,' which was pure, national, German, spiritual and authentic. Civilization pulled Germany to the West, culture to the East. . . . When Germany responded to the pull of the West, it met disaster; when it pursued its destiny in the East, it fulfilled itself." Paul Johnson, *Modern Times* (New York: Harper & Row, 1983), p. 111.

14. *The Social Teachings of Ketteler*, p. 349.

15. Ibid., p. 350. "Nations and states are also such moral organisms in which countless moral forces, like the idea of home and fatherland as well as history itself with its mixture of good and bad fortune, bind men together organically." Ibid., p. 349.

16. According to John XXIII, Pius XII stressed "that private ownership of material goods helps to safeguard and develop family life. Such goods are an apt means 'to secure for the father of a family the healthy liberty he needs in order to fulfill the duties assigned him by the Creator, regarding the physical, spiritual, and religious welfare of the family.' From this arises the right of the family to migrate. Accordingly, our predecessor [Pius XII] reminds governments, both those permitting emigration and those accepting immigrants, that 'they never permit anything whereby mutual and sincere understanding between States is diminished or destroyed.' If this be mutually accomplished, it will come to pass that benefits are equalized and diffused widely among peoples, as the supply of goods and the arts and crafts are increased and fostered." *Mater et Magistra*, 45.

17. "Within his own circle in Heidelberg, Weber exchanged thoughts regularly with men who reflected the forces at the very center of Germany's new anti-modernist wave: Friedrich Gundolf, a leading disciple of Stefan George; and the Hungarian, Georg Lukacs, whose beliefs in these years epitomized the powerful hold of Slavic culture over many German intellectuals." Arthur Mitzman, *The Iron Cage: An Historical Interpretation of Max Weber* (New York: Alfred A. Knopf, 1970), pp. 261–262.

18. See Nietzsche's "Peoples and Fatherlands": "[W]e should not forget that the English with their profound normality have once before caused an over-all depression of the European spirit: what people call 'modern ideas' or 'the ideas of the eighteenth cen-

tury' or also 'French ideas'—that, in other words, against which the *German* spirit has risen with a profound disgust—was of English origin . . . European *noblesse*—of feeling, of taste, of manners, taking the word, in short, in every higher sense—is the work and invention of *France;* European vulgarity, the plebeianism of modern ideas, that of *England." Beyond Good and Evil,* trans. Walter Kaufmann (New York: Vintage Books, 1966), pp. 191–192 (emphasis in original).

19. See the extended contrasts drawn by George Santayana in *The German Mind: A Philosophical Diagnosis* (New York: Thomas Y. Crowell Co., 1968), p. 77 and passim: "In England Fichte did not see the champion of Protestantism, morality, and political liberty, nor the constant foe of Napoleon, but only a universal commercial vampire" (p. 77).

20. "The German-American Catholics . . . were a tight-knit group characterized by devotion to the German traditions, customs, and language, as well as by a stalwart, uncompromising Catholicism. . . . In their view the modern world was far from good; in fact, the primary enemy was liberalism. Ever since the Middle Ages infectious liberalism had brought about a growing individualism and selfishness. . . . This theoretical estrangement of German–American Catholics from the modern world with its manifold liberalism was reinforced by historical circumstances. . . . Even in their native land they had been somewhat estranged. In the United States they found themselves as an immigrant minority speaking a foreign language. In the American context of the nineteenth century their German immigrant status made them all the more isolated and defensive." Charles E. Curran, *American Catholic Social Ethics: Twentieth-Century Approaches* (Notre Dame, Indiana: University of Notre Dame Press, 1982), pp. 92–93.

21. *The Social Teachings of Ketteler,* p. 350.

22. Ibid., p. 327.

23. Ibid., p. 329.

24. Ibid., pp. 329–330.

25. Ibid., pp. 334–335.

26. Ibid., pp. 335–336.

27. Heinrich Pesch, *Lehrbuch der Nationalökonomie,* 5 vols, rev. ed. (Freiburg im Br.: Herder, 1920–1926), 3:547.

28. Ibid., 4:587.

29. "When at a convention in Vienna, Philippovich, an economist of considerable stature, explicitly acknowledged the importance of Pesch's concept of objective goals for the economy, Max Weber entered an almost passionate protest against any goals and purposes, against any value-judgments in socio-economic theory on the grounds that its scientific character must be kept immaculate." Gustav Gundlach, S.J., "Solidarist Economics," *Social Order* 1 (April 1951):182.

30. Quoted in Franz H. Mueller, "I Knew Heinrich Pesch," *Social Order* 1 (April 1951):151–152.

31. See Joseph A. Schumpeter, *History of Economic Analysis,* ed. Elizabeth Boody Schumpeter (New York: Oxford University Press, 1954), p. 765, quoted in Chapter 1, note 4, above. Sombart placed Pesch's work within the "ethical" school of economic thought, by which he meant "non-scientific." See Goetz Briefs, "Pesch and His Contemporaries," *Social Order* 1 (April 1951):159.

32. Quoted in Mueller, "I Knew Heinrich Pesch," p. 151.

33. Friedman says of Galbraith that, "apart from Galbraith's own assertion, *there has been no successful defence of [Galbraith's] view of the world* . . . I know of no scientific studies which have validated that view of the world. . . . Instead of regarding him as a scientist seeking explanations, I think we shall get more understanding if we look at him as a missionary seeking converts." "From Galbraith to Economic Freedom," in *Tax Limitation, Inflation and the Role of Government* (Dallas: The Fisher Institute, (1978), p. 61 (emphasis in original).

34. Richard E. Mulcahy, S.J., *The Economics of Heinrich Pesch* (New York: Henry Holt and Co., 1952), p. 46.

35. See Gertrude Himmelfarb, "Adam Smith: Political Economy as Moral Philosophy,"

*The Idea of Poverty: England in the Early Industrial Age* (New York: Alfred A. Knopf, 1984), pp. 42–63. "The argument of *Moral Sentiments* is subtle, complicated, and not without difficulties, but even the barest statement of it is enough to demonstrate that Smith was hardly the ruthless individualist or amoralist he is sometimes made out to be. Whatever difficulties there may be in the reconciliation of *Moral Sentiments* with the *Wealth of Nations*, it is clear enough that Smith intended both as parts of his grand 'design,' that he had the *Wealth of Nations* in mind even before he wrote *Moral Sentiments*, and that he remained committed to *Moral Sentiments*, reissuing and revising it long after the *Wealth of Nations* was published.

"A close reading of the *Wealth of Nations* itself suggests that political economy as Smith understood it was part of a larger moral philosophy, a new kind of moral economy. Schumpeter complained that Smith was so steeped in the tradition of moral philosophy derived from scholasticism and natural law that he could not conceive of economics per se, an economics divorced from ethics and politics" (ibid., p. 48).

36. Quoted in Mulcahy, *The Economics of Pesch*, pp. 13–14. *Lehrbuch* 1:467.
37. Quoted in Mulcahy, *The Economics of Pesch*, p. 29. *Lehrbuch* 2:316.
38. See Mulcahy, *The Economics of Pesch*, p. 41. *Lehrbuch* 1:552.
39. Summarizing Pesch's objections to liberalism, Goetz Briefs wrote: "Liberalism erred in failing to recognize the basic community of interests between men and the hierarchical structure of society—both arising immediately from radical needs of man's nature —which distinguish society from a mere horde. As a result it erred also in placing its trust completely in the blind mechanics of the market to regulate moral actions. In writing off the ethics of charity and justice under the assumption that the mechanics of competition left no room for them, liberalism not only invited chaos in economic affairs, but inevitably doomed man to a very limited realization of his own innate potentialities." "Pesch and His Contemporaries," pp. 154–155.
40. Ibid., p. 156.
41. On this point, Pesch wrote: "The difficulties of economic life, which economics has to analyze, are tremendous, and the errors of wrong economic doctrines have had devastating consequences for the nations. If the principles of moral law had been applied, we should not be faced with disaster today. Individualistic liberty, socialistic views of human and social life and the 'natural laws' of pure economics have caused the rise of what is called capitalism in the bad meaning of the term. And it is this capitalism, in turn, which explains the rise, the growth and the lure of socialism" (quoted in ibid., pp. 153–154; *Lehrbuch* 1:497).
42. Pesch argued that socialism is based on a false psychology: "To production pertains an initiative which today is supplied by the entrepreneur and which cannot be replaced by a social production." To which Mulcahy adds: "This is confirmed by the familiar fact that, normally, common property is not utilized as efficiently as private property. And not only is entrepreneurial initiative lacking, but in all segments of the economy every personal incentive to better oneself is wanting, since every opportunity for economic and social improvement remains closed" (Richard E. Mulcahy, S.J., "Economic Freedom in Pesch," *Social Order* 1 (April 1951):167). See also Mulcahy, *The Economics of Heinrich Pesch*, pp. 171–78.
43. Quoted in Mulcahy, "Economic Freedom in Pesch," p. 167: "On principle, private property and private enterprise may not be suppressed in any sphere where its continuance and effectiveness can satisfy the common welfare. Rather, only according to the postulates of social justice does a limitation of freedom take place: a substitution of private enterprise by the public enterprise takes place exclusively, solely, and only, in such fields where indubitably the national economic need in reference to the whole rightly demands the suppression of a private enterprise incapable, unsuited or harmful to the needs of the national economy."
44. On this, Pesch cites with approval the words of Schaeffle: "Freedom to determine one's own wants is certainly the most basic fundamental of freedom. If the means of life and culture were somehow measured from without, even to each one according to his own particular want pattern, still no one could live and develop according to his

own individuality. . . . That one fundamental, practical freedom—individually to employ our private revenue according to our free discretion—we would not be ready to sell for all the possible benefits of social reform heaped together" (quoted ibid., pp. 162–163).

45. Quoted in ibid, p. 163: "We owe to free competitive enterprise the great benefits of the last century in the field of knowledge and 'know-how'; in it dwells a never-failing, animated, creative force; it is able to harness forces for the highest production, always creating new goods for the welfare of the people."

46. Concerning Pesch's view on the role of the state, Father Mulcahy writes (ibid., p. 164): "On the general principle that political regulation is permissible only when other forms of regulation are not possible and when the public welfare unconditionally requires it, the state may set up the general legal forms and necessary juridical processes necessary to realize the standards of justice in industrial relations. It may, to the extent required, protect the rights and enforce the duties flowing from the collective agreements. After all, it would be unworthy of the state to leave such matters to the mere relative power of the parties. But labor and management make their own contracts; they themselves determine their terms of agreement." A contract, Pesch writes, "remains above all a matter of the parties concerned. Here the law can determine only the extrinsic limits of what is legally permissible. And insofar as the social factors prove themselves capable of the regulation of the entire collective bargaining, the autonomy required for effective development should be left to them. Political compulsion in all these matters is not the first, but the last thing." Mulcahy adds: "If he had not been misrepresented on this point, it would be superfluous to point out that Pesch rejects the determination of wages by the state."

47. Pesch's concept of "association," of course, tended to the more organic "corporative" model, but his notion of voluntary cooperatives is not altogether disparate from the Anglo-American meaning of "associations."

48. Quoted in Mueller, "I Knew Heinrich Pesch," p. 151.

49. Mulcahy, *The Economics of Pesch*, p. 159.

50. Mulcahy's words in ibid., p. 164.

51. Ibid. *Lehrbuch* 1:440.

52. Mulcahy, *The Economics of Pesch*, p. 166. *Lehrbuch* 2:ix–x.

53. Mulcahy, *The Economics of Pesch*, pp. 169–170. *Lehrbuch* 4:561–562.

54. Ibid.

55. Mulcahy, *The Economics of Pesch*, p. 170. *Lehrbuch* 2:230.

56. Mulcahy's words in *The Economics of Pesch*, p. 178. *Lehrbuch* 2:214.

57. Mulcahy, *The Economics of Pesch*, p. 179.

58. See his *Mit brennender sorge* in *Twelve Encyclicals of Pius XI* (London: Catholic Truth Society, 1943).

59. See Howard J. Wiarda, *Corporatism and National Development in Latin America* (Boulder, Colorado: Westview Press, 1981).

60. Turning often to this theme, John Dewey quoted Emerson favorably: " 'The connection of events,' and 'the society of your contemporaries' as formed of moving and multiple associations, are the only means by which the possibilities of individuality can be realized." *Individualism Old and New* (New York: Capricorn Books, 1930), p. 170.

61. See Chapter 1, note 8, above.

## Chapter 5: A Quintessential Liberal: John Stuart Mill

1. *Quadragesimo Anno*, 54.

2. Ibid., 27.

3. Ibid., 54.

4. J. Laurence Laughlin, "A Sketch of the History of Political Economy" in John Stuart Mill, *Principles of Political Economy*, abridged, with notes and introduction, by J. Laurence Laughlin (New York: D. Appleton and Company, 1884), pp. 31–32.

5. William D. Grampp, *The Manchester School of Economics* (Stanford, California: Stan-

ford University Press, 1960), pp. 2–5: "[T]he Manchester School was not a school in the sense in which classical economics or other intellectual groupings were, because unlike them it did not have a relatively complete or consistent doctrine nor is there an authoritative statement of its ideas about particular issues. . . . Manchester was a school in the sense of being united by a single purpose between 1838 and 1846: the complete and immediate repeal of the corn laws. Before 1838, the school did not exist, although free traders did; after 1846, it consisted of the followers of Cobden and Bright. What they had in common then was no specific purpose or set of beliefs but an admiration for these two capable men, supporting them on certain issues, openly disagreeing with them on others."

6. Joseph Schumpeter, *History of Economic Analysis*, ed. Elizabeth Boody Schumpeter (New York: Oxford University Press, 1954), p. 888.
7. Ibid.
8. Ibid., p. 398.
9. Ibid.
10. Ibid.
11. Ibid., p. 399; Schumpeter might have added that Henry Adams praised Bright and Cobden's efforts to keep Britain out of the American Civil War; see Henry Adams, *The Education of Henry Adams*, ed. Ernest Samuels (Boston: Houghton Mifflin, 1973), pp. 125–126, 183–192.
12. Oswald von Nell-Breuning, *Reorganization of Social Economy: The Social Encyclical Developed and Explained* (New York: The Bruce Publishing Company, 1936), p. 136.
13. Ibid., p. 137.
14. Ibid., p. 129; and Leo XIII, *Rerum Novarum*, 15.
15. *Quadragesimo Anno*, 54.
16. Nell-Breuning, *Reorganization of Social Economy*, p. 135.
17. *Quadragesimo Anno*, 53; see also von Nell-Breuning, *Reorganization of Social Economy*, p. 134.
18. Nell-Breuning, *Reorganization of Social Economy*, p. 137.
19. Schumpeter, *History of Economic Analysis*, pp. 401–402.
20. Ibid., p. 396.
21. Quoted in Jean-Yves Calvez and Jacques Perrin, *The Church and Social Justice*, trans. J. R. Kirwan (Chicago: Henry Regnery Co., 1961), p. 275.
22. Richard Cobden, *Speeches on Questions of Public Policy*, ed. John Bright and James E. Thorold Rogers (London: Macmillan, 1870), 1:362–3; and Calvez and Perrin, *The Church and Social Justice*, p. 275.
23. See *Quadragesimo Anno*, 53; and von Nell-Breuning, *Reorganization of Social Economy*, p. 134.
24. See *Rerum Novarum*, 27; *Quadragesimo Anno*, 53; and von Nell-Breuning, *Reorganization of Social Economy*, p. 131.
25. *Quadragesimo Anno*, 53; Nell-Breuning, *Reorganization of Social Economy*, pp. *131–132*.
26. For a long discussion of the meaning of "corporatism," see Calvez and Perrin, *The Church and Social Justice*, Chapter 19.
27. John Hellman, *Emmanuel Mounier and the New Catholic Left 1930–1950* (Toronto: University of Toronto Press, 1981).
28. John Stuart Mill, *Principles of Political Economy with Some of Their Applications to Social Philosophy* (London: John W. Parker, 1848).
29. Adam Smith, *An Inquiry Into the Nature and Causes of the Wealth of Nations*, ed. Edwin Cannan (New York: Random House, 1937).
30. Mill, *Principles of Political Economy*, J. Laurence Laughlin's edition. (In addition to Mill's text, Laughlin has provided a useful running commentary on certain sections; citations of this commentary will be so identified.) References to Mill's text will be both to the Laughlin edition and to the edition prepared by Sir William Ashley in 1909 and reprinted in 1969 (New York: Augustus M. Kelley). The Ashley edition contains Mill's last revisions. Citations are from the Laughlin edition, followed by the corresponding page(s) in Ashley.

31. John Stuart Mill, *Autobiography of John Stuart Mill* (New York: Columbia University Press, 1924), pp. 174–175.
32. Mill, *Principles of Political Economy*, p. 47 (Ashley, p. 1).
33. Ibid., p. 47 (Laughlin's commentary).
34. Ibid. (Laughlin's commentary).
35. Ibid., pp. 47–48 (Ashley, p. 2).
36. Ibid., p. 48 (Ashley, p. 3).
37. Ibid., pp. 48–49 (Ashley, p. 5).
38. Ibid., p. 49 (Ashley, p. 6).
39. Ibid., pp. 49–50 (Ashley, pp. 6–7, 9).
40. See ibid., pp. 65–68 (Ashley, pp. 54–56). Mill writes: "What, then, is [the manufacturer's] capital? Precisely that part of his possessions, whatever it be, which he designs to employ in carrying on fresh production" (p. 66 [Ashley, p. 55]).
41. Ibid., p. 53 (Ashley, p. 22).
42. Ibid.
43. See Paul Johnson, "Has Capitalism a Future?" in Ernest W. Lefever, ed., *Will Capitalism Survive? A Challenge by Paul Johnson With Twelve Responses* (Washington, D.C.: Ethics and Public Policy Center, 1979), p. 4.
44. Mill, *Principles of Political Economy*, p. 57 (Laughlin's commentary).
45. Ibid., pp. 58–59 (Ashley, p. 32).
46. Ibid., p. 65 (Ashley, p. 32).
47. Ibid., p. 67 (Laughlin's commentary).
48. Ibid., pp. 67–68 (Ashley, pp. 55–56). Mill observes: "The distinction, then, between Capital and Not-capital does not lie in the kind of commodities, but in the mind of the capitalist—in his will to employ them for one purpose rather than another. . . ." (p. 68 [Ashley, p. 56]).
49. Ibid., p. 74 (Ashley, p. 63).
50. Ibid., p. 75 (Ashley, p. 66).
51. Ibid., p. 76 (Ashley, p. 66).
52. Ibid., p. 76 (Ashley, pp. 66–67).
53. Ibid., p. 77 (Ashley, p. 68).
54. Ibid. (Ashley, p. 68).
55. Ibid. (Ashley, p. 68).
56. Ibid., p. 78 (Laughlin's commentary).
57. Ibid., pp. 82–83 (Ashley, pp. 74–75).
58. Ibid., p. 82 (Laughlin's commentary).
59. Ibid., p. 98 (Ashley, p. 99).
60. Ibid., pp. 99–101 (Ashley, pp. 102–105).
61. Ibid., p. 101 (Ashley, p. 113).
62. Ibid. (Ashley, pp. 116–117).
63. Ibid., pp. 105–106 (Ashley, p. 127).
64. Ibid., p. 110 (Ashley, p. 141).
65. Ibid. (Ashley, p. 137).
66. Ibid., p. 119 (Ashley, p. 161).
67. Ibid., p. 112 (Ashley, p. 155).
68. Ibid., p. 120 (Ashley, p. 163).
69. Ibid., p. 121 (Laughlin's commentary).
70. Ibid., p. 122 (Ashley, p. 165).
71. Ibid. (Laughlin's commentary).
72. Ibid., p. 125 (Ashley, pp. 170–171).
73. Ibid., p. 124 (Ashley, pp. 167–170).
74. Ibid., p. 127 (Ashley, pp. 173–174).
75. Ibid., p. 128 (Ashley, p. 174).
76. Ibid., p. 129 (Ashley, p. 175).
77. Ibid., p. 155 (Ashley, pp. 199–200).
78. Ibid., pp. 156–157 (Ashley, p. 202).

79. Ibid., p. 157 (Ashley, pp. 203–204).
80. Ibid., p. 159 (Ashley, pp. 208–209).
81. Ibid., p. 160 (Ashley, pp. 209–211).
82. Ibid., pp. 168–169. These remarks, and the ones cited in notes 83 and 84, below, were inserted into the text by Laughlin and derive from Mill's "Chapters on Socialism," published in 1879 in the *Fortnightly Review*.
83. Ibid., pp. 170–171.
84. Ibid., p. 171.
85. Ibid., (Ashley, pp. 218, 221).
86. Ibid., pp. 171–172 (Ashley, p. 223).
87. Ibid., p. 173 (Ashley, p. 231).
88. Ibid., p. 172 (Ashley, pp. 229–230).
89. Ibid., pp. 173–174 (Ashley, pp. 233–235).
90. Ibid., p. 175–177 (Ashley, pp. 242–244).
91. Ibid., pp. 178–183 (Ashley, pp. 343–344).
92. Ibid., p. 193 (Ashley, p. 361).
93. Ibid., p. 194 (Ashley, p. 362).
94. Ibid., p. 196 (Ashley, pp. 362–363).
95. Ibid., p. 197 (Ashley, p. 365).
96. Ibid., pp. 225–226, 264–272 (Ashley, pp. 417–419).
97. Ibid., p. 267 (Ashley, pp. 461–462).
98. Ibid., p. 522 (Laughlin's commentary).
99. Ibid., p. 518 (Laughlin's commentary).
100. Ibid. (Laughlin's commentary).
101. Ibid. (Laughlin's commentary).
102. Ibid., p. 517
103. Ibid., p. 520.
104. Ibid.
105. Ibid., pp. 532–533 (Laughlin's commentary).
106. Ibid., p. 217 (Ashley, p. 406).
107. Ibid., p. 221 (Ashley, pp. 411–412).
108. Ibid., p. 226–231 (Ashley, pp. 418–421).
109. Ibid., p. 379 (laughlin's commentary).
110. Ibid., p. 385 (Ashley, p. 578).
111. Ibid., p. 387 (Ashley, p. 579).
112. Ibid., p. 386 (Ashley, p. 578).
113. Ibid., p. 388 (Ashley, p. 580).
114. Ibid., p. 389 (Ashley, p. 581).
115. Ibid., p. 389–390 (Ashley, p. 582).

## Chapter 6: From Politics to Economics: Leo XIII and Pius XI

1. Leo XIII, *Rerum Novarum*, 1.
2. Gertrude Himmelfarb, *The Idea of Poverty: England in the Early Industrial Age* (New York: Alfred A. Knopf, 1984) p. 42.
3. Oswald von Nell-Breuning, S.J., *Reorganization of Social Economy: The Social Encyclical Developed and Explained* (New York: The Bruce Publishing Company, 1936), p. 131.
4. *Rerum Novarum*, 1.
5. Ibid., 1.
6. Ibid., 2.
7. Ibid., 3.
8. Ibid., 10.
9. Ibid., 4.
10. Ibid., 15.
11. Ibid.
12. Ibid., 12 (emphasis in original).

13. Ibid., 14.
14. Ibid., 16.
15. Ibid., 11.
16. Ibid., 41.
17. Ibid. 29.
18. Ibid., 27.
19. Josef Schumpeter, *History of Economic Analysis,* ed. Elizabeth Boody Schumpeter (New York: Oxford University Press, 1954), p. 558.
20. Pius XI, *Quadragesimo Anno,* 105–109.
21. Nell-Breuning, *Reorganization of Social Economy* p. 20.
22. Ibid., p. 5, n. 2.
23. Ibid., pp. 268–269.
24. Ibid., p. 272.
25. Ibid., p. 275.
26. *Quadragesimo Anno,* 101.
27. Nell-Breuning, *Reorganization of Social Economy,* p. 274 (emphasis in original).
28. Ibid., pp. 273–274.
29. Ibid., p. 19.
30. George Santayana, *The German Mind* (New York: Thomas Y. Crowell, 1968), pp. 54–64, 169.
31. Nell-Breuning, *Reorganization of Social Economy,* p. 20.
32. Jean-Yves Calvez and Jacques Perrin, *The Church and Social Justice,* trans. J. R. Kirwan (Chicago: Henry Regnery Co., 1961), pp. 133–161; 402–437.
33. "The rule of justice in the relations between men has a much wider field of application than that of politics. . . . The idea of justice is the woof in the pattern of the social doctrine of the Church.
    "This is to be seen in detail in the encyclical *Rerum Novarum,* first charter of this social doctrine, to use the words of Pius XII. Leo XIII condemned, in the name of justice, the mistaken solution put forward by the socialists. 'The remedy they propose is manifestly against justice, for every man has by nature the right to possess property of his own.' It can be reasoned from this affirmation that justice depends from what is interior to the nature of man, who is at the same time individual and social" (ibid., p. 135). This text in Leo XIII is the foundation for the modern papal concept of "social justice." But see Chapter 2, note 35, above, for a still earlier text in *Rerum Novarum.*
34. E. E. Y. Hales, *Revolution and Papacy* (London: Eyre and Spottiswoode, 1960), pp. 278–295.
35. Nell-Breuning, *Reorganization of Social Economy,* p. 16.
36. See Adam Smith, *An Inquiry into the Nature and Causes of the Wealth of Nations,* ed. Edwin Cannan (New York: Random House, 1937), p. 423; and Adam Smith, *The Theory of Moral Sentiments* (1853; reprint ed., Indianapolis: Liberty Classics, 1969), p. 304.
37. Wilhelm Emmanuel von Ketteler, "Freedom, Authority, and the Church," *The Social Teachings of Wilhelm Emmanuel von Ketteler,* trans. Rupert J. Ederer (Washington, D.C.: University Press of America, 1981), pp. 199–203.
38. Conversation with Henry Briefs, Professor of Economics, Georgetown University, Washington, D.C., 10 August 1983.
39. For a thorough discussion of the developing concept of corporatism in Pius XI and XII, see Calvez and Perrin, *The Church and Social Justice,* Chapter 19, "The Church's Plan for Society: Community and Responsibility," esp. pp. 414–437. See also von Nell-Breuning, *Reorganization of Social Economy,* Chapter 11, "Corporate Co-operation," esp. pp. 217–242.
40. Alexis de Tocqueville, *Democracy in America,* trans. Harry Reeve, ed. Phillips Bradley, 2 vols. (New York: Vintage Books, 1945), 2:118: "Nothing in my opinion, is more deserving of our attention than the intellectual and moral associations of America. The political and industrial associations of that country strike us forcibly; but the

others elude our observation, or if we discover them, we understand them imperfectly because we have hardly ever seen anything of the kind. It must be acknowledged, however, that they are as necessary to the American people as the former, and perhaps more so. In democratic countries the science of association is the mother of science; the progress of all the rest depends upon the progress it has made.

"Among the laws that rule human societies there is one which seems to be more precise and clear than all others. If men are to remain civilized or to become so, the art of association together must grow and improve in the same ratio in which the equality of conditions is increased."

41. See Howard J. Wiarda, ed., *Politics and Social Change in Latin America: The Distinct Tradition* (Boston: University of Massachusetts Press, 1982). pp. 20–21. See also Part Four and Conclusion.

42. Heinrich Pesch, *Lehrbuch der Nationalökonomie*, 5 vols, rev. ed. (Freiburg im Br.: Herder, 1920–1926), 1:497: "The difficulties of economic life, which economics has to analyze, are tremendous, and the errors of wrong economic doctrines have had devastating consequences for the nations. If the principles of moral law had been applied, we should not be faced with disaster today. Individualistic liberty, socialistic views of human and social life and the 'natural laws' of pure economics have caused the rise of what is called capitalism in the bad meaning of the term. And it is this capitalism, in turn, which explains the rise, the growth and the lure of socialism."

43. Michel Beaud, *A History of Capitalism 1500–1980*, trans. Tom Dickman and Anny Lefebvre (New York: Monthly Review Press, 1983), p. 229.

44. *Quadragesimo Anno*, 83.

45. Ibid., 84.

46. Ibid., 92–95.

47. Ibid., 95.

48. Ibid., 96.

49. Reinhold Niebuhr, "The Crisis," in *Christianity and Crisis* 1 (February 10, 1941):1–2.

50. Luigi Sturzo, *Church and State*, 2 vols. (Notre Dame, Indiana: University of Notre Dame, 1962).

51. Aminatore Fanfani, *Catholicism, Protestantism and Capitalism* (1935; reprint ed., New York: Arno Press, 1972).

52. Guido Gonella, *The Papacy and World Peace* (London: Hollis and Carter, 1945).

53. The most neglected dimension of Catholic social thought is the achievement of American Catholics. Cardinal Gibbons helped influence Leo XIII to come to the warm support of labor unions. Charles Curran has provided yeoman service in assessing a few of the major intellectual contributions of the Americans in *American Catholic Social Ethics: Twentieth Century Approaches* (Notre Dame, Indiana: University of Notre Dame, 1982).

54. William Roepke, *The Humane Economy*, trans. Elizabeth Henderson (Chicago: Regnery, 1960).

55. See Michael Novak, "Pope John's Session, 1962," *The Open Church* (New York: Macmillan, 1964), pp. 3–16.

## Chapter 7. The Development of Nations: John XXIII and Paul VI

1. .John XXIII, *Mater et Magistra*, 182–183: "We note with deep satisfaction that Catholic men, citizens of the less developed nations, are for the most part second to no other citizens in furthering efforts of their countries to make progress economically and socially according to their capacity.... Furthermore, we note that Catholic citizens of the richer nations are making extensive efforts to ensure that aid given by their own countries to needy countries is directed increasingly toward economic and social progress. In this connection, it seems specially praiseworthy that appreciable aid in various forms is provided increasingly each year to young people from Africa and Asia, so that they may pursue literary and professional studies in the great universities

of Europe and America. The same applies to the great care that has been taken in training for every responsibility of their office men prepared to go to less developed areas, there to carry out their profession and duties."

2. Ibid., 18.
3. Ibid., 23 (emphasis in original).
4. Ibid., 55.
5. Ibid., 57
6. Ibid., 61.
7. Ibid., 65.
8. Ibid., 74.
9. Ibid., 82.
10. Ibid., 83.
11. Ibid., 84, 85, 87.
12. Ibid., 104–108.
13. Ibid., 109.
14. Ibid., 110.
15. Ibid., 112.
16. Ibid., 120.
17. Ibid., 122.
18. Ibid., 151.
19. See Roger Heckel, *Self-Reliance* (Vatican City: Pontifical Commission "Iustitia et Pax," 1978), pp. 4–6.
20. *Mater et Magistra,* 152 (emphasis in original).
21. Ibid., 163, 165.
22. Ibid., 175.
23. Ibid., 189.
24. Ibid., 219 (emphasis added).
25. Ibid., 220.
26. The Pope is indebted to Maritain's *Christianity and Democracy,* trans. Doris C. Anson (New York: Charles Scribner's Sons, 1944); *Man and the State* (Chicago: University of Chicago, 1951); *The Person and the Common Good,* trans. John J. Fitzgerald (New York: Charles Scribner's Sons, 1941), and the Universal Declaration of Human Rights, of which Maritain was one of the authors.
27. John XXIII, *Pacem In Terris,* 9.
28. Ibid., 24.
29. Ibid., 42.
30. Ibid., 45.
31. Ibid., 52.
32. Ibid., 64.
33. Ibid., 65. John XXIII is quoting from his earlier encyclical *Mater et Magistra,* 428.
34. *Pacem in Terris,* 67–69.
35. Ibid., 77.
36. Ibid., 130–135.
37. Ibid., 139.
38. Ibid., 159: "It must be borne in mind, furthermore, that neither can false philosophical teachings regarding the nature, origin and destiny of the universe and of man be identified with historical movements that have economic, social, cultural or political ends, not even when these movements have originated from those teachings and have drawn and still draw inspiration therefrom. . . . This is so because the teachings, once they are drawn up and defined, remain always the same, while the movements, working in constantly evolving historical situations, cannot but be influenced by these latter and cannot avoid, therefore, being subject to changes, even of a profound nature. Besides, who can deny that those movements, insofar as they conform to the dictates of right reason and are interpreters of the lawful aspirations of the human person, contain elements that are positive and deserving of approval?"
39. See also *Mater et Magistra,* 239: "But in the exercise of economic and social functions,

Catholics often come in contact with men who do not share their view of life. On such occasions, those who profess Catholicism must take special care to be consistent and not compromise in matters wherein the integrity of religion or morals would suffer harm. Likewise, in their conduct they should weigh the opinions of others with fitting courtesy and not measure everything in the light of their own interests. They should be prepared to join sincerely in doing whatever is naturally good or conducive to good. If, indeed, it happens that in these matters sacred authorities have prescribed or decreed anything, it is evident that this judgment is to be obeyed promptly by Catholics. For it is the Church's right and duty not only to safeguard principles relating to the integrity of religion and morals, but also to pronounce authoritatively when it is a matter of putting these principles into effect."

40. Ibid., 238.
41. *Pacem in Terris*, 229.
42. The emphasis of *Populorum Progressio* on the Third World brought intellectuals who specialized in economic development into the preparation of the encyclical. Of particular note were Louis Lebret, O.P., Barbara Ward, and George Jarlot.
43. Paul VI, *Populorum Progressio*, 22, 23.
44. Ibid., 26.
45. Ibid., 57.
46. "Raw materials and some tropical food products come from the poor countries to the rich. But the greatest suppliers of wheat, feed grains, coal, wood and wood pulp and cotton fiber are the two North American countries—the United States and Canada. If to be part of the Third World is to be a hewer of wood and a supplier of food and natural products, the United States and Canada are, by a wide margin, the first of the Third World countries and should vote accordingly in the United Nations. The trading corporation has, of course, receded greatly in relative importance." John Kenneth Galbraith, "The Defense of the Multinational Company," *Harvard Business Review* 56 (March/April, 1978):85.
47. *Populorum Progressio*, 58.
48. See Edoardo Rovida, "Intervention of Archibishop Edoardo Rovida, Head of the Holy See Delegation to UNCTAD VI," *International Economics: Interdependence and Dialogue*, (Vatican City: Pontifical Commission "Iustitia et Pax," 1984), p. 9.
49. *Populorum Progressio*, 60.
50. Ibid., 61.
51. Ibid.
52. Ibid., 70.
53. Ibid., Title of Section 4, preceding no. 76.
54. Ibid., 59.
55. Ibid.
56. P. T. Bauer, "Ecclesiastical Economics Is Envy Exalted," *This World*, No. 1 (Winter/Spring, 1982), p. 69.
57. Ibid., p. 61.
58. Ibid., p. 64: "Prevailing attitudes, mores, and beliefs in many ldc's are unhelpful to economic performance and advance, at any rate as these are conventionally interpreted. Examples include the widespread refusal to let women take paid work in Moslem countries, or the reluctance to kill cows and other animals, as in much of South Asia. Some of these mores are deeply ingrained and reflect beliefs which are an integral part of people's spiritual lives." See also P. T. Bauer, *Equality, the Third World, and Economic Delusion* (Cambridge, Massachusetts: Harvard University Press, 1981), esp. Chapter 4, "Western Guilt and Third World Poverty."
59. Paul VI, *Octogesima Adveniens*, 50.
60. *Populorum Progressio*, 49.
61. *Octogesima Adveniens*, 4.
62. Ibid., 5.
63. Ibid., 23.
64. Ibid., 24.

65. Ibid., 25.
66. Ibid., 46.
67. Ibid.
68. Ibid., 26.
69. Ibid., 33.
70. Ibid., 34.
71. Ibid., 26.
72. Ibid., 35.
73. Quoted in Joseph Gremillion, *The Gospel of Peace and Justice* (Maryknoll, New York: Orbis, 1976), p. 9.
74. See Walter Lippmann, *The Essential Walter Lippmann*, ed. Clinton Rossiter and James Lare (New York: Random House, 1963), pp. 176–181.
75. Gremillion, *The Gospel of Peace and Justice*, pp. 12–13.
76. Ibid., p. 15.
77. Quoted in ibid., p. 18.
78. Quoted in ibid.
79. Quoted in ibid., p. 19 (emphasis in original).
80. Quoted in ibid.
81. Ibid. Quotation is from *Octogesima Adveniens*, 45–46.
82. Quoted in Gremillion, *The Gospel of Peace and Justice, p. 20*.
83. Ibid., p. 49.
84. Ibid., p. 81.
85. Ibid., p. 49.
86. Paul VI observed in *Octogesima Adveniens*, 3; "In some other nations, where the Church sees her place recognized, sometimes officially so, she too finds heself subjected to the repercussions of the crisis which is unsettling society; some of her members are tempted by radical and violent solutions from which they believe that they can expect a happier outcome. While some people, unaware of present injustices, strive to prolong the existing situation, others allow themselves to be beguiled by revolutionary ideologies which promise them, not without delusion, a definitively better world."

## Chapter 8. Creation Theology: Pope John Paul II

1. *Selections from the Letters, Speeches, and State Papers of Abraham Lincoln*, ed. Ida M. Tarbell (Boston: Ginn and Company, 1911), pp. 73–74; hereafter cited as *Selections From Lincoln*.
2. See Claire Sterling, *The Time of the Assassins* (New York: Holt, Rinehart and Winston, 1983) and Paul Henze, *The Plot to Kill the Pope* (New York: Charles Scribner's Sons, 1983).
3. See James B. Edie, "William James and the Phenomenology of Religious Experience," in *American Philosophy and the Future*, ed. Michael Novak (New York: Charles Scribner's Sons, 1968), pp. 247–269.
4. See, e.g., Karol Wojtyla, *The Acting Person* (Boston: Reidel, 1979).
5. *Laborem Exercens*, 3. To reduce the number of footnotes referring to the encyclical, one note below frequently covers sequential citations from the same paragraph.
6. Ibid., Preamble.
7. Ibid., 4.
8. Ibid., 5.
9. Ibid., 27.
10. Ibid., 27.
11. Ibid., 7.
12. November 1–7, 1981, "Conference on 'The Common Spiritual Roots of Europe.'" About half the delegates came from Poland. Msgr. Josef Tischner attacked the Marxist conception of work, rooted in Ricardo, as did others. The Pope likewise attributes Marx's errors to capitalist predecessors. The papers delivered at the Conference,

called by Pope John Paul II, have been published at Vatican City, Don Virgilio Levi (editor).

13. *Laborem Exercens,* 7.

14. Ibid.

15. Richard N. Current, ed., *The Political Thought of Abraham Lincoln* (Indianapolis, Indiana: Bobbs-Merrill, 1967), pp. 133–134.

16. The text of Lincoln's letter, written in 1851, runs as follows: "Your request for eighty dollars I do not think it best to comply with now. At the various times when I have helped you a little you have said to me, 'We can get along very well now'; but in a very short time I find you in the same difficulty again. Now, this can only happen by some defect in your conduct. What that defect is, I think I know. You are not lazy, and still you are an idler. I doubt whether, since I saw you, you have done a good whole day's work in any one day. You do not very much dislike to work, and still you do not work much, merely because it does not seem to you that you could get much for it. This habit of uselessly wasting time is the whole difficulty; it is vastly important to you, and still more so to your children, that you should break the habit. It is more important to them, because they have longer to live, and can keep out of an idle habit before they are in it, easier than they can get out after they are in" *(Selections from Lincoln,* p. 13).

17. Smith writes, for example, "Every colonist gets more land than he can possibly cultivate. He has no rent, and scarce any taxes to pay. No landlord shares with him in its produce, and the share of the sovereign is commonly but a trifle. He has every motive to render as great as possible a produce, which is thus to be almost entirely his own. But his land is commonly so extensive, that with all his own industry, and with all the industry of other people whom he can get to employ, he can seldom make it produce the tenth part of what it is capable of producing. He is eager, therefore, to collect labourers from all quarters, and to reward them with the most liberal wages. But those liberal wages, joined to the plenty and cheapness of land, soon make those labourers leave him, in order to become landlords themselves, and to reward, with equal liberality, other labourers, who soon leave them for the same reason that they left their first master. The liberal reward of labour encourages marriage. The children, during the tender years of infancy, are well fed and properly taken care of, and when they are grown up, the value of their labour greatly overpays their maintenance. When arrived at maturity, the high price of labour, and the low price of land, enable them to establish themselves in the same manner as their fathers did before them" (Adam Smith, *An Inquiry into the Nature and Causes of the Wealth of Nations,* ed. Edwin Cannan (New York: Random House, 1937), p. 532).

18. Hamilton writes that when commerce and manufacturing are encouraged, "each individual can find his proper element, and can call into activity the whole vigour of his nature." He observed that "to cherish and stimulate the activity of the human mind, by multiplying the objects of enterprise, is not among the least considerable of the expedients, by which the wealth of a nation may be promoted" (Alexander Hamilton, "Report on Manufacturers," in *The Papers of Alexander Hamilton,* ed. Harold C. Syrett, 25 vols. (New York: Columbia University Press, 1960–1977), 10:255–56).

19. *Laborem Exercens,* 12.

20. *Abraham Lincoln: His Speeches and Writings,* ed. Roy P. Basler (New York: World Publishing Co., 1946), p. 633; hereafter cited as *Lincoln: Speeches and Writings.*

21. Ibid., p. 634. On July 4, 1976, during the bicentennial parade in Cresco, Iowa, the author had occasion to see a woman, age 101, born 15 years after Lincoln uttered these words. During her lifetime, the United States had increased its population to 232 million. And Iowa had ceased being an "underdeveloped country."

22. *Laborem Exercens,* 12.

23. *Laborem Exercens,* 13. The many following citations are also from no. 13.

24. Distinguishing between the wealthy who invest in productive labor and those who invest in unproductive labor (such as retainers and courtiers), Smith wrote: "The proportion between those different funds necessarily determines in every country the

general character of the inhabitants as to industry or idleness. We are more industrious than our forefathers; because in the present times the funds destined for the maintenance of industry, are much greater in proportion to those which are likely to be employed in the maintenance of idleness, than they were two or three centuries ago. Our ancestors were idle for want of a sufficient encouragement to industry. It is better says the proverb, to play for nothing, than to work for nothing. In mercantile and manufacturing towns, where the inferior ranks of people are chiefly maintained by the employment of capital, they are in general industrious, sober, and thriving; as in many English, and in most Dutch towns. In those towns which are principally supported by the constant or occasional residence of a court, and in which the inferior ranks of people are chiefly maintained by the spending of revenue, they are in general idle, dissolute, and poor; as at Rome, Versailles, Compiegne, and Fontainbleau. If you except Rouen and Bourdeaux, there is little trade or industry in any of the parliament towns of France; and the inferior ranks of people, being chiefly maintained by the expence of the members of the courts of justice, and of those who come to plead before them, are in general idle and poor.... Wherever capital predominates, industry prevails; wherever revenue, idleness. Every increase or diminution of capital, therefore, naturally tends to increase or diminish the real quantity of industry, the number of productive hands, and consequently the exchangeable value of the annual produce of the land and labour of the country, the real wealth and revenue of all its inhabitants.... That portion of his revenue which a rich man annually spends, is in most cases consumed by idle guests, and menial servants, who leave nothing behind them in return for their consumption. That portion which he annually saves, as for the sake of the profit it is immediately employed as a capital, is consumed in the same manner, and nearly in the same time too, but by a different set of people, by labourers, manufacturers, and artificers, who re-produce with a profit the value of their annual consumption" (Smith, *Wealth of Nations,* pp. 319, 321).

25. *Laborem Exercens,* 14. The many following citations are also from no. 14.
26. Anticipating the pope's point here, Theodore Roosevelt wrote: "Every man holds his property subject to the general right of the community to regulate it to whatever degree the public welfare may require it." *The New Nationalism* (New York: Outlook Co., 1910), pp. 23–24.
27. These and the following quotations are from *Laborem Exercens,* 14.
28. Ibid., 15.
29. Ibid., 24.
30. Ibid., 25.
31. Ibid., 5.
32. Annual address before the Wisconsin State Agricultural Society, at Milwaukee, Wisconsin, 30 September 1859, published in *Speeches and Writings,* pp. 502–503.
33. Gregory Baum, "John Paul II's Encyclical on Labor," *The Ecumenist* 20 (November–December, 1981):3; see also Gregory Baum, *The Priority of Labor* (New York: Paulist Press, 1982), esp. pp. 80–91. In a remarkable chapter, "Pope John Paul II's Socialism," Professor Baum describes Pope John Paul II as a socialist of a rare species, distinguished by seven features: The pope's is a new socialism which is (1) moral; (2) liberationist; (3) cooperative; (4) internationalist; (5) reformist; (6) "personalist" in a sense learned from Marx (!); and (7) "utopian" but "non-ideological" (i.e., picturing a "concrete, historical social ideal, based on the potentialities of the present"). Baum holds that liberal institutions "oppress" peoples. By contrast, his vision of socialism seems to express *piety,* but conveys virtually nothing about *institutions.* Further, Baum fails to see that Pope John Paul II at every crucial institutional point supports such *liberal* institutions as private property for all, markets, limits upon the power of the state, the principle of free associations, the fundamental rights and liberties of the individual person, and the internalized spirit and practice of voluntary cooperation.
34. Philip F. Lawler, ed., *Papal Economics* (Washington, D.C.: Heritage Foundation, 1982).
35. See John Dewey, *The Public and its Problems* (New York: Henry Holt & Co., 1927), Chapter 5, "Search for the Great Community." The idea of community is also a major

theme in Josiah Royce, *The Problem of Christianity*, 2 vols. (New York: Macmillan, 1913); and Royce, *The Hope of the Great Community* (New York: Macmillan, 1916).

36. See Jacques Maritain, *The Person and the Common Good*, trans. John J. Fitzgerald (Notre Dame, Indiana: University of Notre Dame Press, 1966), p. 49 et seq.

37. Jean-Jacques Serban-Schreiber, *The American Challenge*, trans. Ronald Steel (New York: Avon, 1969), Chapters 5 and 6.

38. An excellent discussion of the role patent law played in the growth of technology and innovation can be found in Douglas C. North and Robert Paul Thomas, *The Rise of the Western World: A New Economic History* (Cambridge: Cambridge University Press, 1973), esp. pp. 2–3, 147–48, 152–53.

39. *Laborem Exercens*, 9.

40. *Laborem Exercens* 9: "Man has to subdue the earth and dominate it, because as 'the image of God' he is a person, that is to say, a subjective being capable of acting in a planned and rational way, capable of deciding about himself and with a tendency to self-realization."

41. See Maritain, *The Person and the Common Good*, Chapter 3, "Individuality and Personality."

42. *Laborem Exercens*, 14.

43. Ibid.

44. Ibid.

45. Alexis de Tocqueville, *Democracy in America*, trans. Harry Reeve, ed. Phillips Bradley, 2 vols. (New York: Vintage Books, 1945), 2:342: "private citizens, by combining together, may constitute bodies of great wealth, influence, and strength. . . . An association for political, commercial, or manufacturing purposes, or even for those of science and literature, is a powerful and enlightened member of the community, which cannot be disposed of at pleasure or oppressed without remonstrance, and which, by defending its own rights against the encroachments of the government, saves the common liberties of the country."

46. Peter L. Berger and Richard J. Neuhaus, *To Empower People: The Role of Mediating Structures in Public Policy* (Washington, D.C.: American Enterprise Institute, 1977).

47. See Peter F. Drucker, *The Unseen Revolution: How Pension Fund Socialism Came to America* (New York: Harper & Row, 1976); and Mortimer Adler and Louis O. Kelso, *The Capitalist Manifesto* (Westport, Connecticut: Greenwood, 1975), Chapter 11, "Measures Aimed at Broadening the Ownership of Existing Enterprises."

48. *Laborem Exercens*, 15.

49. Ibid.

50. As Ronald C. Nairn points out: "Less than 40% of the world's arable lands are being used. Even that estimate may be too low. It is difficult to assess what is and what is not arable. An Arizona desert region which in 1950 supported one breeding cow per 150 acres, under irrigation now produces three bales of cotton and 25 bushels of wheat per acre yearly. A New Zealand hillside, denuded and eroding, produced in the 1950's, under aerial top-dressing and seeding, wonderful stands of clover and rye grass and carried two to four sheep to the acre, often more. In Israel proper use of water (it was as simple as that) increased yields by eight times in less than 20 years. No matter how one measures it, the world has large acres of land, probably more than we farm now, awaiting the agricultural dynamic." *Wealth of Nations in Crisis* (Houston: Bayland Publishing, 1979), pp. 101–102.

51. In its 1981 report on world development, the World Bank observed: "In the past four years, India has imported hardly any foodgrains, and built its stocks up to unprecedented levels. As a result India was able to manage the consequences of a severe drought in 1979 without resorting to significant foodgrain imports. Over the 1970's as a whole, foodgrain production rose at an average of almost 3 percent a year, compared with population growth of 1.1 percent a year." *World Development Report 1981* (Washington, D.C.: International Bank for Reconstruction and Development/World Bank, 1981), p. 80.

52. *Laborem Exercens*, 10.

## Chapter 9. Catholic Social Thought in the Future: Toward a Theology of Commerce and Industry

1. Jacques Maritain, *Integral Humanism*, trans. Joseph W. Evans (New York: Charles Scribner's Sons, 1968).
2. Ibid., Chapter 4, "The Historical Ideal of a New Christendom," esp. "The Notion of 'Concrete Historical Ideal,'" pp. 127 et seq.
3. Roger Heckel, *Self-Reliance* (Vatican City: Pontifical Commission "Iustitia et Pax," 1978), p. 1: "The 'decades for development' were launched with the emphasis on *solidarity*. Inspired by moral conviction and basic realism, developed countries felt that it was their task to assist the third world to move into the realm of a modern economic reality. Appreciable results have been achieved in this sense, but it is now felt that an impasse has been reached which is further aggravated by the world economic crisis."
4. David Morawetz, *Twenty-Five Years of Economic Development, 1950–1975* (Baltimore, Maryland: Johns Hopkins University Press, 1977), Table A-1, pp. 77–80. Marc F. Plattner distinguishes between the *absolute* gap and the *relative* gap; the one can go down while the other goes up. Most of all, he distinguishes between the concept of a gap (whether absolute or relative) and the concept of poverty: *"For the gap is not a measurement of poverty.* The gap may be widening while enormous progress is being made in overcoming poverty and its attendant ills, and it may narrow when the plight of the poor is growing worse (or improving less rapidly)." "Thinking About the 'North-South Gap,'" *This World*, No. 7 (Winter 1984), p. 29; emphasis in original.
5. P. T. Bauer, "Ecclesiastical Economics Is Envy Exalted," *This World*, No. 1 (Winter/ Spring, 1982), p. 61: "The wide differences in economic performance between individuals and groups in the same country with access to the same natural resources again throws into relief the personal and cultural differences behind economic performance. In the Third World examples of group differences in economic performance include economic differences between Chinese, Indians, and Malays in Malaysia; Marwaris, Parsees, and others in India; Asians and Africans in Black Africa; Ibo and others in Nigeria; Greeks and Turks in Cyprus. In some of these examples the most successful groups have been the targets of severe adverse discrimination."
6. See, e.g., Julian Simon, *The Ultimate Resource* (Princeton, New Jersey: Princeton University Press, 1981); Warren T. Brookes, *The Economy In Mind* (New York: Universe Books, 1982); and Shlomo Maital, *Minds, Markets, and Money* (New York: Basic Books, 1982), esp. Part II, "People as Producers," and Chapter 4, "You Are Your Own Most Valuable Asset: The Psychology of Human Capital."
7. *Populorum Progressio*, 41: "Less well-off peoples can never be sufficiently on their guard against this temptation which comes to them from wealthy nations. For these nations all too often set an example of success in a highly technical and culturally developed civilization; they also provide the model for a way of acting that is principally aimed at the conquest of material prosperity.... Developing nations must know how to discriminate among those things that are held out to them; they must be able to assess critically, and eliminate those deceptive goods which would only bring about a lowering of the human ideal, and to accept those values that are sound and beneficial, in order to develop them alongside their own, in accordance with their own genius."
8. See John Stuart Mill, *Principles of Political Economy*, ed. William Ashley (1909; reprint ed., Fairfield, New Jersey: Augustus M. Kelley, 1976), pp. 189–190.
9. *Populorum Progressio*, 24: "It is unacceptable that citizens with abundant incomes from the resources and activity of their country should transfer a considerable part of this income abroad purely for their own advantage, without care for the manifest wrong they inflict on their country by doing this."
10. See John A. Coleman, S.J., "The Christian as Citizen," *Commonweal*, 9 September 1983, p. 460.
11. See Giovanni Sartori, "The Market, Planning, Capitalism and Democracy," *This World*, No. 5 (Spring/Summer, 1983), esp. pp. 68–71.

12. No one has written more eloquently of the universal propensity of the poor to better their condition—and their frequent success in doing so—than P. T. Bauer. See, e.g., his *Reality and Rhetoric: Studies in the Economics of Development* (Cambridge, Massachusetts: Harvard University Press, 1984). Lord Bauer is especially telling in his description of the development of millions of acres of rubber trees in Southeast Asia and cocoa trees in West Africa, most of them owned and developed by indigenous farmers in pursuit of economic incentives. See esp. Chapters 1, 6 and 8.

## Chapter 10. Liberation Theology in Practice

1. The best summary of a sympathetic nature is Arthur F. McGovern, S.J., *Marxism: An American Christian Perspective* (Maryknoll, New York: Orbis, 1980), esp. Chapters 5, "Liberation Theology in Latin America"; 8, "Property, Violence, Class Struggle, Democracy"; and 9, "Personal Reflections: Marxism, Socialism, the United States." The best short critical analysis is probably the Introduction to *Liberation Theology*, ed. James V. Schall, S.J. (San Francisco: Ignatius Press, 1982), pp. 3–126. Three chapters of the author's *The Spirit of Democratic Capitalism* (New York: American Enterprise Institute/Simon and Schuster, 1982) are directed to the Latin American case.

2. Roosevelt enunciated the Four Freedoms in his annual Message to the Congress, January 6, 1941: "In the future days, which we seek to make secure, we look forward to a world founded upon four essential human freedoms. The first is freedom of speech and expression—everywhere in the world. The second is freedom of every person to worship God in his own way—everywhere in the world. The third is freedom from want—everywhere in the world. The fourth is freedom from fear—anywhere in the world."

   In his Inaugural Address on January 20, 1949, Harry S Truman emphasized "four major courses of action," the last of which was to "embark on a bold new program for making the benefits of our scientific advances and industrial progress available for the improvement and growth of underdeveloped areas. . . . For the first time in history, humanity possesses the knowledge and skill to relieve the suffering of these people." United States, President, *Public Papers of the Presidents of the United States* (Washington, D.C.: Office of the *Federal Register*, National Archives and Records Service, 1953– ), Harry S Truman, 1949, p. 114.

3. Alexis de Tocqueville, *Democracy in America*, trans. Harry Reeve, ed. Phillips Bradley, 2 vols. (New York: Vintage, 1945), 2:114: "Americans of all ages, all conditions, and all dispositions constantly form associations. They have not only commercial and manufacturing companies, in which all take part, but associations of a thousand other kinds, religious, moral, serious, futile, general or restricted, enormous or diminutive. The Americans make associations to give entertainments, to found seminaries, to build inns, to construct churches, to diffuse books, to send missionaries to the antipodes; in this manner they found hospitals, prisons, and schools. If it is proposed to inculcate some truth or to foster some feeling by the encouragement of a great example, they form a society. Wherever at the head of some new undertaking you see the government in France, or a man of rank in England, in the United States you will be sure to find an association."

4. See John M. Berry's article on US trade: "Tide Turning Against U.S.," *Washington Post*, 18 December 1983.

5. See the figures and sources given in Novak, *The Spirit of Democratic Capitalism*, pp. 308–310.

6. In his oral remarks at a conference on "Catholic Social Thought and the U.S. Economy" at the University of Notre Dame, December 12–14, 1983, Professor Ernest Bartell, C.S.C., listed these three points. They are alluded to but not developed in his paper given at the conference, "The United States and Third World Poor in the International Economy: Some Economic and Ethical Issues for Discussion," University of Notre Dame, Notre Dame, Indiana, December 12–14, 1983 (mimeo).

7. Since Latin American exports are disproportionately composed of primary goods, the

component of exports constituted by manufactured goods is relatively small. Nonetheless, for many years a variety of experts from many different points of view have argued that a chief condition for the continued economic growth of Latin America is rapid growth both in the manufacturing sector in general and in particular in manufacturing for export. For a variety of reasons, this rapid growth in the manufacturing sector depends to an extraordinary degree on help from outside in the form of capital, investment, management, and facilities for worldwide marketing. See, for example, Robert B. Williamson, William P. Glade, Jr., and Karl M. Schmitt, eds., *Latin America—U.S. Economic Interactions* (Washington, D.C.: American Enterprise Institute, 1974); and in particular the chapter by Jose de la Torre, "Latin American Exports of Manufactures to the United States: The Outlook for the Future," pp. 49–74. On page 72, he summarizes his findings about the growth of Latin American manufactured/ imports in the US market: "The evidence . . . points to a major turnaround in Latin America's penetration of the growing U.S. market for manufactured goods. Latin America's share of this market has been on the increase in the last few years for a large number of product groups, many of which are labor-intensive and based on local resources (for example, clothing, footwear, furniture, leather and wood products, and electrical equipment). While 7.6 percent of the region's 1961 exports to the United States were manufactured goods, the proportion . . . tripled to 22.8 percent in 1972."

8. John Kenneth Galbraith, "The Defense of the Multinational Company," *Harvard Business Review* 56 (March–April 1978) :85; see Chapter 7, note 46, above.

9. The size and number of multinationals from developing countries marketing manufactured goods has expanded greatly over the last two decades. "The fastest-growing group of multinational companies in the past two decades has gone almost unnoticed by most Western managers. The Birla group of India, United Laboratories from the Philippines and Autlan of Mexico are among the several hundred multinationals from the Third World whose overseas subsidiaries have increased from dozens around 1960 to a few thousand today. In Southeast Asia and in Latin America, regional investors are expanding rapidly. Hong Kong already accounts for the second-largest number of nonmineral investors in Indonesia. Even in Africa and the Middle East, a few Latin American multinationals and a considerable number of Asian enterprises have established footholds. . . . The strength of many new Third World multinationals comes from their special experience with manufacturing for small home markets." Louis T. Wells, Jr., "Guess Who's Creating the World's Newest Multinationals," *Wall Street Journal,* 12 December 1983. A fuller account of this phenomenon appears in Louis T. Wells, Jr., *Third World Multinationals* (Cambridge, Massachusetts: MIT Press, 1983).

10. See Paul Lewis, "Socialists Forced to Use Economics of the Right," *New York Times,* 1 December 1983: "It is a paradox that southern Europe's political shift to the left has produced a marked move to the right in economic affairs. . . . Everywhere these Socialist and Socialist-led Governments, all of which have come to power in the last two and a half years, are cutting spending and holding down wages to try to live within their means again and make their economies more efficient. . . . Instead of nationalizing private companies, most are trying to slim down state-owned companies and are speaking of the virtues of free enterprise, making it easier for employers to dismiss surplus workers. . . . 'The road to Socialism no longer passes through the welfare-statism of the 1950's and 60's,' Greece's Finance Minister, Gerassimos Arsenis, said recently. 'Today Socialist goals require restructuring the economy, improving competitiveness. Those are difficult, painful things.'" See also *U.S. News and World Report*'s Special Report "Soviets Loosen Their Grip on Eastern Europe," 5 December 1983, pp. 35–38. This article contains a number of examples of free enterprise activities which Moscow is permitting in Czechoslovakia, Romania, Hungary and Poland.

11. Lawrence E. Harrison, "Nicaraguan Anguish and Costa Rican Progress," *This World,* No. 6, (Fall 1983), p. 29: "Costa Rica . . . has experienced sustained political, economic

and social progress, particularly in the mid-nineteenth century. Today, it is Latin America's most firmly rooted democracy."

## Chapter 11. The Communitarian Individual in Practice

1. Remarks of President Ronald Reagan to the World Affairs Council of Philadelphia, 15 October 1981. United States, President, *Public Papers of the Presidents of the United States, 1981* (Washington, D.C.: Office of the *Federal Register*, National Archives and Records Service, 1953– ), 1982, pp. 938–939.
2. See "War on Poverty is Difficult to Call Off," by Robert Pear, *The New York Times*, 29 November 1981.
3. Alexis de Tocqueville, *Democracy in America*, trans. Harry Reeve, ed. Phillips Bradley, 2 vols. (New York: Vintage Books, 1945), 2:336–37.
4. See Robert Woodson's series of books on mediating structures: Robert L. Woodson, *A Summons to Life: Mediating Structures and the Prevention of Youth Crime* (Washington, D.C.: American Enterprise Institute; and Cambridge, Massachusetts: Ballinger, 1981); Robert L. Woodson, ed., *Youth Crime and Urban Policy: A View from the Inner City* (Washington, D.C.: American Enterprise Institute, 1981); Brigitte Berger and Sidney Callahan, *Child Care and Mediating Structures* (Washington, D.C.: American Enterprise Institute, 1981); Sydney Duncan, et al., *The Urban Crisis: Can Grass-Roots Groups Succeed Where Government Has Failed?* (Washington, D.C.: American Enterprise Institute, 1981); Lowell S. Levin and Ellen L. Idler, *The Hidden Health Care System: Mediating Structures and Medicine* (Cambridge, Massachusetts: Ballinger, 1981); John Egan, et. al., *Housing and Public Policy: A Role for Mediating Structures* (Cambridge, Massachusetts: Ballinger, 1981); Nathan Glazer, *Mediating Structures and Welfare* (Cambridge, Massachusetts: Ballinger, 1981); David Seeley, *Education Through Partnership: Mediating Structures and Education* (Cambridge, Massachusetts: Ballinger, 1981).
5. On minority employment see Walter Williams, "Government Sanctioned Restraints that Reduce Economic Opportunities for Minorities," *Policy Review* 2 (Fall 1977):7–30; and Peter Germanis, *The Minimum Wage: Restricting Jobs for Youth*, Backgrounder no. 147, (Washington, D.C.: The Heritage Foundation, 1981).
6. See David L. Birch, "Who Creates Jobs?" *Public Interest* 65 (Fall 1981):7.
7. Stephen Roman and Eugen Loebl, *The Responsible Society* (New York: Two Continents Publishing Group, Ltd., 1977).
8. For a brilliant, sustained and original argument on this point, see William A. Schambra, "The Quest for Community and the New Public Philosophy," Parts I and II, *Catholicism in Crisis* 2 (April and May 1984).

## Chapter 12. International Economics

1. Paul Steidl-Meier, "Church Ministry in Areas of International Economics and Development," *International Economics: Interdependence and Dialogue* (Vatican City: Pontifical Commission "Iustitia et Pax," 1984), pp. 15–48.
2. Robert Nisbet, *History of the Idea of Progress* (New York: Basic Books, 1980), pp. 352–353.
3. Steidl-Meier, *International Economics*, p. 16.
4. Irving Kristol, "The Disaffection from Capitalism," in *Capitalism and Socialism*, ed. Michael Novak (Washington, D.C.: American Enterprise Institute, 1979), pp. 17–18: "In France, the Enlightenment takes a form in which the premises of the ideas of progress and of human perfectability are radicalized. . . . The French Enlightenment writers without question expected a radical improvement in the human condition to result from a radical restructuring of the social order and, above all, of the religious order. . . . Bourgeois capitalism emerges as a theory, as a way of life, and as an orthodoxy in the Anglo-Scottish tradition, which is also 'enlightened.' But because England was England and Scotland was Scotland, those two countries somehow gave rise

to an enlightenment that was not antireligious. . . . There may have been a hope, as there was in the French Enlightenment, that humanity would evolve beyond the need for churches, but there was no challenge to the actual role of the churches as teachers of moral doctrine from the new class of writers, thinkers, philosophers, and publicists in England and Scotland. . . . They believed that institutional religion, if not good, was necessary—indispensable—to spiritual governance."

5. *The Federalist Papers*, ed. Clinton Rossiter (New York: New American Library, 1961), No. 51, p. 322: "But what is government itself but the greatest of all reflections on human nature? If men were angels, no government would be necessary. If angels were to govern men, neither external nor internal controls on government would be necessary. In framing a government which is to be administered by men over men, the great difficulty lies in this: you must first enable the government to control the governed; and in the next place oblige it to control itself."

6. Steidl-Meier, *International Economics*, p. 16.

7. Ibid., p. 17.

8. Ibid.

9. Ibid.

10. Alexis de Tocqueville, *Democracy in America*, trans. Harry Reeve, ed. Phillips Bradley, 2 vols. (New York: Vintage Books, 1945), 2:131.

11. Steidl-Meier, *International Economics*, p. 18.

12. Herbert Stein, *Presidential Economics*, (New York: Simon and Schuster, 1984).

13. Steidl-Meier, *International Economics*, p. 18.

14. Ibid., p. 20.

15. Ibid., p. 31.

16. Ibid.

17. Ibid., pp. 32–33.

18. Ibid., p. 34.

19. Ibid., p. 35.

20. Ibid., p. 38.

21. Ibid.

22. Ibid.

23. Ibid., pp. 43–44.

# Index